Piety and Nationalism

McGill-Queen's Studies in the History of Religion
G.A. Rawlyk, Editor

Volumes in this series have been supported by the Jackman
Foundation of Toronto.

Piety and Nationalism

Lay Voluntary Associations and the Creation of an Irish-Catholic Community in Toronto, 1850–1895

BRIAN P. CLARKE

McGill-Queen's University Press
Montreal & Kingston • London • Buffalo

© McGill-Queen's University Press 1993
ISBN 0-7735-1130-X

Legal deposit fourth quarter 1993
Bibliothèque nationale du Québec

Printed in Canada on acid-free paper

This book has been published with the help of grants from the Social Science Federation of Canada, using funds provided by the Social Sciences and Humanities Research Council of Canada. Funding has also been received from Multiculturalism Canada.

Canadian Cataloguing in Publication Data

Clarke, Brian P., 1952–
   Piety and nationalism: lay voluntary associations and the creation
   of an Irish-Catholic community in Toronto, 1850–1895
   (McGill-Queen's studies in the history of religion; 12)
   Includes index.
   ISBN 0-7735-1130-X
   1. Irish – Ontario – Toronto – Societies, etc. – History –
   19th century. 2. Catholic Church – Ontario – Toronto – Societies, etc.
   – 19th century. 3. Irish – Ontario – Toronto – History – 19th century.
   I. Title. II. Series.
   FC3097.9.I6C53 1993   971.3′5410049162   C93-090455-9
   F1059.5.T68916 1993

This book was typeset by Typo Litho composition inc. in 10/12 Baskerville.

To Simonne E. and Brock F. Clarke
and
in memory of N. Keith Clifford

Contents

Tables

Acknowledgments

In researching and writing this book I have benefited from the assistance and support of many individuals. The archivists and librarians at the National Archives of Canada, Archives of Ontario, City Archives of Toronto, Archives of the Archdiocese of Ottawa, Archives de la chancellerie de l'archidiocèse de Montréal, and Metro Toronto Central Reference Library were most helpful. I especially thank the staff of the microtext reading room at Robarts Research Library, University of Toronto, for their cheerful cooperation. I am deeply indebted to the late James S. McGivern, sj, who graciously assisted my work at the Archives of the Roman Catholic Archdiocese of Toronto, and to his successor at the archives, Sister Frieda Watson, csj. Sister Watson's reorganization of the archdiocesan archives made my research much easier. My free access to the documents under her care is testimony to her commitment to historical research. My thanks also go to Sister Watson's staff, especially Linda Wicks, for all their efforts on my behalf.

John S. Moir of the University of Toronto helped me in many ways when I first embarked upon this project and, by generously sharing his vast knowledge of English-Canadian Catholic history, has continued to point me in fruitful directions. The study began as a doctoral dissertation for the Divinity School, University of Chicago, and I was fortunate in the direction and counsel offered by my dissertation committee both then and since. Martin E. Marty has been a constant source of intellectual inspiration and, with his characteristic eye for the larger picture, prompted me to keep the project on track whenever it threatened to jump the rails. Those who are familiar with Emmet Larkin's studies of the Roman Catholic Church in nineteenth-century Ireland will recognize my debt to his work. More than that, however, I owe much of what I know of the historian's craft to Larkin's guidance. Jerald C. Brauer, my dissertation supervisor, allowed me to explore many byways, one of which, as it turned out, led to this book. Brauer's commitment to the study of the religion of the people, his wise counsel, and his warm encouragement helped to make researching and writing this work a rewarding and humane experience.

In revising the manuscript for publication I have also incurred a number of debts to other friends and colleagues. Mark McGowan and Michael Cottrell, two of my co-workers in the study of Irish Catholics in Toronto, have demonstrated selfless dedication to scholarship and collegiality in our many conversations over the years, for which I am most grateful. William M. Baker, Ruth Compton Brouwer, C.T. McIntire, Terry Murphy, and Marguerite Van Die commented on portions of earlier versions of this study, much to my edification. Roger Hutchinson, Paul Gooch, Ronald Sweet, and, above all, Muna Salloum made my stay at the Centre for Religious Studies at the University of Toronto both a pleasant and productive one. Since then, I have enjoyed the hospitable environs of the Centre for the Study of Religion, Emmanuel College, and for that I thank Roger Hutchinson (once again) and Phyllis Airhart.

Tirthankar Bose offered expert editorial guidance and immeasurably eased the task of revising the manuscript for publication. At McGill-Queen's University Press, I benefited from Donald Harman Akenson's insight and advice. I am also most grateful to the anonymous readers commissioned under the Aid to Scholarly Publications Programme for their invaluable comments. In Curtis Fahey I found the editor that most authors dream of. My thanks, too, to Michael Power for preparing the index. Finally, I thank Edith Killey, who read nearly every page of my many drafts and commented on them with her usual acumen. Apart from that, without her support this study would not have been completed; without her companionship it could never have been so enjoyable.

Piety and Nationalism

Introduction

"Let each say in his heart," declared Bishop Ignace Bourget of Montreal, "'I hear my curé, my curé hears the bishop, the bishop hears the Pope, and the Pope hears Our Lord Jesus Christ.'"[1] Such was Bourget's understanding of the laity's role in the Roman Catholic Church, and during the middle decades of the nineteenth century this view was increasingly shared by a clergy whose outlook had been shaped by the revival of ultramontanism. Ultramontanes adopted a hierarchical and centralized model of the church in which the papacy in Rome was the true foundation for right belief and practice. Power and authority, as Bishop Bourget's declaration well illustrates, not only flowed from the top down, but it was to remain at all times in the hands of the clergy. Just as the pontiff, the vicar of Christ, was the unquestioned sovereign of the church universal, so too were the bishops and clergy to rule as virtual popes over their own dioceses and parishes.

Activism on the part of the laity posed little challenge to this hierarchical view of the church. Both in principle and in practice lay activism could be subject to clerical authority. By contrast, initiative on the part of the laity flatly contradicted Bourget's conception of the church in which it was the prerogative of the clergy to lead and the duty of the laity to follow their clergy's direction. The purpose of this book is to explore what indeed did happen to lay initiative during the latter part of the nineteenth century when new conceptions of the clergy's power and authority took hold in the Catholic Church. Certainly the clergy did curtail some of the more visible expressions of lay initiative in the church, most notably in their successful campaign to abolish lay trustees.[2] The clergy also ousted the laity from the general management of the parish (a process that was to be repeated as new waves of immigrants came to North America) and so brought the parish under their immediate control. At the same time, however, other institutional changes in the church favoured the expression of lay initiative. One such development was the proliferation of Catholic voluntary associations, which after the mid-century mark fundamentally transformed the institutional face of Catholicism. The renewal of the Catholic Church resulted in the emergence of a wide variety of parochial voluntary associations – confraternities, charitable organizations, temperance societies, literary clubs, and the like – all of which were dedicated to advancing Catholic piety and instilling ultramontane principles.

The role of the laity in founding some of these Catholic voluntary associations was perhaps the most notable example of lay initiative, but lay initiative can be exercised in other ways, as Timothy L. Smith has pointed out. Even in organizations established by the clergy, lay people could and in fact did on occasion gain effective control.[3] Such an outcome may seem surprising in light of the rising authority of the clergy in the parish, and it is one of the purposes of the present study to explain how Catholic voluntary associations contributed to the development of lay initiative. In examining how Catholics organized their associational life, this book explores the cultural and religious mainsprings of (and constraints on) lay initiative, delineates its nature and scope, maps the influence of class and gender on its expression and development, and traces its interaction with and relationship to clerical leadership.

In North America, Catholic associational life was frequently organized along national or ethnic lines. This was most obviously the case when Catholics joined self-consciously national organizations such as the Irish Catholic Benevolent Union or the Central-Verein, but even when it came to generic associations, such as devotional organizations, the laity generally preferred to join those associations that catered to their particular ethnic group. This study focuses upon the voluntary associations of one such group, the Irish Catholics. Not only did Irish Catholics establish and participate in a wide variety of voluntary associations, but their clergy were well known for their authoritarian leadership. This mix of strong clerical leadership and a high level of lay participation in voluntary associations makes the Catholic Irish an object study of what happened to lay initiative at a time when the resurgence of ultramontanism bolstered the clergy's leadership in the Catholic Church.

Irish Catholics joined two types of organizations: those attached to the church and under the supervision of the clergy, and those which, though professedly Catholic, were independent of the church and promoted Irish nationalism. This basic structure of Irish-Catholic associational life was shaped by two movements that arose in Ireland and in Irish-Catholic enclaves overseas during the middle decades of the nineteenth century: the renewal of the Catholic Church, which was ultramontane in inspiration, and the Irish nationalist awakening. Irish nationalism was an international phenomenon, and it offered Irish Catholics a social identity both at home and abroad. The renewal of the Catholic Church was also an international movement, and it fundamentally changed the face of Catholicism. Yet in only a few cases did this renewal so radically affect the religious outlook of the people that it effected a religious revival of such depth and breadth that Catholicism became a constituent element of a national awakening.[4]

It is often supposed that, because the Catholics of Ireland are now a church-going people, they have always been so. Emmet Larkin, in his highly influential article "The Devotional Revolution in Ireland," has pointed out that the Irish were not particularly religious before the Great Famine of 1845–49, at least when measured by the norms of official Catholicism, which enjoined regular attendance at Sunday Mass and the like. Only in the quarter-century following the famine, Larkin argues, did this form of religious observance become common. During that period, the Catholic Church set new standards for religious behaviour.[5] Not only were Roman Catholics expected to discharge their canonical duties, such as attendance at Sunday Mass and the performance of Easter duties, but they were also encouraged to perform a wide variety of devotions, short paraliturgical rituals that could be practised publicly in the parish church or privately at home. This form of piety became so central to the religious life of the laity that within a generation the church effected nothing less than a devotional revolution, as Emmet Larkin puts it.

In Ireland the renewal of the Catholic Church marked such a profound change in the religious practice and sensibilities of the laity that Catholicism became the touchstone for their communal identity and sense of unity. Among Irish Catholics overseas, the pace of the religious revival varied from community to community. Whatever the immediate effects, however, historians are unanimous that the religious renewal proceeded from the top down and have thus cast the laity in a passive role. One consequence of this approach is that the laity appear not so much as participants in their own right but as objects of reform and conversion at the hands of the clergy. Parochial organizations, such as devotional organizations and temperance societies, are therefore seen as the means by which clerical values were communicated to the laity rather than as potential forums for lay initiative.[6]

Most historians have implicitly minimized the existence of lay initiative in at least one other respect: organizations that existed outside the formal structures of the church, no matter how self-consciously Catholic, are generally regarded as a separate and unrelated social world, as though Catholic associational life was bounded by the walls of the parish church. Nowhere is this assumption more evident than in the treatment of the most important voluntary associations that were independent of the church, the Irish nationalist societies.

While it is often recognized that the patriotic passions of these societies' supporters were shared by many of the clergy, the emphasis is usually on the conflict between priests and laity.[7] Irish nationalism thus appears as an external challenge to the church. What is often overlooked in this approach is that even when conflict did break out between the nationalists and the clergy, their conflicts were over issues that were intra-communal in nature and circumscribed by a broad consensus, to which all appealed as the measure of religious and patriotic orthodoxy. Chief among these communal issues was the question of the laity's proper place as activists and leaders in church and community. Nationalist societies frequently did stand up for the laity's right to exercise leadership independently of the clergy, but the fact that not all such affirmations resulted in conflict with the church suggests that the relationship between lay initiative and clerical leadership was a good deal more complex and much closer than is usually recognized.

The presence of lay initiative in nationalist organizations and in associations affiliated with the Catholic Church also has important implications for our understanding of Irish-Catholic ethnicity. Some historians of Irish nationalism have sought to explain the emergence of Irish-Catholic ethnicity as a response to social stress, such as Protestant xenophobia or economic adversity.[8] In this respect, much of the work on Irish nationalism has been informed by the primordialist interpretation of ethnicity. According to that interpretation, pre-modern "tribal" loyalties erupt in response to external provocations.[9] Shocks, such as the trauma of emigrating, Protestant hostility towards Catholic immigrants, or economic hardship, jolt individuals to look inside themselves and to assert their fundamental communal affinity. Ethnicity is deeply rooted in "the core of the individual," a primordial identity that fulfils the individual's need to belong. Only the traditional and, so it is argued, fixed givens of social existence, such as custom, language, kinship, and religion, can satisfy the individual's longing for personal integration and therefore form the basis for ethnicity. Although remarkably resilient, ethnicity – like tradition and custom – is essentially immutable.

Some recent studies on ethnic groups have questioned the primordialist interpretation of ethnicity, suggesting that ethnicity is itself elastic, for group boundaries are drawn and redrawn in different ways over time.[10] Ethnicity, in this understanding, is not a fixed identity that is merely inherited. Rather, ethnicity is constantly in the process of being made and reformulated by people. Culture, including custom and tradition, is mobilized to achieve specific goals in response to a particular social situation and is itself redefined in the process of ethnic formation, a point that is fundamental to Thomas Brown's pioneering work on Irish-American nationalism.[11] Ethnicity, then, is a new social form rather than an Old World survival.

Those historians who emphasize the protean nature of ethnicity have pointed to the critical role played by voluntary associations in the forging of ethnic communities in the New World.[12] Whether they were formally attached to the church or not, voluntary associations were a primary outlet for lay leadership and a principal means by which popular sentiment was both shaped and mobilized. As organizations that operate in specific localities, voluntary associations offer a vantage point from which to observe the external forces acting on an ethnic community as well as its internal social dynamics. In order to capture the associational life of the laity in its lived concreteness and historical specificity, one community, the Irish Catholics of Toronto in the province of Ontario, was selected for an intensive study.

Those who engage in local history do so in the conviction that their chosen locale is of intrinsic interest, and in that respect this study is no exception. Of all the jurisdictions in North America, Ontario had one of the heaviest concentrations of Irish men and women in proportion to its overall population. Those of Irish background comprised about one-quarter of the total population, far outstripping those from other parts of the United Kingdom. The religious composition of the province's Irish population was also unique. Unlike the United States, where Roman Catholics predominated among the Irish, Irish Protestants outnumbered Irish Catholics two to one in Ontario. Catholics were a distinct minority among the Irish of Ontario, but in the Catholic Church itself the Irish so far outnumbered other groups that in many parts of the province Catholicism was synonymous with Irishness.

In addition to the close association between Catholicism and Irish ancestry, the overall pattern of Irish-Catholic immigration and settlement in the province is also striking. As Donald Akenson has pointed out, urban Irish Catholics were outnumbered by their co-religionists and compatriots who lived in the surrounding countryside. The vast majority of Ontario's – and indeed Canada's – Irish Catholics were rural residents, most of whom were engaged in farming. This agricultural background reflected the fact that most Irish Catholics who put down roots in the province had arrived during its formative period of settlement when land was still available. Rather than being a late-arriving minority, as in the United States, Irish Catholics were a charter group in Ontario society.[13]

Why, when so many Irish Catholics in Ontario were rural residents, does this study deliberately focus upon an urban community? The answer to this question lies in the urban origins of Irish-Catholic voluntary associations and the role played by urban centres in the dissemination of these organizations. As the site of the largest Irish-Catholic community in Ontario, Toronto was the leading metropolitan centre for the province's Irish-Catholics. Many Catholic voluntary associations first took hold in Toronto and then spread to the many towns that served rural Ontario.[14] Thus, while this is a study of one community, the issues it raises have implications for understanding the role of the laity in the church elsewhere.

The Irish-Catholic community of Toronto offers several advantages for investigating lay associational life, and these advantages are directly related to patterns of immigration and settlement that are specific to Ontario as a whole and Toronto in particular. The Catholic community of Toronto was overwhelmingly dominated by people who were of Irish background. In such a homogeneous community the development of different forms of associational life, those that were attached to the church and those that were formally independent of the church, is remarkably clear.

Not only was the Catholic Church an unmistakably Green institution, but the city of Toronto was also very much an Irish city. At mid-century, over a third of the city's residents had been born in Ireland. The large number of Irish, together with the all-too-evident rivalry between the Orange and the Green, has led some historians to call Toronto the Belfast of Canada.[15] As a city where traditional rivalries persisted in a New World setting, Toronto provides an excellent opportunity to examine the roots and nature of Irish-Catholic identity.

Toronto's Irish-Catholic community also offers a model case study for the relationship between generational change and the development of ethnicity. Irish Catholics were a charter group in Canadian society with a longstanding presence in Toronto, but at mid-century Toronto was still a young and fast-growing town. Like most other Toronto residents, the majority of Irish Catholics were recent arrivals. Irish-Catholic immigration to the city was heavy throughout the 1840s and 1850s, but then fell off dramatically in the early 1860s. Since large-scale emigration from Ireland occurred in such a short span, the impact of generational change upon ethnic associational life and identity among the city's Irish-Catholic population can easily be traced.

The period covered in this study is determined by the types of voluntary associations found among the Irish Catholics of Toronto. The study begins in 1850, when Toronto's second Roman Catholic bishop, Armand de Charbonnel, arrived in the city. Bishop Charbonnel's arrival set the stage for the emergence of a wide variety of church-based voluntary associations, marking the effective beginning of renewal in the Catholic Church. The closing years of the 1850s saw the introduction to Toronto of Irish nationalism, which in various organizational incarnations was to have a significant presence in the city until the 1890s. After the late 1850s, these two types of voluntary organizations were to form the fundamental structure for Catholic associational life for the next three and a half decades. The study closes in 1895, by which time the independent nationalist societies had entered into decline and their place had been filled by church-affiliated organizations, decisively altering the pattern of lay associational life in Toronto.

Membership in a voluntary association is a form of leisure, and leisure requires both free time and money. Many historians have portrayed Irish-Catholic immigrants, especially the famine immigrants, as being so culturally inept and technologically backward as to lack the skills and the sophistication required to exercise initiative in their community and establish voluntary associations of their own. The present study therefore begins by revising this stereotype through an examination of the cultural and social condition of Toronto's Irish Catholics in the decade and a half after mid-century. Far from being a ghettoized and impoverished people, the majority of Irish Catholics lived throughout the city and belonged to the "solid" working class, many of whom attained the coveted status of homeowners. Furthermore, a significant number of Irish Catholics had gained middle-class status, mainly by establishing businesses catering to an Irish-Catholic clientele. In short, modest prosperity ensured that a ready pool of lay activists and leaders existed in the Irish-Catholic community.

Although the majority of Irish-Catholic immigrants adapted far more readily to the urban and industrial realities than is usually assumed, the sudden arrival of large numbers of immigrants to the city did pose a twin challenge, social as well as religious, to the Roman Catholic Church. These new arrivals, a good number of whom needed assistance after experiencing the rigours of emigration, were a severe strain on the church's modest financial resources. In addition, the church was hard pressed to minister spiritually to the mass of Irish-Catholic immigrants, many of whom were not in the habit of attending church regularly. In order to meet this social and spiritual challenge, the ecclesiastical authorities undertook an extensive administrative reorganization of the church and a thorough reform of its clergy. A reformed and reorganized church, inspired by the zeal and principles of ultramontanism, could then set out to effect the religious renewal of the laity, that is, to devotionalize them.

The most important agencies in promoting this transformation of popular piety were the devotional associations established in each parish by the clergy. The membership of these organizations was predominantly female, a characteristic that was to shape both the manner in which lay initiative was developed and its range of expression. Devotional organizations did encourage lay initiative, though this initiative was typically limited to the parish's social élite. Not only was lay initiative the privilege of the few, but the field for initiative open to women was limited by their lay status and gender. Women were in a doubly subordinate position in the parish, a condition that is thrown into further relief when one examines parish organizations for men.

The apparent lack of religious fervour among men so disturbed the clergy that they willingly endorsed new pastoral methods, including those that arose from the laity. Perhaps the most dramatic example of such lay leadership and initiative was the introduction to the city of the Saint Vincent de Paul Society, whose primary object was to foster male piety. Various factors, religious as well as social, made it possible for the members of the Saint Vincent de Paul Society to gain control over what were matters of vital concern to the clergy: the recruitment of laymen into the ranks of the church and the cultivation of their religious life.

Through its charitable endeavours, the Saint Vincent de Paul Society made a substantial contribution to popularizing the devotions of the church among the Roman Catholic poor, but it failed in its central goal and never recruited laymen in large numbers, mainly because it failed to reckon with the sensibilities and aspirations of the vast majority of Irish-Catholic men. In response to this situation, the clergy founded temperance societies that were devoted to ostensibly secular and recreational pursuits. Temperance was closely associated with the ideals of individual self-reliance and self-respect, and so these societies provide an example of how the clergy attempted to accommodate laymen's needs and interests, including their desire to secure control of their own social life.

The well-springs of Irish nationalism in North America are usually traced to the Irish-Catholic immigrant experience in a predominantly Protestant society. This experience, with its burning resentment of exclusion by the majority, did of course contribute to the emergence of Irish nationalism in Toronto. Nevertheless, Irish nationalism must at the same time be firmly located in its immediate context in the Irish-Catholic community. The founding of nationalist associations that were formally independent of the church was perhaps the most obvious example of initiative among Irish-Catholic men. These organizations were populist in character, and it was on this basis that they advocated national independence for Ireland and promoted lay leadership in the Irish-Catholic community, both of which alarmed the clergy. Not only were the clergy suspicious of the nationalists' insistence that their social life remain free from clerical direction and supervision, but they were also disturbed by the militant nationalists' flirtation with revolutionary politics. Nevertheless, an accommodation between the nationalist associations and the church was possible. Both religion and nation were fundamental to the self-image of Irish-Catholics, and it was this dual nature of their ethnic identity that enabled independent lay initiative to flourish and to coexist with the clergy's leadership in church and community. Even when rifts did open between the lay nationalist leaders and the clergy, as was to happen in the late 1860s, the accommodation was shaken but far from shattered.

During the 1870s the militant nationalists tempered their stance sufficiently to regain the support of the clergy. At the same time, a less militant strain of nationalism, one that placed the emphasis more on religion rather than on nationalism, also emerged in lay circles. Though this form of nationalism was more congenial to the clergy's project of building a religious subculture and appealed to those Irish Catholics who accepted Canada's constitutional and cultural links with Britain, militant lay activists retained their dominance over the Irish nationalist movement in Toronto. These nationalists continued to advocate lay initiative and autonomy from

clerical direction, and at times their views resulted in open conflict
with the clergy. By highlighting the contested boundaries between
lay initiative and clerical leadership, such conflicts reveal the perim-
eters for lay initiative that had gained acceptance among clergy and
people. They also illuminate the changing nature of Irish-Catholic
ethnicity as religion rather than nation became a more effective
rallying cry to mobilize public support. In the late 1880s conflict between the militant nationalists and the clergy broke out once again,
this time over the laity's role on the Catholic separate school board.
Beginning from what seemed to be a position of strength, fortified
by the now traditional nationalist pieties, the nationalists' push for
lay control of the school board soon fizzled, a situation that signalled
that a profound change in the Irish-Catholic community was in the
offing.

During the late 1880s male associational life in the Catholic community began to undergo a massive reorganization. By 1895 independent lay nationalist associations were languishing, and those
organizations for men that thrived were typically fraternal in character and a part of parish life. In a striking departure from the past,
devotional organizations were now for the first time picking up a
substantial following among men. This shift in the organizational
structure of Catholic voluntary associations, and the integration
of laymen's initiative and activism into the official structures of the
church that it effected, heralded a redefinition of Irish-Catholic
ethnicity in which the accent was to be increasingly placed upon
religion.

What follows is the history of one community, and as such it can
hardly be taken as a microcosm of the Irish-Catholics' experience in
Canada, let alone of their experience in North America. Yet, if the
story of Toronto's Irish Catholics was in many respects unique, that
community nevertheless affords an excellent opportunity to study
several important trends in the development of lay initiative and its
relationship to clerical leadership. Lay initiative in Toronto played
an important role in the religious and nationalist organizations of
the people, and this book explores how such initiative contributed to
the formation of an ethnic community based upon denominational
loyalty.

1 The Irish in Toronto

In early Ontario, the arrival of the pre-famine Irish resulted in an Irish population whose religious composition and pattern of settlement were very different from that found in the United States. Before the 1840s, two-thirds of Ontario's Irish were Protestant, and the vast majority of the Irish, whether they were Protestant or not, settled in rural areas. Moreover, since most of Ontario's Irish arrived before the Great Famine of 1845–49, the religious composition of the province's Irish population and the rural nature of their settlement remained much the same despite the influx of Irish immigrants during and after the famine.[1]

Although immigration during the famine and after had little effect on the general contours of the Irish population in the province of Ontario, the bulk of Toronto's Irish-Catholic population arrived during the famine and the decade that followed. This growth in population made it possible for Toronto to emerge as the metropolitan centre of the Irish-Catholic community in Ontario during the 1850s and 1860s; the religious and ethnic institutions established by the Irish Catholics of that city also served Irish Catholics in the surrounding countryside. Despite this and other examples of industry and initiative, historians and contemporaries alike have burdened the Irish Catholics of Toronto with the stereotype of technologically backward and socially inept famine immigrants. This stereotype is overworked. True, Irish Catholics were clustered in the working class, especially among the city's unskilled workers, but the majority of them did at least gain an economic foothold. Though their means may have been modest, most Irish Catholics were determined to build a better life for themselves in the New World, and one of the most notable examples of this aspiration was their determination to organize and become active in voluntary associations dedicated to advancing their individual and collective well-being.

The Great Famine of 1845–49 has often been seen as the archetypical tragedy that symbolized Irish-Catholic emigration to North America. As a result, many historians have stressed over-population and its attendant poverty as the key triggers for the Irish-Catholic exodus to the New World.[2] However, not all Irish Catholics, no matter how poor or hungry, were equally willing or able to leave Ireland. Contrary to the Malthusian assumptions of some historians, the poorest areas of Ireland, in the extreme south and west, had the lowest rates of emigration.[3] In general, the poor across the country were the least likely to emigrate.[4]

Irish-Catholic emigration to British North America increased sharply during the 1830s in the wake of the transformation of Irish agriculture.[5] The rise of commercial agriculture had encouraged landlords to consolidate their holdings at the expense of small, inefficient farmers, who were far from being at the bottom of Irish society. The collapse of Ireland's textile industry after 1815 further reduced the chances of Ireland's increasingly marginalized small farmers of finding other employment at home. As a result of increased literacy, many of them for the first time became aware of economic opportunities abroad. At the same time, declining transatlantic fares brought emigration within the reach of a growing number of families. Under increasing economic pressure, many small farmers and the better-off cottiers left their tiny farms and set out for North America to maintain their independence.

If emigration was now a possibility for many families, it became increasingly a necessity for the sons and daughters of farmers. Lacking opportunities both for employment and – as impartible inheritance became the norm – for acquiring land, young men and women left for the New World in order to improve their lot. After 1830 Irish-Catholic labourers also began to emigrate in large numbers. Still, such emigration remained family-oriented as parents in Ireland and family members overseas contributed the capital necessary for settlement abroad.[6] Some of those who emigrated to British North America were obviously of modest means, but for the most part they were hardly among Ireland's destitute.

This pattern of immigration explains why most Irish-Catholics in British North America failed to resemble the stereotype of the impoverished and unskilled emigrant. True, Irish Catholics were found among the poor in numbers beyond their representation in the general population, especially in Ontario's larger towns where the "low" Irish were a familiar and obtrusive presence, but this visibility masked the reality of social advancement, which passed almost unnoticed by contemporary observers. The detailed study of the 1871 census returns by Gordon Darroch and Michael D. Ornstein reveals that Irish Catholics were well represented in all occupational categories, although they were somewhat under-represented as farmers and significantly over-represented as labourers.[7] Far from being a ghettoized minority, the vast majority of Irish Catholics had secured a position in the social and economic mainstream of Ontarian society. Irish Catholics were thus geographically and socially mobile. During the formative years of agricultural settlement, they worked in the towns and lumber camps of the province to acquire the capital necessary to enter into farming full time.[8] Many fulfilled their dream of modest prosperity and economic independence.[9] Among the urban Irish Catholics, a significant number rose into the ranks of the middle class, for the most part by way of shopkeeping.[10]

Toronto, like other larger towns in British North America, represented something of departure from the province-wide pattern of Irish-Catholic immigration and settlement. Although the published census returns do not cross-tabulate between religion and origin (see table 1), it is possible to provide estimates for Toronto's Irish-Catholic population on the basis of these returns. As in Saint John, New Brunswick, Quebec City, and Montreal, those who arrived during the famine and immediate post-famine period made up the bulk of the Irish-Catholic population. Even so, in 1841 Irish Catholics comprised a sixth of Toronto's population, a significant minority in an otherwise Protestant town. Their numbers are especially striking in that Toronto's pre-industrial economy, unlike that of contemporary American cities, had little need for unskilled labour.[11]

The famine and immediate post-famine influx of Irish-Catholic emigrants took place when Toronto's growth as a commercial and industrial centre resulted in a demand for unskilled and semi-skilled workers.[12] In 1851, while the city's population had doubled to 30,775, the number of Irish Catholics had tripled, bringing their proportion to almost one-quarter of the total population.[13] In 1861, when the next census was taken, the Irish-Catholic community had inched past the one-quarter mark.[14] Thereafter, emigration from

Table 1
Population of Toronto

	Irish Birth	Irish Ancestry	Catholic	Total
1841	–	–	2,401	14,249
1848	1,695	–	5,903	23,503
1851	11,305	–	7,940	30,775
1861	12,441	–	12,135	44,821
1871	10,336	24,101	11,881	56,092
1881	10,781	32,177	15,716	86,415
1891	13,252	–	21,830	144,023

Source: Census of Canada.

Ireland dropped off precipitously as the United States became the main destination for Irish Catholics leaving Ireland, and by 1871 the Irish-Catholic population had declined in absolute numbers, with the result that Irish Catholics accounted for under one-fifth of the city's residents.[15] By 1881, Irish Catholics made up less than 15 per cent of the population.[16]

Despite the influx of Irish Catholics to Toronto during and shortly after the famine, Irish Protestants still outnumbered Irish Catholics. The large number of Irish Protestants together with the presence of Irish Catholics made Toronto the most Irish city in North America. In 1851 over one-third of Toronto's population had been born in Ireland.[17] The figures from the first census to report national ancestry, taken in 1871, are equally telling. Despite the dramatic drop in emigration from Ireland, which dated from the mid-1850s, just over two-fifths of the city's residents claimed Irish ancestry in that year.[18] Even in a province noted for its Irish-Protestant population, the Orange presence in Toronto was indeed formidable.[19] And, as one would expect, the rivalry between the Orange and the Green was intense. When Protestant-Catholic conflict broke out, it was not simply between Protestants of native stock and newly arrived Irish Catholics, as in the United States: it was largely a conflict between the Orange and the Green, with all the historical associations that those party labels evoked.[20]

Unfortunately for Irish Catholics, their traditional opponents were not the only ones to hold them in low esteem. The tragedy of the Great Famine overwhelmed contemporaries, and it fixed their perception of Irish Catholics as an impoverished and degraded lot. In 1847, during the height of the famine exodus, over 38,000 Irish emigrants arrived in Toronto, of whom some 2,000 settled there.

Others never survived the ordeal: over 1,100 Irish died in the fever sheds down by the waterfront.[21] The sudden arrival of the famine Irish, the majority of whom were Catholic, taxed to the limit the charitable resources of the city, especially as the Catholic Church lacked both the institutions and the means to care for its own.[22] Irish-Catholic emigrants arrived in such a "destitute and weak" condition and made such "a very large demand" upon public charity, observed John Elmsley, a leading Catholic layman, that they were in danger of alienating public sympathy.[23] Indeed, their presence in the town did much to create a civic consensus among Toronto's Protestants that, like the Orange tradition of Irish Protestants, was ever vigilant in the defence of Protestant principles and British institutions.[24]

The arrival of the famine Irish reinforced among Toronto's Protestants the prevailing images of Irish Catholics. The large number of destitute Irish Catholics confirmed to many contemporaries that poverty and nationality were intimately associated.[25] Yet as tragic as the exodus of 1847 was, it was hardly typical of Irish immigration to Canada during the late 1840s and early 1850s. The Irish who immigrated to Canada during these years were not quite the dregs of Irish society that contemporaries assumed them to be. Those who were able to leave for Canada were precisely those who had ready money in hand, especially after 1847 when Canadian authorities levied heavy immigrant head taxes.[26] If most of these emigrants were better off than the vast majority of their compatriots, it is also not surprising that Irish Catholics were over-represented on the poor rolls of Toronto. Having scraped together whatever capital they possessed to pay for their own passage as well as that of their family members, not a few found themselves with scant resources in the New World.

Apart from the immediate problem of securing material assistance, Irish Catholics had the problem of finding a place for themselves in the Canadian economy – a problem that was especially acute in a city such as Toronto. The vast majority of the emigrants had been rural residents in an underdeveloped country. Emigration to Toronto required them to make the difficult transition from a rural, partly commercial society to an urban one that was undergoing an industrial revolution.[27] Yet not all Irish Catholics were without skills, and a significant number of them had picked up traditional trades such as carpentry, tailoring, shoemaking, and butchering before emigrating to the New World.[28]

The dramatic increase in the Irish-Catholic population of Toronto coincided with the city's growth as a commercial centre and the early stages of its subsequent industrialization. By 1851 Toronto had established itself as the administrative and commercial hub of what is now southern Ontario. The railway boom of the 1850s not only consolidated Toronto's commercial position but also transformed the city's economy. The railways, by connecting Toronto to a hinterland stretching from the Niagara frontier to the Ottawa valley, secured the city's dominance in the corn and wholesale trades. The rise of the railways was a godsend for carters, a line of work typically dominated by Irish Catholics, but, more important, the prosperity generated by the railways resulted in a building boom, which sent contractors scouting for semi-skilled and unskilled labour. Simultaneously, the development of the railway established a larger market for agricultural produce and thus enabled southern Ontario's farmers to enjoy exceptional prosperity. This new-found rural affluence together with the rise of the railways produced increasing demand for manufactured goods and resulted in the formation of an integrated home market with Toronto at its centre. Toronto's commercial supremacy therefore laid the foundations for its industrial hegemony in southern Ontario. In 1860 Toronto was predominantly a commercial city, and its burgeoning manufacturing economy was still based on small shop and craft production. Though the pace of industrialization was to gain further momentum in the 1880s and 1890s, Toronto's industrial revolution was well under way by 1871, when the bulk of its manufacturing workforce was employed in factories.[29]

Toronto's growth as a commercial centre and the onset of industrialization created an unprecedented demand for skilled and unskilled labour. Industrialization in certain sectors, for example in the metal trades and, initially, the shoe industry, vastly increased the need for a skilled work force.[30] Railway builders, contractors (particularly during the building boom of 1866–73), and clothing manufacturers, however, depended on a ready supply of unskilled labour.[31] Both the swift growth and transformation of Toronto's economy were made possible by the presence of a large unskilled labour force, a large part of which was Irish Catholic.

Sometime in the early 1860s, Father Jean Jamot enumerated the Catholic ratepayers in Toronto (table 2). Because this census was undertaken in order to collect separate school taxes, it is certainly an accurate survey of the occupational status of those household heads who were liable for school rates – house owners and those who rented an entire house. Jamot's census indicates that many Irish Catholics, lacking the necessary skills, entered the industrial labour market at the bottom of the occupational hierarchy. Among male

Table 2
Distribution of Irish-Catholic Occupations,
circa 1860

Category	Total	Men Only
Unskilled	45.0%	37.6%
Semi-skilled	13.5	17.0
Skilled	12.1	15.4
Clerical	2.8	3.6
Business	16.7	21.0
Professional	3.3	4.1
Private Means	6.6	.9

Source: Rev. Jean Jamot, "Census of City Wards," *circa* early
1860s, Archives of the Roman Catholic Archdiocese of
Toronto; city directories.

Irish-Catholic ratepayers, who by any standard had achieved economic success in the form of house occupancy, almost two-fifths of
them were in unskilled occupations.

Broad categories, however, could well obscure the occupational
diversity of unskilled Irish Catholics. In Father Jamot's census,
almost three-quarters of the male unskilled workers were classified
as labourers.[32] Unfortunately, it is not possible to distinguish the
varying grades of labourer: some may have had more or less secure
employment in factories and warehouses, and others could probably
count on regular, if seasonal, employment with Irish-Catholic contractors in the building trades. Carters and drivers made up almost
a fifth of the unskilled Catholic ratepayers. Irish Catholics comprised about a half of the city's hackmen and carters. Unlike watch-
men and caretakers (the third largest group of male workers among
the unskilled Irish-Catholic workforce), who could be sure of year-
round employment, the carter's income was subject to seasonal fluctuations, but many had secure employment with wholesalers,
manufacturers, and the Toronto Street Railway.

While many Irish-Catholic men entered the workforce at the
bottom of the occupational hierarchy, this was even more common
for Irish-Catholic women. All of the working women in Father
Jamot's census were employed as charwomen or seamstresses. The
growing clothing industry, with its large network of outwork and
subcontracting, offered one of the few occupations open to women.
The availability of relatively cheap, mass-produced sewing machines
made it possible for Irish women to do piece-work in their homes.[33]
But with long hours and low piece-work wages, clothing manufac-

turing was a notorious sweated trade. The other major sources of employment for Irish-Catholic women were domestic service and street selling. Women selling apples, oranges, and other snacks were familiar downtown figures, and the accounts in the daily newspapers would seem to indicate that Irish women, particularly the elderly, dominated the trade.[34] Working women in the nineteenth century were trapped in unskilled occupations, usually in the sweated trades or domestic service, and Irish women were no exception. Irish-Catholic women, like most working women in Victorian Toronto, were relegated to low-paying jobs. If anything, because more of them existed at, if not below, the level of subsistence, they were worse off than women from other backgrounds.

While many of Toronto's Irish-Catholic ratepayers were clustered in unskilled occupations, they were well represented in other occupational categories. A significant number of them, some 30 per cent, all of them men, had gained entry into the semi-skilled and skilled trades (table 2).[35] Among the semi-skilled, carpenters, painters, butchers, and printers made up the bulk of Irish-Catholic workers. Skilled Irish-Catholic workers were heavily represented among tailors and shoemakers, both traditional but declining trades.[36] Many Irish Catholics were also employed as brakemen, switchmen, and conductors on the railways, especially the Grand Trunk Railway.[37] In Saint Lawrence Ward, about half of the semi-skilled and skilled householders were employed at the Gzowski Rolling Mills, the most advanced factory in Toronto during the 1860s and a mill widely known for its high proportion of Irish-Catholic workers.[38]

There were few Irish Catholics in the professions or clerical positions, but as table 2 indicates there was a sizeable Irish-Catholic business class. For Irish Catholics, going into business meant opening a bar and boarding-house or a grocery catering to the needs of their fellow countrymen.[39] A few became prominent businessmen, such as John McGee, who built up one of the largest foundries in the city; Patrick Hughes, the founder of a prosperous dry goods store; and Frank Smith, one of the leading wholesalers in the province and later owner of the Toronto Street Railway. Most of the Irish-Catholic businessmen had more modest aspirations. Irish-Catholic grocers and tavern keepers, such as Charles Burns, Michael Murphy, and Owen Cosgrove, were working-class entrepreneurs who had managed to set aside a little capital to go into business on their own account. In addition to the keeping of taverns and groceries, a growing number of Irish Catholics went into the contracting business, encouraged by the Catholic Church's building spree in the late 1850s and 1870s. Petty capitalism, rather than the professions or white-collar occupations, was the main avenue for Irish-Catholic mobility out of the working class.

For unskilled Irish-Catholic workers, poverty was an ever-present threat.[40] Labourers earned about a dollar a day but would need to bring in at least four and half dollars a week to support a wife and two children at a level not much above subsistence. For all families, economic well-being depended on their primary wage-earner having steady work and a regular income, and this was especially the case for families whose household heads were unskilled and worked for low wages. Some Irish-Catholic labourers, employed in factories or steadily employed by compatriot contractors, could expect to work between 200 and 230 days of the year and thus could provide for their families, but still the margin was very slim.[41] By contrast, many casual outdoor labourers averaged only $3.60 a week, far below the level of subsistence. In such families, the earnings of older children and wives would be critical. Seasonal or cyclical unemployment, illness, and death could easily disrupt the precarious subsistence of labourers' families. Winter, with its slackened demand for labour and lower wages when work could be had, inevitably meant misery and cold. Illness or death of a labourer – constant dangers in the fetid slums of Toronto – could mean disaster for his family: deprived of the earnings of the family's main wage-earner, wives and children would have to rely on the help of kin and charity. Even among the most established labouring families, poverty always loomed.[42]

Semi-skilled workers were more comfortably off. Painters and carpenters, when employed, could expect on average to earn about $7.85 and $8.85 a week. Their work tended to be seasonal, so that in many cases their yearly income may not have exceeded that of labourers who held steady jobs. Tailors, moulders, and pressmen, with an average income of $9.50 a week, were relatively prosperous because their high wage rates were not usually vitiated by seasonal unemployment. Though many skilled workers periodically faced unemployment, especially during economic recessions, they could usually afford in good times to rent a house or, better yet, buy one and so secure a measure of security against economic hardship. Their accumulated savings also enabled skilled and semi-skilled workers to go into business, and it was from these occupations that the Irish-Catholic business class originated.

As Father Jamot's census indicates, therefore, occupational differentiation was already established by the 1860s, even among unskilled workers. Many Irish Catholics had entered the trades, and not a few had started in businesses. This differentiation illustrates that many Irish Catholics had adjusted successfully to an urban and industrial labour market. True, many Irish Catholics were at the bottom of the occupational hierarchy, and this marked them as a community of unskilled workers in the eyes of Protestant Torontonians. But for the Irish Catholics themselves, their advancement was real; after all, they were still comparing their present achievements in Toronto with their Irish past. One of the major symbols of security became, for them, home ownership. Owning a house was something that they could only dream about in Ireland, and Irish Catholics in Toronto made tremendous sacrifices in order to realize that dream. Father Jamot's census indicates that some 45 per cent of Irish-Catholic family heads either owned or rented whole houses.[43] To earn that security, Irish Catholics in Toronto strained every scrap of their meager means. This quest to become homeowners best reveals how successfully Irish Catholics adjusted to an urban milieu. By adapting the traditional family economy to industrial capitalism, they were able to amass capital and acquire homes.

Single-family, two-storey houses ranging from fourteen by twenty to twenty-eight feet square were the most typical form of shelter available in Toronto. Prices averaged between three and four hundred dollars for a small cottage, and between six hundred and eight hundred dollars for a larger roughcast house. Rents for a two-storey roughcast varied from eight to fifteen dollars a month. The purchase of even a small house represented a substantial investment which would require the diversion of the family's entire financial resources. In order to buy a home, Irish Catholics not only systematically shaved their expenses to a minimum but also set family members to work. As well, most homeowners needed to take in boarders, at some five dollars a month for a room, in order to pay off the mortgage.[44] For workers with some modest means, renting a house and subletting the top floor provided an additional source of income and a measure of insurance against unemployment or illness. The crowded living conditions, in some cases a family to a room, were no worse than what they had experienced in Ireland, and for many were a definite improvement.

By taking in boarders, some Irish Catholics were able to use inherited cultural patterns to achieve economic security. This perpetuation of a household economy can most readily be seen in the attempts of Irish-Catholic householders to achieve modest independence by planting vegetable gardens and raising chickens and pigs. Both boarding and domestic industry were an extension and adaptation of the traditional household economy of Ireland, which centred on the production of eggs, chickens, and pigs for sale at the local market. In the city, the household economy generated income through subletting and domestic industry. The putting-out work done by women and children in the home was absolutely crucial to family survival. In particular, this form of domestic industry allowed women to combine housework with industrial work and to supplement the erratic income of the male family head.

The family economy made it possible for Irish Catholics to put down roots in Toronto, and in conjunction with Irish-Catholic patterns of householding and residential concentration created an essential informal network for the development of ethnic awareness. In the early 1860s Toronto was a commercial city and large-scale residential segregation had not yet occurred. There were no dense concentrations based on class or religion; Irish Catholics were spread throughout the city but were over-represented in Saint David's and Saint Lawrence wards, both of which had large numbers of poor, Protestant as well as Catholic.[45] Though residential clustering was usually on a small scale, readily observable over a few blocks or within a block, Irish Catholics were unique for their relative concentrations in different parts of the city.[46] Many Irish Catholics lived below Queen Street along the waterfront, but within this broad belt there was marked clustering in the east and west ends of the city, in the swampy flats along the Don River in Saint Lawrence Ward, and in the area around King and Bathurst streets in Saint George's Ward. Later, as the city grew, another concentration arose along Dufferin Street between College and Bloor streets.[47]

These concentrations were a reflection of growing residential segregation along class and religious lines as the city underwent industrialization. This process reinforced the concentration of Irish Catholics, but at no time did they come close to dominating or taking over an entire neighbourhood. Irish Catholics were always one group among many in working-class neighbourhoods, and their clustering was usually observable only along a single street or in a city block. Within these confines, not only were Irish Catholics mixed with residents of different national origins, but the social and economic status of the Irish Catholics themselves varied greatly.[48] Irish-Catholic businessmen and skilled workers lived alongside Irish-Catholic labourers. And despite these concentrations, Irish Catholics throughout the city intermingled to a remarkable degree with other city residents. The Irish-Catholic ghetto was less a place than a state of mind.

The Irish were "a social people," lamented Archbishop John Joseph Lynch of Toronto, who preferred "the pleasure of being amongst their neighbors" in the city to the isolated yet wholesome life of the country.[49] Lynch was mistaken in his belief that the Irish were a peculiarly urban people in Ontario, but his observation about their sociability was accurate. Small-scale clustering on the city streets was the most obvious manifestation of this sociability, or rather, it was the most visible aspect of the support network developed by Irish-Catholic immigrants. Coping with an urban and industrial environment so different from that of rural Ireland, Irish Catholics naturally sought out the company and support of their compatriots and relatives. Neighbours and kin provided food when one had hard luck, passed on news of available work, helped out with the laundry, minded the children on occasion, and kept watch on households struck by illness, ready to assist should the need arise. Contacts with neighbours and family gave the Irish essential support in their adjustment to Toronto and integrated them into the Irish-Catholic community.

Married Irish women turned to kin and neighbours for companionship and assistance. Shared housework and afternoon visits for a cup of tea or something stronger gave Irish women a sense of place and identity within the Irish community. Visiting was, of course, an essential element in Irish social life. In fact it is difficult to tell which was the worse social sin: to turn a neighbour away from the door or to refuse an offered drink. Women developed bonds with other women within the domestic sphere defined by housework and child-rearing. The kitchen was the place for women's companionship. The social life of most men, however, centred on the street and in the tavern, not the kitchen. The separation of workplace from household placed new strains on the family, and the sexual division of social life was one way of creating new bonds of support.[50]

One other significant aspect of small-scale clustering among Irish Catholics was the close relationship between home ownership and subletting which played an important role in the formation of an Irish-Catholic community. Although recent arrivals might have stayed at commercial boarding-houses, most Irish-Catholic boarders rented a room from a family. Only a few lived in tenements, mostly in the area around King and Yonge or King and Parliament streets, which in any case were rare in Toronto.[51] Some 45 per cent of Irish-Catholic family heads either owned or rented whole houses. By taking in boarders, these householders probably accounted for at least three-fifths of all Irish-Catholic households.[52] The prevalence of subletting helped to integrate recent immigrants and Toronto's floating workforce into the established Irish-Catholic community.

The drive towards home ownership and the family economy it required, as well as the small-scale clustering it resulted in, were essential for the emergence and development of an ethnic community. So too were occupational differentiation and mobility. The sizable number of Irish-Catholic businessmen and skilled workers provided an economic basis for community life. Most of the services immigrants required could be obtained within the Irish-Catholic community: when shopping for groceries, treating their friends to a drink, building a home, or burying their dead, Irish Catholics took their business to their countrymen.[53] The ties that developed as a result of this economic self-sufficiency reinforced ethnic awareness. By the early 1860s many Irish Catholics had become fully integrated into a rapidly growing urban economy and had achieved modest working-class prosperity – a steady job, a house, and a savings account.

Side by side with this established and successful group of Irish Catholics was a substantial minority who lived in poverty. The presence of so many impoverished Irish Catholics, especially in comparison to the number of Irish Catholics in the city, was one more factor that set Irish Catholics apart from the rest of the population. The Irish-Catholic poor inhabited some of the worst housing in the city: anyone wishing to see the slums of Toronto would visit in the course of their investigation streets inhabited by the "low" Irish.[54] Living among the foundries, soap factories, tanning shops, and abattoirs in the shanties along the Don River in Saint David's Ward or in the dilapidated houses near the wharves in Saint Lawrence and Saint David's wards, these Irish Catholics were exposed to the worst filth and stench in the city.[55] Contaminated well-water and overflowing privies, whose contents then flooded into basements after a downpour, were all too common.[56] In Fish Alley, near George and Duchess streets, which was inhabited by about fifty people and contained nine "apologies for houses," one newspaper reporter observed that "there are no backyards to the miserable hovels, and slop and filth and dirt are thrown out in front [of] the doors. At one end of the lane the necessary is in a fearful state and it is credibly believed that a well situated a short distance from it received the sewage."[57]

Next to filth, overcrowding marked the living conditions of these Irish Catholics. In a house on Stanley Street, a *Globe* reporter was horrified to discover that in two small rooms, their walls blackened and "broken to pieces," there were "no less than sixteen human beings, men and women, lying indiscriminately." A table, two chairs, a stove, and a box were the only pieces of furniture.[58] On Dummer, a street also well known for its poor Irish-Catholic residents, a reporter saw families in tattered clothes – barely enough to cover

Table 3
Irish Arrests as Percentage of Total Arrests,
1858–65

Year	Percentage
1858	67.3
1859	64.0
1860	67.5
1861	69.2
1862	63.9
1863	61.2
1864	54.9
1865	55.4

Source: *Globe, Leader,* and Toronto City Council Minutes,
1861–66.

themselves decently, it was noted – keeping warm in their beds, which were a "compound of a few rags, and a few handful [sic] of straw."[59] Living as these Irish did in dirt and squalor, with little furniture and even less clothing, it is not surprising that the average mortality rate for the entire Irish-Catholic community was substantially higher than that for the rest of the population.[60]

The dramatic poverty of Irish Catholic slum dwellers naturally drew public attention. Contemporaries were less struck by Irish Catholics who were living in modest neighbourhoods and quietly striving for working-class respectability than by the destitute Irish Catholics whom they frequently saw on the street, especially when these Irish Catholics freely violated middle-class sensibilities. Stanley, Dummer, Centre and Pine streets, with their large number of unruly Irish Catholics, illegal grog shops, and prostitutes stood out not because they were typical but because they offered sensational scenes and provided the police-court reports in the daily press with their staple of brawlers, drunkards, prostitutes, and lurid figures of Toronto's low life.[61]

Between 1858 and 1863 the Irish accounted for some three-fifths of all arrests. Unfortunately, the police force's annual crime returns did not report religious affiliation. Yet the frequency of Irish surnames in the police-court reports that appeared in the daily press leaves little doubt that Catholics accounted for a large proportion of the Irish arrested, as contemporaries were well aware. The high crime rates for this identifiable group reinforced the image of Irish Catholics as an unassimilable and degraded mass. While the Irish

Table 4
Irish Arrests as a Percentage of Total
Arrests by Sex, 1860–65

Year	Male	Female
1860	59.0	84.4
1861	65.1	83.1
1862	59.6	77.7
1863	54.4	74.6
1864	52.8	64.0
1865	49.0	65.5

Source: Toronto City Council Minutes, 1861–66.

Catholics accounted for a little over a quarter of the city's population in 1861, their arrest rate probably ran from twice to as much as two and a half times that of the population at large (table 3). An especially striking feature of the situation was the high arrest rate for women (table 4). Nevertheless, high arrest rates do not necessarily support the stereotype of violent and lawless Irish Catholics. Relatively few arrests in Toronto involved violent crime, and a good many arrests were occasioned by infractions against the code of middle-class propriety, which an Irish-Protestant dominated police force was very likely to enforce when Irish Catholics were involved.

What crimes were the Irish likely to be arrested for? The published returns on arrests do not provide this information, since references to the national background of those arrested are not cross-tabulated with another list of references to the offences for which these people were charged. Nevertheless, a general trend can be detected in these statistics. For example, in 1865, of the 1,108 women arrested, of whom 749 were Irish, 41 were charged with assault and 104 with larceny or suspected larceny. The vast majority of arrests, 704 in all, were for drunk and disorderly conduct. In the same year, of the 2,123 adult males arrested, drunk and disorderly behaviour accounted for 943 arrests, followed by larceny with 228 and assault with 225. In all, violent crime accounted for only one-eighth of the arrests made in 1865. Confirming this overall picture are police-court accounts in the daily newspapers, which indicate that Irish Catholics were mainly arrested for incidents resulting from drunkenness and occasionally for theft.[62]

The publicizing of Irish-Catholic crime in the daily press, of course, fostered the image of Irish Catholics as turbulent and lawless. In addition, Irish Catholics, with their readily identifiable names and accents, were well known to newspaper readers for their occasional attacks on the police in their attempts to "rescue" their comrades from the clutches of the law.[63] Irish Catholics, it seemed, were repeatedly undermining the legal process. Witnesses were unable to recall events essential to the prosecutor's case, the accused mocked the police magistrate's efforts to maintain decorum by addressing him as "honey," and not a few, when all else failed, lapsed into poetic nonsense: "The man was out, the stars were shining, and the lamps were alight," but nothing was seen and nobody was "fingered." One old lady, on taking the witness stand and being asked to swear on the Bible, declared, in a thinly veiled religious protest, that she "never had such a book in all her life and it was not worth her while doing it now." The courts with their King James bibles were an alien institution to many Irish Catholics, who preferred to look after their own and administer their own form of justice. However much they might disagree with one another, even to the extent of exchanging blows, calling in the "peelers" broke the bonds of community and loyalty to one's group, and it was not uncommon for victims to post bail for their arrested assailants.[64]

Accounts of Irish-Catholic couples lying on their babies in a drunken stupor, of inebriated Irish labourers beating their children or kicking their pregnant wives in the belly, and of stabbings, fights, and late-night brawling parties further confirmed anti-Catholic prejudice.[65] Even relatively mild reports, such as the story of Bridget Judge, appearing "in puris naturalibus" and with dishevelled hair, who was found "fighting· with herself" and pummelling "a fence most lustily," or that of Ann McCabe, "found lying in the gutter ... with her children playing about like little pigs," reinforced the image of Irish Catholics as a drunken and degenerate blight upon the landscape of the Queen City.[66] The association of crime, poverty, and profligacy with Irish Catholics is all the more interesting since most of the streets well known for their "low" Irish denizens, such as Stanley and Dummer, were inhabited by Protestant as well as Catholic Irish. Nevertheless, in this context Irish became synonymous with Catholic, as Irish Catholics well recognized.[67]

The stereotype of Irish Catholics as drunken brawlers appears not only in contemporary accounts but also in the historical literature. For example, Kenneth Duncan and Murray Nicolson base their respective interpretations on this stereotype rather than exploding it as a myth. Kenneth Duncan claims that the disorderliness of the Irish Catholics was but a sign of the "successful" retention of the peasant values of rural Ireland in an urban environment.[68] Murray Nicolson believes that, because Irish Catholics lacked the cultural skills to adjust to city life, they sought refuge in their traditional culture by indulging in what he identified as the customary peasant pastimes of rioting and heavy drinking. Nicolson tendentiously maintains that this "individualistic and anti-group" behaviour was not without some benefits: because of their riotous ways the Irish Catholics were not assimilated and absorbed by the Protestant majority. This in turn, Nicolson argues, allowed the Catholic Church free rein to create a new group identity and therefore to save Irish Catholics from the danger of conversion to Protestantism.[69]

The Irish-Catholic adjustment to Toronto was much more varied than such analyses claim. As we have noted earlier, the drunkards and the brawlers represented, for all their visibility, a minority group within the larger Irish-Catholic community. To see them as typifying the Irish-Catholic community is to assume that the part represents the whole. The truth is that, although more Irish Catholics than people of other nationalities were clustered at the bottom of the occupational scale, they nonetheless showed an ability and an eagerness to fit into the social and economic patterns of industrial life. By the early 1860s many Irish Catholics, indeed a large plurality, had become householders and had achieved moderate prosperity. The majority of Irish Catholics had become an integral part of Toronto's workforce. Their participation in the trade-union movement among the carpenters and shoemakers during the early 1850s amply demonstrates their willingness to engage in corporate action to advance their interests.[70] Irish Catholics in rural Ireland had a long tradition of resistance to defend their communal rights. Such traditional tactics as the boycott and vigilantism were extremely useful in the labour struggle. In Toronto, however, Irish Catholics were not simply reacting to external challenges to their community's moral code. Rather, they were organizing to achieve new goals, such as improved wages and control of their trades. In these circumstances, gang action, which had served so well in Ireland, was insufficient. The new form of labour activism required a new type of organization, an association of like-minded individuals devoted to achieving specific objectives and capable of steadily pursuing these goals over time. In short, the labour movement was sustained by the voluntary association, or more specifically, the labour union.

The ingenuity displayed by Irish-Catholic workers in combining traditional patterns of resistance with new forms of labour activism demonstrates that Irish Catholics were capable of organized and sustained collective action. This type of collective action, as Irish Catholics were well aware, could also be applied to ethnic objectives. Irish Catholics thus possessed a vital and adaptable culture that enabled them to undertake corporate initiatives to build their own community organizations. Moreover, their prosperity, modest as it may have been, gave Irish Catholics the economic resources necessary to develop their own rich associational life.

The laity's passion for voluntary associations was to affect their largest institution, the Roman Catholic Church. Religious voluntarism had a long tradition in Ireland, where the Catholic Church depended upon the free financial support of the laity, and despite their modest means Irish Catholics generously contributed to the church.[71] The parish church that the laity had known in Ireland was generally unable to provide sufficient accommodation for them on Sundays, let alone to offer them much in the way of social services (which it was later to do). In Toronto, lay expectations of the church changed dramatically. In a city where public institutions were dominated by Protestants, Irish Catholics looked to their church – the one institution familiar to them from Ireland – not only to provide them with material relief and social services but also to act in defence of their national interests.

The Catholic Church during the 1840s, however, was an unlikely candidate to become the principal ethnic institution for Irish Catholics. Because its rudimentary social services and ramshackle administrative structure were stretched to the limit by the arrival of the famine Irish, the church first had to undergo extensive administrative reform and reorganization before it could live up to the laity's expectations. Church-based voluntary associations were to play an essential role in this campaign of renewal, which eventually would make the Catholic Church the dominant social institution not only for Toronto's Irish Catholics but also for those in the surrounding countryside.

2 Reform of the Roman Catholic Church

The reform of the diocese of Toronto was initially an outgrowth of the Lower Canadian Catholic revival in the 1840s, which itself was part of the international movement of renewal known as ultramontanism.[1] This reform had three goals: establishing episcopal authority, creating a professional clergy, and "devotionalizing" the laity. Internal reform of the church was to result in the consolidation of the bishop's authority over his clergy, thereby giving him control over the local parish. Besides extending the bishop's authority, church reform also brought about an effective change in the standard of clerical behaviour, reorienting the clergy along professional lines. Many of the Irish-Catholic immigrants who came to the province were not in the habit of attending church. To reach the laity and influence their religious conduct, much more was required than a conscientious and zealous clergy. As part of the reform and reorganization of the church, the episcopacy established church-operated social institutions, such as schools, orphanages, refuges, and other social services, to bring people who did not regularly attend church into the ambit of the parish. Ecclesiastical reform resulted in the Catholic Church offering a cradle-to-grave culture separate from that of the Protestant majority, a development that was to have decisive consequences for Irish-Catholic associational life.

The revitalization of the Catholic Church had a direct impact on the development of Toronto's Irish-Catholic community, but it also unexpectedly contributed to community formation by provoking a

Protestant reaction. The energetic activity of the Roman Catholic Church made the ethnic character of the Irish-Catholic immigrants more visible and therefore more of a target of Protestant antipathy. Anti-Catholicism was to become part of the warp and woof of militant Protestant nationalism, which excluded Irish Catholics from its vision of Canadian society. While this antagonism was by no means the prime cause of the emergence of Irish-Catholic ethnicity, it certainly reinforced the development of Irish-Catholic separatism, a necessary feature of Irish-Catholic community building in Toronto.

Under Bishop Alexander Macdonell, vicar apostolic of Upper Canada from 1817 and bishop of Kingston from 1826 until his death in 1840, the Roman Catholic Church in Toronto was dominated by members of the Family Compact, the oligarchy that held sway over Upper Canadian politics during the 1820s and 1830s. Bishop Macdonell strengthened this gentry's influence in ecclesiastical affairs by appointing lay administrators from among its ranks to supervise the clergy and oversee parish finances. The Compact took full advantage of this arrangement. By restricting the vote for the parish wardens to pewholders of wealth and substance, for example, the Compact attempted to eliminate the Irish from the management of congregational affairs and so perpetuate its own dominance over the local church.[2] Regarding the parish church as their fiefdom and viewing the clergy as their personal chaplains, Compact members resembled the English gentry who dominated the Catholic Church in England prior to 1820.[3] As in England, however, élitist congregational government could not cope with the arrival of large numbers of Irish Catholics and the challenge that they posed to the church.[4]

As already noted, the image of Irish Catholics as a devout people, which has gained credence because of the extraordinarily high level of religious observance common in Ireland from the 1870s till today, is misleading. In pre-famine rural Ireland, the majority of Irish Catholics did not attend church regularly and many rarely received the sacraments. After 1820, the Catholic clergy began a campaign to inculcate canonical religious practice among the laity, but limited resources and popular resistance to this new form of piety prevented great headway till after the famine. The same situation prevailed in Upper Canada. Many Irish-Catholic immigrants in Toronto were not in the habit of attending Sunday Mass. The Catholic Church in the city was confronted with the enormous task of transforming these immigrants into regular churchgoers – a goal beyond the reach of a church that represented the interests of Toronto's Catholic gentry.[5] Moreover, the presence of large numbers of poor Irish Catholics necessitated new charitable and social institutions. The renewal of the parish and the development of social institutions that would help to integrate Irish-Catholic immigrants into the parish depended on a revitalized clergy under the direction of an activist episcopacy.

The erection of the diocese of Toronto as a suffragan see of Quebec was one result of the rise of ultramontane influence during the Catholic revival of the 1840s.[6] At the instigation of Bishop Rémi Gaulin of Kingston, Bishop Ignace Bourget of Montreal, the leading Canadian ultramontane, orchestrated the French-Canadian hierarchy's petition for the new diocese and gained its support for the appointment of his vicar-general, Michael Power, as its first bishop.[7] As Power was born in Nova Scotia of Irish parents, the bishops agreed that Power's background suited him to lead a predominantly Irish diocese.[8] Following the death of Bishop Power in 1847 from typhus contracted while ministering to Irish-Catholic immigrants in the fever sheds, Bishop Bourget again used his influence to fill the see with the candidate of his choice. After determining that no priest in the diocese was capable of undertaking the responsibilities of episcopal office, the bishops of the province of Quebec set out to recruit from either the United States or Ireland a priest of Irish origin. After a lengthy but fruitless search, the bishops realized that the quickly deteriorating state of the diocese of Toronto necessitated prompt action. Bourget then canvassed the support of the bishops to secure the elevation of Armand-François-Marie de Charbonnel to the vacant see.[9] Charbonnel, a former professor of dogmatic theology and scripture at Lyons, France, and a well-known preacher at parish retreats, had attracted the attention of Bourget soon after coming to Montreal in 1839. Charbonnel's experience of ministering to Irish Catholics during his chaplaincy at the Montreal General Hospital and his dedication to ecclesiastical reform persuaded Bishop Bourget to nominate him as bishop of Toronto.[10]

As a foreign-born cleric, Charbonnel always felt uneasy leading a diocese whose population was predominantly of Irish origin. An Irish flock, he believed, required an Irish shepherd. To achieve this goal, he attempted to secure an Irishman as coadjutor with right of succession. After several unsuccesful attempts Bishop Charbonnel finally discovered the Irish-born John Joseph Lynch, then rector of the Seminary of Our Lady of Angels at Niagara Falls, New York.[11] Though the French-Canadian hierarchy exercised little influence in the appointment of Lynch to the episcopacy in 1859, it played an active role in the elevation of Toronto to the status of archdiocese. At the 1868 Provincial Council of Quebec, the French-Canadian bishops took the lead by addressing the pope on this matter. In so doing they ensured that Ottawa with its large French-Canadian population would not be incorporated into the new and Irish-Catholic-dominated ecclesiastical province of Ontario.[12]

The first task the bishops of Toronto faced was to reform a clergy who were unaccustomed to immediate episcopal supervision. In order to establish their authority, the bishops enacted and enforced new standards of clerical conduct. In 1843, several days after visiting one rural church in an almost ruined state, its altar covered with dirt, Bishop Power severely rebuked the parish priest, declaring that "I have not yet recovered from the state of shock I received when I first saw the State of that altar on which our Redeemer descends truly and really whenever you celebrate the adorable sacrifice of the Mass."[13] Early efforts to improve the quality of parish worship were evidently unsuccessful; few years after Power's death Bishop Charbonnel sadly reported to Cardinal Giacomo Filippo Fransoni, prefect of the Propaganda Fide, that "le culte public était misérable."[14] Few Masses were said punctually at the appointed hour at Saint Paul's church in Toronto, and the choir were continually arguing over the selection of music or the choice of soloists while Mass was in progress – that is, if they bothered to show up at all.[15] Not surprisingly, Charbonnel observed, few assisted at Mass and even fewer received the sacraments.[16]

The purpose of clerical reform in the view of bishops Power and Charbonnel was to revive the parish and make it an effective agency for pastoral care. Such reform was ultramontane in inspiration, for it drew upon Roman standards and usages for pastoral practice and clerical discipline. In keeping with their ultramontane ideals, both Power and Charbonnel emphasized the sacerdotal office of the priesthood. At the centre of parochial life lay the Mass, the indispensable means of sanctification. The role of the priest, Bishop Charbonnel insisted, was to edify the people "by giving a shining example of religious [life] in the worship of God & the performance of sacred rites ... by continual, solid, practical & short instructions; by facilitating the frequenting and fervent receiving [sic] of the two sacrament [sic] of a Christian life."[17] This emphasis on the sacramental nature of the priesthood raised the status of the clergy and at the same time separated them from the laity. The replacement of the trousers and frock coat by the soutane and Roman collar was the most visible confirmation that the clergy were a distinct order. This shift in the conception of the clergy from ministry to priesthood was also reflected in the change in the form of address, from "Reverend Mister" to "Father."[18] Ultimately, the new conception of priesthood depended on the enforcement of ecclesiastical discipline along ultramontane lines.

The greatest problem facing the bishops was the shortage and low quality of the priests. When Bishop Power arrived in May 1842 he found only fifteen priests to care for some 40,000 Catholics in the diocese. By 1854, as a result of Bishop Charbonnel's efforts, there were fifty-three priests. After the subdivision of the diocese in 1856, however, there were only thirty priests in a diocese containing some 40,000 Catholics. The number of parish priests remained stable till the early 1870s. Then, after a gradual increase, the total reached forty-four by the close of the decade.[19]

The bishops experienced tremendous difficulties in recruiting suitable priests. Although Bishop Charbonnel had brought in forty-two priests between 1850 and 1854, he had expelled fourteen priests for insubordination and other flagrant breeches of clerical discipline in the same period.[20] Without their own seminary and with few vocations from the diocese, the bishops had to depend on peripatetic priests with unreliable testimonials and exeats.[21] The results were all too predictable. One priest, Bishop Charbonnel was horrified to discover, not only neglected to preach or hear confessions but rarely said Sunday Mass; in addition, he appropriated the parish funds and took in a housekeeper who was only twenty years old, much to the scandal of his parishioners.[22] This was obviously an extreme case, but the neglect of parochial duties, especially Sunday Mass and the instruction of parishioners, was common.[23] Generally, clerical laxity was the result not of contempt for church practices but of poor training: many priests were simply unprepared for what was expected of them, and some were almost entirely ignorant of the basic teachings of the church. Such priests could hardly fulfil their duties to their congregations.[24]

Another frequent problem was the tendency of priests to exercise their ministry outside their parishes, particularly in the case of marriage. As the decrees of the Council of Trent had not been published in the diocese, such marriages were valid, though illicit, and the clergy competed to perform them because marriage fees were a major source of their income.[25] This competition among the clergy was just one facet of the widespread avarice that characterized the church. Priests, Bishop Power warned, should not "be always talking money," as if "the *alpha & omega* ... is *money, money.*"[26]

The greed of the clergy, as in the case of illicitly performed marriages, undermined the parochial system. In their search for

better, more valuable livings, some of the clergy forged alliances
with lay trustees in order to resist the authority of the bishop. The
attempt by lay trustees to maintain control of their churches was
trouble enough for the bishops, and the quarrels among the clergy
over the allocation of Christmas collections and pew rents offered
the laity ample opportunity to demonstrate their support for one or
another of the contending parties. In at least one case, a priest called
upon the "boys" to throw a priest appointed by the bishop out of the
church while he was saying Mass.[27]

Many churches, because they had farms attached, were rich pick-
ings indeed. By renting these lands out, priests could substantially
increase their income by about sixty to two hundred dollars a year.
Some priests were tempted by the potential income of parochial farms and attempted to farm the land themselves. Others suc-
cumbed to the temptation of land speculation, as did one priest who
accumulated at least three farms in addition to nearly three thousand dollars in cash. Some priests were preoccupied with the business of running their farms and with land speculation to the neglect
of their parishioners. Others were so taken by greed that they used
their office to exploit their parishioners, and in one instance a parish
priest refused the sacraments to parishioners who were unwilling to
plow his fields.[28]

Though in the early years of the diocese some priests treated ecclesiastical property as if it was their own, for example by selling off
firewood from church lands, outright peculation, though not entirely unknown, was rare.[29] Far more common were exorbitant fees.
One priest was known to ask couples wishing to be married to pay a
fantastic fee of twenty-two dollars.[30] The avarice of the clergy did
little to encourage the confidence of the laity in their church, and
made the revival of parochial life, essential for the inculcation of the
laity with the doctrines and piety of Catholicism, almost impossible.

Next to greed, moral turpitude was probably the most objection-
able clerical offence in the eyes of the hierarchy and the laity.
Although sexual transgressions were unusual, alcoholism was a
continuing scourge among the clergy and was likely caused by a
combination of boredom and loneliness.[31] One rural priest described his daily routine in this way: "Rise 6 [;] 6 1/2 prayer and
meditate; Mass; breakfast; Sundry; dinner 1:00; Sundry; 6 1/2 dinner [;] 8 3/4 spiritual reading & prayer; door locked and no stranger
admitted (sick calls excepted) after 9 1/2 o'clock."[32] The repeated
use of "sundry" indicates that rural priests often had little to do.
With few opportunities for socializing – however modest their education may seem by current standards, priests were far better educa-

ted than their parishioners – many of them sought comfort in the bottle.

Much of clerical overindulgence was confined to the presbytery, but it was usually impossible to conceal for long. One priest, while travelling on a steamer on Lake Ontario, got so drunk that his embarrassed parishioners had to carry him off the boat. Another went on a binge, hopping from one hotel to another in Orillia until he finally started brawling. The parishioners, quite naturally, were reluctant to take him on; finally, the aid of several Protestant men was necessary to subdue him.[33] In any diocese that was perpetually short of priests, the ravages of alcoholism hit especially hard. As a result of drunkenness Masses went unsaid, confessions unheard, and children uncatechized. How serious the problem was may be judged from Archbishop Lynch's comment that he would have to "pay and answer" for this insult to God and he could only hope that God would be merciful.[34] Besides leaving their religious duties undone, in an alcoholic haze priests spent parochial funds and wildly contracted large debts, sometimes to support their habit but more often out of sheer impulsiveness and inability to balance the books.[35]

The lack of familiarity with the doctrines of the church and the responsibility of the priest, ecclesiastical "poaching," stubborn independence, and alcoholism – in short, the neglect of pastoral duties – prevented the development of parochial life and devotions. So horrified was Bishop Power that he launched an internal reform of the church in what is now southern Ontario. Imbued with the ultramontane fervour of his mentor, Bishop Bourget of Montreal, Power sought to impose new standards of behaviour on his clergy. One of his first steps was to introduce diocesan retreats, where he could more closely question his clergy about the performance of their duties and ascertain whether they had acquired an acceptable knowledge of the doctrines of the church. Fee schedules were established, and priests now had to account for dispensation moneys, which were the property of the bishop.[36] To prevent lay control of the parish churches and ensure that priests could be easily transferred at the pleasure of the bishop, Power insisted that the clergy and parish trustees vest all parochial property in the Roman Catholic Episcopal Corporation, which was the "body corporate" of the bishop and his successors. If trustees refused to transfer the deed, they would simply have to do without a priest.[37]

Bishop Power's new regulations on clerical dress, the performance of sacerdotal duties, such as preaching and Sunday Mass, and his requirement that baptisms and marriages be performed in the parish church, all were an attempt to impose clerical discipline. Yet these regulations were of little use without close personal supervision. It was only in 1846 that Power appointed rural deans to oversee the parish clergy, and the effectiveness of this move was vitiated by the fact that one of his vicars-general, William P. McDonough, refused to change his old ways.[38] In any event, the death of Power in 1847 temporarily ended episcopal efforts at modest reform. During the three-year period following his death, some of the clergy believed that they had little to fear and openly challenged the authority of the diocesan administrators.[39] Such dissension was to be short-lived.

Bishop Charbonnel extended the tentative reforms initiated by Power and brought about a fundamental reorganization of the Roman Catholic Church. By establishing the Cathedraticum, a tax of one-tenth of all parochial revenues, including fees, collections, and pew rents, Charbonnel was able to make parish priests accountable to the bishop for all moneys received. He continued Power's practice of holding diocesan retreats and conferences, and under his guidance rural deans efficiently uncovered clerical abuses and disciplined the perpetrators. Unlike his predecessor, Charbonnel ruthlessly expelled recalcitrant and unruly priests, so that between 1850 and 1855 sixteen priests had their faculties withdrawn and were banished from the diocese.[40]

Bishop Charbonnel also addressed the shortage of clerical manpower. First in France and then later in Ireland when candidates became available, the diocese recruited philosophy students, who were sent to the Grand Séminaire in Montreal for their theological studies. Vocations were also encouraged within the diocese and prospective seminarians received their philosophical training at Saint Michael's College, Toronto, founded in 1852. Finally, some postulants were taken in by the parish clergy to learn the rudiments of theology before being sent to the Grand Séminaire in Montreal.[41]

By 1860, as the result of these efforts, the worst was over. The responsibility of consolidating Charbonnel's achievements was left to his successor, Archbishop Lynch: retreats were now held annually, and the supervision of deans and vicars-general became increasingly routinized. Archbishop Lynch also continued the trend towards centralized administration by insisting that the clergy submit detailed annual reports on the financial and spiritual state of the parishes. The growing dependence of the parish clergy on the episcopacy was reinforced by the establishment of the Infirm Priests' Fund in 1863. With the provision of retirement benefits, the archbishop had greater freedom to transfer older priests to less demanding and less lucrative parishes or to retire them altogether.[42]

Alcoholism remained a serious problem, especially since the shortage of priests forced the archbishop to be relatively lenient with his fallen clergy. Still, these were a small minority. The overall impression one gains sifting through the archbishop's correspondence is of a zealous, if all too human, clergy. By the early 1870s, all the priests in the diocese had been educated in Canadian or Irish seminaries and were thus thoroughly exposed to the new standards of clerical behaviour. The result was a clergy imbued with missionary zeal who were determined to elevate the spiritual condition of the people.

While the church was certainly molded by the ultramontane ideals of its episcopal reformers, the ethnic loyalties of the laity also played a role in its development. The Catholic population of Toronto was overwhelming Irish, and this ethnic concentration shaped the laity's perception of their church. As early as 1828, Irish Catholics rebelled against the dominance of the non-Irish Family Compact in the affairs of Toronto's parish church, Saint Paul's.[43] Through a complicated voting system in which only those who held pews renting at five pounds a year could participate, the Compact had excluded the vast majority of Irish Catholics from having a voice in the administration of their parish. In reaction to this situation, the Irish-Catholic laity eagerly took up the banner of universal suffrage. The conflict, which lasted until 1835, centred on ethnic control of the church. Among Irish-Catholic immigrants, the church was a familiar institution from back home, and for this reason they insisted that it function as their ethnic institution and respond to their social needs.[44] This was particularly true for the poor who desperately needed the necessities of life, but better-off Irish Catholics also looked to the church for social services and institutions that would confirm their cultural distinctiveness.

Under Bishop Power, the Catholic Church in Canada West had little to do with the day-to-day life of the laity. Bishop Charbonnel developed a new approach to pastoral care by establishing a network of social institutions which would parallel those supported by Protestant charities. During the 1850s the danger of proselytism by Protestant-controlled social institutions came to alarm Catholics, and many feared that the Irish-Catholic poor were particularly vulnerable to Protestant evangelization.[45] In part, then, the rise of Catholic charitable organizations was a response to the humanitarian impulse among Protestant voluntary associations.[46] The development of Catholic social institutions was not, however, simply a defensive reaction. Catholic social institutions, having as their primary aim spiritual reform and conversion, were aggressive as well. They sought to reach not only the poor but all Irish Catholics regardless of class in order to create an inclusive community informed by Catholic principles. Nowhere was the new ultramontane spirit better exemplified than in Charbonnel's push for separate schools.

The public school system in Canada West was modelled on the Irish school system. The Irish school system had a number of attractions for educational administrators in the Canadas, and chief among them was its goal of offering a standard, non-denominational education that would appeal to a diverse population.[47] In Ireland non-denominational education never became a reality, but the ideal of non-denominational education was to cast a long shadow over the Ontarian landscape. Under Bishop Power, state-supported separate schools were intended as a last resort, "a protection from insult" when attempts at educational accommodation failed.[48] In short, Power, who accepted the chairmanship of the Board of Education, believed that in most cases the education of Catholics and Protestants in non-denominational public schools would not be inimical to the religious faith of Irish Catholics.[49]

With the arrival of Bishop Charbonnel, the climate changed appreciably. Following the precedent set by the Irish hierarchy at the Synod of Thurles in 1850, Charbonnel condemned the province's public school system.[50] "The infernal system of mixed schools," Charbonnel affirmed, "is the ruin of religion, and a persecution of our church." In this view, mixed schools were inimical to the idea that true education must be informed and guided by Catholic teaching. "We must have, and we will have," Charbonnel therefore insisted, "the full management of our schools."[51] Separate schools were an inalienable right, for only in separate schools could Catholic parents discharge their duty to provide their children with a Catholic education. This demand reflected the ultramontane ideal that the church was a complete society in which the education and the socialization of the whole person must necessarily take place under its direction and control. In this way, separate schools reflected a fundamentally new pastoral approach. Their purpose was to integrate Irish-Catholic children into the religious and social framework of the parish, and through them their parents as well.

After a protracted legislative battle, Charbonnel and Lynch secured, with the aid of French-Canadian representatives from Canada East, state support and local revenues for separate schools. In 1851 Bishop Charbonnel recruited two new religious orders, the Sisters of Saint Joseph from Philadelphia and the Christian Brothers from Montreal, to operate his schools, and by the mid-1850s primary schools were attached to each of the city parishes.[52] In 1863, the first year for which there are reliable enrolment statistics, 81 per cent of all Catholic children attended separate schools, a figure roughly comparable to that of Protestant children at public schools.[53] With their imposing edifices and Protestant personnel, the public schools were an alien institution for most Irish Catholics. By contrast, the separate school was an extension of the parish and thus a more familiar environment to Irish-Catholic parents and their children.[54] It was, moreover, an institution they strongly identified with, as popular participation in separate school board elections well illustrated.[55]

In addition to schools, charitable organizations were essential if the church was to become the central social institution for Irish Catholics. Until Charbonnel's arrival, the church had no charitable institutions of its own. The only Catholic charity, a private orphanage, was operated by a committee of Roman Catholic women from the leading families in the city. With a small number of financial contributors, the orphanage was regularly hard pressed to care for the growing number of Irish-Catholic orphans, especially following the influx of immigrants in 1847. In 1855 Bishop Charbonnel took over the orphanage from the committee, which was now unable to continue operating the home without the assistance of a religious order or the financial resources of the diocese.[56] When the House of Providence was opened in 1859 for the care of "invalids," the orphanage was transferred to the new building. This new institution, operated by the Sisters of Saint Joseph, made a substantial contribution to Irish-Catholic welfare. Within one year of its opening, it had 407 residents, of whom 241 were orphans.[57] Charbonnel's successor, Archbishop Lynch, established two other homes. The Saint Nicholas Institute for homeless children opened its doors in 1869, and the Notre Dame Institute began accepting young working women and Normal School students in 1871. In 1875, the Sisters of the Good Shepherd founded a home for prostitutes. The mid-1870s, then, saw the completion, with the exception of a hospital, of a comprehensive Roman Catholic network of charitable and educational institutions that served and were supported by Irish Catholics in both town and country.

The church's network of social institutions contributed directly to the development of Irish-Catholic ethnicity. Irish-Catholic immigrants in Toronto were remarkably heterogeneous in terms of their counties of origin.[58] The majority came from the south of Ireland, but virtually all regions of the country were represented in the city's population. Furthermore, because Irish-Catholic immigrants came from a country divided by a highly regionalized culture and intense local loyalties, the Catholic Church was one of the few things they had in common.[59] For this reason, the clergy regularly appealed to the patriotic sentiments of the laity when seeking their mite for the church's religious and social institutions. In identifying itself so closely with the needs and aspirations of the laity, the church became an institution that Irish Catholics could call their own. Through its social agencies and parish network, the Catholic Church provided Irish Catholics with communal institutions that had a purchase on their allegiances whether they lived in town or in the country. Not only did the church foster the emergence of ethnic consciousness, but it gave this ethnicity a particular cast. The social services offered by the church provided an institutional framework that resulted in a form of ethnicity in which religion was central.

Conflict between Protestants and Catholics reached such intensity during the 1850s that this decade has come to be known as "the fiery fifties." The influx of large numbers of Irish Catholics into Toronto during the 1840s and 1850s certainly contributed to Protestant antipathy. The continual parade of Irish Catholics at the morning sessions of the police court, along with their teeming presence in the slums of the city, led many Protestants to believe that Irish Catholics – unlike Irish Protestants – were an unassimilable mob, incapable of benefiting from the generous freedoms bestowed by the British crown. This attitude was intertwined with the Protestant perception of Catholicism. For many Protestants in Canada West, the transformation of the Catholic Church challenged the pan-Protestant consensus that was just then in the making.

   The Protestant population of Canada West was in fact both religiously and ethnically diverse. Each denomination contained members of English, Scottish, and Irish extraction, and likewise each of these national groups was denominationally diverse. In the 1840s, while Protestant-Catholic relations were characterized by relative tolerance, Protestants themselves were divided by divergent visions of society. That was to change in the 1850s. In the Victorian period, W.L. Morton has observed, "all Canadian politics were sectarian," and at no time was this more true than during the 1850s.[60] In both Catholic Canada East and Protestant Canada West, nationalist crusades to establish a religious and cultural consensus took on a political expression, with the result that the United Canadas were wracked by sectional and religious conflict.

In Canada East, the revival of Catholicism resulted in the rise of a French-Canadian nationalism suffused with the ideals of ultramontanism.[61] While a renewed Catholic church reshaped French Canada in its own image, the rise of evangelical Protestantism intensified anti-Catholic sentiment among Protestants in Canada West. In addition, the institutional consolidation of evangelical Protestantism during the 1850s coincided with the emergence of nationalism among the Protestants of Canada West. From that crucible emerged a self-conscious, colonial nationalism that fused evangelical Protestantism with British loyalism. This national vision was shared by many Protestants across the denominational spectrum and included people of all political stripes.[62] Even so, no single group benefited more from the emergence of Protestant militancy than the Irish Protestants.

Despite their large numbers, Irish Protestants and their fraternal organization, the Orange Order, were not initially part of the social establishment. The standing of Irish Protestants changed dramatically, however, as Orangeism appealed to a wider Protestant constituency. Drawing on the traditional pride of Irish Protestants as the loyal colonists of the British crown, the Orange Order offered a timely and appealing vision of the United Canadas as a thoroughly British and Protestant colony. All Irish were not alike, and by differentiating themselves from Irish Catholics on the basis of religion and British loyalism, Irish Protestants reinforced the image of Catholicism as an alien threat. As a consequence, many regarded Irish Protestants in general and the Orange Order in particular as defenders of public order and a dependable bulwark against the inroads of Catholicism.[63]

As an institution charged with instilling and transmitting a common culture and religion, the public school system became the lightning rod for popular fears of Catholic subversion.[64] Bishop Charbonnel's arrival in Toronto in 1850 coincided with the "Papal Aggression" controversy over the restoration of the Roman Catholic hierarchy in England. The controversy soon saw the firing of the opening salvos in the sectional confrontation between Canada West and Canada East, a confrontation that grew increasingly tense as public uneasiness focused on the ultramontane designs of the Catholic Church. When Charbonnel began his campaign to extend the separate school system in the spring of 1851, he threw the Irish-Catholic community into the middle of the sectarian quarrel between the two Canadas.

By the fall of 1851, sectarian conflict between Protestant Canada West and Catholic Canada East had become so heated that fully one-half of the representatives elected in Canada West were Clear Grits dedicated to the abolition of separate schools and the dissolution of the union of 1840. In this heated atmosphere Irish Catholics were now a suspected fifth column, all the more to be distrusted since their bishop was French-born.[65] The Catholics' demand that their particularity be inculcated and sustained by their own state-supported schools was a fundamental challenge to the province's British and Protestant moral order. At the same time, the large numbers of Irish-Catholic poor, who could be seen begging daily in the streets, simply confirmed in the minds of many that they were not merely an unassimilable lump but a degraded one as well. And their religion, inimical as it was to Protestantism and progress, provided a ready explanation for their condition. For many Irish Catholics, then, the virulence of anti-Catholic sentiment was an ever-present reality. In their search for employment they were frequently confronted by the refrain, "no Irish need apply."[66]

While Protestant antipathy certainly reinforced the belief of Irish Catholics that they were a people apart in a Protestant-dominated town, anti-Catholicism was not the primary cause of the development of their ethnic consciousness. Such hostility cannot explain why the Catholic Church became the focus of the Irish Catholics' social identity. To be sure, Irish Catholics responded to conditions in Toronto, including Protestant provocation; however, in order to understand how they went about constructing their world, one must examine the impact of the devotional revolution on their outlook and identity.

3 Renewal

Under the leadership of the ultramontane reformer, Bishop Charbonnel, the Catholic Church in Toronto effected, to use Emmet Larkin's term, a devotional revolution, a dramatic change in the nature of popular religious practice. The performance of canonical obligations such as Sunday Mass became more regular, and devotions recently authorized by the papacy – the rosary, the *Quarant' Ore*, the stations of the cross, and the benediction of the Blessed Sacrament – became part of the devotional repertoire of the laity.[1] These forms of piety so marked the style and ethos of lay religious practice that the Catholicism of this era can be accurately described as devotional Catholicism. The new style of piety was parish-centred in nature, and so the key to religious renewal lay in the revitalization of the parish.

Much of popular religion in pre-famine Ireland was independent of the parish and uninfluenced by the newly instituted norms of the Catholic Church. This pattern of religious practice reflected the church's weakness as a pastoral organization. Before 1830, poor discipline and training among the clergy contributed to pastoral neglect. Even though the quality of the parish clergy had become much better by the time of the famine, there were still far too few of them to serve the population. Between 1800 and 1850, the proportion of priests to laity did not improve much beyond a rate of one to 2,100;

no clergy regardless how zealous could have ministered effectively in such circumstances. Moreover, the shortage of clergy was aggravated by the lack of sufficient accommodation for congregational worship. In response to these twin problems, the clergy visited various localities in their parishes once or twice a year to say Mass and hear confessions.

As a result of the conditions described above, the religious observance of many Irish Catholics at the beginning of the nineteenth century fell far short of the canonical minimum of attendance at Sunday Mass and the fulfilment of Easter duties.[2] By 1830, however, reformers had rooted out the worst clerical excesses, and the church's program of church construction was well under way. The clergy's efforts to revitalize the religious observance of the faithful after 1810 resulted in over 40 per cent of the total rural population attending Sunday Mass in 1834, though regional variations were considerable.[3] At the same time, the new devotional practices promoted by the clergy made some headway, but their diffusion was still largely limited to the prosperous social classes and, in general, to the English-language regions of the country. Even in areas such as the southeast, where the devotions had made significant progress, religious observance had not yet reached anything like the universal level it was to gain in the three decades after the famine.[4] Nor did devotional practice match the intensity and the quality that marked post-famine Ireland.

The failure of ecclesiastical discipline, the low quality of the clergy, and the lack of resources cannot fully explain why the church faced so many difficulties in promoting canonical religious practice. The true explanation is that in pre-famine Ireland a wide range of unofficial religious practices and beliefs were part of the people's traditional culture. As long as this culture retained its resiliency – and it did so in many parts of Ireland until the Great Famine – the precepts of canonical Catholicism were unlikely to take hold among the people.

The religion of the Irish peasant was above all a localized religion. The popular religious festivals, known as "patterns," that were held in honour of a patron saint at a holy place, usually a well, combined a religious pilgrimage with social festivity. By stressing the relationship between the community and its patrons as well as the mutual obligations that bound the pilgrims to one another, these festivals reinforced communal solidarity. In addition to patterns, there were also country-wide annual festivals which expressed the community's dependence on the supernatural for its well-being. Many of these festivals marked the major turning-points in the agricultural cycle:

Saint Bridget's Day (1 February) signalled the beginning of agricultural work; Saint Patrick's Day (17 March) marked the sowing of the fields; May Day was associated with putting the cattle out to field; and Saint John's Eve, or Midsummer Eve (23 June), was celebrated when the days began to grow shorter. Magic ritual was also a part of these festivals, such as weaving protective charms from straw on Saint Bridget's Day.[5]

Perhaps the oldest communal religious celebration in pre-famine Ireland was the wake. With the corpse laid out in its Sunday best, often in full view, friends and neighbours gathered for a night or two of festivities. Story-telling, singing, and heavy drinking were common at wakes, and some of the amusements held at them, such as mock marriages, were explicit expressions of sexuality. Unlike other popular religious festivals, the wake had no inherent relationship to agriculture. Consequently, in contrast to those celebrations tied to agriculture, the wake survived the change in social structure and cultural patterns that followed the famine, albeit in a much modified and subdued form. Indeed, the tenacity of the wake resulted largely from its vigorous assertion of communal continuity and vitality in the face of death and profound social change.[6]

Because of their essential link to agriculture, unofficial religious practices were also a vital part of day-to-day life in which the sacred and profane intermingled. Precautions against the magical theft of dairy produce, the use of charms provided by "fairy doctors" to protect cattle, the propitiation of fairies to prevent them from abducting a child and leaving in its place a "changeling" – these and other practices attest to the extent to which dimensions of the supernatural frowned upon by the church impinged on the daily lives of Irish peasants.[7] Some popular beliefs were assimilated into canonical Catholicism. Many holy wells were dedicated to Christian saints, and Celtic festivals were incorporated into the church calendar, sometimes unchanged: the celebration of the festival of Imbolc as Saint Bridget's Day was a notable example. Other times the reverse occurred, such as the modification of Catholic practices to suit popular beliefs. Quite often official and unofficial religion overlapped; when leaving their magical tokens at patterns, pilgrims recited Catholic prayers, and the straw crosses woven on Saint Bridget's Day were sprinkled with holy water. Unlike the laity, most of whom made little distinction between official and unofficial religious practices, the clergy believed that canonical Catholicism and popular rituals were competing spiritual systems. The open recourse to unofficial rituals that provided direct access to the supernatural necessarily lessened the laity's dependence on the clergy and the church.[8]

Before the famine, the new religious practices promoted by the church had made gains in the more commercialized regions of Ireland, particularly among substantial and middling farmers. The rise of commercial, market-oriented agriculture created a thriving farming middle class open to outside influences and to new standards of propriety and respectability. The success of devotional Catholicism in this period owed much to the novel aspirations of this prosperous farming class. It was this class that most experienced the inroads of English-speaking culture and agrarian capitalism. Only after the famine, with the collapse of the Irish language and culture that supported the unofficial religious practices of the lower classes, did devotional Catholicism and an extraordinarily high level of religious observance become the norm.[9]

The vast majority of Irish-Catholic immigrants in Toronto arrived in Canada during or shortly after the Great Famine. What exposure would these immigrants have had to the beliefs and practices of the Catholic Church in their home counties before departing for North America? Religious practice in pre-famine Ireland was differentiated along both class and regional lines. Substantial farmers and their families were the most likely to attend church and, as a class, were the backbone of devotional Catholicism. But it was agricultural labourers, not substantial farmers, who were the mainstay of Irish-Catholic emigration to Canada in the famine and immediate post-famine period.[10] Official Catholicism in Ireland had made few inroads among these people, who tended to stay away from church on Sundays as at any other time.[11] Other Irish-Catholic immigrants to Toronto, albeit a minority, came from modest backgrounds either in small-scale farming or in the trades.[12] The exposure of these immigrants to the official teachings and rituals of the Roman Catholic Church would vary according to where they grew up in Ireland.

Information on the regional origin of Irish-Catholic immigrants is exceedingly rare. Fortunately, parochial marriage records make it possible to paint a regional profile of young adult immigrants married in Toronto between 1850 and 1859.[13] The vast majority of these immigrants, nearly one-half of the total, were from Munster. Those from Leinster came in a distant second, comprising a little over one-quarter of the sample. Immigrants from Connaught and Ulster together made up the remaining quarter. Of all these immigrants, only a handful came from cities or towns, where church attendance was generally high – between 60 and 80 per cent – and sometimes nearly universal.[14]

In rural Ireland, the Catholic church was weakest in Ulster and, above all, Connaught. In these two provinces, the population far outstripped the institutional resources and personnel of the church and, as a consequence, the majority of people did not attend church regularly. The situation was somewhat better in Munster, but even here people's contact with the church was minimal. For example, in many parts of counties Limerick, Tipperary, and Cork, which ranked consecutively after Clare in the number of immigrants recorded in the parish marriage registers of Toronto, the church's parochial network was greatly overextended. By contrast, in Leinster, with the exception of the counties to the north, church attendance was generally high.[15]

In sum, because of their standing in society or their regional origins, many of those who emigrated could hardly have had extensive exposure to the official beliefs and practices of the Catholic Church. Yet most Irish-Catholic immigrants brought with them a deep attachment to the church, even though that attachment might be more to the idea of the church than to its practices. The wide circulation of the prophecies of Pastorini in the middle 1820s, which foretold the violent overthrow of Protestantism in Ireland by a resurgent Catholicism, revealed the depth of popular identification with the church.[16] Immigration was to intensify this attachment, in part because unofficial religious practices and beliefs were local in nature and did not travel well.

In Upper Canada, the leaders of the Roman Catholic Church were deeply disturbed by the laity's lack of religious conformity, and under Charbonnel's leadership the clergy of the diocese became a disciplined corps devoted to pastoral reform.[17] According to them, the primary obstacle to religious renewal was the laity's culture. One of the aspects of that culture that the clergy found most worrisome was the laity's ignorance and indifference in religious matters. "J'ai rencontré partout une grande ignorance et intempérance," Bishop Charbonnel sadly observed some two years after his arrival in Toronto.[18] Some were "five, seven, and twenty years from confession," as one of Charbonnel's parish priests reported, and many more rarely attended Sunday Mass.[19] Besides ignoring the religious obligations of canonical Catholicism, too many Irish-Catholic immigrants, Charbonnel believed, were totally ignorant of "the Lord's Prayer, Hail Mary, the Apostles' Creed, the Commandments, how to hear Mass, to make one's confession ... and how to receive communion" – all of which he considered to be the bare minimum of observance.[20]

Besides ignorance and indifference, there was drunkenness, which, Bishop Charbonnel confided to Cardinal Giacomo Filippo Fransoni, prefect of the Propaganda Fide, had reached disastrous proportions among the Irish-Catholic population.[21] The annual reports of the chief of police leave no doubt as to the devastating impact of alcohol abuse, but the bishop was not simply referring to the moral and social effects of individual incidents of intemperance. Charbonnel was certain that the dissolute pastimes of the Irish Catholics were responsible for their indifferent religious observance. What was at stake was a way of life. The bishop was intent on both changing Irish-Catholic religious behaviour and remaking their culture. In fact, the two were related. The Roman Catholic clergy, like their evangelical counterparts, set out to reform popular recreation; dancing, drinking, "parties and amusements" were denounced as "immediate occasions of sin alike to those who indulge in them and to willing spectacles [sic]."[22] Wakes were especially singled out for condemnation by the clergy because of the heavy drinking and the "dangerous intercourses" and "familiarities" that were part of the celebrations.[23] The work cycle of the Irish, with its intense activity followed often by equally intense festivities and drinking, no doubt led many to miss Mass on Sunday morning. If the clergy faced a real competitor, it was the sheeban, which was open for business on Sunday as on any other day.

Equally disquieting in the clergy's view, the seemingly erratic alternation of work and leisure was incompatible with the demands of the Catholic Church, which stressed the regular performance of religious duties at a precise time and place. The rationalization of social life and the promotion of the regular and punctual discharge of religious duties went together, and thus the connection drawn in clerical jeremiads among religious indifference, idleness, and "extravagant expenses" was not coincidental. In such a perspective, the exuberance and spontaneity of the people's pastimes could be the result only of dissipation and idleness. The clergy realized that orderly habits – the virtues of industry and self-discipline – were essential for the regular and faithful performance of religious duties.[24]

Charbonnel feared that the religious indifference of Irish Catholics was particularly dangerous in a country where they were constantly exposed to Protestant influences. In such an environment, the reckless ways of Irish Catholics portended cultural dissolution and the danger that they could easily succumb to the wiles of Protestantism, which, in true ultramontane fashion, he associated with religious indifference.[25] "Leakage," the loss of souls to Protestantism, became Charbonnel's chief preoccupation.[26] Certainly many of the immigrants the bishop met were innocent of the basic doctrines of the church, but what he saw as ignorance was also a manifestation of the immigrant's religious eclecticism. Although many of their unof-

ficial religious practices did not take root in the New World, many
Irish Catholics continued to ignore most Catholic rituals, much as
they had done in Ireland. Indifference to Catholic ritual did not
mean that Irish-Catholic immigrants were indifferent to Catholicism, nor did it signify that they were not Catholic. For example,
though Irish Catholics felt that one could safely miss Sunday Mass,
to die without receiving extreme unction was considered cata-
strophic. Irish Catholics believed extreme unction and the wake to
be essential rites of passage, and hence both were thought to be
equally Catholic. Almost all Irish-Catholic immigrants identified
strongly with the Roman Catholic Church, but many also believed
that being religious had little to do with obeying the precepts of
official Catholicism. Yet it is unlikely that they took their attachment
to Catholicism lightly or that, given their traditional hostility to
Protestantism, many would take the drastic step and convert to
Protestantism.[27]

Why, then, did the clergy take the threat of leakage to heart? One
reason is that in their pastoral work they were often frustrated by
what they considered to be lay independence or, as Charbonnel revealingly termed it, stubbornness. Perhaps the most serious manifestation of lay independence in the clergy's opinion was mixed marriages between Catholics and non-Catholics. The clergy, as they re-
luctantly admitted, had little choice but to perform these marriages.
If they refused, the couple would simply apply to the nearest Protestant minister or justice of the peace. Whatever influence the clergy
could hope to have over the couple and, more important, their future offspring would then be lost forever. "I may secure all," commented Timothy O'Mahony, auxiliary bishop to Archbishop Lynch,
"if the marriage take place; I am sure to lose all if it is not performed." So concerned were the clergy about leakage through
Catholic-Protestant unions that such marriages could be performed
only after the couple had pledged to raise their children as Catholics
and a dispensation had been issued by the bishop. These obligatory
dispensations, which were granted by Rome to the bishop in lots of
fifty, were strictly controlled, and each case was personally reviewed
by the ordinary.[28]

Actually, mixed marriages were relatively rare during the mid-
nineteenth century: between 1864 and 1870 only twenty-seven
dispensations were granted in the city of Toronto.[29] Yet much of the
time, the clergy, especially the hierarchy, feared the worst. Father
W.P. Harris declared in 1886 that, because of mixed marriages,
Catholicism "in the next twenty years will be struck with death."
Evidently, Archbishop Lynch shared Father Harris's apprehensions,

for the next year he refused to grant dispensations for marriages to Protestant women.[30] Such a response was hardly commensurate with the pastoral problem mixed marriages posed for the clergy. However much individual cases may have caused them anxiety, mixed marriages simply were not a major source of leakage.

The preoccupation of the clergy with what they believed to be the excesses of popular culture and the problem of leakage indicated their desire to create an all-inclusive culture under the auspices of the church. The social institutions of the church – the separate schools, the orphanages, and old age homes – were a part of this effort to create a religious subculture. If the clergy were to win the laity to the church, they would have to bring religion to the people and present the tenets of the church more forcibly than before. The success of the clergy in transforming the religion and culture of the laity would depend on the revitalization of the parish.

The first step in transforming the religious behaviour of the laity was to make the church more accessible and to provide a proper setting for the practice of devotions. In 1845 Bishop Power began building Saint Michael's Cathedral, a great Gothic structure that was completed in 1848. When Bishop Charbonnel arrived in 1850, the two Catholic churches in Toronto, Saint Michael's Cathedral and Saint Paul's, completed in 1826, could probably sit about 55 per cent of those Catholics who were obligated under canon law to attend Mass.[31] As the churches were reasonably well attended on Sundays, though far from packed, it is likely that around two-fifths of the city's Catholics who were required to attend Mass actually did so, a rate of attendance similar to that found in pre-famine rural Ireland. With only two priests to serve almost 8,000 Catholics in the city, this was a remarkable rate of attendance for a church that had such minimal resources and was ministering to many Catholics who were not in the habit of attending Sunday Mass.[32]

While Bishop Charbonnel could have reasonably taken solace in the Roman Catholic turnout on Sundays, he saw things rather differently. For Charbonnel, the less-than-packed churches demonstrated how much still needed to be done to make Toronto's Catholics a church-going people. In this task the church faced a number of obstacles. The shortage of priests, the lack of sufficient space in the existing churches, and the location of both these churches in the eastern part of the city prevented the Catholic Church from reaching many of its flock. Catholics living in the west end of the city would have to walk at least two miles each way on Sunday mornings to attend Mass. To cater to the needs of the Irish Catholics in the west, a new church, Saint Mary's, was opened in 1852, and it obtained its first resident priest in 1853.[33] Two years later, in 1855, Saint Basil's, the small Gothic church attached to Saint Michael's College in the north part of the city, was built. Finally, in 1858, the Catholics living between Saint Mary's, to the west, and Saint Paul's, to the east, received their own church, Saint Patrick's. With the construction of Saint Patrick's, later rebuilt in 1869, the first phase of church building came to an end, and it was almost fifteen years before the Catholic Church resumed its parish-building program.

In 1872 Saint Mary's parish built a new church, Saint Helen's, to the west in Brockton. In the same year, Saint Peter's, a small roughcast church on Bathurst Street near Bloor, was opened as a chapel-of-ease to Saint Mary's. Three years later, in 1875, Saint Helen's became a parish in its own right; Saint Peter's was finally raised to parochial status in 1896, a year after Saint Cecilia, a small chapel purchased from the Presbyterians, was declared a parish to serve the workers in the Junction Triangle, some two miles north of Saint Helen's. To the east, Saint Joseph's Church in Leslieville, originally served from Saint Paul's, was founded as a parish in 1878. In 1886, two new parish churches were opened: the Church of the Sacred Heart on King Street East for the French-Canadian residents of the city; and Our Lady of Lourdes, the only domed church in Toronto, which took over a part of the old parish of Saint Paul's. Two of the older Catholic churches in Toronto, Saint Paul's and Saint Mary's, were rebuilt in 1889, the earlier modest churches being replaced by a large Romanesque palace and a Gothic edifice respectively, each almost as large as the cathedral itself. Despite this later expansion, the first five parishes – Saint Paul's, Saint Michael's, Saint Basil's, Saint Mary's, and Saint Patrick's – constituted the main parochial divisions and remained the leading parishes in the city.

All the city parishes were overwhelmingly Irish and contained a cross-section of the Catholic community, but each had a distinctive character and congregation. Perhaps the most prosperous parish, if the least populated, was Saint Basil's, where suburban professionals, the remnant of the Family Compact, and college students attended Mass. Even in this parish, however, the upper class and upper-middle class did not comprise the bulk of the congregation. When they went to church, especially at the earlier Masses, they mingled with the domestics and gardeners employed by the upper-class and middle-class Protestants of the area. Still, the number of civic notables was by no means inconsiderable. At Saint Michael's Cathedral, although the general run of parishioners was from the city's Irish-

Catholic working class, many of the Catholic élite held pews. Eugene
O'Keefe, a leading brewer in the province, Patrick Hughes, owner
of one of the city's largest dry goods emporiums, Mrs John W.
Crawford, wife of the lieutenant-governor of Ontario, and J.J. Foy,
later provincial attorney-general from 1905 to 1916, regularly
attended High Mass at ten-thirty.[34]

Other parishes similarly comprised a diverse population. Saint
Paul's parish in the east end was an example. Within its boundaries
were the casual labourers living on the Don Flats, industrial workers
from the city's foundries, and the largest concentration of middling
shopkeepers and businessmen in the city. In the west end, at mid-
century, the area around King and Bathurst streets was sparsely
populated by impoverished immigrants. As a result of the general
rise of both small-scale and large-scale manufacturing, however,
Saint Mary's parish contained by the 1870s a diverse and relatively
prosperous working-class population. Even the poorest parish in the
city, Saint Patrick's, showed this mix. Rebuilt in 1869, Saint Patrick's
church ran up a building debt that still remained unpaid some
twenty years later when the parish was taken over by the Redemp-
torists. Saint Patrick's certainly lacked the financial resources of
other parishes, but its population was mostly "solid" working class,
with a sprinkling of clerks, tavern keepers, and small shop owners.[35]

The church's building boom, which could only have been achieved
at great financial sacrifice on the part of ordinary Irish-Catholic men
and women, reflected the pervasive and intense support for the
church among Irish-Catholic immigrants.[36] The churches, declared
Father Joseph Laurent of Saint Patrick's, are "a monument to attest
to your children and your children's children the piety and generos-
ity of this generation; a monument to speak of you when you have
passed away, and to plead for you when you stand before the judgement seat."[37] In the early 1880s, with three Masses each Sunday
morning, the churches could probably accommodate most, if not all,
of the city's adult Catholics. But these "monuments of Faith," though
they affirmed and, perhaps because the laity saw in them the celebration of ancestral ways in the New World, solidified Irish-Catholic
attachment to the church, could not by their sheer presence alone
transform the behaviour of the laity.

To reach non-practising Catholics, the church needed a more
numerous and zealous clergy. After the appointment of a priest at
Saint Mary's in 1853, there were still only three priests to serve a
Catholic population of some 8,000. By 1860, there were nine priests
besides the Basilians at Saint Michael's College. Yet those priests now
had to care for over 12,000 Irish Catholics. Still, in seven years, the

proportion of priests to laity rose from one per 2,860 in 1853 to one per 1,150 in 1860, a much more favourable ratio.[38] The clergy in the city of Toronto were an activist group: besides saying Mass, hearing confession, teaching catechism, attending the sick, and preaching, they regularly sought out Irish Catholics, visiting them in their homes and inducing them to attend church.[39] Most of the clergy lived up to the high standards demanded by their ordinary, and only one parish, Saint Helen's, fell into neglect as a result of the failings of its two incumbents between 1875 and 1882.[40]

The strengthening of the hierarchical structure of the church, together with the increased emphasis on the sacramental role of the clergy, led to clericalism. The priest, declared Father Francis Rooney of Saint Mary's parish,

offered the Holy Sacrifice of the Mass daily for the living and the dead. He administered the sacraments, he visited the sick and afflicted, and he gave to the dying the pardon and peace of consolation and strength which only the priest of the Catholic Church can give. He frequently visited the schools, watching over the progress of their children and instructing them in the tenets of their holy religion. His whole life was devoted to the service of God and of the Church and by his zeal and piety he edified priests and people.

The priest, Rooney concluded "is our most disinterested friend."[41]

It may be argued, of course, that the clergy were exaggerating their place in the Catholic community and were doing so precisely because the laity did not give them their due. Such arguments are disproven, however, by the formal addresses presented to the clergy. In these addresses the leading laymen of the parish would praise the parish priest for his constant "tender paternal attention" in his role "as our spiritual guide" and "faithful friend." The laity saw the ideal priest as a "pastor, director, and friend," and the clergy in turn praised their parishioners for being "docile and obedient," as Father Joseph Laurent of Saint Patrick's parish put it.[42] While this clerical authoritarianism was often cast in paternal and sentimental rhetoric, it nevertheless conveyed the clergy's determination that the laity give due regard to their sacerdotal office.

The source of the clergy's prerogatives was their role as sacramental mediators, and church buildings soon reflected this new emphasis upon sacramental authority. The first Catholic church in Toronto, Saint Paul's, was a plain red brick structure, no different in appearance from non-Anglican chapels.[43] Later churches did not so easily blend into the cityscape. The Gothic-inspired Saint Michael's Cathedral, for example, was an expression of ultramontane ideals of worship. Catholic churches, no matter how small, were to be "grand temple[s] for the glory of God."[44] Indeed, because they housed the host, they were literally "the House of God."[45] The growing emphasis on the real presence of Christ in the consecrated host was accompanied by a proliferation of side altars, usually dedicated to the Virgin Mary, Saint Joseph, and other saints. Stained-glass windows depicting the apostles and other saints, but invariably incorporating "the great sacrifice of the cross" and the mysteries of the Catholic faith, added colour to dark church interiors and so heightened the image of the church as a sacred space set apart from the mundane world. Life-like statues, with the all too vivid wounds of Christ crucified or the Sacred Heart, served both to communicate forcefully the religious world mediated by the church's piety and to reinforce the impression that only in the Roman Catholic Church could salvation be gained.[46] These colourful, decorative additions underscored the claim that the parish church was at the centre of Catholic devotional life, the key to which was the Mass.

As the compendium of God's mercy for the salvation of humanity, the celebration of the Mass was "the first and necessary act of religion."[47] "In this journey," warned Archbishop Lynch, "we require strength and grace from God to withstand the many assaults of our enemies, and conquer the world and the flesh." "Without the sanctifying grace of God in our souls," the archbishop affirmed, "we can make no progress towards eternal life." Were it not for the Mass, he concluded, men and women would die in sin "to forever bear its punishment in hell."[48]

As a result of this emphasis on the centrality of the Mass, both as the principal means of grace and as a distinctive mark of Catholicism, the celebration of the Mass became more frequent. After Bishop Charbonnel's arrival, week-day Masses were said regularly, and by the mid-1860s the major city churches offered three Masses on Sundays.[49] The first two Masses were plain Low Masses. The priest would enter with an altar boy or two and in a low, scarcely audible voice would say the Mass in Latin. Throughout the Mass, besides the low voice of the priest and the rustling made as the congregation knelt and rose, only the whispers of people, mostly women "telling their beads," could be heard. At the elevation of the host, a bell would ring and all would bow their heads. "Not only quiet reigned supreme," observed John Ross Robertson, a well-known Protestant journalist, "but all motion of life seemed suspended." Shortly after the distribution of communion, the priest would read the weekly announcements and ask the congregation to pray for the souls of the recently departed before leaving the sanctuary. Lasting no more than thirty minutes, the Low Mass was a simple, but solemn, service.[50]

By contrast, grand High Mass, the service commonly attended by "society" and those who could afford pews, was an elaborate, musical, and extremely visual ritual. With the altar "a mass of light," the procession led by altar boys would enter the church to the accompaniment of the choir and organ. The parish choir's singing, the chants of the priests wearing elaborate vestments embroidered with gold and silver thread, the altar boys moving in unison, and the clouds of incense swirling around the chalice and paten impressively and powerfully conveyed the mystery of the sacrifice of the Mass. In the dramatic ceremonies of the Catholic Church, the *Globe* commented, "objectiveness plays the chief part, while subjectively the great theme is kept before the hearers ... to the eye is directed the principal part of the teaching." At High Mass the means of grace were elaborately represented and the sermon of the day was delivered. These sermons, lasting no more than thirty minutes – and often much less – were delivered in "simple elegant language" and explained the doctrines of the church.[51]

The development of parochial worship in Toronto, which centred on the regular celebration of the Mass, fostered a major shift in popular religious practice. Not only did attendance at Sunday Mass increase, but also the growing emphasis on the necessity of union with the suffering Christ, so strikingly represented in the sacrifice of the Mass and in the images decorating the parish church, led to the more frequent reception of the sacraments of confession and communion.[52] This new form of piety was also reflected in the private devotions of the laity; for example, Catholics now entered the church to pray before the tabernacle, where the consecrated host was reserved.[53] The emphasis on the real presence led to a change of behaviour within the church. Instead of chattering and amusing themselves, Catholics responded with awe and reverence while inside the parish church. This change in behaviour was especially noticeable when members of the congregation approached the altar and either genuflected or bowed before it.[54]

There were thus two aspects to the revolution in Catholic religious practice during the nineteenth century: a dramatic alteration in the physical setting for Catholic devotions, and a vast change in religious behaviour and decorum. Congregational involvement in the Mass was essential for the revitalization of parochial worship. Attendance at Sunday Mass became more regular and reception of the sacraments more frequent, and the devotional repertoire of the laity was also expanded and enriched. The performance of short devotions, paraliturgical rituals such as the rosary, the benediction of the Blessed Sacrament, and the like became the mark of a practising Catholic.[55]

Most of these devotions were not new; indeed, many had their origins in the Counter-Reformation, but despite their Tridentine roots these devotions now took on a distinctly ultramontane cast. The papacy's promotion of such devotions throughout the Catholic world and its standardization of devotional practice according to Roman norms and usage meant that they were closely associated with the the pope's Petrine authority. The result was to transform the style and ethos of Catholic piety as it was recast into a complex of interrelated devotions, each one of which was characterized by the repeated performance of ritualistic actions – an example being the recitation of the rosary. Devotions became so much a part of the style and ethos of the church that the Catholicism of this era can be aptly described as devotional Catholicism.

The relationship of paraliturgical devotions to the Mass illustrates how they structured and informed the laity's worship. Many devotions emphasized the sufferings of Jesus and the real presence in the consecrated host, and because of this close connection with the Mass they vividly imparted to the laity the distinctive doctrines of the church. The "unbloody sacrifice" of the Mass was nothing less than a repetition of Christ's death and the miracle of the atonement. Through his real presence in the Eucharist, "Christ Himself thanks His Eternal Father for the mercies bestowed upon the entire world." The devotions were designed to prepare the faithful for the Mass so that they would approach "the Lord with a firm belief of his real presence ... joined with a firm confidence in the mercies of the Redeemer." Devotions, then, provided the ritualistic and symbolic context for religious practice and so shaped the laity's understanding of the Mass.[56]

The most common devotion to the Blessed Sacrament was the service of evening vespers and benediction of the host that took place almost every Sunday evening in the city parishes. "The altar was flooded with light around the present Savior, veiled in his sacrament of love," wrote a reporter from the *Canadian Freeman*. While the congregation knelt, the choir sang the vesper prayers. Then the priest approached the tabernacle, wrapped his stole around the monstrance containing the sacred host, and raised it, slowly and reverently, three times to the ringing of the altar bell. While the host was displayed, the people bowed their heads, because, as John Ross Robertson explained, "the sight of it is so holy that no eye must gaze upon it."[57] The forty hours' devotion, or *Quarant' Ore*, during which the Blessed Sacrament was exposed for three days, was a more extended form of the devotion to "Our Lord in the Blessed Sacrament." In this devotion, the laity were encouraged to pray continuously, usually in shifts provided by the parish confraternities, in a perpetual adoration before the displayed sacrament. The purpose of this intense and elaborate devotion was to encourage the laity to receive communion at the spectacular High Mass, complete with procession of the host, which marked the end of the forty hours' devotion.[58]

Perhaps the devotion that most graphically impressed on the laity the sufferings of Christ crucified was the *Via Crucis*, the stations of the cross, erected along the walls of the parish church. This devotion was especially encouraged during Lent, when the parish priest would lead members of the congregation through the stations.[59] Dwelling on the "flayed and mangled" body of Christ, the laity were to remind themselves that "for a creature so unworthy, didst thou suffer ... Surely all this should suffice to wound my heart with love, and make me detest so many transgressions."[60] Through its graphic depiction of the passion, the stations of the cross encouraged the laity to atone for their sins by adoring the Blessed Sacrament, "the bread of sorrow."[61]

The stations of the cross illustrate the close connection that existed between the devotions to Jesus and those directed to the Virgin Mary. In contemplating the passion, the laity were reminded "how deep a wound was inflicted upon the heart of Mary."[62] "The sharpest thorn," was like a "sword of grief, that passed through the heart of that disconsolate lady."[63] Devotions bonded the Virgin Mary's sorrows with the sufferings of Christ. By associating the intercessory power of Mary with her sorrows, and thus with the sacrifice offered by Christ, the devotions led to the parish church's confessional and altar rail.

The benediction of the Blessed Sacrament, the *Quarant' Ore*, the *Via Crucis*, and the devotions associated with the cult of Mary were, as the *Catholic Weekly Review* explained, "the summing up of the Gospel." By encouraging the laity to avail themselves of the means of grace offered by the church through the sacrifice of the Mass, these devotions were crucial "for attuning our hearts to the harmony and unison with God."[64] The new forms of piety placed the parish church at the heart of religious life. If the church found members who rarely entered the parish church or others who, once fervid in their faith, had fallen away, then it offered them even more elaborate and emotional devotions designed to lead them back.

The purpose of the parish mission was to reclaim the indifferent and lukewarm. Mission preachers sought to transform nominal Catholics into practising ones by communicating forcefully and dramatically the claims of the Catholic Church and the consequences of sin. In an Irish-Catholic immigrant community, the mission served to integrate new arrivals into the parish. Missions usually lasted eight days – though two weeks were not uncommon if a mission was offered separately for men and women – and followed a prescribed pattern. On each day, the first Mass was celebrated at four-thirty in the morning and was followed by a sermon at five o'clock, which was early enough that working men and women could have breakfast afterwards before going off to work. The exercise was repeated again at eight o'clock in the morning. The morning sermons were intended to impart the principal teachings of the Catholic Church and to instruct the faithful in the nature of the sacraments as well as on how they were to be received. These catechetical talks were followed in the late afternoon by a tour of the stations of the cross and perhaps an address on the use of devotional aids such as the rosary, the miniature *Via Crucis*, or the *Agnus Dei*.[65]

In the evening, at seven-thirty, the rosary would be said before the evening sermon, the centrepiece of the parish mission. Unlike the earlier sermons which were instructional and catechetical in nature, the evening sermon was an exhortation to convert.[66] These "soul stirring sermons" were not "brilliant oratorical exhibitions that dazzle for the moment but are soon forgotten. Their words go straight to the heart, and make an impression on it that cannot be effaced."[67] Indeed, the themes emphasized in the evening sermons made forgetfulness highly unlikely. "The only things we know about death," one mission preacher warned, "is that it is nearer to us all to-night than it was last night ... nearer, perhaps, than any of us knows." "Since we were here last night," he pointedly reminded his audience, "a sinner has died in sin. Last night he was alive, last night he could have shaped the judgement ... the last warning has been turned away, the last grace has been rejected."[68] After graphically portraying the torments that awaited sinners in hell, the preacher would then draw a riveting picture of eternal bliss: "The avenue of grace," commented one observer, was "explained in terms that gave hope and encouragement to the truly penitent."[69]

Annual retreats and the holy week devotions preceding Easter followed the same pattern. So did other colourful and elaborate rituals such as triduums, jubilees, pilgrimages, and the forty hours' devotion. At once highly ritualistic and emotionally charged, these services encouraged personal conversions that culminated in the reception of the sacraments.[70] At the same time, they made the religious world of the parish a part of the laity's daily life. Private devotions were a major means of instilling the "habit" of a religious life. Devotional Catholicism, especially in its private devotions to the Virgin Mary or the Sacred Heart, was a discipline of piety.

The church's mission to the Irish-Catholic immigrants of Toronto resulted in a revolution of popular religious beliefs and behaviour. Of pre-famine religion, only the wake survived. The Eve of Saint John was forgotten, and holy wells became an expression of nostalgia for old Ireland.[71] Traditional Irish folk beliefs, no longer part of the Irish-Catholic immigrant's daily experience,[72] survived only in the form of literary entertainment.

Perhaps the clearest indication of the transformation of popular religious practice was the marked increase in the performance of canonical duties. Some 68 per cent of Irish Catholics of the age of obligation and older fulfilled their Easter duty in 1864.[73] In early 1882, a religious survey taken by the *Globe*, patterned after the British religious survey of 1851, revealed that slightly over 70 per cent of all Irish Catholics attended Sunday Mass.[74] The survey also indicated that evening vespers with the benediction of the Blessed Sacrament was an extremely popular service. On the Sunday enumerated by the *Globe*, 3,793 attended this service, which meant that on average the parish churches were filled to almost 90 per cent of their capacity. The large attendance at the benediction of the Blessed Sacrament is proof of the popularity of devotions.

By the 1880s, therefore, devotional Catholicism – a religion that stressed the importance of paraliturgical rituals – had triumphed. The contribution of lay devotional organizations to this remarkable change in religious practice in Toronto is examined in the next chapter.

4 The Parish and the Hearth: Women's Confraternities and the Devotional Revolution

In latter part of the nineteenth century Canadian Protestant women joined in unprecedented numbers a wide variety of voluntary associations, such as benevolent, missionary, and reform organizations, of which the best known are the Young Women's Christian Association and the Woman's Christian Temperance Union.[1] During the same period, Catholic women became involved in associations of their own. Although these associations were fundamentally different from those of Protestant women, they were similar in two important respects. Both had a religious impetus and both profoundly affected the larger cultures of which they were a part.[2]

In contrast to the diversity of aims and objects of voluntary associations among North American Protestant women during the nineteenth century, Catholic women's associations were typically organized under church auspices and dedicated to charitable or devotional purposes.[3] As a form of visible behaviour and self-expression, such associations were the principal vehicle of social activism among Catholic women. An examination of them, accordingly, allows us to map the progress of devotional Catholicism among Irish-Catholic women in Toronto and to determine the role that women themselves played in its rise. At a more general level, it offers us a glimpse into these women's personal and social world.

The associational life of women in the church had its origins in the interplay between the clergy's strategy for pastoral renewal and

women's response to that strategy. The result was a pattern of associational organization and affiliation very different from that of
men. To reform the religious practice of the laity the clergy adopted
new methods of evangelization and new approaches to parish ministry. Missions and jubilees were one method by which they sought to
awaken the laity. Such services successfully introduced many lay
people to the various devotions of the church and revived the religious practice of many others who had become casual in their observances. Yet the sporadic and episodic character of these services
meant that the clergy had to turn to other means to sustain the laity's
commitment to the church and its piety. It was to address this situation that the clergy founded devotional organizations or, as contemporaries informally called them, confraternities.[4]

Devotional organizations had two aims: to make devotions an essential part of worship in the parish and to integrate these devotions,
together with the religious and moral universe that they evoked, into
the daily lives of their members. Each confraternity created a social
setting in which devotions could be easily learned and practised.
Given this educational purpose, confraternities for children were
commonly attached to the separate schools. Little is known about
these confraternities except that they, like the separate schools with
which they were affiliated, enrolled children of both sexes, albeit in
segregated sections.[5]

Bishop Charbonnel began founding parish confraternities during
his first year as part of his campaign for religious renewal. These organizations were initially introduced to follow up the retreats that he
had organized in parishes across the province.[6] By the early 1860s
two of the largest confraternities, the Sodality of the Blessed Virgin
Mary and the Association of the Children of Mary, had become well
established in the city's parishes. The Apostleship of Prayer, also
known as the League of the Sacred Heart, was introduced to the city
by Charbonnel's successor, Bishop Lynch, during the mid-1860s,
and by the following decade its branches had become a fixture of
parish life. The one significant latecomer, the Archconfraternity of
the Holy Family, was not generally organized in the parishes until
the early 1880s.[7]

The devotions promoted by these confraternities differed substantially in style from earlier forms of piety popular among educated English-speaking Catholics during the late eighteenth and early
nineteenth centuries. This earlier spirituality was reserved, even
ascetic. By contrast, a strong emotional strain ran through the new
devotionalism. Although Catholicism in this era placed a heavy emphasis on doctrinal orthodoxy and precise dogmatic formulation, it

was also very much a religion of the heart. The elaborate and highly visible rituals and church decorations, the powerful appeals of the mission sermons, and the vivid meditations associated with the new Roman devotions, all testified to the emotional and sentimental focus of Catholic piety. The devotions favoured by the ultramontanes sought to induce the faithful to forge a personal and familiar bond with Jesus, Mary, or one or another saint.[8]

By entering into a relationship with these supernatural beings through the performance of devotions, the believer could participate in the communion of the saints and share in the salvation offered to the faithful through the intercession of the Roman Catholic Church. Through Mary, the mother of God, the manual for the Archconfraternity of Holy Family assured the faithful, "We have the most certain means of obtaining [the] inestimable gift of divine love, since she has been appointed by her Son, the Treasurer and Dispenser of all graces, and is therefore our most compassionate intercessor and advocate with God."[9]

Among all the devotions, it is perhaps the resurgence of Marian piety that most clearly reveals the development of piety among Irish-Catholic women in Toronto. All of the parish devotional organizations – the Children of Mary, the Sodality of the Blessed Virgin Mary, the Archconfraternity of the Holy Family, the Confraternity of the Scapular of Our Lady of Mount Carmel, the Apostleship of Prayer or League of the Sacred Heart – promoted devotions to Mary, especially the saying of the rosary. The rosary was a series of prayers, usually counted on a string of beads, in which the faithful recited fifteen decades of the Hail Mary, with each decade being preceded by an Our Father and followed by a Glory be to the Father. Associated with each decade was a meditation on the life of Mary and Jesus that linked Mary's purity and maternal solicitude with the salvific work of Jesus.

The popularization of the rosary transformed the nature of devotional life among Irish-Catholic women. The rosary, unlike many other Catholic devotions, did not require the mediation of a priest and could be easily performed in the home as well as in the church. Consequently, the rosary became an intensely private devotion. During the celebration of the Mass, the attention of many women was usually directed towards saying the rosary.[10] Few could understand Latin, and Catholic prayer books, a result of Pope Pius IX's prohibition of translations of the liturgy, usually provided only "Mass devotions and meditations" rather than liturgical texts.[11] Like other devotions, the rosary was the prism through which the laity interpreted the Mass. Yet, far from isolating its devotees, the rosary inevitably led to communal affirmation through the reception of the sacraments.

The purpose of the rosary, Bishop Charbonnel explained, "is to unite ourselves, in the course of our daily actions and sufferings to the Blessed Virgin Mary, to Her thoughts, Her Judgments, Her feelings, Her conversations, so that we may live and die as she did for God alone."[12] Mary's devotion to Jesus provided lay women with a model of true piety and maternal solicitude. As the mother of God and a divine mediator, Mary was the spiritual mother of the faithful. Mary's graces and spiritual favours, purchased through her sacrifice and suffering, led her devotees to Christ crucified.[13] In the meditations the laity were encouraged to engage in while reciting the rosary, the sufferings of Mary were associated with Christ's sacrifice and his loving offer of salvation. The passion was thus central to the rosary, as it was to all other devotions.

The rosary stirred women to emulate Mary's self-denying love. Yet this life of piety could be sustained only by the sacraments of the church. Devotions bridged the seemingly infinite gulf between the sacred and profane and therefore made the sacraments much more accessible to the laity. By establishing such an intimate relationship with Mary, a relationship that was rooted in Christ's passion, the rosary inspired Irish-Catholic women to receive the sacraments and so unite themselves with Christ. Without the sanctifying grace conveyed by the sacraments, Archbishop Lynch warned, "we can make no progress towards eternal life."[14] When informed by the sacraments, "the most indifferent works become eminently meritorious and of truly apostolic efficacy."[15]

All women's confraternities advocated the frequent reception of the sacraments.[16] (When the confraternities were first introduced to the city, "frequent" meant monthly.) In the interval between the reception of the sacraments, the performance of daily devotions such as the rosary served to reinforce the sacramental relationship between the faithful and the divine. Although the rosary could be performed almost anywhere, it was nevertheless essentially a parish-centred devotion designed to suffuse day-to-day life with the sacraments.[17] Like all Catholic devotions, it fostered a distinctive way of life for Irish-Catholic women, one that revolved around the parish.

Besides disseminating the rosary, women's devotional organizations encouraged daily prayers, usually the reciting of the Our Father and the Hail Mary, as well as the use of devotional aids: the crucifix with or without the miniature *Via Crucis*, the *Agnus Dei*, scapulars, medals, and prayer cards. These portable aids – one confraternity, that of the Holy Family, advocated raffling them to encourage their use – promoted the practice of private devotions among Irish-Catholic women.[18] The day of a confraternity member was punctuated by short devotions such as the litany of the Blessed Virgin Mary, short exclamatory prayers ("My dear Jesus, I love you"), and, if possible, a visit to the Blessed Sacrament or a statue of the Blessed Virgin in the parish church.[19] As with the rosary, the purpose of these devotions and devotional aids was to make the sacraments part of the faithful's daily lives and so draw them to the parish church where the host was reserved in the tabernacle.

Most women's confraternities encouraged their members to make regular devotions to the reserved host, and two societies, the Apostleship of Prayer and the Sodality of the Blessed Virgin Mary, were especially active in promoting the perpetual adoration of the Blessed Sacrament or the forty hours' devotion.[20] By honouring "Our Lord's presence in the Holy Sacrament," the laity could make "reparation for the Outrages Our Lord and Savior received during his Passion and those He daily received in the Holy Sacrament of our Altars."[21]

One of the more spectacular manifestations of this veneration of the suffering Christ was the devotion to the Sacred Heart of Jesus advocated by the Apostleship of Prayer. The Sacred Heart of Jesus, often depicted surrounded by a crown of thorns and pierced by a sword dripping blood, vividly conveyed the sufferings of Christ, but it also symbolized a heart of divine love.[22] Through the "infinite bounty" of the Sacred Heart, the members of the Apostleship of Prayer gained "the graces we stand in need of."[23] The devotion to the suffering Christ exemplified the close connection between the incarnation, the sacraments, and good works in Catholic piety. Devotions encouraged lay women to lead holy lives committed to the performance of good works and thus to make reparation for their past sins. And to renounce sin was to renounce the world.[24]

The devotions to the suffering Christ energetically promoted by the parish confraternities, especially the Apostleship of Prayer, marked the Catholic Church's retreat from the modern world. The same was true of another devotion, that centred on the person of the pope. This devotion reflected the growing authority of the pope in the church (which culminated in the declaration of papal infallibility at the Vatican Council in 1870). It also reflected, however, the papacy's declining power in the secular world. With the conquest of the papal states in the same year as the Vatican Council, the devotion to the pope increasingly came to express the faithful's sympathy for their beleaguered pontiff. In protest against the usurpation of his temporal power, Pius IX shut himself in the Vatican and refused to recognize the Italian government now installed in Rome. Venerated as the "Prisoner of the Vatican," the pope symbolized the church's withdrawal from a world that it now saw as profoundly sinful.

All parish confraternities for Irish-Catholic women, with their papal indulgences and exhortations to pray for the intentions of the holy father, promoted the cult of the pope.[25] The idealization of the pope as the spiritual father of the faithful resulted in the church becoming a family of faith.[26] In this family, the faithful became tied to their superiors, both in heaven and on earth, through the devotions of the church and the economy of salvation that they represented and made available to the laity. The affinities generated by this piety – at once formal and informal, distant and immediate – were removed from the outside world and identified with the nurturing and emotional bonds of the family. Indirectly, but in a manner that nevertheless made an indelible impression on the faithful, the devotion to the pope, like all devotions associated with the revival in the church, reinforced the personal and private character of faith.

In the world, especially the working world of "shops and manufactories," warned Archbishop Lynch, "vice and profanity" flourished. The sacraments were a shield against these worldly and corrupting influences.[27] With the clergy increasingly referring to the church as "the Mother Church," the emphasis was placed less on preparation for Christian action than on withdrawal from the world.[28] As with the devotion to the pope, this form of piety equated true religion with domesticity, in its case by identifying the Roman Catholic Church with Mary. Just as a mother and wife in the home protected her husband and children from the "narrow, selfish, and impious" spirit of the world and nurtured their religion, so too did the church protect and nurture the faithful. Like the home, the church was a haven in a materialistic and immoral world.

Devotions, especially those to the Sacred Heart and to the Virgin Mary, also revealed a markedly sentimental strain. The devotions cultivated an intense private emotional life that was both sustained and expressed in public rituals in the parish church. One manifestation of this sentimentalism was the devotion to the Blessed Sacrament, in particular the forty hours' devotion. In the Archconfraternity of the Holy Family, the women members were encouraged to dwell on the passion as represented in the Blessed Sacrament:

His sacred hands and feet are pierced through and through with wide nails hammered deep in the wood; his kingly head is crowned with thorns, his sacred body is covered with marks of cruel scourges; and his unspeakable agony appears in his dying eyes and the convulsions of his suffering limbs.

Who is it? And what is the cause of this bloody spectacle? Ah! sinner it is your Saviour, and your sins have brought Him to this sad extremity. Yes for your sake He became man, for the pardon of your sins He suffered and died ... cruel sinner, who in our day still crucify their [sic] Lord, and mock at his pains.[29]

Devotions induced an affective state in which the faithful identified with the suffering of a supernatural figure. Louisa White, a student at Loretto Abbey, wrote to her father that the sight of the crucifix atop the tabernacle where the Blessed Sacrament was reserved was "so dolorous that I imagined I could almost perceive the tears."[30] Through the intercessory prayers of the various devotions of the church, the faithful called upon Jesus, Mary, or their patron saint for the divine assistance that would soften their hearts.[31] This form of piety heightened the dependence of the faithful on their supernatural patrons and at the same time associated this dependence with the cultivation of virtue. The practice of piety was thus a means of acquiring virtue. The virtues cultivated through these devotions – love, service, and self-sacrifice – made manifest the bond between votary and patron. Such attributes, through their association with the affective relationships women forged in the domestic circle, represented virtue as a habit of the heart nurtured in the family of faith.

The very object of the devotion to the Sacred Heart illustrated the private and personal character of devotional piety. This devotion marked a turning inwards from the usual emphasis on the exterior of the body of Christ to the interior of that body.[32] Each transgression, it was said, caused a shot of pain to run through the Sacred Heart.[33] In performing devotions, devotees united themselves with the Sacred Heart and so offered reparation for their sins. The private nature of this devotion strengthened emotional identification with Jesus, but the personal quest for holiness was also characterized by the performance of visible acts of piety. All the devotions were highly ritualized "minute individual observances."[34] How they were performed was absolutely crucial: proper comportment and the correct and timely gesture were integral to Catholic piety.[35] Though Catholic devotions were intensely private, the accompanying emphasis on exterior acts reflected and supported the vigorous moralistic strain within Victorian Catholicism. In this active piety, right living and orthodox religious behaviour went together. Life was prayer in action, and so the devout Catholic was "to offer up faithfully and with regularity all the actions of the day."[36] The other side of Catholic moralism was a strong emphasis on religious behaviour.

The life of piety was a rigorous one that many found difficult to sustain on their own. Parish missions and other services, such as the *Quarant' Ore* and jubilees, introduced new devotions and galvanized the laity, but their impact was short-lived.[37] The parish confraternities were to feed the spark set off by the parish mission and to finish its work of converting people to a life of faith and piety.[38] As the proponents of the confraternities understood, this life of faith and piety was best imparted and sustained in intimate groups rather than in the general anonymity of the larger congregation. Through their regular bi-weekly or, more commonly, monthly meetings in which the collective performance of devotions were the central activity, confraternities created a setting in which Irish-Catholic women could practise piety and absorb its view of the world.

Most devotional organizations had meeting-rooms where their business was conducted and various religious exercises were practised. These rooms were also used by the smaller devotional circles into which most confraternities were divided. In the privacy of these smaller circles, each member was encouraged to participate and contribute to the group's activities. The repeated performance of the devotions not only cemented the members' commitment to the Catholic Church but also enabled members to get to know each other better and to form new friendships. These friendships were further developed and strengthened in the confraternities' informal meetings in the homes of members, where women gathered to sew and bake as part of their efforts to raise funds for the parish.[39] Members of the devotional societies offered each other mutual support and encouragement, and they did so by creating a social world in the parish that was part and parcel of women's sociability and domestic rituals. The bonds of friendship nurtured in this social world bestowed a sense of belonging and an identity of purpose that sustained women in the practice of piety and enabled them to internalize the religious world of Catholic piety.[40] Through their devotional organizations women forged a distinctive way of life, one that can best described as a culture of piety. This culture of piety encouraged women to become active in the parish and to contribute to its spiritual vitality.

Confraternities helped to revitalize the parish by extending the range of devotional observances. In addition to disseminating private devotions, which were related in a variety of ways to the sacrifice of the Mass, women contributed in a more direct fashion to the public worship of the parish. Confraternities played a critical role in the development of the public performance of devotions in the parish church, such as vespers, the benediction of the Blessed Sacrament, and the forty hours' devotion. When these parish-centred devotions were first introduced in the early 1850s, it was primarily the women members of the confraternities who assisted at them.[41] Public ceremonies of this kind were, of course, orchestrated by the clergy, but the confraternities made an invaluable contribution. The leading role taken by the members of the confraternities in church processions, at vespers, and at the forty hours' devotion galvanized the parish and acted as leaven, encouraging others to participate in the devotions of the church. By the 1880s these parochial devotions, as the *Globe's* survey of church attendance in 1882 revealed, had become popular indeed, and on Sunday evenings, when vespers and the benediction of the Blessed Sacrament were celebrated, the parish churches were filled close to capacity.[42]

Parish confraternities were a critical agency in popularizing the Roman Catholic Church's private as well as public forms of piety. The devotional program promoted by these parish organizations effected a revolution in the scope, nature, and style of Catholic piety. Confraternities vastly expanded the range of Catholic religious practice, and in so doing they set a new standard for religious observance among Catholics. The devotional revolution forged by confraternities resulted in the piety of the church becoming standardized along Roman lines. The close identification of the devotions with the papacy, both formally through the papacy's endorsement and in their content, as in the devotions to the pope, meant that for clergy, as well as for a growing number of women, the performance of these devotions was the mark of a practising Roman Catholic.

The rise of devotional Catholicism, as Roger Aubert has observed, represented the "true triumph of Ultramontanism" within the Catholic Church.[43] Not only did this distinctive form of piety distinguish Roman Catholics from other Christians, but it served to separate the devout from the lukewarm within the Catholic Church itself. The religious universe entered through these rituals also served to communicate and, perhaps more important, internalize the world view of ultramontanism. The piety promoted by the devotional organizations was an active and exterior piety, characterized by intense adoration and by the repeated ritual performance of prescribed acts.[44] At the same time, this form of piety cultivated among the faithful a rich interior life of marked emotional intensity, most notably in their personal relationships with spiritual figures. Both the exterior and interior aspects of this piety fostered a drive for personal sanctity,

and in this pursuit of holiness the members of the devotional organizations made the religious rituals and universe of the parish
church a part of their daily lives.

The purpose of the confraternities and sodalities was to popularize
Catholic devotions. Yet how many Catholics in fact joined these parish organizations? Were some Catholics more likely to enrol than
others? Unfortunately, complete and detailed reports on parish confraternities before 1895 are extremely rare; only one such report,
from Saint Mary's parish in 1881, has survived. In this parish of
5,000 there were some 1,620 confraternity members, or almost a
third of the total congregation. This figure apparently includes 570
school children, who, if deducted from the total membership, leave
1,050 or roughly a quarter of the parish's adult population.[45] Such
large enrolment was not at all unusual. At about the same time, the
Apostleship of Prayer had some eight hundred members in Saint
Paul's parish alone. Still, while a substantial segment of the parish
population joined confraternities, the available figures do not indicate where the true strength of these organizations lay. Women
dominated the membership of the devotional organizations, but just
what proportion of the membership did they in fact comprise?

Only one nominal roll, that of the city-wide Saint Joseph's Bona
Mors Society has survived, but its detailed membership list makes it
possible to fix an upper limit for male membership in devotional
organizations. In this society men accounted for only a tenth of the
membership, and three-fifths of them were married to women who
belonged to the society.[46] As a city-wide association, the Saint
Joseph's Society was not typical of the parish devotional organizations, but it is unlikely that men were more prominent in the parish
confraternities than in the Saint Joseph's Society. In contrast to the
parish devotional organizations, the Saint Joseph's Society did not
require its members to attend meetings and to participate regularly
in collective devotions. Moreover, the material benefit offered by the
Saint Joseph Society in return for a twenty-five cent annual membership fee was significant – a free funeral Mass. The religious requirements of the Saint Joseph's Society were far from onerous, and for
many men joining the society must have been an easy way to appease
their wives' anxieties over their spiritual state.

All of this leads to the following conclusions. First, it can be assumed that women made up least nine-tenths of the confraternities'
adult membership in Saint Mary's parish. Second, if it is further

assumed that the proportion of Irish-Catholic women in the parish reflected that of the general population, thereby comprising about half of the parish's adult population, then some two-fifths of all women in that parish belonged to one or another of the parish's confraternities.[47] Even these figures probably discount the full impact of the parish confraternities on the female population. The Saint Joseph's Society, for example, had an average membership of 158, yet over ten years some 336 people, the vast majority of them women, at one time or another belonged to the society.[48] This turnover indicates that static membership figures underestimate women's involvement in the parish confraternities. Saint Mary's may not have been a typical parish, but it is nonetheless clear that confraternities enjoyed substantial support among Irish-Catholic women by the early 1880s. By the next decade, parish devotional organizations were to enjoy almost universal support among Irish-Catholic women. In 1895, the Apostleship of Prayer had some 6,000 members city-wide – more than nine out of ten of all Catholic women in the city.[49]

The large membership of Saint Mary's devotional organizations in the early 1880s indicates that devotional Catholicism among Irish-Catholic women had come of age. Without more detailed membership statistics from earlier decades, it is difficult to determine precisely when the devotional revolution began and was consolidated among Irish-Catholic women, but the general trend is nonetheless clear. Parish devotional organizations first appeared in the 1850s, assumed a distinct institutional structure in the 1860s, and attained widespread influence in the 1870s. It was the decade of the 1860s, then, that represented the turning-point both in the development of devotional organizations and in the history of the devotional revolution itself.

The timing of the profound change in women's religious practice underscores the central role of the parish confraternities in the making of the devotional revolution. The women who joined these devotional organizations in the 1860s were for the most part first-generation residents of Toronto. They were much less likely to have grown up having had extensive contact with the church than second-generation Irish-Catholic women, who had been familiar with separate schools and other Catholic social institutions since childhood. Parish devotional organizations, which could recruit women in large numbers, were thus a linchpin in the Catholic Church's campaign to reach immigrant women and transform their religious practice.

The paucity of membership rolls makes it difficult to determine the class backgrounds of the parish societies' members. As noted

Table 5
Membership of Saint Joseph's Society, 1863–73

Category	St Joseph's Society members	Irish-Catholic ratepayers, circa early 1860s
Unskilled	38 %	45.0%
Semi-skilled	13.1	13.5
Skilled	8.3	12.1
Clerical	3.4	2.8
Business	17.2	16.7
Professional	2.8	3.3
Private Means	17.2*	6.6

* All widows
Sources: "Register of the Saint Joseph's Bona Mors Society,"
and Rev. J. Jamot, "Census of City Wards," circa early 1860s,
Archives of the Roman Catholic Archdiocese of Toronto;
city directories.

before, only one membership list, that of the Saint Joseph's Bona Mors Society, is available. This source is a particularly useful one, however, since it lists the home addresses for nearly all the members on its rolls. By locating these addresses in city directories, it is possible to reconstruct the occupational backgrounds of just under one half of the women in the Saint Joseph's Society.

At first glance, the figures in table 5 seem to suggest that the occupational profile of the women who joined the Saint Joseph's Society was roughly similar to that of Irish-Catholic ratepayers, with the notable exception of widows and those from unskilled backgrounds. However, the use of city directories to trace occupational backgrounds significantly understates the presence of lower-class and economically marginal women. City directories were published to provide businessmen with access to services and labour, and so their listings nearly always include occupational backgrounds.[50] Yet the directories' coverage was far from complete. Unskilled men, for example, were significantly underrepresented in the directories, a situation that significantly affects the representation in table 5 of women who were from unskilled backgrounds by virtue of their husbands' occupations. Single women were even less likely to be listed in the directories. Only women who were longstanding residents of the city, usually householders such as widows, or who were known to offer services to the public, such as washerwomen and seamstresses, were listed.

Although the evidence is admittedly fragmentary, the percentage of members who could be identified through the directories as widows does indicate that the society did appeal to the economically marginal. Moreover, of the women from unskilled backgrounds who could be traced through the directories, over one-fifth were working women, a figure that only hints at their true number on the society's membership roll. The most telling indication of the women's social standing, however, is the large number of members who could not be traced through the city directories, even though they may have lived in the city for years. The social bias of the directories excluded many people of the lower classes from their listings, particularly in the case of single working women. These observations lead to the conclusion that, although women from all ranks in the Irish-Catholic community joined devotional organizations such as the Saint Joseph's Society, women from lower down the social hierarchy and whose status was insecure were more likely to enlist than their more prosperous sisters.

Lower-working-class women did have an economic incentive to join the parish devotional organizations. During hard times it was these women who sought charitable relief on behalf of their families. Membership in a confraternity established a woman's respectability, as well as that of her family, and it brought her into contact with the parish priest, who could intercede on her behalf in time of need.[51] Belonging to a devotional organization was similar to taking out an insurance policy. This was no small consideration, but the possible economic benefits of membership alone cannot explain the success of devotional organizations in recruiting Irish-Catholic women. As women's responsibility for securing charitable relief suggests, gender – the culturally and socially constructed differences in the social roles of women and men – was a salient factor in influencing women's decision to join a parish devotional organization.[52]

While there are marked differences that are related to class in the participation of women from various social backgrounds in the parish devotional organizations, these organizations were remarkably successful in recruiting women from all classes. The influences of class were indeed significant, but in the case of membership in a devotional organization they must also be placed within the general context of gender. Fundamentally, it was the connection between the philosophical outlook of devotional organizations and the new social role of Irish-Catholic women, particularly their role in the family, that explains why devotional practice gained such a large following among women and why it was especially popular with Irish-

Catholic women from the lower and more economically insecure strata of society.

In pre-famine Ireland, the family functioned as an economic unit; the men worked in the fields while the women provided essential income from the sale of poultry and dairy produce as well as the products of their domestic industry. Men and women not only performed different tasks and made different contributions to the household economy, they also led separate social lives. So separate were the social lives of Irish men and women that in the home they rarely ate or sat together. Men and women spent little time together, and recreation outside of the home was male-dominated. Women were also were expected to defer to men: for example, they could sit down to eat only after the men had had their fill and left the table. Even though women's economic contribution to the family was vital, such a male-centred culture relegated women to a subordinate and segregated position in the family and on the farm.[53]

The industrial labour market in Toronto fundamentally altered both the structure of the household and the nature of women's work in the home. As Toronto industrialized, men's work became separated from that of the household. One consequence of this development was the differentiation between paid and unpaid labour along sexual lines in the household, with unpaid labour being associated with women's work in the home. Women's work in the home was essential to the family's welfare, but the economic significance of this contribution to the household was frequently not recognized. Unlike in Ireland, where their paid labour was quite visible and constituted a significant part of a family's annual cash income, most women in Toronto could earn only a fraction of what men could earn through unskilled labour. The sexual division of labour created by industrialization left most women economically dependent on men.[54]

One response to these new economic and social conditions was the formulation by middle-class opinion-makers of an ideology of "separate spheres." Although the work women did as wives was productive and as essential as men's work for the survival of the household, the identification of the home with women's sphere of work made it appear that their labour had escaped the economic calculus, which was now associated with the workplace outside the home. As a separate sphere, cut off from the cash nexus of the working "world," the home was a moral haven from materialism and competitiveness. In this haven women provided their husbands and children with the spiritual leaven essential to their salvation in a competitive market-place.[55] The Catholic clergy eagerly embraced this vision of domesticity and its idealization of "true womanhood".[56]

The vision was prescriptive in nature, and one may well wonder how much it reflected women's own experience, especially that of Irish-Catholic women in working-class families. Women's experience of life in general and of the domestic environment in particular differed from that of men, but that did not make the home a "separate sphere," one that was peculiarly feminine in character, as the proponents of domesticity liked to believe. For most Irish-Catholic women from working-class backgrounds, domestic privacy scarcely existed.[57] Many rented rooms in someone else's house, and those fortunate to own a home in turn rented out rooms or in some cases an entire floor. In large families, where practically every room would be used for sleeping quarters, there would be even less privacy. Furthermore, the cooperation between households to help make ends meet and to lessen the burden of domestic chores resulted in a near constant traffic of neighbours and children.

Yet, if the gap between myth and reality was large, there is considerable evidence that the cult of domesticity and its notion of a "separate sphere" appealed to working-class women. To understand why this was so, it is necessary to look at the home as part of the organization of social life of women and men.[58] The home was contested terrain, and this was the case precisely because it was critical to the social organization of the sexes.

The general expectation, certainly one very much encouraged by the church, was that women would marry, unless they were destined for religious life. While the evidence is admittedly scanty, it would appear that the vast majority of Irish-Catholic women did eventually marry.[59] Many women would have worked outside their homes before marriage, either as domestics or in the city's clothing and shoe factories, and this experience shaped their expectations of marriage. Since most single working women could at best earn a subsistence income, marriage was a practical necessity.[60] Once married, women were economically dependent on their husbands, a position that was reinforced by their departure from the workplace. The significant number of impoverished widows and wives who had been abandoned by their husbands reveals the precarious nature of this dependence.[61]

Because they were especially vulnerable to the exigencies of working-class life, women – above all women whose husbands' economic standing was insecure – were very much concerned with acquiring authority within the family. The separation of men's work from the home meant that women were increasingly responsible for the household and its relations with the outside world. Women did the shopping, managed the weekly pay packet (or what portion of it they could lay their hands on), arranged for credit with shopkeepers or pawnbrokers, sold piece-work to help make ends meet, and during hard times interceded with the parish priest for relief.[62] In short, women were expected as a matter of course to mediate between the public and the private spheres. Given women's economic dependence on their husbands, however, wielding authority in the home commensurate with their responsibilities was another matter.

The cult of domesticity was a middle-class social ideal, but one that was supported by Catholic piety. In performing their devotions women entered into a religious universe that gave new meaning and authority to their role in the home. One way Catholic devotions sanctioned women's authority in the home was by undermining cultural conventions of sexual segregation. According to the Catholic understanding of domesticity, when a man was in his home, he was shielded from the dangers of the world, especially those of the tavern, by the comforting and virtuous influence of his wife. It was the wife's responsibility to encourage her husband's religious observance. Catholicism was seen as a religion learned on the mother's knee, and women ensured the religious education of their children, as well as that of their husbands, by protecting the sanctity of the home.[63] Only as mothers and wives and as celibates devoted to God's service could women fulfil their function as models of virtue and piety.[64] While wives' economic contribution to the household was discounted in this view of domesticity, their authority in the home, especially in religious and moral matters, was vastly expanded. At the same time that piety validated women's domestic role, it legitimized their authority in the home. Devotional Catholicism enabled women to claim a moral power and influence over those upon whom they were dependent.

Industrialization had permanently altered the role of women in the family, but the piety advocated by the ultramontane reformers cast this new social role as a religious vocation. By associating the ideals of domesticity with female virtue and influence, Catholic devotionalism transformed the home into an extension of the parish church. The Catholic church had long praised the family, the cornerstone and "the root of society," as a sacred institution. "Woman is ennobled by chaste matrimony," declared Archbishop Lynch and, he added, in such a family her children will "rise up and call her blessed."[65] Each woman in her own way could emulate the Blessed Virgin Mary and make her family a holy family. This image of the

family and its home as a sacred refuge led many families to recreate
the atmosphere of the parish church by placing on the wall litho-
graphs of the sacred heart, the Virgin Mary, the life of Christ, or
Pius IX, which could be purchased for twenty-five cents apiece.[66]

Nevertheless, the relationship between the domestic hearth and
the parish church was a problematic one for Irish Catholics. Because
devotions were church-centred forms of piety, the parish undercut
the religious function of the family and, in particular, that of the
male head of the household. Most devotional organizations, for example, did not advocate family prayer. Even the Archconfraternity
of the Holy Family, which sought to introduce piety into the home,
encouraged only the performance of devotions by family members
as individuals.[67] This emphasis on personal piety strengthened the
religious role of women in the home. To them fell the responsibility
of teaching their children Catholic prayers and providing their husbands with a model of piety. Devotions sanctified the woman's role
in the family, a process that is especially apparent in the cult of
Mary.

The Virgin Mary represented feminine attributes raised to a
supernatural level. Her divine qualities were precisely those that
women were expected to fulfil, albeit on a more mundane level. Further, these qualities were not mere attributes, but virtues. If the Virgin Mary represented the sum total of feminine qualities, she also
embodied virtue *tout court*. Nor was this combination of femininity
with virtue in the person of Mary coincidental, for the two were seen
as synonymous. In this sense, the Virgin Mary personified the idealization of womanhood, and a very particular type of womanhood at
that: woman as the repository and embodiment of self-sacrificing
virtue, purity, and motherhood.

In the Virgin Mary, as the following prayer demonstrates, female
virtues were elevated to a sacred status:

Mary gloriously crowned in heaven
Mary crowned through her seraphic love
Mary crowned through her angelical purity
Mary crowned through her profound humility
Mary crowned through her perfect obedience
Mary crowned through her holy prudence
Mary crowned through her admirable patience
Mary crowned through her ardent gratitude.[68]

The characteristics of "true" women were meekness, humility, and
obedience; in short, service and suffering. "Think of Mary," Bishop
Charbonnel urged Irish-Catholic women, "choosing to be a servant

in the temple." "Suffer patiently," he continued, for "this is blessing worthy before God." Women should remember that "Christ also suffered for us, leaving us an example that you should follow in his steps."[69] Suffering was the way of salvation, but it was the lot of women, it would seem, to suffer more. By embracing it, as did the Virgin Mary, they proved themselves all the more virtuous. Because of this direct relationship between femininity and virtue, only though self-denial could women truly achieve self-fulfilment.[70]

Suffering and acceptance were not, of course, the only reason that Virgin Mary was praised. She was honoured because she was the mother of God and, in a very real way, the mother of humanity.[71] Her "sacrifice of [her] One and only Son for others is above any other service"; it was this sacrifice that made possible humanity's redemption.[72] Mary "seated at the right hand of Jesus" was "our advocate in Heaven."[73] In her role as "our mediatrix in Heaven," the Virgin Mary fostered those virtues essential for salvation.[74] In particular, she was an inspiring example that motherhood and nurture entailed self-sacrificing service and dependence on others.

Many Irish-Catholic women could readily identify with these requirements. Unlike their husbands, women were more likely to deny themselves on behalf of their families, and in the breach they would take on putting-out work in addition to household chores to make ends meet. Just as Mary's suffering served a redemptive purpose, so too did the wife's self-sacrifice serve a religious purpose in the domestic circle. The shattering of the family circle, as the clergy repeatedly stressed, would result in a mother's or a wife's broken heart.[75] Not only did the pangs of the heart thereby become a feminine attribute, but at the same time they were also domesticated. Self-sacrifice was an expression of the ideal of domesticity, the wife who kept the warm glow of the hearth going for her husband and family. Because Irish-Catholic women devoted themselves to others, sometimes at tremendous cost to themselves, they could more easily embrace the virtues embodied in the figure of the Virgin Mary. Of course, the passive, meek, and obedient female was a convenient, even self-serving, figure for Irish-Catholic men, clergy included. The clergy encouraged women to emulate the Virgin Mary and make their households a Holy Family by performing their own devotions and instructing family members in the faith.[76] The myth of female virtue gave women considerable authority in the home, but in following the Blessed Virgin as a "model of maternal solicitude" they gained very little outside it.[77]

Although the clergy often stressed that it was the duty of parents "to edify their children," to "sow the seeds of piety ... in their hearts," it was recognized that the mother was the likelier parent to introduce religion into the home and instruct the children in the devotions of the Catholic Church. "From the mother, far more frequently than from the father," commented the *Canadian Freeman*, "does the child's character receive the stamp which shall distinguish it through life; and it is an oft' repeated truism that, upon the mother's knee are those impressions made upon the opening mind which outlive all others, and which amid the distracting and corrupting influences of the world, rise from time to time with an ameliorating power almost divine."[78] In such pronouncements, not only were women deemed more particularly fitted for raising children and instilling in them a religious sensibility, but the inherently religious nature of women was central to God's plan. The implied contrast between the home and the world was also revealing: if the "world" was impious and corrupt, the home was a haven of religion and virtue, signified by the presence of statues of the Madonna.[79]

This ideology of separate spheres proved to be an ambivalent one. While it was enthusiastically promoted by men to keep women meek and subservient, it was accepted by women because it enabled them to counter male authority by undermining sexual segregation. During his leisure hours, especially on Sundays, the man would be exposed to the natural religious influences of his wife.[80] Devotional Catholicism held out the promise to women that it could intensify familial bonds and give them influence in their familial relationships. The ideal of the woman's sphere, then, is not to be confused with the segregation of geographical space, though women and men did at times occupy distinct spaces. Rather, it enjoined the proper use of social space and regulated its meaning as a construct of gender.[81] Nor can the woman's sphere be simply equated with the private sphere.[82] One of the sources of women's authority lay in their ability to mediate between their families and the religious world of the parish. As mothers and wives, women were to lead their families in the path of faith, and in doing so they integrated the family into the public world of the parish.

The confraternities' influence extended well beyond their predominantly female constituency. In this respect, the impact of the confraternities depended as much on the social location and responsibilities of their members as on the size of their membership rolls. Many women, perhaps the majority, at one time or another participated in these societies, and women, who were usually responsible for child-rearing, were also the most devout and the most likely to impart the devotions and ideals of the parish confraternities to their families. Many sons and daughters, not to mention husbands, were introduced to devotional rituals by confraternity members. The appeals of these women in the privacy of their homes are now unfortunately beyond the reach of the historian, but there is no doubt of their effectiveness. Through their membership, parish confraternities and the devotions they promoted reached most Irish-Catholic families. Women were responsible for rearing children, and it was they who could ensure that their children attended separate schools for instruction in the beliefs and practices of the Catholic Church. Second-generation Irish Catholics grew up in homes saturated with the ethos of devotional Catholicism.

With the triumph of ultramontanism, Jay Dolan has observed, the parish priest came to enjoy "a supremacy over the laity not unlike that of the Pope over the entire church."[83] As a result of this exercise of clerical authority, the lot of the faithful was to pray, obey, and, of course, pay the bills.[84] At first glance, the founding of parish devotional organizations seems to confirm the view that the laity played a largely passive role in the parish. Devotional organizations, like other parish associations, were founded by the clergy and provided an institutional framework that reached down to the grass roots and incorporated the laity into the authority structures of the church. As will be seen, however, these organizations also gave the laity an associational context through which they could become activists in the parish, and this activism included the exercise of initiative by the laity both as individuals and as a group.

Bishop Charbonnel's ultramontane-inspired reform of the church resulted in a dramatic change in the laity's role. In his hierarchical conception of the church, the laity were to occupy a subordinate position in which they would be guided and directed by the clergy. To this end, Charbonnel replaced the parish wardens elected by the local congregation with *ad hoc* committees appointed by the pastor to deal with specific administrative problems. Most of these parish committees were dominated by wealthy Irish-Catholics. In Saint Michael's parish, for example, the wholesaler Frank Smith, the leading Catholic dry goods merchant Patrick Hughes, and the brewer Eugene O'Keefe often served on committees. Occasionally, less socially prominent laymen, such as Mike Murphy, bar owner and president of the Irish nationalist organization the Hibernian Benevolent Society, and James Britton, a butcher, were also approached by the clergy for advice. In Charbonnel's view, the laity were expected to aid the church, but it was for the clergy to decide how and when their talents and efforts could best be used. Since parish committees served at the pleasure of the priest, the laity were deprived of a crucial institutional base in the parish for exercising leadership independently of the clergy.

The clergy's conception of their authority, it would seem, allowed little in the way of lay initiative. Parish priests were the "fathers of their flocks" and the "filial duty" of the parishioners was to obey them.[85] "The people," declared Father Francis Rooney of Saint Mary's parish, "must accept the teachings of the priest" and "obey him ... in all that relates to faith and morals" – and the operation of the parish devotional organizations was pre-eminently a question of faith and morals.[86] Lay leaders were thus to concern themselves solely with "material administration."[87] The manner in which the clergy directed these societies and appointed their leadership was unmistakably paternalistic. The clergy exercised their prerogative as *ex officio* presidents and, when free from other duties, presided over the meetings of these organizations. Significantly, in contrast to the literary clubs for men founded in the 1880s, where elections for the executive prevailed, the parish clergy usually appointed the devotional organizations' officers.

The women appointed to the executives of these organizations were typically the "leading ladies" of the parish. The confraternities' leadership thus reflected the parish's social hierarchy. For example, in Saint Mary's parish, Mrs Mary Treanor, who took over her husband's grocery after his death, Mrs Patrick Burns, wife of a coal and wood dealer, and Mrs John Mulvey, wife of a grocer, were among the confraternity leaders. While in Saint Mary's parish the leadership was solidly middle class, the women at the head of Saint Basil's and Saint Michael's confraternities included many from the upper class.[88] In these parishes, women of high social standing, such as Mrs John Crawford, wife of the lieutenant-governor of Ontario, Mrs Frank Smith, whose husband was one of the wealthiest men in Toronto, and Mrs Patrick Hughes, whose husband owned one of the largest dry goods emporiums in the city, were active in one or another confraternity.

Class had its privileges, as well as its responsibilities, and in the operation of the confraternities the prerogatives of class are quite evident. The women who led these organizations were certainly no strangers to the cultural conventions of deference prescribed for their sex. At the same time, however, they were accustomed to exercising influence and authority in managing their households, in their dealings with their social subordinates, and, for some, in conducting a business either with their husbands or on their own. In short, these women were conscious of the privileges and prerogatives that accompanied their social status. The clergy may have appointed them to office in the parish devotional organizations on the basis of their social status alone, but their background and experience suggest that they were not likely to be simply honorary leaders.

Although middle-class women dominated the executive of the devotional organizations, they depended on a large number of activists who occupied lesser positions of leadership to keep their organizations running smoothly. Most devotional organizations, such as the Apostleship of Prayer or the Archconfraternity of the Holy Family, were divided into prayer circles with no more than twenty-five members, each with its own leader. A large parish confraternity would need some forty circle leaders to conduct its bi-weekly or monthly meetings. Devotional organizations thus required a large number of leaders, activists who were willing to commit their time and talent to the confraternity week in and week out.

The identity of these activists is not so clear. Catholic newspapers generally took little notice of parish devotional organizations and their leaders, except when they were raising funds for the church. Even then, newspapers tended to emphasize the contributions made by the wives of well-known Irish-Catholic laymen; the others were referred to by their last name only, if they were noticed at all. The anonymity of confraternity activists shows that confraternities, like women's work in general, were undervalued by the male leaders of the church and of the Irish-Catholic community. Still, despite the anonymity of the vast majority of parish activists, some tentative conclusions regarding their social background can be offered. The pool of middle-class and upper-class women that the devotional organizations could draw on was a limited one, and certainly the Irish-Catholic middle class was not large enough to provide leadership on this scale. Although one cannot be certain, it is likely that most of these confraternity activists, long ignored by the Catholic press because they were not married to prominent Irish-Catholic laymen, were from the same general social background as the rank-and-file membership.[89] The middle-class officers of the devotional organizations thus led and collaborated with a large and socially diverse body of activists who occupied the lower rungs of leadership.

The composite structure of the confraternities had important consequences for the development of lay leadership and for the emergence of lay initiative among Irish-Catholic women. Most confraternities had plenary sessions as well as assemblies of the individual circles. The plenary meetings usually had a set format and often required the presence of the parish priests to offer instruction, initiate new members, or perform the benediction of the Blessed Sacrament. By contrast, there were so many separate meetings of the confraternity circles that an overworked clergy must have left the circle leaders to their own devices. Once a devotional organization was in the hands of capable and zealous activists, Father Edward Kelly of Saint Paul's parish remarked in the early 1920s when reviewing the Apostleship of Prayer's work in his parish over the years, "there is not much required from the pastor in the working of the Society."[90] The clergy founded the devotional organizations and exercised pastoral oversight but, as Father Kelly recognized, these organizations acquired a life of their own, and they did so because of the leadership and direction of their lay officers.

In the regular meetings of the devotional organizations, which were usually held bi-weekly or monthly, circle prefects would lead their members through a set round of devotions. They were also expected to offer a short instruction and to demonstrate ingenuity in devising the meeting's program so that it would be both lively and entertaining. Each circle leader was also responsible for the general administration and well-being of her circle: she was to collect fees, keep track of attendance, visit members at home, console sick members, reassure the faint-hearted, and recruit new members. As the instructional manuals stressed, the smooth operation and prosperity of a devotional organization required not only organizational and leadership skills but also invention and experimentation by the laity in conducting the organization's activities so as to stimulate interest and sustain the commitment of members.

Devotional organizations provided women with an organizational base from which to participate in the larger arena of the parish itself. In the parish, women made their most visible contribution in their capacity as fund-raisers. Women rarely took an organizational role in the staging of entertainments, but they did take a very active part in the planning of bazaars and picnics, both of which were a regular feature in the parish's social calendar. Once the date had been set by the ordinary of the diocese, the parish priest would call on the members of the devotional organizations to make the necessary preparations. At this point the women would take over much of the organization of the bazaar or picnic. While men, usually members of the Saint Vincent de Paul Society, sat on the committee of management to supervise financial arrangements, it was the women who prepared the food, decorated the hall, and made fine-point articles and the like to be sold or auctioned off at the bazaars and fairs. In addition to formal planning meetings held in the parish church, the women would hold many more informal meetings in their homes where, while sewing or baking, they would further discuss the arrangements. Given the amount of planning required to allocate responsibilities, to line up articles for sale and to prepare the refreshments, many such informal meetings would have been necessary to coordinate the large number of women involved, particularly when the city's confraternities collaborated in holding the annual picnic for the House of Providence or in organizing the occasional bazaar for a diocesan social institution such as the Notre Dame Institute or the Saint Nicholas Institute.[91]

On the day of the bazaar or picnic, women played an especially prominent role. At these events the leading ladies of the parish, such as Mrs Lawrence Coffee, wife of a grain merchant, Mrs Thomas McCrossan, wife of a well-known Toronto hatter and publisher of the *Ontario Tribune*, Mrs Eugene O'Keefe, and Mrs Patrick Hughes, together with the many lesser-known women of the parish, staffed the tables loaded with home-made crafts and goodies. With entreaties well calculated both to provoke pangs of conscience and to foster appreciation of the goods on sale, these women enticed the public, men in particular it is alleged, to part with their money. So persistent were they, and so graceful were they in their persistence, commented a *Globe* reporter, that it was "hard for the unwary stranger to pass by without first making a purchase."[92]

Women's devotional organizations were indeed the most successful parish fund-raisers, and the church's coffers benefited enormously from their strenuous efforts; bazaars and picnics for Catholic social institutions usually netted around fifteen hundred dollars, while those for parishes could bring in between five and eight hundred dollars.[93] The fund-raising of the confraternities was essential not only for the expansion and continuing operation of the parishes but also for the church's social services, either through its institutions, such as the House of Providence, or through its voluntary associations, such as the Saint Vincent de Paul Society. By 1872 Catholic church buildings and social institutions were valued at over half a million dollars, far outstripping any other denomination in Toronto, an impressive achievement for a denomination that had such a large lower-working-class constituency.[94] This institutional growth and the diocesan-wide services that these institutions provided would not have been possible without the financial contribution and organizational ingenuity of Irish-Catholic women.

A few women's parish societies were directly involved in the church's charity work. Most confraternities donated funds to one or another Catholic charity. In order to aid the poor more directly, women in most of the city parishes joined benevolent societies, popularly known as sewing societies, which were usually led by the same women who held office in the devotional organizations. Like their male counterparts in the Saint Vincent de Paul Society, the women members of benevolent societies sought out potential recipients of their charity, and they frequently used their own judgment, quite independently of the clergy, as to whether these poor were worthy of relief.[95] In their benevolent work women were expected to extend the spiritual benefits gained through their membership in a devotional society and to share these riches with the poor women and children of the parish. In 1885, at the request of the Saint Vincent de Paul for assistance in visiting female patients at Toronto General Hospital, the parish sewing societies combined to form the Lady Visitors to the Hospital, which gave women activists in the sewing societies a permanent forum for city-wide cooperation and leadership.[96]

Women's role in the church was defined not only by their lay status but also by their sex; together these attributes relegated women to a position of deference and service. Important as the contribution of the devotional organizations was in making the parish a vibrant religious and social institution, the work of these societies reflected the role of their major constituency, women. Much of the practical work done by the devotional organizations was an extension of the domestic sphere. Women cleaned the altar cloths, baked cakes for the parish picnics, and cleaned up after the parish bazaar, but serious business was left to the financial committees run by men and to the parish priests. In the home or in the parish, the vocation of women was service. Women could exercise leadership among themselves – in the circle of the confraternity or in the sewing society meeting – but at public gatherings their role was more limited. In the safe confines of the bazaar and picnic, women were expected to exhibit suitable female accomplishments and graces.

Women's activism and leadership were of community-wide significance, but within the male-dominated structures of the church they were typically located in the devotional or sewing circle and so remained largely invisible. This disregard for the significance of women's activism had two consequences for their leadership in the parish. First, unlike Protestant women with their denominational missionary societies, Catholic women did not possess a recognized institutional base from which they could play a prominent role in the public life of their church. Secondly, their activism was directed towards the social and religious world of the parish. As a consequence, again in contrast to many Protestant women, Catholic women could not draw on religious traditions of moral and social reform to legitimatize their collective activism outside the church.

The women's benevolent societies provide perhaps the most telling example of how women exercised lay initiative while at the same time demonstrating due deference to ecclesiastical authority. The origins of the societies can be traced in only two parishes, Saint Michael's and Saint Basil's, but in both these cases the leaders of the parish devotional organizations were responsible for establishing the parish benevolent society on their own initiative.[97] The founding of the Society of Our Lady of Perpetual Help, a women's benevolent society in Saint Michael's parish, was typical. The wives of some of the wealthiest laymen in the parish, who were also prominent in the parish's devotional organization, respectfully requested Archbishop Lynch to call a meeting so that the society, which now had numerous members, could be "properly organized." They further asked that the archbishop "speak in favourable terms of it in the Cathedral."[98] The society was already organized, but its leaders recognized that a proper show of deference was essential in order to obtain the necessary ecclesiastical sanction. Without official approval, the organization could not operate in the parish, nor could it have secured popular support, as the women were well aware. The founding of the Society of Our Lady of Perpetual Help exhibits the limits to women's initiative and the stratagems women developed so that they could realize their objectives. These women obviously knew what they wanted and how to get it, but their petition to Archbishop Lynch also demonstrates that in exercising their initiative they had to act through the clergy to achieve their goals.

The deferential relationship of the devotional organization's leadership with the clergy was in keeping with the latter's hierarchical and authoritarian conception of the church. Yet the women who led the devotional organizations did not understand this to mean that they would simply follow the clergy's lead, as the founding of Society of Our Lady of Perpetual Help in Saint Michael's parish indicates. One constitution of a women's benevolent society has survived, that of the Association of the Sacred Heart in Saint Basil's parish, and it offers a first-hand glimpse into aims and aspirations of the leading women of the parish when they founded their society in 1877.[99] These women gathered together to draw up their own constitution and by-laws under which they committed themselves to serve Jesus and Mary by working for the material and religious welfare of the poor as well as for their own spiritual improvement. To this end, the women established an executive that was to be elected by and thus directly accountable to the general membership, unlike the officers in the devotional organizations who served at the pleasure of the parish priest.

The pastor did have a recognized role as a spiritual adviser in the Association of the Sacred Heart: to offer from time to time a spiritual exhortation or reading and to offer guidance when, in the judgment of the members, the poor who requested assistance were "doubtful cases." Even so, the founders of the association gave their executive a rather free hand: the association's by-laws authorized the officers to admit members, lead the members in religious exercises, organize and appoint the teams of visitors, administer the society's finances, and arrange for the collection, repair, and distribution of clothing throughout the parish. While the clergy offered much needed support, in general it was the responsibility of the members of the executive to direct the society in its good works. The leaders of this devotional organization wished to expand lay activism and initiative in the parish, and they did so by founding an association in which effective control was in lay hands.

The connection between women's initiative and their piety was a close one, as the Association of the Sacred Heart's motto, "All for the Heart of Jesus Through the Heart of Mary," illustrated. Devotional organizations set a new and far more rigorous standard for religious practice. Not only were the faithful to lead an active life of piety, but they were to demonstrate their commitment to this life of piety by becoming involved in a devotional organization. The confraternity activist was someone to be emulated, for an active life of piety entailed service to others whereby each woman contributed to her own salvation. Though the clergy usually associated the woman's sphere with domesticity, their conception of that sphere nevertheless envisioned an arena for women's activism and leadership outside the home. Women were to lead a life devoted to the care and nurture of others. Just as they were responsible for keeping the home hearth warm, so too were they to devote their energies to the devotional organizations, which like the family existed to nurture its members in a life of piety. By identifying religion with the woman's sphere in this way, devotional Catholicism gave women a distinct moral impetus to participate in the associational life of the parish and engage in religious outreach.

Devotions imparted to the members of the confraternities a social as well as a religious identity that were mutually reinforcing. Women introduced other women to the associational life of the parish and then led and sustained their sisters in the practice of piety. As leaders of their parish devotional organizations, women activists had long been accustomed to take responsibility for organizing their associational life. In developing and exercising their leadership skills, these women activists acquired a sense of personal usefulness and common purpose. At the same time, they created their own informal networks. Practical activities, such as sewing bees in their front rooms and baking parties in their kitchens, were essential to the operation of a devotional organization. Through these informal networks the leaders of the devotional organizations became conscious of themselves as a group and so gained the confidence to exercise corporate initiative.

Many women found the religious and social life of the parish confraternity and benevolent society to be an attractive one. For one thing, the Roman Catholic church provided one of the few respectable forms of recreation available to Irish-Catholic women outside the home. The sexual division of work and recreation limited much of women's social life to their homes and immediate neighbourhood. Moreover, most working-class women would have had little spare time to themselves. The meetings of the parish devotional and benevolent organizations enabled women to escape their daily round of household chores for a few hours on a Sunday afternoon or weekday evening. Women's parish associations made the religious world of the Catholic church both immediate and personal, and so encouraged women to become involved in their church and community. In the parish confraternity women could form close friendships and collaborate with other women of their own choosing who shared their interests and ideals. Not only could women associate and socialize with other women, formally as well informally, in their parish associations, but they could also engage in corporate action with them.

As has been seen, middle-class women were the moving force in the parish devotional and benevolent organizations, and they were the ones most likely to secure the clergy's support for women's initiatives. Yet these middle-class leaders depended on working-class women at the grass roots to make the devotional organizations a vibrant part of parish life. Devotional organizations became such vital parish institutions because they created a social space for women's activism that wedded women's self-expression and sociability to Catholic devotionalism and its world view. Through their joint efforts women created a religious and social world centred in the parish. Within the male-dominated Roman Catholic Church they could not make that world in any way they chose, but in creating it they successfully claimed a social vocation both at home and in the parish. Women may not have gained power in the larger world of the parish; however, to borrow Carroll Smith-Rosenberg's distinction, at least some of them did gain influence, and this influence enabled them to carve out a niche where they could exercise leadership and initiative.[100]

Women's devotional organizations embodied the new and exacting standard for Catholic religious practice established by the clergy.

Not only were devout Catholics to attend Mass regularly, but they were to perform a wide variety of devotions as part of their public and private worship. In this regard, the fact that few men joined devotional organizations reflected the general difference in religious observance between men and women. Fewer men than women attended Mass regularly, and fewer men took up the devotions of the church and made them part of their daily life. Yet men's religious behaviour must be understood on its own terms. Most Irish-Catholic men saw themselves as religious, and as time went on the religious observances of a growing number of them conformed to the minimum standards set by the church. By the 1880s a majority of them at least fulfilled their canonical duties, and many performed private devotions, even if they did not join a devotional organization.[101]

The improvement in religious practice among Irish-Catholic men was considerable, but for the clergy it simply underscored how much had yet to be accomplished in this pastoral field. After the 1850s, the clergy measured lay religious behaviour by a far more exacting standard than that which had prevailed previously. Not only did most men's religious behaviour fall short of this standard, but the selective nature of their observances appeared to betray an ineradicable strain of religious indifference. Such was far from the case, but the reluctance of men to join devotional organizations most certainly challenged the clergy's vision of the church as an inclusive religious and social community. Especially disturbing for the clergy was the religious behaviour of young men. Well after devotional Catholicism had become the norm among Irish-Catholic women, young men were still notably absent from church on Sunday mornings.[102] The clergy's concern for the spiritual welfare of young men explains why they periodically established devotional organizations for them.

In addition to devotional associations, the clergy also attempted to reach Irish-Catholic men, especially young men, by establishing church-based recreational associations, the first of which was the Catholic Literary Association, founded in 1847. Besides sponsoring a debating club, the association organized a parochial library which eventually contained some 600 volumes. After reaching a peak of over 200 members in 1853, the association lost public support and was dissolved in 1856.[103] Six years went by before another church-based organization for young men was established. Archbishop Lynch founded his first organization for young men, the Saint Joseph's Society, in 1862. This society, however, never attained even the limited success of its predecessor and folded within a year of its founding. Following this failure, Archbishop Lynch waited a decade before launching in September 1872 the Catholic Young Men's Literary Club, which he hoped would foster the "mutual improvement of its members and [the] promotion of Catholic interests among our young men." This second effort was also unable to attract sufficient members, and it too folded in less than a year.[104]

Two years later, in November 1875, Archbishop Lynch, still undeterred, inaugurated the Catholic Young Men's Association. This association, open to "Catholic young men of good moral character, and who are practical members of the church," was intended to promote "the religious, social and intellectual improvement of its members."[105] Lectures, debates, readings, and concerts were organized, all with a suitable focus on Catholic themes, and the association offered a reading room stocked with Catholic newspapers and Toronto dailies as well as two parlours for its members' use.[106] This program of recreation to foster cultural self-improvement, which resembled the social activities of the lay-led and working-class-dominated Irish nationalist societies, was intended to attract Irish-Catholic men from all social backgrounds. The organization did attract several men who later became prominent laymen, most notably J.J. Foy, who was a major Conservative Party power broker under the provincial government of James Whitney, and D.A. O'Sullivan, who in the 1880s was one of Lynch's most trusted advisers and a well-known lay spokesman for the church. Yet the Catholic Young Men's Association never succeeded in broadening its support beyond the relatively small Irish-Catholic middle class. Unable to reach the mass of Irish-Catholic men, the association sank without a trace two years after it was founded.

Laymen had a narrow range of options when it came to the fraternal organizations that they could join, for canon law and diocesan regulations proscribed a variety of non-Catholic societies, such as the Masons and Odd Fellows. Set in this context, the church's failure to recruit young men to its voluntary associations was a severe setback.[107] "What shall we do for our young men," lamented the *Catholic Weekly Review*, the diocesan newspaper. Parish clubs, the *Review* insisted, are "necessary as protectives and safeguards and sources of strength for our young men."[108] Archbishop Lynch also realized that only through recreational clubs could young men "harbor themselves from street gatherings, gambling rooms, saloons etc., presently the scourge of the city."[109] In addition to this protective function, these organizations also served in a more positive way to integrate men into the social and religious life of the parish, as Lynch and his clergy well recognized.[110] Some ten years after the failure of the Catholic Young Men's Association, three parishes finally founded Catholic recreational and social associations for young men, and unlike Lynch's earlier efforts these societies proved to be successful.

In 1887 two parish literary societies for young men, one in Saint Basil' parish and the other in Saint Paul's, were established, quickly followed by the Saint Alphonsus Young Men's Literary Society of Saint Patrick's parish in 1888.[111] These societies were devoted to "mental improvement" and to encouraging "a healthy Catholic spirit."[112] Unlike earlier literary societies, they appealed to the sensibilities of laymen at the grass roots. The clergy realized that, in order to enrol Irish-Catholic men in large numbers, the new societies would have to allow members to select their own leaders and to provide opportunities for members to exercise leadership in a variety of capacities. In these literary societies, accordingly, members held elections for the executive officers, sometimes with competing slates.[113] This display of lay democracy, in which the lay leadership was held accountable to the membership at large, was a part of the literary societies' attempt to offer attractive recreational activities for young men. Their leaders enjoyed more responsibility than was formally acknowledged by the clergy in the parish confraternities. Though the clergy were the recognized patrons of the literary societies, once they founded a society the parish priests usually limited themselves to a supervisory role and left the leaders to develop the society's social program. At least one of the literary societies, the Saint Paul's Literary and Debating Society, owed its inception to the grass-roots initiative of the young men of the parish.[114] Such initiative reveals that laymen found in literary societies a congenial environment to exercise lay leadership and to participate in the social life of the parish.

Under the direction of lay leaders such as Charles J. McCabe, a lawyer, George Duffy, proprietor of a clothing store, Andy Cottam, manager of the publisher Peter F. Collier's Toronto operations, Daniel P. Cahill, a bedding manufacturer, and James I. Travers, a printer, these societies created a rich and varied social program, which, unlike the activities of earlier literary associations, was rooted in the recreational pastimes popular among young men. Besides the traditional literary pursuits, the members also organized boxing and tug-of-war events.[115] Without these "manly" activities, the lay leaders and clergy agreed, it would be impossible to attract young men. The attempt to join manliness with religion was also reflected in the rhetoric of the *Catholic Weekly Review*: "A Catholic young man who fears to lose political or social prestige by a frank and open avowal of his creed," the *Review* insisted, "is only half a man at best," at worst, "a coward." "Joining the ranks of Catholic manhood, and nobly assisting each other in true Christian fraternity," the *Review* endeavoured to explain, was the height of manhood.[116] By stressing athletics activities, establishing banjo clubs (which enjoyed an enthusiastic following), offering free tobacco at their concerts (in which the musical program was interspersed by rounds of boxing and other athletic exhibitions), and providing smoking, reading, and billiard rooms which were open to the members on weekday evenings (an alternative to the city's numerous taverns), the lay leadership ensured that the parish literary societies were appropriate vehicles for Irish male sociability and self-expression.[117]

Only three parishes established clubs for men, but in these parishes the societies achieved at least moderate success, with two of them gaining about 150 members each, the largest recruiting over 700 members.[118] Yet the composition of the literary societies' leadership indicates that these societies probably did not enrol single young men in great numbers. Few of the rank-and-file members appear in contemporary newspaper reports, but those that were noticed by the press tend to confirm the profile of the literary societies' leadership. Most of these men were well established and in many cases had started families of their own. If these activists reflected the membership as a whole, it would appear that the prime constituency of the organizations was comprised of men who had recently married or who were about to marry, that is, men in their mid-twenties to early thirties.

Two of the clergy, Bishop Timothy O'Mahony of Saint Paul's parish and Father Henning of Saint Patrick's, were apparently so impressed with the success of the men's literary associations that they founded literary societies for young women.[119] The establishment of literary associations for young women was a significant departure from the usual organization of women's associational life in the parish, which was dominated by the devotional organizations and their adjuncts, such as sewing societies, altar societies, and the like. These societies were the first to offer women a wide range of recreational pursuits under the official auspices of the parish. Literary clubs were also the first to provide young women from all social backgrounds with the refinements usually associated with middle-class women.[120] In effect, the program of these societies was a popularization of the private Catholic school curriculum for young ladies.[121] Unlike the literary societies for men, however, the executive as well as the rank and file of the literary societies was dominated by young single women.[122] Women such as Minnie Lawlor, daughter of Doctor Michael Lawlor, and Kate Mallon, daughter of the assessor James J. Mallon, organized the weekly meetings in which members recited poetry, read essays, engaged in debate, and played music.[123] Perhaps the clergy hoped that the presence of single women in these parish societies would encourage men who were of an age to embark on marriage to become active in the parish. Certainly, the joint entertainments organized by the women's and men's sections of the literary societies proved to be among the high points of the parish's social calendar.

The success of the parish literary societies for men and, in particular, the way this success was achieved disturbed some tender consciences. The *Catholic Weekly Review* complained that too many answered the needs of young Catholic men by replying, "Give them gymnasiums, billiard rooms, smoking-rooms, provide and encourage indoor and outdoor exercise, sports and games." "Indeed," commented the *Review*'s editors in a burst of indignation, "it is difficult to understand why some clubs are called 'Catholic.'"[124] In making such remarks, the *Review* misconstrued both the purpose and nature of the parish societies for men. These societies, like all parish organizations, were integral to the clergy's project of making the church an inclusive religious and social institution that would incorporate the social life of the laity into the parish where it could be informed by the official tenets of the church. School children, both boys and girls, had long been enrolled in separate school devotional organizations dedicated to the Sacred Heart or the Virgin Mary, but after they had left school men rarely joined parish confraternities. The tepid response to the clergy's earlier efforts to found devotional organizations for men clearly indicated that if the clergy were to realize their social ideal for the church they would have to develop new approaches to reach and recruit men.[125] The success of the parish societies for men thus marked a major turning-point in the organization of associational life in the Catholic Church.

The parish societies for men were recreational societies, and religious observances, as the *Catholic Weekly Review* correctly perceived, were only indirectly part of their program. Yet these societies did bring Catholic men under the "protecting aegis" of the parish church and the watchful eye of the parish priest. In their debates and public readings, members dwelt on issues of general interest to Catholics and so affirmed their cultural and religious distinctiveness as Catholics. Religion may have been, so to speak, smuggled in by the back door, but its influence was nonetheless very real. In these societies, accepted "manly" activities and other forms of male sociability were fused with a leaven of cultural and religious uplift. This ambience reflected the moral earnestness of the Catholicism of the era, and attendance at Sunday Mass and the regular reception of the sacraments was enjoined on members. Then, too, the exhortatory talks by the clergy and the occasional attendance of the societies as a group to assist at devotions in the parish church very likely persuaded some members at least to take up devotional observances and to sustain others who already had. If these societies were not imbued with the devotional atmosphere that traditionally typified the parish organizations for women, they nonetheless encouraged men in the performance of their religious duties and, in some cases, inspired them to extend the range of their religious practices beyond this minimum.[126] In joining recreational societies, the *Catholic Weekly Review* approvingly declared, Irish-Catholic men would find themselves "more directly in accord with the clergy in all questions."[127] The democratic ethos of the literary societies offered men an attractive way to participate in the social and religious life of the parish in an associational setting that featured popular forms of recreation that were largely under the direction of laymen. Collaboration between lay leaders and the clergy resulted in the creation of a social life in the parish that appealed to men, and it appealed to men because it enabled them to appropriate the beliefs and practices of devotional Catholicism in their own way and on their own terms.

The success of the parish literary societies was a portent of the church's major drive to establish devotional organizations for men. Over time, devotional Catholicism became more closely intertwined with male social life, and the recreational societies that flourished in the 1880s played an important role in this development. Within a few years of launching literary societies, the church embarked on a campaign to extend its devotional organizations, long the preserve of women, to men. In 1892 the clergy established the Men's League, a city-wide branch of the Apostleship of Prayer, and by 1895 the league had recruited some 760 men.[128] The rise of the Men's League signalled the triumph of devotional Catholicism among Irish-Catholic men, for it indicated the direction that Catholic associations for men would take in the future. After the turn of the century, the Holy Name Society, a devotional organization dedicated to the veneration of the name of Jesus, was to gain a following among Catholic men that numbered in the thousands.[129]

This achievement was well over a generation in the making. Until the 1890s, male voluntary associations differed substantially from those of Irish-Catholic women. Despite the founding of a variety of parish associations for men, such as the Saint Vincent de Paul Society and temperance societies, nationalist associations that were independent of the church dominated men's associational life. The recreational societies of the 1880s succeeded where their predecessors had failed, and their success marked the general realignment of Catholic voluntary associations for men that was to take place in the late 1880s and early 1890s. By 1895 all Catholic associations for men, including the Irish nationalist societies, had become affiliated with the church, and membership in a devotional organization was to become common among Catholic men. Why, then, did devotional organizations fail to recruit Irish-Catholic men in significant numbers in the three decades following Bishop Charbonnel's arrival in the city? The reasons for the failure of devotional organizations for men to take root can be seen in the most notable attempt to transform the religious practice of Irish-Catholic men, that of the Saint Vincent de Paul Society.

5 "To Bribe the Porters of Heaven": Poverty, Salvation, and the Saint Vincent de Paul Society

Although the clergy had been able to effect a devotional revolution among Irish-Catholic women, largely through the influence of the parish confraternities, Irish-Catholic men had remained aloof from the parish devotional organizations. Perhaps the Roman Catholic Church's most notable instrument to inculcate the new devotional practices among Irish-Catholic men was the Saint Vincent de Paul Society. Founded in 1833 by Frédéric Ozanam for practising Catholic men over the age of eighteen, the Saint Vincent de Paul Society was an integral part of the nineteenth-century revival of French Catholicism. Although well known for its acts of charity, the organization was primarily concerned with fostering the faith of its members as well as that of the poor and with encouraging them in the practice of piety.

The structure of the Saint Vincent de Paul Society was a vertical one, with its parish conferences accountable to the city's coordinating body, the Particular Council, which reported to the society's Canadian board of directors, the Superior Council, which in turn was under the guidance of the General Council of Paris, the supreme governing board of the society. This vertical structure ensured that the aims and methods of the society would be transplanted to Toronto with little or no modification. The activity of the society in Toronto was not an *ad hoc* response to local conditions but rather conformed to the ultramontane religious and social program set out in the association's *Manual* and monthly bulletin. However, the particular contribution of the society to the development of Catholicism in Toronto depended very much on local circumstances.

When Bishop Armand de Charbonnel arrived in October 1850, he faced two immense challenges in alleviating the material and spiritual wants of the laity. The large number of Irish-Catholic poor was perhaps the most obvious problem confronting the bishop. Without social institutions and labouring under heavy debts, the Catholic Church was singularly unable to provide material relief.[1] Only a month after his arrival, Bishop Charbonnel formally approved the founding of the first Toronto conference of the Saint Vincent de Paul Society. He believed that the society, with its lay visitors organized in parish-based conferences under the direction of a local governing board, the Particular Council, was well adapted to deliver outdoor relief efficiently and cheaply.[2]

The neglect of canonical religious obligations by the majority of Irish Catholics, together with their unfamiliarity with the most elementary Catholic devotions and doctrines, was of even greater concern to Charbonnel than their material deprivations. As a French ultramontane bishop intent on reforming the religious behaviour of the laity, Charbonnel viewed the Saint Vincent de Paul Society as a valuable agency in disseminating the new devotions of the church among the poor as well as among men who were better off. The society's strategic importance to the church's campaign for religious renewal makes it an ideal case study to trace the roots and the development of activism and initiative among laymen and to examine the nature and significance of lay participation and leadership in the life of the parish. As it turned out, however, this type of activism and initiative had a limited appeal for the mass of Irish-Catholic men, and the laity's cool response was to influence the clergy's approach in the associations they established for men.

Many people today think of the Saint Vincent de Paul Society as simply a charitable organization that supplies second-hand clothing and furniture to the poor. In fact, when the Saint Vincent de Paul Society was introduced to Toronto it had two distinct but related goals: the salvation of its members and the conversion of the poor. The primary object of the society was, in the words of the *Manual of the Society of St. Vincent of Paul*, "the salvation of souls, and in particular the souls of the members themselves." The society existed to sustain its members in the practice of a Christian life, or, as the

Manual put it, to achieve the "sanctification of the members by the personal performance of acts of Charity." Charity was the means by which the members of the Saint Vincent de Paul Society gained their salvation. Visiting the poor was not chiefly a philanthropic exercise; on the contrary, this activity was the special object of the society because it was a form of Christian virtue that, as the *Manual* of the society pointed out, required but little time and could be easily practised by men who lived in the world.[3]

In the charity sermons for the Saint Vincent de Paul Society, the clergy repeatedly stressed that without charity it was impossible to be saved. Through good works the charitable could lay up in heaven a treasure of merit. "What was given to the poor was only lent to God," asserted Father J.J. McCann of Saint Paul's parish.[4] The corollary, of course, was that the loan would be repaid to the faithful at the time of death; or as Archbishop Lynch explained, "When the soul is balancing between two eternities, happy or miserable, he will repay principal and interest."[5] Charity offered the laity strong protection in their hour of need, and as James G. Moylan, editor of the *Canadian Freeman* and a member of the Saint Vincent de Paul Society, noted, "How near that may be who can say?"[6]

This charitable impulse was nurtured by the sacraments of the Roman Catholic Church. "Christian works belong to God alone, the sole author of all good," and thus, as an active Christian virtue, charity became truly meritorious only as a result of the sanctifying grace communicated through the sacraments of the church.[7] Good works were essential for salvation, but their efficaciousness depended on sanctification. Without the aid of the sacraments "our charity would be ... but cold compassion – a virtue completely human – praiseworthy no doubt, but imperfect in the eyes of faith."[8]

In the weekly conference meetings of the Saint Vincent de Paul Society, piety and charity intermingled and reinforced one another. While other members kneeled, the conference president opened the meeting with prayers.[9] After reciting together the Ave Maria, the members would take turns in reading a selection from the *Imitation of Christ*, *The Bulletin of the Society of Saint Vincent of Paul*, the *Manual* of the society, or the gospels. Before taking up the cases for relief, the members would consider the meditation for the week. These meditations, taken individually or together, poignantly expressed the fundamental goal of the society. Members were urged to dwell on the "small number of the Elect" and the "Certainty of Death." "The shortness of Life & the length of Eternity" only served to underscore the "Folly of Neglecting our Salvation" and being preoccupied by "the vanity of worldly things." Hence, the "Necessity of

Charity" and "walking in the ways of God" to avoid the "danger of an unprovided death."[10]

The Saint Vincent de Paul Society sought to secure the salvation of its members in this world and the next by promoting devotions, especially those dedicated to the sacraments. In its weekly meetings the society set out to inculcate a life of piety that would "preserve the divine flame of charity" communicated by the sacraments.[11] The society encouraged its members to participate frequently both in private devotions, such as the rosary and the miniature stations of the cross, and in such parish-focused devotions as the forty hours' devotion and the benediction of the Blessed Sacrament.[12] Because they stressed the real presence of Christ, as in the case of the forty hours' devotion to the Blessed Sacrament, and the necessity of union with the suffering Christ, as in the stations of the cross, these devotions were calculated to encourage the reception of the sacraments. In addition, members were expected to receive communion monthly, an unusually high frequency for Catholic men in mid-Victorian Toronto. Through the "brotherly union of prayer" and the sacraments of the church, the Saint Vincent de Paul Society sought to cultivate the spirituality necessary for "the practice of a Christian life."[13]

The indulgences that the papacy liberally granted to the Saint Vincent de Paul Society also illustrate the close connection between the new devotions and ultramontanism.[14] It is also significant that when Archbishop Lynch called a public meeting to demonstrate Catholic sympathy and support for the pope in 1860, shortly after Victor Emmanuel had overrun most of the papal states, nearly all the lay speakers were members of the Saint Vincent de Paul Society.[15] The papal indulgences and the new forms of piety not only served to strengthen the identity of the members of the Saint Vincent de Paul Society as Catholics and as a people apart, but also underscored the connection between piety and charity. Charity was not simply a particular act but rather a way of life. As an embodiment of ultramontane ideals and devotional piety, the society encouraged its members to integrate the devotions of the Catholic church into their daily life.

The idea of "holy poverty" neatly expressed the connection between Catholicism and charity that was at the heart of the Saint Vincent de Paul Society's mission.[16] The poor were God's children; indeed, because the poor were the "representatives of Jesus Christ," it could be said that "they are Himself."[17] The privations of the poor resembled those of Christ, explained Father John Teefy of Saint Basil's parish, for Jesus Christ, "though he was rich, yet for your souls He became poor."[18] The sufferings of the poor represented the agony of the cross, and therefore charity to the poor was similar to performing devotions to the sacraments. The garret of the poor is "the tabernacle where Jesus Christ veils himself under the rags of misery, as on the altar he conceals himself beneath the Eucharistic species."[19] For those who were well off, holy poverty thus entailed a life of service to the poor.

Holy poverty meant something quite different to the poor. The charity of the rich could help the poor to resign themselves to their condition. The poor could then, in effect, make a virtue of necessity. By accepting their lot, the poor could realize their calling as God's children and gain sanctification.[20] As well, if they derived spiritual benefit from material privation, their poverty would truly become holy poverty and a source of salvation to their social superiors. The poor, especially those who had achieved holy poverty, held the keys of salvation for the rich. As our divine saviour "wishes to be recognized under the features of the poor," the members of the Saint Vincent de Paul Society could be certain of "the efficacy of the prayers of him who is so near to God, and who is destined to come to your house."[21] In attending to the needs of the poor, the members of the Saint Vincent de Paul Society gained the patronage of those who were near to God. "Let us," declared one members, "devote ourselves to the poor and so 'bribe these porters of heaven.'"[22] Because the poor in their suffering resembled Christ, their prayers could indeed open the gates of heaven.

Jesus Christ, Catholics were repeatedly reminded, pronounced "woe against the rich, saying it was easier for a camel to pass through the eye of a needle than for a rich man to enter heaven."[23] It was by being poor in spirit, by giving alms, and by engaging in self-sacrifice that the rich could gain salvation. The members of the Saint Vincent de Paul Society were urged to ask themselves how their caprices could be equal to the needs of the poor. "Should I dare treat Jesus Christ as I have hitherto treated the poor? ... I have sometimes spent nights in worldly pleasures, how many have I spent at the bedside of the indigent sick?"[24] Alms-giving was the best antidote against extravagant living and wasteful consumption.[25] Thus, the "sight of so many privations is the best preservation against the abuse of riches." The presence of poverty encouraged acts of self-denial and the habit of a simpler life among those who were better off, and thereby inspired them to devote their surplus to alms.[26] Through charity, the rich atoned for past transgressions and avoided future relapses.[27]

Not only did the existence of poverty contribute to the salvation of wealthy Christians by giving them a singular opportunity to engage in charity, but it could also be said that the poor redeemed society as a whole.[28] Although poverty was natural result of the Fall, "the day of man's first and most keenly felt poverty," property was instituted by God for the well-being of society and the salvation of humanity.[29] The inequalities of society, stated Bishop Timothy O'Mahony, the auxiliary bishop of Toronto, were "doubtless for the common good," for without them society could not exist. People must occupy different stations in life. "If all were rich," he asked, "who would come down to fill the humble offices of the poor and render the duties that comprise all the workings of society?"[30]

The doctrine of holy poverty presupposed a hierarchical society, a society in which classes were bound by reciprocal duties and in which a premium was placed on charity and resignation. But while the hierarchical ordering of society was necessary for the common good, it was still more critical for the realization of salvation. Each rank in society had its duty. "The rich gave material assistance," explained Father John Teefy of Saint Basil's parish, "and the poor man prayers and gratitude, his spiritual graces."[31] Because it provided "the most magnificent field for the exercise of Christian virtue," the order of society was in effect a divine scheme for salvation.[32]

Far from promoting social change, viewing society from the perspective of holy poverty resulted in an emphasis on charity as a religious responsibility. The socially disruptive consequences of a growing urban and industrial society were the direct result of individualism: the rich forgot their duty of charity and the poor were discontented with their lot. Only Catholicism with its sacramental aids and inducements could restore the proper relations and harmony of society. The Protestant, declared *Canadian Freeman* editor James Moylan, is charitable "*naturally*, with as much earnestness and strength as any other man," but his religion "by denying the religious value of works of charity, has taken from him the strongest inducement to struggle on patiently in the work of providing for [the] aged or infirm."[33] All spiritual reform, therefore, began with a return to the Roman Catholic Church. Individual spiritual reform, properly understood, was the key and only legitimate basis for all social action. Charity, which had as its aim the salvation of souls, reinforced the hierarchical order of society, and by engaging in charity the rich could ensure that society fulfilled its true purpose as an arena for the salvation of souls.

Though salvation took place in the world and was effected through the proper ordering of society, the Roman Catholic emphasis on holy poverty reveals a fundamental distrust of the world in general and of worldly pleasure in particular. For the poor, deprivation offered an opportunity to embrace their lot and so offer to all the model of an exemplary life of humility and selfless sacrifice. Those who were better off were called to lead a life of poverty in the spirit, whereby they denied themselves the pleasures and comforts they could easily afford and led a life of spiritual simplicity. Only a life of denial could lead, when infused by the sanctifying grace of the sacraments, to salvation. The laity lived in the world but were not to be of it. Detachment from the world could be achieved only through a life of service and devotion to the sacraments.

Pledged to securing the salvation of its members, the Saint Vincent de Paul Society sought to introduce Catholic men to the devotions of the church and to create a social environment in which laymen could integrate Catholic sacramental piety into their daily lives. Yet, at the same time that the Saint Vincent de Paul Society attempted to popularize Catholic piety among laymen, it also set out to form a spiritual élite. The society's repeated emphasis on holy poverty indicated that it expected from its members an unusual degree of spiritual commitment and a highly disciplined way of life.

The Saint Vincent de Paul Society conceived itself to be a "Christian Brotherhood."[34] In a brotherly spirit the members were to take advantage of the "ready-made friendship" that comes from Catholic charity and to encourage one another to work for their sanctification.[35] The society sought to accommodate itself to men living in the world, but its ideals were obviously those of the religious orders. It was the religious orders, the Sisters of Charity and the Sisters of Saint Joseph, that provided the society with its model of Christian action, for they "are truly the inheritors" of Saint Vincent de Paul's virtues – his humility, his self-denial, his charity.[36] Holding before all the example of a religious body devoted to the poor and the church, imbued by the piety of devotional Catholicism, the Saint Vincent de Paul Society was certainly an ideal organization in the eyes of the clergy.

Unfortunately for the church, the clergy's enthusiasm was not shared by the Irish-Catholic laity. The seven founding members of the Saint Vincent de Paul Society were among the élite of the Catholic community and only one was Irish. Five were well-off merchants, one had been a member of the Legislative Council of Upper Canada, and the other was the clerk to the Legislative Assembly.[37] Within some six months the society had gained some ten additional members. Of these, seven were clerks, two were businessmen, and one was a student of law clerking in the attorney-general's office.[38] Though the society had quickly broadened its social base to include

Table 6
Membership of Our Lady Conference, 1853–57

Category	Number	Percentage
Unskilled	1	2.1
Semi-skilled	6	12.5
Skilled	10	20.8
Clerical	8	16.6
Business	18	37.5
Professional	4	8.3
Private Means	1	2.1

Source: Minutes of Our Lady Conference, Archives of the
Roman Catholic Archdiocese of Toronto; city directories.

Table 7
Membership of Our Lady Conference, 1866–82

Category	Number	Percentage
Unskilled	12	10.7
Semi-skilled	10	8.9
Skilled	18	16.1
Clerical	22	19.6
Business	39	34.8
Professional	9	8.1
Private Means	2	1.8

Source: Minutes of Our Lady Conference, Archives of the
Roman Catholic Archdiocese of Toronto; city directories.

a sizable number of clerks, with few Irish-Catholic members and
without any working-class support it could hardly be said that
the society's membership was representative of the Irish-Catholic
community.

The Saint Vincent de Paul Society did become an Irish-Catholic
organization within a year of its founding, yet the minute books of
the Our Lady Conference of Saint Michael's parish and of the Saint
Patrick Conference of Saint Patrick's parish show that the middle
class continued to dominate the organization with well over half of
the membership (tables 6–9).[39] In the Our Lady Conference, out of
fourteen officers, eight were businessmen, two were professionals,
two were in clerical occupations, and only two were skilled workers.
In short, only two of the officers came from the working class. There
were even fewer men from a working-class background on the exec-

Table 8
Membership of Saint Patrick's Conference,
1874–79

Category	Number	Percentage
Unskilled	12	19.4
Semi-skilled	9	14.5
Skilled	8	12.5
Clerical	12	19.4
Business	19	30.6
Professional	2	3.2
Private Means	–	–

Source: Minutes of Saint Patrick's Conference, Archives of the
Roman Catholic Archdiocese of Toronto; city directories.

Table 9
Membership of Saint Patrick's Conference,
1882–90

Category	Number	Percentage
Unskilled	10	9.4
Semi-skilled	26	24.5
Skilled	15	14.2
Clerical	25	23.6
Business	25	23.6
Professional	5	4.7
Private Means	–	–

Source: Minutes of Saint Patrick's Conference, Archives of the
Roman Catholic Archdiocese of Toronto; *Might's City Directory.*

utive of the Saint Patrick's Conference, a significant result since the
congregation was well known for its lower-working-class composition. Of the six men who held office from 1882 to 1890, only one was
a worker.

While labourers formed the bulk of the male Irish-Catholic working population, their numbers in the Saint Vincent de Paul Society
were exceedingly low. Even in absolute terms, workers accounted
for a third to less than a half of the society's membership and were
virtually excluded from the executive, which was almost a business-
man's monopoly. Although all occupational categories were represented in the Saint Vincent de Paul Society, middle-class occupations
predominated. The large number of businessmen in the society

most likely reflects the fact that small business, particularly the neighbourhood grocery and shop, was for Irish Catholics the most readily available form of upward mobility into the middle class.

The representation of the clerical occupations among the ranks of the Saint Vincent de Paul Society is also notable. Perhaps this indicates that more Irish Catholics were gaining entry to the middle class through white-collar occupations, albeit at the lower end of that class. Yet the position of the clerk was always an insecure one in the nineteenth century.[40] This was true not simply in terms of income but also of occupational stability. Their lower-middle class standing could herald the arrival of better days, but just as easily could be a momentary plateau, to be followed by a slide back from where they came. Certainly many clerks had deeply held middle-class aspirations, and membership in the Saint Vincent de Paul Society was one way for these men to claim the badge of middle-class respectability as their own. The same was likely true for other Irish-Catholic men. Even though the Saint Vincent de Paul Society was modest in its ways – members did not wear ribbons or other paraphernalia – it was in fact the most prestigious organization for men in the parish.

The predominance of the middle class in the society meant, given the largely working-class character of the Irish-Catholic population in Toronto, that the Saint Vincent de Paul Society had failed to attract the largest group of men in the community – Irish-Catholic workers. By 1865 the Saint Vincent de Paul Society had gained only 205 members.[41] Two decades later the society had but 248 members, its largest enrolment, even though the Roman Catholic population had grown by nearly 50 per cent.[42] The membership of the society, then, never exceeded 5 per cent of the adult male Catholic population. The rate at which the Saint Vincent de Paul Society founded parish conferences also indicates the society's slow growth. From 1853 to 1864, the establishment of the society's conferences accompanied the development of the city parishes. The society abruptly completed the first phase of expansion in 1864, three years after the founding of the last of the old city parishes, Saint Patrick's, and then did not expand for nearly twenty years despite the creation of new parishes. When the society founded new conferences in the 1880s, the growth was more apparent that real. In 1882, three new conferences – Saint Peter's, Saint Helen's, and Saint Joseph's – averaged only eleven members each, compared to approximately forty for each of the other conferences.[43] Any increase in the membership of the Saint Vincent de Paul Society throughout the 1880s depended upon growth in the older parish conferences.

Although the minutes of the society are for the most part silent as to how individuals were recruited for membership, there are a few tantalizing hints. In some instances members' sons were encouraged to join.[44] This was not a particularly effective method, and most of the sons did not remain in the society for long. Others were nominated by their employers or by fellow artisans in the same trade.[45] Not infrequently, new members would be suggested by the parish priest or recruited from one of the short-lived parish confraternities for men.[46] What is clear, however, is that the society, although originally founded for young men, proved to be unable to recruit younger members. This problem was repeatedly mentioned in the society's annual reports. Too many young men, lamented a leading member, saw joining the Saint Vincent de Paul Society as "one of the processes of 'making their souls,' to be undertaken only when white hairs begin to appear." Many were passive Catholics who were content to let the priest act "like an eastern prayer-wheel, operating for the benefit of the parishioners, without much volition on their part."[47]

The most obvious reason for the Saint Vincent de Paul Society's failure to recruit members, not only among the young but among the Irish-Catholic community at large, was its predominantly middle-class membership. Working-class men, one suspects, wished to associate with others from a similar background. In addition, as the leaders of the Saint Vincent de Paul Society well recognized, the organization's religious earnestness was as much a handicap as a strength. The society did in fact demand a great deal of its members. During the winter months, when poor relief was distributed, members would have to devote most if not all of their spare time to the society's activities. For many Irish-Catholic men, the issue was not only the degree of commitment demanded by the society, but also the nature of that commitment. In this respect, the difficulties faced by the Saint Vincent de Paul Society in recruiting Irish-Catholic men were similar to those experienced by the devotional organizations.

The Saint Vincent de Paul Society, like the devotional organizations, urged its members to lead a way of life radically different from that of most Irish-Catholic men. Members were expected to exemplify the virtues of probity, propriety, and self-denial in their daily lives by distancing themselves from the pastimes of street and tavern, which the clergy regularly denounced as occasions for sin.[48] As in the case of other parish organizations for men, the Saint Vincent de Paul Society was to provide a wholesome alternative to such popular pastimes. Many men probably saw no conflict between being a faithful Catholic and indulging in a few drinks in the company of friends at their favourite tavern and, not unreasonably, they preferred not to be placed in position where they could be asked to choose between the two. The Saint Vincent de Paul Society was also at a disadvantage because, like the devotional organizations, it offered little in the way of organized recreation to act as a counter-attraction to the pastimes popular among Irish-Catholic men in the city. The vast majority of Irish-Catholic men expected their associational life to be an extension and embodiment of the social world of male pastimes and conviviality, but the focus of the Saint Vincent de Paul Society on charity and piety left little room for these familiar forms of sociability.

In the case of the Irish-Catholic middle class, the Saint Vincent de Paul Society's emphasis on piety and personal service to the poor restricted its appeal. For those middle-class Irish Catholics who did join the society, part of its attractiveness lay in its promotion of the ideals of respectability that were then taking root in Canada and elsewhere. Not only were the virtues advocated by the Saint Vincent de Paul Society central to the work ethic of the middle class, but they were also integral to its world of leisure. The purpose of leisure, most middle-class Victorians agreed, was to effect the moral improvement of the self and to elevate the moral tone of society as a whole.[49] In serving their God and their community, the members of the Saint Vincent de Paul Society exemplified this ideal of the proper use of leisure.

The Saint Vincent de Paul Society's low membership should not be mistaken for lay apathy. The society sought to encourage the formation of devotional "high achievers," and this spiritual élitism undercut its ability to recruit the mass of Irish-Catholic laymen. The way of life advocated by the organization, with its emphasis on piety and service to the poor, resembled in many respects that of the clergy, and only a few laymen were prepared to rise to such heights of spiritual heroism.

For the clergy, the Saint Vincent de Paul Society's mission to the poor was of central importance. The poor, the clergy feared, were in greatest need of spiritual reformation but were also the least likely to attend church or send their children to the separate schools, where they could be instructed in the Catholic faith. Through its close connection with the clergy, the Saint Vincent de Paul Society became a vehicle for creating a cohesive lay minority – a lay army of the church – intent on disseminating devotions among the poor. Yet, if the members of the Saint Vincent de Paul Society were to expose the poor to the ideals and piety of the Catholic Church, it was first necessary for the society's visitors to reach them. Poor relief was thus but a means to an end. In order to determine how the society's religious goals influenced its charitable efforts, it is necessary to outline briefly the nature of poverty in Victorian Toronto and then to evaluate the nature and extent of the society's outdoor relief.

Lack of skills and low wages left many Irish Catholics particularly vulnerable to the cyclical and seasonal fluctuations of the economy. Labourers could earn about a dollar a day but would need to bring in at least four or four and a half dollars a week to support a wife and two children adequately. Irish-Catholic labourers who enjoyed steady employment could expect to work between 200 and 230 days of the year and thus provide for their families if contributions from other family members filled the gap, but still the margin was very slim. Most casual outdoor labourers were not so fortunate in their search for work.[50] In these families the earnings of older children would be absolutely essential to fend off starvation.[51] For families of unskilled workers surviving on what was at best a subsistence income, any interruption in employment would bring with it extreme hardship. Although it was during the recessions of 1857–59 and 1873–79 that unskilled workers experienced the severest deprivation, even in good times they regularly faced unemployment because of the seasonal slow-downs of Toronto's economy.[52] During the winter months not only did outdoor work such as construction come to a standstill, but factories were also closed.[53] Because of the fierce competition in an oversupplied labour market, those lucky enough to find work would accept deep cuts in their wages.[54] When food was already dear and the cost of heat – almost a dollar and a half a week for a family – would have strained a full wage packet, workers found themselves without the means to meet the rigours of winter.

Illness or accident, too, could cast a family into poverty. However brief the illness, a working-class family deprived of its main source of income experienced great hardship. If the illness, however brief, of a family's main wage-earner forced them to rely upon the aid of kin and charity, the death of the husband was nothing short of disaster. The higher incidence of mortality among Irish-Catholic men compared to the general male population, together with the proclivity of some Irish-Catholic men to abandon their families in their peripatetic search for work, meant that their wives and children were especially vulnerable to the depredations of extreme poverty.[55] Women's wages, even during the best of times, were insufficient to support a family.[56] The sexual division of labour condemned these now single women and their children to a life of indigence.

In keeping with the prevailing middle-class consensus that poverty was essentially a seasonal phenomena, the Saint Vincent de Paul Society's outdoor charity was distributed only during the winter months and limited to the barest necessities for those either unable to find work or incapable of working. The society's main form of relief was an allotment of oatmeal or barley, bread, and wood. Contemporary accounts leave no doubt as to how crucial this assistance was. One *Globe* reporter visiting the slums on Adelaide Street was shocked to find "a spectacle of misery and wretchedness." In one room he found a family with only one piece of furniture – a bed which had icicles that reached to the floor.[57] Without fuel or even clothes, many a family huddled in bed to keep warm.[58] Food, of course, was also scarce. Another *Globe* reporter noted that the poor were reduced to eating stale bread crusts, which they had purchased from bakers at a discount.[59]

Most families on the Saint Vincent de Paul Society's rolls received between six and eight pounds of bread and two pounds of grain a week.[60] While contributing a major staple to the diet of the poor, this allotment of bread was no substitute for a balanced diet.[61] Nor would the society's additional allocations of tea and sugar or cash grants, which were sparingly dispensed and never exceeded fifty cents, help poor families close the nutrition gap.[62] If such families were to survive they would have to find other ways to obtain food.

The cold of winter, with its ever present danger of death from exposure, rivalled the lack of food as a threat to the poor. The Saint Vincent de Paul Society's distribution of a quarter of a cord of wood as needed to the families on its rolls ensured that the poor would not freeze to death in their damp and dingy rooms.[63] Some families who were without wood heaters also received stoves.[64] In addition to providing stoves and fuel, the Saint Vincent de Paul Society, in cooperation with the parish sewing societies, distributed clothing such as trousers, coats, and boots. The society rarely disclosed the extent of its own clothing distribution, but as the Saint Patrick's Conference during the winter of 1887–88 gave away 1,100 pieces of clothing to 163 of the 207 individuals on its books, it would seem that many of the families supported by the Saint Vincent de Paul Society received clothing.[65] The society also provided bedding and blankets, surely no luxury in the cold and damp dwellings of the Irish poor, and bedsteads to prevent "frightful moral disorder." Given the overcrowded conditions of Toronto's slums, with several families sharing very cramped quarters, the Saint Vincent de Paul Society's fears that the poor would lie "together promiscuously" were perhaps not unreasonable. In any event, the society's visitors could console themselves that the distribution of bedding and bedsteads contributed to the health of Toronto's Irish-Catholic poor by keeping them warm during the cold nights of winter.[66]

Some of Toronto's poor, the secretary for the Saint Mary's Conference noted, had sold all in order to pay their rents and were left with "nothing but the clothes on their backs, & some had hardly sufficient to cover them."[67] The Saint Vincent de Paul Society on occasion paid the back rents of the poor on its rolls.[68] The society also intervened with pawnbrokers to make good the debts of those who had pawned their furniture and clothing to meet the exactions of their landlords.[69]

The society's allotment of bread and grain offered the poor little in the way of nutrition. Nonetheless, the society's bread allocation alone could save a poor family up to forty cents a week, no small consideration for Toronto's desperate poor.[70] The society was able to clothe some of the worst off but could not clothe all the poor on its rolls, nor was its program intended to provide the poor with a varied wardrobe. Similarly, the society's payment of rent, important as it was to a select number of beneficiaries, was an extraordinary measure, and most of the poor aided by the society had to find other ways to pay their rent. The society's allocation of wood was an unambiguous contribution to the well-being of the poor. The quarter-cord of wood, which was regularly replenished as supplies ran out, ensured that the poor won at least one battle against the vicissitudes of winter. In sum, if the society's relief was not extensive enough to guarantee the survival of the poor, it was still absolutely crucial for those without any other means of support.

Although most of the poor on the Saint Vincent de Paul Society's books, such as widows and abandoned wives with children, were unable to work, the society did attempt at times to help those Irish Catholics who were able to work gain the means of livelihood. Skilled workers were provided with tools to pursue their craft, peddlers with goods to sell.[71] Members of the society also used their influence to obtain jobs for those on relief, and one conference established an employment agency.[72] For many of the poor, however, the prospects in Toronto were not promising. The only alternative was to leave the city in the hope of meeting up with more affluent relatives or finding employment elsewhere, and the Saint Vincent de Paul Society regularly purchased fares for poor migrants.[73]

There were those – the old, the ill, and the incurable – who could not leave. The Saint Vincent de Paul Society conferences would obtain and pay for medical treatment and, if need be, petition the mayor to gain them admission to the General Hospital.[74] Also, in consultation with the parish priest, the conferences would place the old, the handicapped, and the incurable, all those no longer able to look after themselves, in the House of Providence, the Catholic home run by the Sisters of Saint Joseph.[75] Inmates at both the General Hospital and the House of Providence were visited by members of the society. Besides providing books and magazines, the society ensured that the patients were provided with underclothing and socks, along with tobacco for men and woollen jackets for women.[76] Spectacles, crutches, and artificial legs were also distributed.[77] Thus, whether ill or without means of support, the Irish-Catholic poor of Toronto could look to the Saint Vincent de Paul Society for assistance. Nor were they abandoned in death, which for some came all too suddenly but for others not soon enough. The society would not only pay for the undertaker's expenses and the burial of the indigent but also arrange for a requiem Mass, thereby relieving relations, if there were any, of a costly burden.[78]

The Saint Vincent de Paul Society assisted only those with children who were or had been married and were without other means of support. Unmarried men and women were not assisted by the society. The constitution and rules of the society forbade members to visit or assist women who had not been married for fear that such contact would bring the visitors to temptation and, in any event, would give rise to suspicion.[79] As for single men, the society believed that since they had few responsibilities they ought to be able to get along without assistance. Families born of the legitimate union of man and woman, who represented the hope of the future and, as all agreed, were the innocent victims of economic vicissitudes, were the object of the Saint Vincent de Paul Society's charity.[80] While the society did provide aid to families with husbands who were unable to work, the conference minutes indicate that women with children whose husbands were either absent or dead were most likely to receive relief from the society. The extent to which families headed by women dominated the society's rolls is revealed when the figures in table 10 are reviewed.[81] In 1851 almost two-thirds of the families on the rolls were headed by women. As late as 1886, slightly more than one-half of the families on relief had women as heads. By 1888 single-parent families made up only one-third of the families receiving relief from the Saint Vincent de Paul Society. This shift possibly reflected the relative decline of single-parent Irish-Catholic families, but it was also a direct result of the Saint Vincent de Paul Society's improved finances, which widened the range of those relieved.

Because some of the donations to the society, most typically clothes, staples, and stoves, were given in kind, the published ac-

Table 10
Relief Provided by the Saint Vincent de Paul Society, 1850–88

Year	Expenditure	Families	Adults	Children	Bread (in pounds)
1850–51	$320	69	85	136	2,076
1852	$520	81	113	171	–
1864	$724	–	107	190	9,485
1865	$775	–	165	265	15,710
1882	$1,677.79	–	–	–	–
1885	$2,500	c. 303	(c. 1,000 in all)		–
1886	$2,061.16	248	372	463	–
1888	$2,800	322	536	703	–

Source: Saint Vincent de Paul Society, "Summary Statement," 2 May 1851, in Documentary History, 36; Families Relieved, 1850–53, ARCAT; "Minutes of the First General Meeting of the Saint Vincent de Paul Society in Toronto," July 1854, in Documentary History, 32; Canadian Freeman, 28 April 1864; "Twenty-Fifth General Meeting," in Documentary History, 60–1; Superior Council Report 1882; Superior Council Report 1885; Rapport du Conseil Supérieur 1886; Report Superior Council 1888.

counts of the Saint Vincent de Paul Society underestimate the cash value of its aid to the poor. Nonetheless, it is still evident that the number relieved by the society in its early days was restricted by its limited finances. In 1850 the society spent close to one-third of its budget on bread, the rest of funds being used to purchase wood and to pay rents.[82] With bread and fuel accounting for the bulk of the society's expenditures, the society naturally concentrated its resources on the neediest of the poor – widows, abandoned wives, and their children.

Over time, the financial resources of the Saint Vincent de Paul Society increased considerably, more than doubling in the fifteen years after 1850. In part, this growth in financial resources was an indication that as Irish Catholics became settled in the city they had more discretionary income that they could devote to charitable causes. The Saint Vincent de Paul Society's charity sermons, concerts, and picnics were major community events for the Irish Catholics of Toronto. If few men were willing to be actively involved in the society, many were willing to contribute their mite. After the mid-1860s, not only did the society's financial situation improve, but it also regularly received donations of fuel.[83] The society was therefore able to spend 50 to 70 per cent of its budget on bread.

As its financial resources grew, the Saint Vincent de Paul Society's impact on the Irish-Catholic population increased: in the early 1850s between 2.5 and 3.5 per cent of the Irish-Catholic residents of Toronto benefited from the society's charity, and by the mid-1880s the figure was in the range of 4.5 to 6 per cent. These statistics, however, do not reflect the society's impact accurately. Once the totals are analyzed by age and sex, quite a different picture emerges. In the 1850s almost 6 per cent of adult Catholic women received relief, and by the 1880s as many as 9 per cent of all Catholic women were under the society's care. The proportion of children under twelve years of age on the society's rolls increased from 7 per cent in the 1850s to as high as 12 per cent in the 1880s.[84]

Yet the true impact of the Saint Vincent de Paul Society can be measured only by the proportion of poor families that it assisted. Unfortunately, it is impossible to estimate how many Irish-Catholic families faced poverty sometime or another during the winter. The Saint Vincent de Paul Society's figures for relief do indicate, however, that it did reach a substantial number of families in poverty headed by women. Despite improved finances, the society still focused its mission on women with children. Women with children were singled out for relief not only because they were the most exposed to the ravages of poverty. They were also thought to be especially vulnerable to the blandishments of Protestant-operated charities, and the Saint Vincent de Paul Society's relief was seen as a means of keeping these poor in the Roman Catholic Church.

With public charities under the management and direction of Protestants, Catholic fears of "leakage" were easily aroused. Catholic denunciations of "souperism" – the alleged use of hot meals by Protestant charities to proselytize Catholics – and of Protestant "proselytising mills" were common throughout the latter part of the nineteenth century.[85] "It is high time to protest against the outrageous and indefensible conduct of these would be philanthropists," thundered the *Canadian Freeman*. By taking advantage of the adverse circumstances of the Irish-Catholic poor, these charities were, the *Freeman* insisted, setting snares to entrap Catholics.[86] The Saint Vincent de Paul Society therefore undertook to combat "leakage" to Protestantism by providing outdoor relief in direct competition with the largely Protestant and city-supported House of Industry. In fact, as explained earlier, whatever little evidence there is indicates that "leakage" was simply not a significant phenomenon. Irish Catholics of the time, however, saw matters differently, and it was their perception of reality rather than reality itself that determined their actions. Furthermore, while Protestant-dominated agencies did not actually draw Irish Catholics to Protestant churches, they could undermine the Catholic Church's efforts to reach the Catholic poor and to transform their religious behaviour. In short, only Catholic charitable organizations, of which the Saint Vincent de Paul Society was a prime example, could be relied upon to bring the Irish-Catholic poor into the religious sphere of the parish and its social institutions, especially the separate school.

This leads to the question of how the Saint Vincent de Paul Society's approach to poor relief differed from that of the Protestant-dominated charitable agencies. During the middle of the nineteenth century, liberalism, and with it the conviction that the vast majority of the poor were undeserving, gained ascendancy in Toronto's official circles.[87] The poor, the laws of political economy revealed, were impoverished because of their listless and extravagant ways. People, declared the *Globe*, the foremost advocate of liberal political economy in Canada, "have only themselves to blame." Work was a virtue, and to provide relief would simply confirm the poor in their destructive habits. Indiscriminate relief, thundered the *Globe*, "has done more to make a pauper class than anything else." If relief were extended, it would be found to be "one of the greatest encouragers of reckless improvidence and vicious indulgence to be thought of."[88]

As a result of the influence of liberal political economy, Protestant-supported charities in Toronto offered relief on the basis of the moral distinction between "deserving" and "undeserving" poor.[89] The deserving poor were individuals of good moral character who were destitute not through any failing of their own but rather through misfortune and chance. Although Catholics were usually quick to denounce liberalism and its suspicion of the poor as the authors of their own misfortune, poverty did elicit contradictory responses among better-off Catholics. "Indulgence, idleness, medicity [*sic*], intemperance and all immoralities," Bishop Charbonnel observed, "are too often sisters living together."[90] Even if immorality was not the root cause of poverty, some of the poor had become so corrupt as to be undeserving. Without the leaven of the church's spiritual influences, poverty was a threat to moral and religious well-being.

The question naturally arises: how did the Saint Vincent de Paul Society determine who the "deserving" poor were? Upon recommendation of a case for relief by a member of the society or parish priest, the conference would appoint two visitors to investigate.[91] Members were not to be appointed visitors in cases where they had nominated individuals for relief, nor were visitors to be acquaintances of or related to those recommended for assistance.[92] For the most part, the conferences acted on the advice of the visitors, and relief tickets were accordingly issued. Thus, the poor were spared the trial of appearing before a committee of trustees, as was the case at the House of Industry.[93] Visitors of the Saint Vincent de Paul

Society were urged "to use discrimination and to seek out worthy objects of their charity." The deserving poor would not seek to draw attention to themselves because their "retiring delicacy" leads to "concealment of their distress." "The virtuous poor," Father Francis Rooney claimed, "must be sought out in their humble abodes and made happy by your alms and sympathy."[94] Others, however, would take advantage of the society's desire to minister to the less fortunate. W.J. Macdonell, president of the Particular Council, the local governing board of the society, strongly objected to giving relief to those "who are well able to get along without and who ... in many instances boasted that it was unnecessary for them to work as they could always count on getting relief from the St. Vincent de Paul Society."[95] The visitors were particularly concerned to establish that the families applying for relief were without resources.[96]

Although the society did distinguish between deserving and undeserving poor, this distinction did not always govern its administration of relief.[97] The minute books the Saint Vincent de Paul Society's conferences indicate that, as long as the applicants to the society were without means, relief was often granted irrespective of other considerations when children were concerned, particularly in families headed by women. In such cases, even when it was a question of flagrant intemperance, the conferences were usually reluctant to refuse relief "as they were in an impoverished state."[98] Perhaps what is notable is that the distinction between deserving and undeserving poor does not appear in the Saint Vincent de Paul Society's minutes as frequently as one would expect.[99] One reason why it was not often invoked is that the society rejected the assumption shared by many Protestants that the majority of the poor were undeserving. As James Moylan, a leading member of the society and one of its best-known spokesmen, pointed out in the pages of the *Canadian Freeman*, in direct opposition to the *Globe*: "The vast majority of ... the poor and destitute ... are so through no fault of their own." "Vicissitudes of trade, change of fortune, failing health, accident" – these were the true causes of poverty. To attribute poverty to the failings of the poor, the *Freeman* concluded, "is not consistent with justice and truth."[100]

All the same, much was made of the "keenness" of the Saint Vincent de Paul Society's visitors' "practiced glance" and the "searching nature of their investigation." If any impostor escaped the society's detection, declared James Moylan, they "must be clever indeed." In any case, the undeserving poor were a tiny minority, and "the [political] economy practiced by our City Salons is ... false economy."[101] The poor were indeed the representatives of Christ, and as loyal

sons of the church the members of the Saint Vincent de Paul Society
had a duty to assist them.[102] The representatives of Christ could not
be easily refused the charity of Catholics.

While the society endeavoured to foster the habits of self-control
and self-help, relief was not, and probably could not, be granted
solely on the basis of these virtues. Should the society's visitors be too
demanding, poor families could simply turn to one or another Protestant charitable organization for assistance. Besides, however degenerate the parents may seem to the visitors, the children could still be
saved for the Catholic Church. Religious considerations were central
the Saint Vincent de Paul's Society's administration of relief. Thus,
on a practical level, the division of the poor into the deserving and
industrious and the undeserving and shiftless was irrelevant to the
Saint Vincent de Paul Society's administration of relief. Such a practice would only alienate the poor, and then the society would be unable to fulfil its religious mission to them. The purpose of charity
was to save souls. It would be presumptuous of the visitors to judge
the poor, who were fulfiling a divine purpose and whose conversion,
as a result of Catholic charity, would take place in God's own time.[103]
As long as there was hope for a religious conversion, aid could be
continued in all good conscience. Given the immense pastoral challenge the visitors of the Saint Vincent de Paul Society faced, hope
was a welcome inspiration.

For a clergy imbued with the reforming zeal of ultramontanism, the
poor's casual attitude towards their canonical religious obligations
was nothing less than apostasy. The physical wants of the poor, the
members of the Saint Vincent de Paul Society were reminded, is "the
least of their misfortunes."[104] Their spiritual poverty was of far
more serious consequence since the fate of their souls hung in the
balance. The society exhorted its members to "sit on the half-broken
chair which is offered us" and to talk with the poor.[105] Outdoor relief was a way of gaining the confidence of the poor and effecting
their spiritual improvement.[106]

The conversion of the poor, the second major aim of the Saint
Vincent de Paul Society, was inextricably linked with the salvation of
its members.[107] The members recognized that, with its limited resources, the society could do little to alleviate the material wants of
the poor.[108] Yet, because the members could "command the very
graces of God himself," the spiritual alms of the society were inexhaustible. Zeal for the salvation of souls, not philanthropy, characterized the Saint Vincent de Paul Society.[109] By placing themselves

under the protection of the church, the members could practise every virtue to atone for past deeds, and what could be more virtuous than the "active love of our neighbour" to aid his salvation?[110] In strengthening the faith of the poor, the members would be edified by the poor's patient resignation in the face of adversity.[111] It was therefore "not sufficient that religious improvement take place among the poor; it is necessary ... that the Conference should know it has been effected."[112] In accepting their sufferings, the poor displayed the virtues of holy poverty and became worthy models for the visitors and members of the Saint Vincent de Paul Society.

The members visited the families on the society's rolls weekly and deliberately avoided visits at fixed times "so that the families may not be prepared, or 'got up' for their reception." The purpose of these visits was to determine whether the families were "worthy objects of their charity."[113] Although temperate habits were highly desirable, the visitors' most detailed questions were designed to elicit the nature of the families' religious practice and to assess the potential for religious reform. Did the family regularly attend church on Sunday? How frequently did members of the family receive the sacraments? Did the children attend Catholic schools where they would be educated in Catholic doctrine and piety? Had the children received baptism, confirmation, or first communion? Did they know how to recite the Lord's Prayer? These were the questions that concerned the visitors of the Saint Vincent de Paul Society.[114]

Such questions illustrate that the society's visitors sought to introduce the poor to the devotional life of the parish and that they were especially concerned with the piety of children. As Father Joseph Laurent of Saint Patrick's parish put it, "On the youth of to-day will mainly depend the progress of the Catholic church in the future."[115] In order to initiate Catholic children into the sacramental life of the church, the Saint Vincent de Paul Society took charge of the supervision that the parents were supposed to undertake, but which they sometimes neglected.[116] The first task of the society was to enrol the children in the separate schools or the catechetical classes conducted by the society where they could be instructed in the values and ideals of the church. Accordingly, during their visits to the family home and in the schools, the members sought to oversee the children's educational and spiritual progress and to ensure that they attended separate schools. At the same time, the visitors applied moral suasion to make sure that the children were confirmed and made their first communion – the initiations into the full sacramental life of the church – and that they said their daily prayers and regularly attended Sunday Mass.[117] If the parents proved recalcitrant, the society would frequently threaten to remove the children and arrange for them to be adopted by a pious family where the children would be nurtured in the observance of official Catholicism.[118]

In order to have any impact on the children's spiritual development, the society had to recast the religious practice of their parents. Adults, too, were encouraged by the visitors to attend church regularly and fulfil their Easter duties.[119] But the visitors were not satisfied with this minimal canonical observance. They distributed rosaries, crucifixes, prayer books, and religious literature.[120] These devotional aids were a means of popularizing various forms of piety: the cult of the Virgin Mary, the devotions to the Sacred Heart, and the pilgrimage of the stations of the cross.[121]

Religious literature in particular played a critical role in the dissemination of piety by the visitors of the Saint Vincent de Paul Society. Because the visitors "may be embarrassed in the choice of words" in instructing the poor, observed W.J. Macdonell, president of the Particular Council, such books could be an indispensable aid for explaining devotions and "so fortify the faith of the poor." After having read the tracts aloud, the visitors could then question the poor in order to determine the effects of the society's efforts to instill Catholic orthodoxy.[122] Perhaps the most visible effort of the society to influence the ways of the poor was its attempt to curtail wakes. The society not only paid for the funerals of the poor, but the members also "prayed in the houses by the corpses" and attended the funerals to prevent wake games and amusements.[123]

Right living was just as important as assiduous praying in the discipline of piety popularized by the Saint Vincent de Paul Society. For the poor this meant embracing a life of holy poverty. The poor were God's children: by accepting their lot they could gain sanctification. Poverty, instead of being an obstacle to salvation, could become the means by which salvation could be gained. The other side of this sanctification of poverty was a rigorous moralism: parties, dancing, drinking, easy familiarity with members of the opposite sex, even between children, were all condemned, and the members of the Saint Vincent de Paul Society did not hesitate to use their weekly visits to enforce this strict moral code.[124]

Although the Saint Vincent de Paul Society's emphasis on holy poverty led it to stress the virtues of obedience and passivity for the poor, it also promoted the habits of thrift and self-help. The key to self-help, the members believed, was education. Without education, one member asked, how can Irish Catholics "be able to keep pace with our 'going ahead' times of the nineteenth century?"[125] The idea was not that education would necessarily raise the poor out of poverty; rather, the hope was that education would enable the poor to make the best use of the few opportunities available to them and at the same time instruct them in moral habits. The members of the Saint Vincent de Paul Society also hoped that education would ensure that those who were living close to the margin of subsistence would not needlessly fall into poverty because they lacked self-discipline and foresight, the virtues that Catholic education was supposed to impart.

In 1883 the society began to operate two night schools, one at the Saint Nicholas Institute, the Catholic home for working boys, the other at Saint Patrick's School.[126] In these evening classes, instruction was confined to "secular" subjects. Reading, writing, composition, and arithmetic were taught, and special attention was given to the drafting of business forms such as accounts and receipts. Over the winter of 1887–88 the Saint Nicholas night school had thirty students and the Saint Patrick's school twenty-three. The Saint Basil conference also started up a young men's club with twenty-two members, which met two nights a week in the society's reading-room in the basement of the church. Though their numbers were small, this club and the night schools illustrate the society's efforts to promote self-improvement and divert Catholic youths from spending their time "with much less profit to themselves."[127]

The visitors of the Saint Vincent de Paul Society sought to impress on the poor that living on charity was "very precarious" and endeavoured to induce them to "exert themselves to earn their livelihood."[128] The society would attempt to secure employment for the Irish-Catholic poor, and at least one conference attempted to foster thrifty habits among the working poor by establishing a savings bank.[129] The most important effort to "encourage economy and forethought amongst the poor, and direct the useful employment of their means" was the founding of the Toronto Savings Bank in 1854 by Bishop Charbonnel with W.J. Macdonell as president and D.K. Feehan as manager.[130] Both were members of the Saint Vincent de Paul Society.[131] The bank's charitable goals, to aid the development of Catholic business and to devote its surpluses to Catholic charity, ensured that it developed close ties with the Saint Vincent de Paul Society.[132] Of the thirty-six lay directors of the bank prior to 1872, at least twenty-four were members of the society.[133]

The Toronto Savings Bank never managed to gain the support of the Irish-Catholic workers of Toronto. The bank accepted deposits as low as twenty-five cents, which, compared to the usual minimum of a dollar at other banks, was well within the means of many workers. Nevertheless, its business hours, from 10 a.m. to 3 p.m., meant that many workers could not get to the bank before the end of their working day.[134] When the Toronto Savings bank finally extended its business hours from 7 p.m. to 9 p.m. in 1873, it was already in deep financial difficulty. As a result of bad loans, the bank had amassed colossal debts by 1872, and changes in the federal law regulating savings banks made its demise inevitable.[135] Archbishop Lynch won a reprieve for the Toronto Savings Bank, but in the end only a charitable trust remained to fulfil the bank's original object, and the bank's assets were taken over by the Home Savings and Loan Company.

The members of the Saint Vincent de Paul Society had few illusions that the virtues of self-help and self-discipline would vastly improve the material lot of the poor. Such virtues might enable the poor to stretch further their meager resources, but the truly indigent could hardly be expected to raise themselves out of poverty. Nonetheless, the ethic of self-help and self-discipline was essential to the religious program of the Saint Vincent de Paul Society. It was one way to prepare the poor for the church's discipline of piety, which demanded that religious observances be fulfilled regularly and with propriety.

Although the society rarely made relief directly contingent on religious conversion, the complete dependence of the poor upon the resources of the society undoubtedly persuaded many to cooperate. Such external compliance, however, would have been as ephemeral as it was artificial. The ability of the Saint Vincent de Paul Society to influence the poor was based on the immigrants' inherent loyalty to their church. Catholicism had become by 1830 an inextricable part of the Irish communal consciousness. Although many of these immigrants were not practising Catholics when judged by the norms of official Catholicism, they themselves had no doubt that they were Catholic and thoroughly identified with the Catholic Church. Such sentiments would have led many Irish Catholics to turn to the Saint Vincent de Paul Society for assistance, as would have their long-standing resentment of Protestant "souperism."[136]

Especially during the 1850s, visits by members of the Saint Vincent de Paul Society would have been the first exposure that many of the poor would have had to the doctrines and devotions of the Roman Catholic Church. The response of the poor to their teachings was determined by sex and age. Many of the poor women and children on relief, it would seem, adopted the piety promoted by the society. During the late 1860s and after, contemporary observers were especially struck by the large number of poor women and children at church on Sundays.[137] These poor, whose spiritual fate particularly worried Bishop Charbonnel, had become church-goers. Besides discharging this canonical minimum, there is also evidence that poor women and children practised devotions. By the 1880s, the society's visitors could rely on children to read religious tracts to their parents and answer the questions that arose during these readings. This level of literacy demonstrates that poor children had attended separate schools long enough to gain a basic knowledge of Catholic dogma and practice.[138] At the same time, the large number of poor women and children in the parish confraternities would seem to indicate that the Saint Vincent de Paul Society was successful in popularizing devotions and in fostering support for the church among this part of the Irish-Catholic population.

The Saint Vincent de Paul Society's policy of focusing its efforts on women and their children meant that it had less contact with poor men. The evidence in this case is both impressionistic and fragmentary. Still, it would seem that by the 1880s many Irish-Catholic men attended church regularly, and a significant number of them had taken up devotional observances.[139] The Saint Vincent de Paul Society contributed to the creation of a social climate in the Irish-Catholic community in which religious conformity would become the norm before the end of the nineteenth century.

"Essentially Catholic," declared the *Manual of the Society of St. Vincent of Paul*, "our society should always maintain as a singular honor a close connection with the Parochial clergy and Bishops of the Diocese."[140] "Its intimate union with the Church," the *Manual* further maintained, "is for the Society of Saint Vincent of Paul, as for all Catholic works, an indispensable condition of stability, and the most necessary of duties." Because the members of the society were dependent on the sacraments of the church for the efficacy of their work, "we should always remember that we are only laics" ,and should therefore "observe and follow with an absolute docility the directions which our ecclesiastical superiors may think fit to give us."[141] "It is the office of pastors to expose our duties to us," the *Manual* concluded, "it is ours to discharge them."[142]

The members of the Saint Vincent de Paul Society were to be the "servants" of the church, the "auxiliaries" of the clergy, and it was with this expectation that Bishop Charbonnel approved the introduction of the society to Toronto.[143] Perhaps the most notable example of the members' auxiliary status was their role in the general affairs of the parish. With parish trustees playing little or no role, the parish priests enjoyed a monopoly in the management of parochial property.[144] The laity, usually officers of the Saint Vincent de Paul Society, were appointed to serve, at the parish priest's pleasure, on *ad hoc* committees established by the clergy to deal with limited and specific parochial issues.[145] Members of the Saint Vincent de Paul Society often acted as ushers in the parish churches and frequently helped the women's devotional organizations put on bazaars, picnics, and garden parties to aid the parish building fund or to liquidate the parish debt.[146] Because of these contributions, so essential to the operation of any parish, the Saint Vincent de Paul Society was, as Father Joseph Laurent of Saint Patrick's parish phrased it, the right hand of the clergy.[147] In recognition of the members' role in the parish at large, the clergy usually placed the Saint Vincent de Paul Society at the head of the religious processions held on ecclesiastical festivals, such as the feast of Corpus Christi.[148]

Like many aspects of parish life, the role of the leaders of the Saint Vincent de Paul Society in the quotidian affairs of the parish is largely unrecorded. One example of how the leaders acted as the spokesmen of a parish, however, was reported in some detail, largely because it set the stage for a confrontation with the archbishop. Unusual as this incident was, it does throw light on how the leaders of the Saint Vincent de Paul Society understood their place in the parish and in the authority structures of the church. In January 1881 a delegation of members from the Saint Vincent de Paul Society conference in Saint Patrick's parish met with Archbishop Lynch in the hope that the archbishop would reconsider his decision to transfer their parish priest, Father Joseph Laurent. As the discussions proceeded, a few members lost their temper and began shouting at the archbishop, whereupon Lynch quickly brought the audience to an end. "It is almost certain," the *Globe* predicted, "that His Grace's views will be accepted" – and so they were. The parish conference leadership dissociated the society from this "unseemly conduct" of a few hotheads and, as loyal sons of the church, they defended their archbishop's prerogatives and accepted his decision. If the society's leaders were upset at the offence given to their archbishop, they were also concerned that the disrespect shown for ecclesiastical authority undermined their role as the natural spokesmen of the parish. The leaders of the Saint Vincent de Paul Society could best "express the wishes of the people," William Burns affirmed on behalf of the parish conference, and so could well do without the interference of others.[149]

The origins of the first conference of the Saint Vincent de Paul Society in Toronto illuminates how the leaders of the Saint Vincent de Paul Society came to see themselves as the natural spokesmen and representatives of the parish. G.M. Muir, who had been active in the society in Quebec City prior to his move to Toronto, gathered together six other laymen to organize the first parish conference in the city. Once he secured Charbonnel's approval for this project, Muir then took steps to have the conference officially constituted by the society's national council, which was based in Quebec City.[150]

Muir's gambit resulted in the creation of an institutional framework for lay leadership and activism that enjoyed the church's blessing. As has been seen, the clergy occupied a place of honour in the Saint Vincent de Paul Society. In their capacity as chaplains to the society, the clergy offered spiritual direction and guidance as well as providing practical support. From time to time, they would suggest cases for relief, seek out new members for the society and, when asked to evaluate difficult petitions for relief, offer their advice.[151] Yet, though the clergy were entitled to attend the society's regular weekly meetings, they rarely did so, with the result that most of the time the lay officers were left to run the society on their own. The society's officers led the society's weekly meetings and devotions, administered the society's finances, organized teams of visitors, vetted candidates for membership, and ensured that the members properly monitored the spiritual and moral progress of the society's charges. Not only did these leaders organize the society's programs for social and religious outreach, but they also ensured that the society nurtured its members in the practice of piety.

The Saint Vincent de Paul Society was a society of lay activists, as its leaders emphasized, in which the members worked for their own sanctification by personally aiding the poor and by participating in the society's meetings and devotions.[152] In visiting the poor, members were expected to use their own judgment and ingenuity in the religious instruction and moral reform of the poor, two areas that were normally the clergy's prerogative. Through the Saint Vincent de Paul Society laymen could participate in the church's apostolate, and in recognition of this role the society's members were able to become spiritual and social counsellors to the poor. The rank and file were also involved in making decisions that affected the operations of the society, although only in a limited way. Decisions to admit new members and to adjudicate cases for relief were made in a collegial manner, but the structure of the Saint Vincent de Paul Society was unmistakeably hierarchical.

Authority in the Saint Vincent de Paul Society was concentrated at the top. The leaders of the parish conference – the president and vice president – were selected by the city's Particular Council, and they were to serve in office until such time as they submitted their resignations. The society was thus led by a self-perpetuating oligarchy, many members of which were from the Catholic community's social élite, and this leadership was in no way formally accountable to the rank and file. Activism, therefore, was the responsibility of the many, but leadership was the prerogative of the few. The officers of the Saint Vincent de Paul Society led their members in a life of piety and of service to the poor, and the authority they had for this endeavour was delegated to them by the clergy.

The program and goals of the Saint Vincent de Paul Society were laid down in detail in its *Manual* and monthly *Bulletin* but, as the leaders of the society well recognized, innovation was necessary if the society were to hold its members' interest and if it were to fulfil its apostolate to the poor.[153] The society's most important local forum for leadership was its city-wide Particular Council. Formed in 1854 by the officers of the three parish conferences then in existence in Toronto, the Particular Council brought together the leaders of the city's parish conferences four times a year. At the Particular Conference meetings, which were always chaired by a priest, the leaders of the Saint Vincent de Paul Society exchanged information on their activities, coordinated the outreach of the parish conferences, shared ideas to make the weekly meetings interesting for members, and discussed how the society could best use its slender resources to edify the poor.[154]

The Particular Council also developed new initiatives for the society's apostolate to the poor – such as night schools, lending libraries, and a special board of visitors to serve Toronto General Hospital and the House of Providence – for which they of course secured approval from the proper ecclesiastical authorities.[155] In the Saint Vincent de Paul Society, lay initiative and leadership coexisted with due deference to the clergy's prerogatives. The clergy chaired the Particular Council's meetings, but usually their role in that capacity was unobtrusive. As the reports of these meetings make plain, it was the laity who introduced, discussed, and voted on new initiatives. Ultimately, it was the clergy who set the boundaries for the members' endeavours, but within those bounds the scope for leadership and initiative was considerable.

The leaders of the Saint Vincent de Paul Society exercised leadership over their members and engaged in corporate as well as individual initiative in developing new structures and programs. In contrast to their role in the parish at large, where they acted from time to time in an advisory and auxiliary capacity to the clergy, in their own society these men made the decisions that directly affected the general membership and the operation of Saint Vincent de Paul Society as a whole. The leadership and initiative of these men resulted in the Saint Vincent de Paul Society becoming a linchpin in the church's network of social institutions that provided social services and religious outreach from the cradle to the grave. Under their direction, the rank-and-file members of the Saint Vincent de Paul Society visited the most marginalized members of the Irish-Catholic community – the impoverished women and children of the city – and integrated them into the social and religious world of the parish. The Saint Vincent de Paul Society was a vitally important agency of the church, and its officers led in the church's efforts to reach and convert the poor. In recognition of this role its leaders occupied an honoured place in the parish in the eyes both of the clergy and of the general Catholic public. It thus came naturally to these leaders to act as spokesmen and representatives of the parish, as indeed the clergy frequently called on them to do.

As in the devotional societies for women, the impulse for lay activism and initiative was the desire for personal salvation. In working to save the souls of others members gained merit for themselves, and in the process they were spurred on to new acts of virtue and of service to others. For the members of the Saint Vincent de Paul Society, charity began at home, so to speak, in strengthening their fellow members in the practice of virtue and piety. Having appropriated the outlook and ethos of devotional Catholicism, laymen cooperated with each other to create a fraternal life in the parish that would unite them in the spiritual bonds of charity and prayer. Such bonds sustained members in their religious life and strengthened their commitment to the church. So close was their identification with the church that the members of the Saint Vincent de Paul Society saw in their practice of charity the very symbol of Catholicism.[156] Devotional Catholicism imparted to the members of the society a responsibility to serve both church and community, and it was this mandate that inspired the members' activism.

In their social and religious mission to the poor, the members of the Saint Vincent de Paul Society played a critical role in the formation of a religiously informed community and culture in Victorian Toronto. Yet, in contrast to its successful efforts to evangelize the poor, the society failed to recruit Irish-Catholic men in large numbers. Its emphasis on deference to hierarchically constituted authority, both clerical and lay, was alien to many laymen's sensibilities and their expectations for fraternization in their associational life. For these men, voluntary associations that offered familiar forms of conviviality in a more egalitarian social atmosphere had a much greater appeal, and they were to find such a social life in parish societies dedicated to apparently more secular pursuits.

6 "Heroic Virtue": Parish Temperance Societies and Male Piety

The small size of the Saint Vincent de Paul Society's membership illustrated the difficulties that any parish organization dedicated to devotional purposes faced in recruiting Irish-Catholic men. One way for the clergy to surmount this difficulty was to introduce voluntary organizations that emphasized secular pastimes and so establish an associational environment in the parish that would prove more amenable to Irish-Catholic men. Temperance societies were a notable example of this strategy. Given the importance of alcohol to male sociability, drink was a natural target for a clergy determined to reform the cultural life of Irish-Catholic men and to leaven it with the influence of the church. The clergy's object in founding these societies was religious, but the aspirations to self-improvement and self-respect implicit in temperance had deep roots in the culture of Irish-Catholic men. Temperance societies offer a unique prism to examine the interplay between clerical direction from the top down, and lay activism from the grass roots up, in the creation of church-based associational life for men.

Traditionally, poteen was an integral part of Irish-Catholic social life: weddings, wakes, religious festivals, work, and fireside visits by neighbours were marked by drinking.[1] The landless Irish peasant or cottier lacked either the means to distill poteen or the ready cash to purchase it regularly, and thus the consumption of liquor was usually limited to major social occasions.[2] In the Canadian city, however, the situation was much different.

In 1859 the civic authorities of Toronto issued some 550 shop and tavern licences, creating a ratio of one tavern or liquor shop per eighty-one city residents. Though the number of licensed premises was reduced to 312 by 1865, the *Globe* complained that there were still "man traps at every twentieth pace for the corruption of the young and the destruction of the unwary."[3] Unlicensed taverns and groceries – the "low grog shops" and "sheebans" – flourished despite, or perhaps because of, the city council's efforts to limit the number of licensed premises. In the last fifteen days of July 1865, for example, over forty shop and tavern keepers were charged with selling liquor without a licence.[4] The following year, in one massive raid, sixty-five individuals were arrested for violating the liquor licence law. Despite periodic crackdowns, however, the grog shops prospered. One liquor-licence inspector estimated that, as late as 1875, there were some 250 unlicensed taverns and shops.[5] Only after the passage of the Crooks Act in 1874 and the appointment of licence inspectors for Toronto in 1876 was the number of illicit establishments reduced substantially, and by 1881 there were only some fifty unlicensed grog shops in the city.[6]

The supply of alcohol was also increasingly restricted by Sunday closing laws and the limitations placed upon licensed grocers. After the enactment of the Dunkin Act of 1864, taverns were required to close at seven o'clock Saturday evenings, instead of eleven o'clock as on weekdays, and remain closed on Sundays. The police commissioners' initial reluctance to enforce the law for fear of violent protest was removed by the passage of the Crooks Act of 1874 and the undoubted shift in public opinion that the act represented. Still, there were many difficulties in enforcing the Sunday closing laws. Many taverns were located in the front rooms of boarding-houses. In such cases, it was often difficult for the crown to prove that the bar was in fact open and that the room was not simply being used by boarders as a living-room.[7]

More serious from the point of view of the authorities was the impossibility of controlling the sale of alcohol by grocers. Grocers, of necessity, remained open Saturday evenings so that workers could buy their provisions after having been paid.[8] Customers, while still flush with cash, could have liquor sent out to them or bring in their own jar and have it filled.[9] Moreover, many grocers, the *Globe* complained, contravened the law in doing "all the work of a tavern" by selling alcohol by the glass.[10] Such cases were hard to prove without the aid of informers, and Irish Catholics were particularly adept at discouraging informers through self-administered justice – the informers' inevitable fate of ostracism and being pummelled to within an inch of death. Irish Catholics, with their traditional suspicion of the legal system and their emphasis on self-administered justice, were adamant in refusing to "turn informer." Irish-Catholic witnesses, by acting "thick," frequently made a mockery of the police-court proceedings, as they no doubt intended.[11]

In order to gain a conviction against the unlicensed taverns or shops, prosecutors had to establish that the liquor had been paid for.[12] No one could be convicted for treating their friends, and without the informers' testimony that cash had changed hands, conviction was impossible. Even with the aid of informers, the essential evidence for the crown's case was hard to come by. By carefully concealing supplies off premises, shopkeepers could, in "treating" their customers, evade the licence laws. Money placed on a table mysteriously disappeared: how, no one could or would say. When the licensed taverns were closed, Irish Catholics in search of a drink could easily find a grog shop and enjoy the company of their compatriots into the wee hours of the morning.[13] Many of the taverns in Toronto were operated by the Irish: of the 209 saloon and tavern licences issued in 1869, Irish men and women held 91, or 43 per cent, of the licences issued.[14] Further, police-court reports in the *Globe* indicate that the Irish were also prominent in the illegal liquor trade as owners of grog shops and sheebans. As many of these were located on streets where Irish Catholics were concentrated, it would appear that the popular perception equating low grog shops with sheebans was not without foundation.[15]

Despite the efforts of the authorities, then, alcohol was freely available in Toronto. It was also relatively cheap. A glass of lager cost three cents, a glass of whisky five cents, and a pint of whisky went for twenty-five cents.[16] For a labourer receiving only a dollar a day, alcohol could, of course, quickly slim down his all-too-thin wage packet, but there were few other beverages available to Irish-Catholic workers. The quality of Toronto drinking water, when it was available, was at best uneven; at worst it was no more than strained sewage.[17] Soft drinks, such as soda water and ginger beer, were not easily available, and milk, though only five cents a quart, was often adulterated. None of these, of course, offered an escape from the weekly round of work and the anxieties of adjusting to urban life in the New World. The constant threat of unemployment, brought on by the downturns in the economy, illness, or accident, accentuated the precarious nature of all efforts at thrift and industriousness and encouraged a fatalistic outlook on life. If alcohol was not necessary in order to face the vicissitudes of this world, neither did the saving of a nickle seem worth the sacrifice of one of the few luxuries that life offered.[18]

Alcohol not only offered an escape; it also provided access to a rich social life. Irish-Catholic women tended to drink at home with their kin and neighbours, especially after the civic authorities closed down the low grog shops that populated Irish-Catholic neighbourhoods. Liquor played a crucial role in visiting and hospitality among Irish-Catholic women: neighbours would share a jug when visiting or simply helping out with the wash. Women would also regularly "lend" a half-pint of whisky when their neighbours ran short unexpectedly. Such mutuality drew neighbours closer, thus providing women with much needed emotional support. Not only did the reciprocity involved in this exchange help to ease their daily routine, but it also enabled them to form personal networks that could be drawn upon for aid in time of need.[19]

Drink was also an integral part of male working-class life. In some trades, apprentices were expected to treat the journeymen in return for their training. Beer drinking marked the stages of an apprentice's career and punctuated the rhythm of work in the crafts.[20] Among day labourers, one "acted square and treated the boys." "Do you think," a labourer replied to a puzzled reporter, "I would see him stuck for a drink? No, Sir! I have more heart in me than that!"[21] Much of this mutuality took place in taverns, which after the 1860s had become largely male social clubs. While the tavern was a recognized male working-class institution, the tavern also helped Irish-Catholic men to create their own separate culture and social life, and the price of admission to the tavern with its diversions, entertainments, and companionship was more than reasonable from their point of view.

In Toronto, as in many North American cities in the mid-nineteenth century, neighbourhoods were not segregated along class or ethnic lines.[22] With Irish Catholics dispersed throughout the city and with neighbourhoods representing a relatively diverse cross-section of the city population, taverns gave Irish-Catholic males a focal point for their communal identity, a club they could call their own. In a tavern presided over by a patriotic tavern keeper, so easily stereotyped in the temperance lecture, the Irishman could enjoy the company of his own compatriots and neighbours. There the Irishman could exchange neighbourhood gossip, read the religious and nationalist press, freely discuss the news from "home," and play a few rounds of quoits.[23] The tavern did not simply sustain and consolidate the links between old-time residents. Newcomers, especially those boarding in taverns, had easy access to the social life of the tavern and the ties to the Irish-Catholic community that it had to offer. Drinking, with its traditions of treating, implied reciprocity and equality free from the deference to authority associated with the workplace. The tavern provided a haven of male sociability, where Irish-Catholic men could consolidate the bonds of friendship formed in the workplace and in the neighbourhood. With its nationalist toasts – "here's to ould Ireland, may her enemies be confounded" – the Irish tavern helped to create both a nationalist sentiment and a sense of community.[24] By joining camaraderie with patriotic sentiment, the tavern imparted a sense of community among its patrons. It was central to the self-esteem of Irish-Catholic men both as workers and as Irish Catholics.

Alcohol also helped to solidify the bonds of community by bringing Irish-Catholic men and women together. Wakes, weddings, and house-warmings were marked by copious consumption of liquor.[25] Funerals, weddings, and religious festivals were as much social events as they were religious celebrations.[26] But, if drinking helped to cement the bonds of community, it also promoted strife and dissolved social ties between Irish-Catholic men and women. For labourers subsisting on a marginal wage of a dollar a day, when they could find work, the spree inevitably resulted in familial hardship. The early Saturday closing laws were intended to protect the worker's wage packet.[27] The later hours of the grocery store and the illicit trade of the sheebans ensured that some of these wages did not find their way home. Wives usually controlled the family funds, but only after their husbands had handed over their wages.[28] For families that lived continuously on the edge of poverty in the best of times, husbands' binges brought disaster. Even among those families who were initially better off, a husband's repeated binges could mean financial ruin for his family. Wives retaliated and their refusal to give a nickle for more liquor could and often did signal the start of a fight.[29] Husbands, likewise, could arrive home and find their room and cupboard bare, their wives having pawned the family's possessions and provisions to an obliging tavern keeper for liquor.[30] But, in general, it was the women who pleaded with their inebriated husbands to go to the parish priest and take the pledge before the family's funds were dissipated in a drunken spree.[31]

For some Irish Catholics, without skills, with hopes but without the means to realize them, alcohol offered an escape. This combination of whisky and despair bred violence. Wife-beating and fights between neighbours were all too common. The attacks on wives by husbands, and more rarely on husbands by wives, with a poker, a hammer, or whatever else came to hand, with the obvious result of black eyes and horribly battered faces, were regular fare in the police-court reports.[32] The high incidence of alcohol abuse accounted for much of the violence, petty crime, and disruption of families among Irish Catholics. This spectacle of human misery was especially disheartening to the Catholic clergy. The degradation it entailed and, moreover, the loss of souls that it caused demanded a response. Lives cut down before their prime, the hardship endured by families when wages were dissipated by drink, all this was bad enough. The loss of faith, precluding any possibility of repentance, was nothing short of catastrophe.

The moderate use of alcohol, as of all things created by God, had, of course, long been accepted by the Roman Catholic Church. Moreover, the practice of temperance was inextricably linked to the sacramental system of the church: virtue, "a special gift of God" conveyed through the sacraments, was a "necessary qualification of a christian's hope" and a "necessary means for avoiding sin."[33] The emphasis on the virtue of temperance, however, did not necessarily entail support either for temperance societies or for the total abstinence that some advocated. Most notable of those advocates were Father Theobald Mathew in Ireland, Cardinal Henry Manning in England, and Bishop Ignace Bourget of Montreal, all of whom were impelled by the degradation and misery brought on by excessive drinking and were influenced by Protestant teetotal advocates.[34] The campaign of Father Mathew represented a turning-point, for its impact was to change Catholic attitudes to teetotalism. Mathew's spectacular crusade, with thousands taking the pledge at a time, persuaded some Catholics to accept the total-abstinence platform. Henceforth, total abstinence was the object of legitimate debate within the Catholic community – a sure sign that it was increasingly considered to be a viable option.

Father Mathew's campaign, relying as it did on the individual's unaided pledge, was nevertheless inherently unstable.[35] Without an organizational structure, it was inevitable that the movement would collapse. The failure of his pledge movement was to result in the reformulation of Catholic efforts in curbing intemperance. For some of the Catholic hierarchy in North America, the main weakness of Father Mathew's promotion of total abstinence was that he excluded religious influences from his pledge.[36] The response of many in the hierarchy was a concerted effort to incorporate temperance within the Catholic Church and to establish temperance societies on a paro-

Table 11
Catholic Temperance Societies in Toronto, 1850–95

Parish	Societies	Years
St Paul's parish	Catholic Total Abstinence Society	1851–*c.* 1857
	St Paul's Temperance Society	1876–77
	League of the Cross	1892–?
St Michael's parish	Catholic Total Abstinence Society	*c.* 1853–*c.* 1856
	Father Mathew Total Abstinence and Literary Association	Dec. 1862–63
	St Michael's Temperance Society	Jan. 1883–?
St Mary's parish	Catholic Total Abstinence Society	1853–*c.* 1856
	St John's Temperance Society	1862–63
	St Mary's Temperance Society	*c.* 1873–77
St Patrick's parish	St Patrick's Temperance and Benevolent Society	1871–81
Other	Father Mathew Temperance Association	1871–83

chial basis. Temperance, many clergy now maintained, was not the result of individual effort, an exercise in self-help, but rather an integral part of the life of the church. Prayer and the sacraments were essential aids in the development of an abstinent, Christian life.

Bishop Charbonnel was one of the first members of the hierarchy in North America to adopt a sacramentalized understanding of temperance, quite possibly because he was inspired by Bishop Ignace Bourget's pioneering efforts in the diocese of Montreal.[37] The focus in the new Catholic view of temperance was on individual moral reform and spiritual regeneration rather than on reform of the social order through prohibition. Because this variety of temperance represented an ideal of Christian life, it was also, through its connection with the church, a means to recruit the laity to the church. It quickly gained ground in the English-speaking Catholic world, and by the late 1850s temperance societies were a common organization for pastoral outreach in many Irish parishes throughout North America.[38] Much as the clergy or laity may have disagreed over the relative merits of total abstinence versus temperance (the abstention from hard liquor only), the connection between temperance, however it was interpreted, and the church was unquestioned. Temperance societies were established for one purpose – to save souls.

The immigrants' spiritual and moral poverty, Bishop Charbonnel believed, had its roots in their social life and customs. He was particularly disturbed by what he took to be the predilection among Irish Catholics to take to drink, and he was certain that the poor were especially prone to this vice.[39] Although the bulk of Irish Catholics were not nearly as dissipated as Bishop Charbonnel imagined, their rhythm of work and leisure followed a pre-industrial pattern common among many workers in Canada that was task- rather time-oriented. Drinks punctuated the working day, and periods of frantic work were followed by equally intense rounds of celebration. The bishop feared that this rhythm of work and leisure ran counter to the orderly and disciplined way of life that was necessary for the punctual and dignified discharge of religious duties.[40] In the eyes of Charbonnel and his clergy, alcohol was the pre-eminent symbol of a diseased culture that was inimical to the cultivation of the religious life. According to this view, the tavern was the church's direct competitor, especially since it provided men with a convivial social environment for recreation and conviviality that was separate from the parish and so immune from its wholesome influences.

When Charbonnel arrived in Toronto in 1850, the Catholic Church was vastly over-extended by the continued influx of Catholics from Ireland. With few resources and personnel, temperance was one of the few means available to the bishop to effect religious renewal among the masses of recently arrived Irish Catholics, many of whom had little contact with the church. Taking the pledge to abstain from intoxicants was an act of conversion in which people renounced sin and committed themselves to the sacramental and devotional life of the church. To this end, Charbonnel founded the Catholic Total Abstinence Society of Toronto in 1851, and soon the society was the largest Catholic voluntary association in the city. By 1854 it had recruited over 4,500 members out of a Catholic population of about 8,000. Unlike later temperance societies, which were aimed at men only, the Catholic Total Abstinence Society in its membership drive appealed to all the Catholics in the city, and it was not uncommon for whole families to take the pledge and join the society.[41]

The Catholic Total Abstinence Society was one among several of Charbonnel's initiatives in his campaign for religious renewal, but in the short term it proved to be the most effective voluntary association established by the church in reaching the laity and incorporating them into its social fabric. Yet, while the mass character of Charbonnel's temperance crusade was a testimony to the Catholic Total Abstinence Society's success, it also revealed the society's greatest weakness. With so large a proportion of the city's Catholic population on its rolls, one suspects that a good number of them were members in name only. The Catholic Total Abstinence Society indeed persuaded many to take the pledge, but it failed to offer them an on-going social life in an associational setting that could sustain its members' commitment to the cause, and by 1858 it had ceased to exist.[42]

By the early 1860s Catholic temperance societies in Toronto, as elsewhere in North America, had undergone a fundamental change in both their constituency and their character. In Toronto, as in many other places on the continent, temperance societies became exclusively male organizations and so no longer recruited members regardless of age or sex. This is not to say that the church lost interest in promoting temperance among women and children. Mission preachers regularly called on women and children as well as men to take the pledge, but temperance societies did not usually recruit women and children. The institutional context for Catholic temperance work among women was the devotional organization; among children, it was the separate school, except in the mid-1870s when junior temperance societies were established for older boys. Unfortunately, the paucity of contemporary records and accounts makes it impossible to investigate the contributions of the parish mission, the devotional organization, and the separate school to the cause of temperance in Toronto. By contrast, the temperance societies for men – especially those that flourished in the 1870s – received extensive coverage in the Catholic press, and an examination of these organizations reveals why the clergy in Toronto made them an important part of their pastoral work.

Clerical temperance advocates repeatedly drew graphic pictures of sin as manifested by intoxication. "The bloated countenances, the glazed-cast eyes, the sickly emaciated form," observed Brother Arnold, the president of the Father Mathew Temperance Association (FMTA), "all plainly indicate the ruin and disgrace brought about" by intemperance.[43] Drunkenness, besides hastening men to early graves, also sealed their eternal fate. "Terrible, indeed," warned Father A.J. O'Reilly of the cathedral parish, was "the demon power that could blast reason, higher than anything else in creation."[44] Because drink "foments our passions and disturbs our guiding principle, the brain," declared Father Michael Stafford, the best-known Catholic temperance lecturer in the province, it was "the only thing in creation that will make a man do immoral acts."[45]

Alcohol lured the drunkard onto the path that led to hell.[46] "By degrees a cold indifference ... takes possession of his mind," observed Archbishop Lynch, until finally "he ends giving up the duties which, as a Christian, he owes to God."[47] Hardened in his habits, the drunk was a classic example of a sinner. Having turned away from God, he refused to receive the benefits of the sacraments of the church, the one sure way to reform his life and gain his salvation. Not only was the drunkard unable to lift himself out of the gutter, he was incapable of realizing the true precariousness of his situation. The drunkard, then, was the very embodiment of sin, the falling away of man from the Roman Catholic Church, the means of salvation. It was this understanding that formed the religious basis of the clergy's temperance program. Yet the clergy's graphic descriptions of the drunkard should not be taken as literally applying to the members of the temperance societies, few of whom were reformed alcoholics. Unlike the temperance crusade of the 1850s, which organized teams of visitors to reform those who were down and out as a result of alcohol abuse, temperance societies during the 1870s did not attempt to rescue the poor ravaged by drink. Nor did they publish accounts, as the earlier temperance societies had done, boasting of the number of drunkards, whether poor or well off, they had reformed.

The clergy dwelt on the drunkard as the embodiment of sin for the following reason: they wished to bring the moderate drinker to the moment of decision and at the same time reassure those moderate drinkers who had renounced alcohol that they had taken the path of faith and virtue. Moderate drinkers who relied on self-control unaided by divine grace, the temperance clergy believed, were all too vulnerable to the wiles of drink.[48] The moderate drinker, they insisted, had to be rescued "from the brink to which their self-sufficiency is hurrying them."[49] Prevention was the critical task of the Catholic temperance crusade, and all agreed that the individual's perseverance in sobriety depended on the sacramental intervention of the church.[50]

Catholic temperance was not to be an exercise in self-help. The pledge was first and foremost a religious commitment to enter the sacramental life of the church. The "help and the strength necessary to draw the sinner from the depths of vice," declared Archbishop Lynch, came from God alone. Only through conversion, by turning to God and resorting to the means of grace – the sacraments of the church – could a person hope to persevere in faith and sobriety. As a "heroic virtue" temperance was a gift from God.[51] This allusion to Christian heroism or the saintly life is revealing. Temperance, like the clerical or religious state, was a divine calling for the few. Like the clergy, temperance men stood "on a higher grade of perfection than ordinary christians." As they had imposed upon themselves "a restraint which many pious persons will not endure," temperance men were all the more in need of the sacraments that alone could guarantee their perseverance both in faith and in temperance.[52]

The image of the drunkard and the perilous state of the moderate drinker, so often invoked by the clergy in their temperance lectures, drove home the point that nothing less than the layman's eternal salvation was at stake. The contrast between purity and sin, between temperance and intemperance, in these temperance appeals was an expression of the religious impetus of the Catholic temperance movement. If intemperance symbolized the complete degradation of sin, the pledge represented the way of salvation. Temperance served to strengthen the emotional commitment of Irish-Catholic laymen to the Catholic Church. It was with this expectation that the provincial council of 1875 urged the clergy to establish parish temperance societies.[53] These societies were to be the means of exposing laymen to the sacraments and to encourage them to practise the devotions of the church. Members of the societies were to receive communion in a body at least twice a year and to receive individual communion frequently.[54] Besides attending evening vespers and the benediction of the Blessed Sacrament, members were usually invited to participate in the processions of Corpus Christi and at diocesan synods.[55]

The link between Catholic temperance and the sacraments was also underscored by the granting of indulgences: a plenary indulgence was granted on the day of admission to a temperance society, and "for every good work performed" the members received an indulgence of one hundred days.[56] While contemporary accounts do not discuss whether the temperance societies disseminated private forms of piety such as the rosary, these indulgences, together with the societies' public devotions, do reveal that the clergy founded temperance societies in the hope that they would popularize the church's piety among Irish-Catholic men.

Temperance also appealed to the clergy's secular ambition to raise the social status of their flock, an aspiration that many Irish-Catholic men shared as well. Temperance was a "holy war and grand cause ... involving no less than the prosperity and well being of our people in this life, and their eternal happiness in the next."[57] In the view of the world held by temperance advocates, the key to achieving both prosperity and salvation lay in self-improvement. Temperance and self-improvement were, in fact, very closely allied, according to Archbishop Lynch, since total abstinence would result in a "marked improvement, spiritually and temporally, among our people."[58] Acutely conscious that Irish Catholics were held in low esteem by many Protestants, the clergy hoped that temperance societies would advance the image and status of Irish Catholics and belie the widely accepted caricature of the Irishman's fondness for the whisky bottle. If an Irishman did "but half the wrong of any other man," Archbishop Lynch bitterly noted, he would receive "twice the blame," a sentiment that was widely shared by Irish Catholics.[59] Temperance societies affirmed Irish-Catholic sobriety and respectability, and they did so by appealing to lay aspirations for social advancement. If Irish Catholics "are to take their place – and places are open to them and must be filled," insisted Father Michael Stafford, those places would be theirs only if they qualified themselves for them through education, self-improvement, and sobriety.[60]

The badges of one temperance society were emblazoned with the motto "Religion Temperance Science" – a message proclaiming the unity of religious and secular ideals promoted by the temperance societies.[61] "Literary effort and improvement," asserted Brother Arnold, president of the Father Mathew Temperance Association, "are second only to the main object" of temperance.[62] By joining temperance societies, as Archbishop Lynch succinctly put it, Irish Catholics would "be able to lay by some money" and thereby "add to their respectability."[63] Not only would the temperate Irishman be able to lay up money for the support and education of his children, but he could also save enough to buy a nice house.[64] If he could give up his three glasses of beer a day, Father Stafford averred, "no man of 27 years of age need be unmarried for want of means." Temperance promoted industry, self-improvement, and thrift. By leading sober and industrious lives, Irish-Catholic men could gain a decent living and make happy homes for themselves.[65]

In addition to success, domesticity figured prominently in the clergy's appeals for temperance. Although clerical temperance lecturers rarely praised the joys of family life, the virtues of the home, family, and motherhood did play a large role in the denunciation of sin. Under the corrupting influence of alcohol, the clergy would point out, the young husband begins to care less for his wife and "will transfer his love to the whiskey seller's bottle." "The much loved wife is first an object of indifference, then of contempt, then of cruelty." The drunkard's natural affections for his family, his mother, his wife, and his children are displaced by cold indifference, and violence finally ensues.[66] In their vivid descriptions of shattered families, neglected children, abused wives, and hopes of mothers bitterly disappointed, temperance lecturers stressed that it was sin and vice that caused both poverty and dissolution of family ties. The happy family, where parents fulfilled their obligations to their children and where husbands respected their wives, was an ideal to be cherished.[67]

Of course, ideals of self-help and domesticity were at a variance with the church's ideals of holy poverty. "The poor," Father Stafford affirmed, "are everywhere made and kept poor" by the "hellish traffic" in liquor.[68] After describing the misery and vice that poverty created "in every form and shape," Father Stafford asked, "Do you find that 'blessed' is the lot of the poor?"[69] Clearly Stafford had no intention of delivering a homily on the virtues of poverty. Far from offering the gospel of resignation to poverty, the temperance lecturers preached the gospel of success and thus departed from the ideals of holy poverty advocated by the Saint Vincent de Paul Society. They did so partly because of the constituency temperance societies sought to attract and also because of the internal dynamics of the temperance crusade.

Catholic temperance societies directed their most fervent appeals to those who were already sober and industrious. The temperance lecturers' graphic denunciations of the horrors of a dissipated life were calculated to reinforce the commitment of such men to the values of self-discipline and self-help. The clergy promoted the gospel of success in the temperance societies because it was there that the gospel of success made the most sense. If intemperance, that symbol of the depredation of sin, brought on wretched poverty and listlessness, it seemed obvious enough that temperance would bring about both material and spiritual prosperity. Temperance advocates appealed to the self-made man as the embodiment of the temperance ethic. No doubt the clergy were influenced by the example of Protestant teetotalers, but, more important, theirs was a pragmatic response to the message of self-improvement inherent in temperance.[70] In promoting the temperance cause, the clergy preached a dual message of religious uplift and social success.

Catholic temperance societies had a sporadic existence in Toronto, as table 11 illustrates. Such societies gained a stable existence in only a few of the city's parishes, and some parishes, such as Saint Helen's and Saint Peter's in the west end, never had a temperance society attached to them. In Saint Michael's, the cathedral parish, no temperance society lasted for more than a year. Nor did Saint Paul's have much success in promoting temperance societies until a branch of the League of the Cross was established in 1892. Compared to these lack-lustre efforts, the temperance activity in Saint Mary's parish, with the Saint Mary's Temperance Society active for four years, stood out.

Information on the membership of the Catholic temperance societies in Victorian Toronto is quite scarce. It is possible to chart with relative accuracy the growth and decline of only two societies, the Saint Patrick's Temperance and Benevolent Society and the Father Mathew Temperance Association. The early reports in the *Irish Canadian* proclaimed that the membership of the temperance societies was "steadily on the increase." The predictions that these societies would soon have all the parishioners on the abstinence rolls, with the result that "the liquor traffic in this city will be sensibly lessened," were not so much a reflection of the actual growth of the parish societies as of the wave of optimism that marked the launching of the temperance movement in Toronto in the early 1870s.[71] The Father Mathew Temperance Association, with thirteen members at its inaugural meeting in December 1871, quickly grew to some 150 members a year later.[72] In 1873, the association had 188 adult members, the largest it ever had on its rolls.[73] By 1874, however, the membership had declined to about one hundred members.[74] The growth of the Saint Patrick's Temperance Society was even less impressive. Though it quickly signed up seventy members in its first two weeks, the society never exceeded 100 members.[75]

The total city-wide membership of the temperance societies reached a peak of some 300 to 350 men in the mid-1870s.[76] If the demographic composition of the Catholic population was similar to that of the city population as a whole, this figure represented between 8 and 9 per cent of all Irish-Catholic men.[77] During much of the decade, the adult membership probably ranged between 200 and 250, or from 5 to 7.5 per cent of the eligible population. Such membership, though it paled in comparison to that of the nationalist societies which had some 700 members, was not an inconsiderable accomplishment. By the end of the 1870s, however, the temperance societies had lost their vitality. Of the two surviving temperance organizations, the Saint Patrick Temperance society folded in 1881, and when the Father Mathew Temperance Association dissolved in 1883 it had no more than thirty men on its membership roll.[78]

A few words are now in order concerning the social background of members of Catholic temperance societies. Although member-

Table 12
Saint Patrick's Temperance Society Officeholders,
1871–80

Category	Number	Percentage
Unskilled	12	35.3
Semi-skilled	4	11.8
Skilled	9	26.5
Clerical	4	11.8
Business	5	14.7

Source: Irish Canadian and city directories.

Table 13
Father Mathew Temperance Association
Officeholders, 1871–83

Category	Number	Percentage
Unskilled	4	7.7
Semi-skilled	10	19.2
Skilled	6	11.5
Clerical	12	23.0
Business	16	30.8
Professional	3	5.8
Private Means	1	1.9

Source: Irish Canadian and city directories.

ship lists for the Toronto temperance societies have not survived, it
is possible – again by relying in part on city directories – to compile
an occupational profile of the members who held office in the Father
Mathew Temperance Association and the Saint Patrick's Temperance Society. In the Saint Patrick's Temperance and Benevolent
Society three-quarters of those who served on the executive were
workers, over half of whom were unskilled (table 12). In the Father
Mathew Temperance Association, however, only 38 per cent of the
officers were workers (table 13). Middle-class occupations dominated the executive of this association, with businessmen being the
most prominent group. Still, working-class involvement at the executive level was quite considerable, and both semi-skilled and skilled
workers were well represented in the association. Unskilled workers
were not so well represented as to reflect their status as the largest
segment of the Irish-Catholic workforce. Nevertheless, the overall
statistics for the membership of both the Father Mathew Temper-

ance Association and the Saint Patrick's Temperance Society indicate that Catholic temperance societies did recruit Irish-Catholic workers in significant numbers.[79]

The occupational pursuits of the middle-class officeholders in the two temperance societies is also significant. Professionals were poorly, if at all, represented among the executive of these societies. Nor were the societies able to attract those businessmen "who from their wealth and position, might give encouragement and, by their example, aid the good cause."[80] An examination of the businessmen who were on the FMTA executive reveals that, for the most part, they were not among the elite of the Irish-Catholic community. Among the sixteen businessmen were ten shopkeepers, two each in the building and undertaking trades, a bottler, and a newspaper proprietor. Most of the merchants on the executive of the FMTA were modest businessmen who were successful artisans-turned-businessmen. With the exception of John Herbert and Matthew O'Connor, who were active in separate school and municipal politics, they were not of the stature of such leading Catholic businessmen of the city as Frank Smith or Patrick Hughes.[81]

When the profile of these temperance societies' executives is compared to that of the nationalist societies that flourished during the same decade (table 15), it would appear that small businessmen and, in particular, clerks were better represented among the ranks of temperance organizations than they were in the nationalist ones. At first glance, it may be thought that the presence of men from these backgrounds confirms the often-made proposition that temperance expressed the aspirations of Catholic men for upward mobility and middle-class success.[82] Still, even though some occupations were better represented in the ranks of temperance than others, temperance activists did in fact come from a wide variety of social backgrounds, including the working-class, and few working-class men could realistically hope to enter the middle class or to emulate its ideals. The clergy certainly appealed to middle-class ideas of success in their temperance lectures, but the social diversity of temperance activists does raise the possibility that temperance may have meant different things to different people. One way to understand what Irish-Catholic men made of temperance is to examine the social life of the temperance societies and the role of lay activists in creating this social life.

Temperance societies were essentially religious associations, and as such the clergy could legitimately claim to lead them.[83] According to the official pronouncements of the church, the laity were to support and aid the clergy in the operation of temperance societies, but only so far as the laity's "limited means and respect due to ecclesiastical authority permit."[84] In keeping with these directives, all the temperance societies in Toronto – with the exception of the Father Mathew Temperance Association, which was led by the director of the Christian Brothers – were founded and usually maintained under the presidency of the parish clergy. As pastors and chief executive officers, the clergy were directly involved in the operation of the temperance societies: they recruited members, had a hand in drawing up the program for the societies' regular meetings, which they frequently chaired, and in general exercised oversight over the societies' activities.

The clergy were the unquestioned leaders of the temperance societies, but the laity also took an active role. Their activism is especially evident in the societies' recreational pursuits. Catholic temperance societies offered their members a continual round of meetings, reunions, lectures, gala concerts, picnics, and excursions, all of which were made possible by the efforts of lay activists. At their regular meetings, held weekly or twice a month in the parish hall or school, the temperance societies strove to provide a varied program of songs, recitations, and debates.[85] The centre-piece of the two-hour meeting was the forty-five-minute lecture. Lectures on temperance were the most common but the variety of subjects treated was notable. Lectures by lay members and invited clergy on such subjects as "The Spanish Inquisition," "The Catacombs of Rome," "The Preparation of the World for the Advent of the Messiah," and "On Liberty and the 'Deluge' of the French Revolution" were obviously apologetic and contributed to the self-consciously Catholic tone of the societies.[86] Other lectures, such as those on "The Discovery of America and its Results" and "Gravitation," along with the weekly debates and recitations provided members with a regular opportunity for literary effort and improvement.[87]

The regular meetings of the temperance societies could hardly fill their members' leisure hours with wholesome recreation, as temperance activists well recognized. Lending libraries were one way to encourage temperance men to devote their leisure hours to cultural improvement. A lending library, temperance supporters pointed out, was an "institution which goes a long way in enlightening the mind" by providing men with wholesome literature that they could read in the company of their wives and children.[88] Temperance societies invested considerable financial resources in their libraries. The Saint Patrick's Temperance Society, for example, could boast a library of some six to seven hundred volumes, "by the best Catholic authors," which included works of high culture as well as those of a lighter character.[89] Not only did temperance men stock extensive libraries, they also borrowed books regularly. In 1879 M.D. Murphy, the librarian for the Saint Patrick's Temperance Society, reported that on average members borrowed two books a week.[90] Murphy did not indicate what the lending library's contribution to domesticity might be, but if the members did in fact read a few pages of the two books a week that they borrowed, they may well have spent more time at home than they otherwise would have.

The temperance societies' pastimes also had a public aspect to them. Promising a "first class program" with well-known performers and brass bands, concerts organized by the temperance societies drew audiences of 700 to 800 people.[91] The audience would hear old favourites, and most concerts would close with Irish airs, including the inevitable "St. Patrick's Day."[92] Such concerts occupied temperance members for weeks in preparing the program, devising skits, designing sets, and making decorations for the theater hall, and it was not unusual for a temperance society to put on three or more concerts over the winter season.

During the summer, when the lecture and concert circuit was over, temperance men occupied themselves in the equally demanding task of organizing picnics and excursions, which among other things involved negotiating with pleasure-park and cruise-ship owners, lining up entertainment, arranging for publicity, and selling tickets. At the picnics themselves, temperance men hotly competed in foot races, lacrosse, football, and hurling, and no picnic was complete without its quadrille band and dancing. Not only did the young men take the opportunity of showing what they could "do on the 'light fantastic,'" but the sober and staid old heads, the *Irish Canadian* assured its readers, also shook the "historic toe." The moonlight harbour cruises and the excursions to Mimico, St Catharines, or Niagara Falls by the temperance societies probably provided some members with a rare opportunity to escape the oppressive heat and summer stench of the city. Excursions, costing about two dollars for travel in addition to the refreshments and food purchased, offered many a relatively cheap way of enjoying the cool breeze of Lake Ontario, and one that demonstrated financial prudence as well as a commitment to wholesome recreation and sobriety.[93]

Other opportunities for socializing were available to the members of temperance societies. Brass bands, with their countless hours of rehearsal, were well suited to occupy temperance men in a profitable pursuit and at the same time sustain their interest in the temperance cause by promoting camaraderie among band members. Music to the Victorian mind was undoubtedly a self-improving pastime, one that elevated the intellect as much as it refined the senses. Brass bands had the added advantage that when the temperance members took to the street in their smart parade uniforms they publicly proclaimed their commitment as well as that of their church to sobriety and uplift. With their repertoire of popular tunes and nationalist airs, the temperance bands were worlds removed from the discreet spirituality of the parish confraternities, but they gave men a familiar outlet for self-expression and the affirmation of self-esteem.[94]

Temperance societies attempted to recreate the social atmosphere of the tavern with its ethos of male camaraderie, equality, and autonomy. Temperance men repeatedly referred to the "utmost harmony, good fellowship and decorum" that prevailed at temperance excursions, picnics, and concerts.[95] At these social events, temperance supporters "beaming with health, intelligence and happiness" could affirm the distinctiveness and value of their way of life.[96] "When the head is cool and the brain is master of all its facilities," the *Irish Canadian* proudly proclaimed without a hint of humour, a "man generally knows what he is about."[97] Sobriety and self-control went hand in hand. The social-club atmosphere of temperance social activities also celebrated manly vigour and pride, especially when temperance men engaged in competitive sports or marched with their brass bands. Surrounded by the "contentment and smiles" of their comrades, temperance society members were confident that their fellowship was both manly and industrious.

The various recreational pursuits offered by temperance societies affirmed in one way or another the respectability of temperance men. The comportment of Catholic temperance men, noted Brother Arnold, head of the FMTA, had earned them "the encomiums even of those who differed from them in religion."[98] Temperance was widely recognized as a badge of respectability, but the respectability that these societies espoused appealed to a cross-section of the community precisely because it was not exclusive to the middle class. Indeed, respectability was an ideal that carried a variety of meanings, as were the other virtues with which it was associated, such as self-improvement and self-control.[99] At the heart of respectability for both middle- and working-class men lay a sense of independence and moral worth. Yet how these aspirations were understood depended very much on their class background as well as on their future expectations. Among modest businessmen and clerical workers, taking the pledge was an affirmation of upward mobility and their determination to maintain their middle-class status. For most workers, the independence that came from being one's own boss or the moral worth signified by the white collar was simply unattainable.

Among working men, independence meant earning enough to support their families in modest comfort and the ability, through the exercise of thrift and sobriety, to make real choices in how they led their lives. Significantly, most of the workers on the temperance societies' executives were householders who were well established in Toronto. They were in fact among the more economically successful members of the city's Irish-Catholic community. Such men were anxious to preserve what they had already accomplished. Self-help was a means to maintain a measure of economic security and to avoid being dependent on the good will of others.

Temperance societies not only stressed the importance of individual self-help, they also fostered collective self-help. For many Irishmen, the maintenance of personal honour depended on a proper funeral and a decent burial. The twenty-five cent monthly fee of the Father Mathew Temperance Association and of the Saint Patrick's Temperance Society assured a death benefit of twenty-five dollars which would cover the expenses of a requiem Mass and an appropriate funeral.[100] Both societies also provided members three dollars a week during illness in addition to free medical attendance and medicine.[101] This aid, though less than what would be needed to sustain a man with a family, was absolutely essential.[102] It could help to forestall eviction or the rapid depletion of savings, and it did provide temperance society members with medical care when it was needed. The reciprocity involved in the temperance societies' mutual aid was a concrete expression of the members' camaraderie and their obligations to one another.

In both symbolic and practical ways, temperance men affirmed their commitment to the family circle. The tavern, affirmed Edward Mahon, a member of the FMTA, led men to seek the pleasure of company of their peers rather than of the domestic circle, and eventually love for alcohol would result in a man's "cold indifference" to his family.[103] If a man took the pledge, argued Boyle, "a few five cent pieces formerly deposited on the bar-till" would instead be spent to provide for his children and wife and, better still, he would spend time at home with his family.[104] Temperance men saw sobriety as a pledge of devotion to family and home. It would result in practical benefits for the family, such as in the domestic comforts that were made possible by thrift and industriousness, and it would restore men to the family circle.[105]

Temperance men also saw their pledge as an affirmation of their commitment to community and church. Sobriety and patriotism, temperance men believed, were of piece. Nationalism was part of the very fabric of temperance life. Each week members would hear orations commemorating Ireland's national heroes, celebrating its patriots' glorious deeds, and recounting the latest political developments of the day.[106] Perhaps the temperance societies' most public display of their nationalist sentiments was their participation in the Saint Patrick's Day parade organized by the city's nationalist societies. On such occasions, as well as at other times, temperance men believed that their sobriety proved for all to see that Irish Catholics were "industrious, law abiding citizens" of Toronto.[107] In claiming that Irish Catholics were worthy of recognition and acceptance by the Protestant majority, temperance men declared their allegiance to their community and their fidelity to its church. When attending Mass in a group in their smart suits decorated with temperance rosettes or marching on Saint Patrick's Day with their brass bands, the members of temperance societies demonstrated that the road to self-respect began with the unequivocal affirmation of one's faith.

Catholic temperance societies largely succeeded in their task of offering recreational pursuits that would foster fraternalism, sobriety, and self-improvement. The extent to which they changed the religious behaviour of Irish-Catholic men, however, is another matter. When looking back on his involvement in the Father Mathew Temperance Association, Patrick Boyle nostalgically recalled that "it was a real pleasure ... to come together for a few hours every week, exchange views, and cement closely friendships already formed."[108] As a former vice-president and president of the association, Boyle's testimony cannot be easily ignored. For him, and undoubtedly for many others as well, the chief attraction of the temperance society lay in its being a social club.

Another member of the FMTA, William A. Lee, understood his membership in the society in rather different terms. "We rely for success upon the grace of God," Lee declared, and this grace was "communicated to us through the sacraments of the Church."[109] Similarly, a temperance man pointed out in an anonymous letter to the *Irish Canadian* that temperance societies succeeded in bringing men to the faith while retreats and missions failed to do so.[110] Religion did indeed occupy an important place in the life of the temperance societies. Members took the pledge of initiation before the

altar, usually after vespers, and, as noted before, they also attended
vespers (which sometimes included the benediction of the Blessed
Sacrament) and received communion in a body several times a year.
In addition, temperance men were expected to attend Sunday Mass
and receive communion on a regular basis. That said, however, the
devotions that marked the meetings of the parish confraternities for
women were notably absent from the temperance societies' weekly
reunions, in which short prayers were said only at the opening and
closing of the meeting.

In the temperance meeting, religion was introduced obliquely in
the guise of the gospel of success and of literary improvement.
Temperance societies offered men a way to demonstrate their attachment to the church that conformed to their aspirations for
manly independence and expectations for fraternal camaraderie.
Not only was the manner in which temperance societies initiated
men into Catholic piety different from that of the women's devotional organizations, but the range of piety enjoined on temperance
society members was also substantially narrower. Although temperance men fulfilled their religious duties and from time to time attended paraliturgical ceremonies such as vespers, the performance
of personal devotions was usually left to their own discretion.

The temperance societies' approach recognized, at least implicitly,
that devotional practices (as opposed to church attendance or the reception of the sacraments) were a private matter for many men. This
approach was consistent with the public persona of temperance
men. As Ann Taves has pointed out in her important study of
Roman Catholic piety, practitioners of devotions entered into a dependent relationship with a supernatural figure, which in many respects was similar to that between child and mother. Such a
relationship was an awkward one for men who saw their masculinity
in terms of independence and self-reliance.[111] Temperance men associated their role as breadwinners and upright citizens, those typical symbols of manhood, with their role as loyal Catholics, faithful
husbands, and devoted sons.[112]

While temperance societies certainly fostered the bonds of family,
their record in promoting devotional practice among temperance
men is more difficult to assess. An approach that respected male sensibilities may well have encouraged men to extend their practice of
piety to include private devotions, but at this point the historical trail
runs cold – and, perhaps, that is how temperance men wished it to
be. Temperance societies in effect sanctioned a sexual division of religious practice among Irish Catholics. Whereas the clergy expected
women to perform private devotions several times a day, they were

apparently relieved if men attended Sunday Mass and occasionally participated in the public devotions of the church.

The adaption of Catholic piety to male sensibilities and expectations was not only the challenge facing temperance societies. They also had to address male aspirations to autonomy and initiative in their social life, and this challenge required the clergy to walk a fine line. Although the direction of the temperance societies was the prerogative of the clergy, the gospel of success that the clergy preached sanctioned lay self-reliance and equality. Social subordination, the gospel of success proclaimed, was inimical to self-respect, of which taking the pledge was just one such affirmation.

The contradiction basic to temperance societies is obvious. On the one hand, temperance societies upheld an hierarchical understanding of the clergy's authority in which the laity were to play but an ancillary role in Catholic associational life. On the other hand, these societies undermined traditional notions of deference based on status and rank. Although the clergy recognized that an ethos of mutuality and equality was central to the temperance societies' appeal to Irish-Catholic men, this ethos still made them uneasy.

If the clergy made concessions to satisfy expectations of mutuality and equality, as when they allowed temperance men to elect their own officers, it is nonetheless clear that they wished to keep temperance social life on a short leash. Not only was the clergy's leadership in the temperance societies quite visible, as newspaper accounts of temperance meetings made clear, but such was their eye for detail that little escaped their attention. Temperance societies were essentially religious organizations, and as such only the clergy could legitimately claim to lead them.

By the end of 1870s the temperance crusade that had begun in the late 1860s was in decline, and the last temperance society from this wave disbanded in 1883. Some blamed the clergy's apathy for the temperance societies' decline. "Have we no Mannings and Irelands among us," asked the Patrick Boyle, at times a vehement critic of the Ontario hierarchy. "Have we," he continued, "no dignitary who will take the monster [liquor] by the throat and strangle it?"[113] Even the *Catholic Weekly Review*, published with the approbation of the Ontario hierarchy, took the clergy to task for ignoring the cause of temperance.[114] Despite Archbishop Lynch's encouragement of temperance, for most of the parish clergy temperance societies were a low priority, mainly because they faced heavy pastoral demands. Sick calls, the annual visitation of the families in the parish, the visiting of the poor, catechism classes, sodality meetings, sermons, confessions, masses, and other religious services took much, if not all, of their time.[115] After attending to these usual pastoral duties, many parish priests could spare neither the time nor the energy to become active in temperance societies.

The causes of the temperance societies' decline were complex. Temperance was inherently a minority movement, especially among working-class men. In taking the pledge Irish-Catholic men separated themselves from their fellow countrymen as well as their co-workers. Those who had taken the pledge promised in effect to change their way of life, and often this must have meant changing their friends as well. Abstainers were an isolated handful incapable of fitting into the majority's rhythms of work, recreation, and drink. As the clergy and many members of these societies were well aware, temperance required heroic virtue that was in constant need of strengthening. The demands placed on the temperance societies were considerable: they had to offer the individual both reinforcement of his ideals and a social environment in which he could go some way to realizing the new way of life he had chosen. If in the end the temperance societies failed in their task, the challenge they faced was one that would have confounded organizations with far greater resources.

The constraints the clergy placed on lay initiative also limited the temperance societies' prospects. Temperance societies offered wide latitude for self-expression through recreational pursuits, but they also offered few opportunities for corporate initiative by the lay members on these societies' executives. In contrast to the Saint Vincent de Paul Society, which was frequently free of the clergy's direct supervision, the parish priests remained in control of the temperance societies. In the hands of an energetic and imaginative pastor, temperance's message of manly independence could secure recognition for his leadership in the parish. The priest, declared the members of one temperance society in an address, was "more than a father," for he "nurture[d] our society" by acting "as a good friend" and "a model to ourselves."[116] Dependence on the clergy, however, was also a source of vulnerability for temperance societies. When a pastor who was at best lukewarm to temperance took over a parish, the chances that a self-sustaining cadre of lay activists would emerge to carry on the good work were exceedingly slim.

Through temperance societies the clergy hoped to integrate Catholic men into the parochial life of the Roman Catholic Church and thereby create a religious subculture. While most temperance societies were too short-lived to accomplish such an ambitious task, their impact should not be underestimated. Because of their efforts a significant number of Irish-Catholic men became practising Cath-

olics, and with the demise of these societies laymen lost a unique opportunity to participate in the social life of the parish. Furthermore,
although the vast majority of Irish-Catholic men did not join in the
associational life of the church, many of the values upheld by the
temperance societies – an acutely self-conscious respectability and a
demonstrative identification with the Catholic Church – were more
widely shared among Irish-Catholic men than the membership in
the temperance societies alone would suggest. The extent of their
appeal was especially evident in the independent nationalist societies
– organizations that, unlike temperance and devotional associations,
elevated lay initiative to the status of a fundamental principle.

7 "A Pariah among Nations": The Rise of Irish Nationalism in Toronto

In the classic work that has informed all subsequent studies of Irish nationalism in the United States, Thomas Brown argued that the roots of this nationalism lay in the Irish-Catholic experience of inferiority and estrangement in a new land where popular prejudice and economic insecurity were common occurrences. In other words, Irish-American nationalism was "directed chiefly toward American, not Irish, ends." Such nationalism, Brown concluded, expressed Irish-Americans' aspirations to social acceptance and, in particular, to middle-class respectability, the American dream of success.[1]

Brown's ground-breaking work has engendered considerable debate among historians over the origins, constituency, and aims of Irish nationalism in the so-called diaspora. In the most sustained analysis of the Irish experience in North America to date, Kerby Miller has traced the roots of Irish-American nationalism, and the alienation from American society that it expressed, to the persistence of a traditional world-view that both molded their identity and caused them to resist the demands of modern society.[2]

Whatever the sources of Irish-American nationalism – anxiety about social status, the fear of popular prejudice, or the persistent grip of traditional culture – it is commonly agreed that a pervasive sense of alienation was fundamental to the emergence of nationalist consciousness. Yet, as recent studies have demonstrated, Irish-American nationalism was a diverse movement both in its constituency and in its aims. Irish-American nationalism attracted working-class as well as middle-class support. At times, Irish nationalism encouraged cultural accommodation and assimilation, though occasionally in ways unanticipated by Brown, such as the Irish-American enthusiasm for mainstream labour activism. At other times, Irish nationalism was associated with an Irish-Catholic cultural militancy that fostered ethnic separatism.[3] Irish nationalism was a protean phenomenon whose character was a function of the complex interplay of social and cultural factors.

While historians have by and large focused on the broader social and cultural currents that gave rise to and shaped Irish nationalism, few have attended to its rich associational life, which, as R.V. Comerford has observed, was one of its salient features and for many its chief attraction.[4] The proliferation of nationalist associations during the latter half of the nineteenth century is one measure of the importance in Irish-Catholic communities across North America of lay activism and initiative independent of the institutional structures of the church. In Toronto, as in other North American cities, a radical form of Irish nationalism was to dominate the city's autonomous lay associations for much of this period.

The Hibernian Benevolent Society was the first organization in Toronto to advocate this variety of Irish nationalism. Protestant attacks on Catholics provided the immediate occasion for the founding of this society. The Irish-Catholic response to such provocations, however, was shaped by their cultural traditions, and it was these traditions that made it possible for laymen to take an initiative independently of the church and to form an associational life of their own.

Toronto's Irish Catholics were undoubtedly a besieged minority in a Protestant town. Not only were they outnumbered nearly three to one in the early 1850s, but their presence in the city offended the religious and patriotic sensitivities of many Protestants. The most prominent institutional expression of this antipathy to Irish Catholics was the Loyal Orange Lodge. Originally founded in the north of Ireland as a Protestant paramilitary organization during the religious warfare of the mid-1790s, the Orange Order embodied the communal consciousness of Irish Protestants. First introduced to Canada as an ethnic organization for Irish-Protestant immigrants, the order quickly attracted a wider Protestant following.[5] Its origins in Ireland made it a natural exponent of militant patriotism and an aggressive form of British colonial nationalism, especially during the sectional conflict between Protestant Canada West and Catholic Canada East.[6]

One of the reasons why the Orange Order could assume an important role in the cultural development of the province was that Irish Protestants, the order's natural constituency, composed at least one-quarter of Canada West's Protestant population.[7] Another reason was the fact that the Irish Protestants' longstanding presence in the province, together with their devotion to Canada's constitutional connection to the British monarchy, gained them acceptance as a charter group. As a result, the Orange Order was able to recruit members in significant numbers from the general Protestant population, although those of Irish background continued to dominate its membership rolls. By the 1850s, then, the order had become a mainstream association devoted to maintaining Protestant hegemony in the United Canadas and upholding the colony's British character.[8] In its support of the British and Protestant ethos of Canada West, the Orange Order appealed to Protestants from all denominational backgrounds on the Conservative side of the political divide, but Reformers also took up the banner of opposition to Catholicism.[9]

The anti-Catholic sentiment embodied in the Orange Lodge was a pervasive aspect of Toronto's Protestant culture in the 1850s. According to the *Globe*, the organ of Canada West Reformers, the "monstrous delusion of Catholicism" was "the enemy of the human race."[10] "The Canadian people have cause to keep this ever in mind," the *Globe* explained, "that Rome means tyranny, and has for its mission the subversion of the civil and religious liberty of the masses."[11] Irish-Catholic immigrants were thus as great a curse to Canada West "as were the locusts to the land of Egypt." "Settle the Roman Catholics in masses," the *Globe* concluded, "and we shall have a second Connaught, a second District of Quebec, a second Naples. No schools, no roads, no progress."[12] Only through the protection afforded by the twin bulwarks of Protestantism and the British connection could the corrosive infiltration of Catholicism be contained and the liberties of free Britons be preserved.[13]

With the high concentration of Orange Lodges in Toronto, anti-Catholic sentiment was visible to Irish Catholics in the figure of the Orangeman. The presence of Orangemen drove home to Irish Catholics that their traditional place in Ireland as the majority group was now reversed in Toronto, as it was in the province as a whole. Not only was the Orangeman a familiar figure, but since the Orange Order was allied to Conservative politicians, who controlled the municipal government of Toronto through most of the 1850s, he impinged directly on the daily life of Irish Catholics in ways that further underlined their marginal status in Toronto.[14] The licensing of taverns, carters, cabmen, public works, and, until 1858, the

the police force were all under the control of the Orange municipal corporation. The order thus controlled a major employer of unskilled labour, and through its influence in the licensing of public houses it regulated a major Irish-Catholic social institution. Moreover, the police force was the primary agency for enforcing Protestant middle-class respectability, and the one outside institution that had frequent contact with Irish Catholics.[15]

Yet Irish nationalism in Toronto was not rooted primarily either in the power of the Orange Order or in the popular hostility to Irish Catholics. On the contrary, the origins of nationalism were largely internal to the Irish-Catholic community. One proof of this can be found in the connection between nationalism and the cultural legacy of Irish-Catholic immigrants.

The identification of Catholicism with Irish nationalism had arisen in Ireland during the late eighteenth and early nineteenth centuries. The movement that consolidated that identification was Daniel O'Connell's campaign for Catholic emancipation from civil disabilities in the 1820s and his crusade in the 1830s to repeal the Act of Union which had incorporated Ireland into the United Kingdom by abolishing the Irish legislature.[16] In part, the connection between this movement and Catholicism was a natural result of the parish clergy's active role as local organizers in both the emancipation and repeal movements.[17] More important, throughout the drive for emancipation and repeal, O'Connell associated the Catholic Church with Irish national aspirations. "The Catholic church is a national church," O'Connell maintained, "and if the people rally with me they will have a nation for that church."[18] This fusion of Irish nationalism with Catholicism had an obvious attraction for the Catholic clergy of Toronto. For them, nationalism was a logical vehicle to promote Irish-Catholic allegiance to the church.

The Catholic Church's most significant initiative to promote a religious form of Irish nationalism was to elevate Saint Patrick's Day into a major religious and national festival.[19] Under Bishop Charbonnel's predecessor, Michael Power, Saint Patrick's Day was a muted affair observed with a small procession and a brief low Mass held without the sermon that usually marked the principal Mass on Sundays or the major festivals of the church. Beginning in 1852, Charbonnel followed the American custom, and Saint Patrick's Day was celebrated with a parade complete with marching brass bands. With various Catholic organizations, such as the Catholic Total Abstinence Society and the Catholic Literary Association, and the separate school children joining the line of march, the parade became a public assertion of Irish-Catholic religious and national particular-

ity. This affirmation culminated in the annual Saint Patrick's Day
Mass, which now had the ceremonial trappings of a major feast day
of the Catholic Church. As Bishop Charbonnel had hoped, the Saint
Patrick's Day celebrations brought Irish Catholics by the thousands
into the city streets and into the cathedral. There each year, the
clergy commemorated Ireland's national faith – the unchanged
and Catholic religion bequeathed to them by Saint Patrick and preserved by their ancestors down through years of persecution and
hardship.[20]

The clergy might hit some of the notes, but usually they could not
carry the nationalist tune. The non-Irish Bishop Charbonnel's well-
meaning appeals to Irish nationalism lacked a sure touch, and his
nationalist addresses were typically both awkward and perfunc-
tory.[21] Still, by proclaiming Saint Patrick's Day a religious holiday,
the bishop had managed to establish a tentative connection between
nationalism and the church. Despite this promising beginning,
Charbonnel's Irish-born clergy proved unable to compose a clerical
version of the Irish nationalist libretto. The vision of Ireland as a nation with its own legislature was central to Irish nationalism. In the
clerical orations on Saint Patrick's Day, however, Irish nationalism
was shorn of its demand for repeal of the union with the United
Kingdom. The result was that, while the clergy could offer a religious understanding of Ireland's past tribulations, they failed to address its present-day political aspirations and its future destiny as a
nation. Indeed, when confronted with the political and social issues
of the day in Ireland, the clergy counselled patience and passivity.
"Suffer all things with Christian patience," Father John Synott ad-
monished, for "the Lord will not permit any to be tried beyond his
strength."[22]

The middle-class activists in the Catholic temperance societies had
quite a different understanding of Irish nationalism. For them, the
political struggle for Ireland's rights was essential. In their speeches
they extolled Daniel O'Connell's fight for repeal and looked forward
to the day when Ireland would be a free nation. These lay leaders
delivered what their audience expected to hear, and their calls
for repeal were invariably greeted with enthusiastic cheers and
applause.[23]

The Irish Catholics of Toronto, therefore, could not look to the
church for leadership in the nationalist cause. The logical alternative
was voluntary associations that were independent of the church,
where the laity could freely affirm their national allegiance. These
nationalist organizations offered the laity an autonomous organiza-

tional base for lay leadership and initiative without at the same time denying the authority of the clergy. However, the search for an associational life independent of the church was to lead many Irish-Catholic men a long way from clerical national traditions, in some cases to significantly different, even radical, ones.

Besides O'Connellite nationalism and the clergy's religious form of nationalism, the laity could draw on another nationalist tradition: the Young Ireland rebels of 1848. William Smith O'Brien's ill-considered cabbage-patch uprising was doomed to failure, but, as R.F. Foster has observed, it was to be "far more influential in how it was interpreted than in what it did."[24] One might add that Young Ireland's subsequent influence on the course of Irish nationalism owed much to its vision of Irish history and, above all, its celebration of the United Irishmen's rebellion of 1798. Rural protest societies in Ireland, most notably the Ribbon societies, preserved the memory of the brutal suppression of the '98 rebellion by the British authorities and so nurtured an abiding hatred of England.[25] Yet the image of the United Irishmen remained inchoate until the Young Ireland rebels of 1848 gave shape to the vague laments of Ribbonism. Instead of the shameful defeat depicted by traditional lore, these Young Irelanders transformed the rebellion into a source of pride. They did so by celebrating the noble band of United Irishmen who in their martyrdom effected the greatest triumph of all – a national catharsis that would lead to the regeneration of the Irish people.

In remaking the United Irishmen in their own image, the Young Ireland rebels recast the Irish past into a succession of struggles for independence led by men of action and patriotism. This mythology was to exercise a powerful hold on the Irish imagination even if it distorted historical reality.[26] The revolutionary republican faction was always a small minority in the Young Ireland movement, one frowned on by the movement's moderate and cautious leadership, but it was the ideals of these Young Irelanders and their vision of the Irish past that were to be celebrated as embodying true patriotism by later revolutionary nationalists. And these revolutionary nationalists were to find their greatest following among the Irish abroad.

With the founding in Dublin of the Irish Revolutionary Brotherhood on 17 March 1858 by James Stephens, a participant in the 1848 revolt, and the simultaneous launching in New York City of the Fenian Brotherhood by another veteran of '48, John O'Mahony, revolutionary nationalists were to set the mold for the development of Irish nationalism in North America.[27] The Fenian leaders had been mere subalterns in the Young Ireland rebellion, but unlike the

leading Young Irelanders they had no reservations about the use of
physical force. The Fenian leadership was thus in a better position
than the senior statesmen of Young Ireland to celebrate the insurrection of '48 and thereby capture the mantle of Young Ireland.
To this end the Fenians forged a chain of apostolic succession in
which the banner of armed revolution was passed from generation
to generation, from the United Irishmen to the Young Irelanders
and then to the Fenian Brotherhood. The Fenians not only turned
the legacy of Young Ireland to their own purposes but at the same
time constructed a tradition of insurrectionary nationalism that was
to assume the status of orthodoxy among advanced nationalists.

Events in 1856–58 set the stage for the founding in Toronto of an
organization dedicated to the defence of Irish Catholics and the promotion of Ireland's national cause. It all began when Robert Corrigan, a convert to Protestantism, was cruelly battered to death by a
gang of Irish Catholics in the parish of Saint Sylvestre, south of
Quebec City, in February 1856. The acquittal of the accused by a
Catholic jury in Canada East convinced Protestants in Canada West
that there was one justice for Protestants and another for Catholics
in Canada East.[28] "How long," protested the *Globe*, "are Protestants
to be killed like dogs and the Government permitted to shield their
murderers?"[29] Protestant outrage immediately greeted the announcement of the jury's verdict in the Corrigan case; placards appeared in
Toronto calling on Protestants to prevent "Dogan" processions and
prepare themselves to seek revenge for the Corrigan murder, an
ominous threat since it referred to the processions of Irish-Catholic
school children filing to and from church.[30]

Over the winter Toronto remained calm, but the summer of 1857
saw an outbreak of religiously and ethnically motivated violence that
was to culminate in the Saint Patrick's Day riot of 1858. On 12 July
Constable Devlin, an Orangeman returning home from church with
his wife, was assaulted on Stanley Street by five or six Irish-Catholic
men who took offence at Devlin's Orange rosette, comparing it to a
piece of shit. The fight soon attracted a large and heated crowd
as Devlin's Orange comrades came to the rescue, and the police
managed to restore calm only with great difficulty.[31] Under such
provocation, Orange retribution was swift and highlighted the religious basis of Orange-Green antagonism. The following night, 13
July, after the annual Twelfth of July Orange parade, the windows
of Saint Michael's Cathedral, the Episcopal Palace, and the convent
of the Sisters of Saint Joseph were smashed by roving gangs of

Orangemen.[32] Only a month later an attempt to set fire to the House of Providence was uncovered. Although no culprit was ever found, Catholics naturally suspected that Orangemen were responsible for the attempted arson.[33]

On Saint Patrick's Day, 1858, the parade held to mark the occasion had arrived, without incident, at Saint Lawrence Hall on King Street in the late afternoon. After a butcher's wagon had been turned back by the marshals, a cab man, John Ritchey, attempted to disrupt the procession by driving through the crowd. Some of the processionists pursued Ritchey, shouting abuse and landing a few blows. William Lennox, owner of a nearby tavern and stable, on hearing that one of his employees, John Howlett, had been assaulted, was heading down West Market Square towards Saint Lawrence Hall when he came upon the processionists pursuing Ritchey. Lennox, who was among those who had rescued his fellow Orangeman, Constable Devlin, at the Stanley Street riot the previous 12 July, was immediately recognized by the crowd, who forgot all about Ritchey and proceeded to set upon Lennox in revenge for his actions the year before. Lennox's stable hands came out to his aid and in the ensuing confusion Matthew Sheedy, one of the Irish-Catholic processionists, was stabbed in the lower abdomen, as contemporary reports delicately put it. Sheedy died two days later without naming his assailant.[34]

On the evening of the seventeenth, a Protestant crowd determined to seek revenge on Lennox's attackers still milled about West Market Square, where the Young Men's Saint Patrick's Association (YMSPA) intended to hold its Saint Patrick's Day dinner. Though a few policemen were posted at the National Hotel on Colborne Street, off West Market Square, the civic authorities made no effort to disperse the crowd. The police clearly anticipated trouble, but were not willing or able to take adequate measures to restore order.

After the YMSPA, a Catholic pro-Reform society led by John O'Donohoe, had exchanged fraternal delegations with the Protestant and Conservative Saint Patrick's Society, the crowd became restive. Thomas D'Arcy McGee, a Montreal member of the Legislative Assembly and the leading Irish-Catholic Reformer in the United Canadas, barely escaped injury on leaving the banquet when his carriage was followed and pelted by an angry mob. Once the chase had been given up, William Lennox – once more in the thick of things – led the crowd in stoning the National Hotel. With glass shattering all around them, terrified men, women, and children dove for cover in the stairways and inner lobbies of the hotel. Others, however, began to search for firearms, and soon a dozen shots were fired on both sides. An eerie silence followed the shots; shaken and sobered by this sudden outbreak of violence, the attackers quietly dispersed. The riot had ended as quickly as it had started.[35]

The man accused of murdering Sheedy, John Howlett, was never sent to trial, and of the four Catholics arrested during the fight outside Lennox's stables, three were convicted of assault. The four Protestants, including Lennox, who were committed to the assizes after the wrecking of the National Hotel were acquitted.[36] Catholics suspected that the Loyal Orange Lodge had rendered justice for Catholics a farce, a suspicion that was confirmed by the investigation of George Gurnett, the city magistrate, into the National Hotel riot.[37] The Orange members of the police force, he concluded, protected their Orange brethren by being less than forthright on the witness stand.[38] A petition to the Legislative Assembly captured the Irish-Catholic reaction to the Orangemen's acquittal. As long as Orangemen served as jurors or as members of the police force, the petition asserted, the judicial system would continue to be "nothing but a delusion, a mockery, a snare," and Irish Catholics would therefore "be obliged to arm in defence of their lives and properties."[39] The movement for organized militancy had begun.

Perhaps the best barometer of the besieged and increasingly militant outlook of the Irish-Catholic community was the *Canadian Freeman*, edited by James G. Moylan, which was the semi-official diocesan weekly until its demise in 1873.[40] During the spring of 1859, Moylan became preoccupied with a string of attacks and unsolved fires involving Roman Catholic churches in rural southern Ontario. Such incidents, Moylan warned in the *Freeman*, would be merely the first in a series by the Orange Order.[41] Nor could Irish Catholics depend on the police for protection. Alluding to the police who were to protect the National Hotel, Moylan wryly commented that "as well as might the vulture be placed over the lamb to protect it from the pounce of the cowering evil."[42] Though the Orange Order "may burn and destroy, threaten and assassinate," Moylan promised that "the Catholics of Western Canada will stand firm" and organize for their self-defence.[43]

As a supporter of D'Arcy McGee's alliance with George Brown's Reformers, the *Freeman*'s comments had a partisan tinge: the governing Conservatives who drew on the Orange Order to man their political machine were an easy and obvious target. The *Freeman*'s hatred of the Orange Order, however, went far beyond political animus. Even after the *Freeman* went over to the Conservatives, it continued to denounce Orangemen as "the very scum of creation."[44]

Persecution played an important role in Irish nationalist rhetoric and ideology, but it would be misleading to assume that nationalism was an instinctive reaction to Protestant hostility towards Irish Catholics in Toronto. The *Canadian Freeman*'s equation of Protestant bigotry with the Orange Order was one indication of how the interpretation of Protestant-Catholic hostility was itself shaped by the framework of Irish nationalism. "Ireland, prostrate, crushed, bleeding," the *Freeman* lamented, "presents to the world the saddest and direct proof of England's wanton cruelty."[45] Orange gangs, rapacious English landlords, and a heartless English government had engineered Ireland's degradation, all in the name of preserving the British connection. Similar forces were at work against Irish Catholics in Canada, the *Freeman* contended. As a result of the Orange Order's presence in Canada West, the *Canadian Freeman* insisted, there are "more disgusting acts of red-hot bigotry, and low dastardly acts of intolerance than in any other civilized country."[46] The Orangeman was a recognizable figure, one whose presence symbolized the Irish-Catholic people's historical experience of oppression. In Canada West the Orangeman was a figure all the more threatening for his ubiquity, and one who could be used to rally Irish Catholics across the province to the nationalist cause.

James Moylan appropriated the nationalism of Young Ireland, and drew the logical conclusion.[47] "To know and respect themselves," the *Freeman* asserted, Irish Catholics "must struggle against persecution, tyranny, and oppression" both in Ireland and in Canada.[48] The Irish must take action and seize control over their own destiny, as Young Ireland had instructed them. In an affirmation that was the pure milk of Young Ireland nationalism, Moylan predicted that Ireland's rise to nationhood was to be the salvation of the Irish both at home and abroad. "Ireland must soon grow too strong for her Anglo-Saxon masters," the *Freeman* warned, and will soon "no longer be a Pariah among the nations of the earth."[49]

It was against this background that organizations independent of the church and committed to the defence of Irish Catholics were formed.

The first Irish societies independent of the Roman Catholic Church, such as the Saint Patrick's Society founded in the early 1830s, included both Protestants and Catholics and were essentially political organizations.[50] The Young Men's Saint Patrick's Association, established in 1855, was the first exclusively Catholic organization free from the church's control.[51] Its formation was an assertion both of independent lay leadership in the Irish-Catholic community and of lay nationalist militancy. In 1856, the middle-class leaders of the YMSPA seized control of the Saint Patrick's Day festivities from the clergy and transformed them into a nationalist demonstration. Not only did YMSPA use the occasion to demonstrate its support for Irish legislative independence, but it also took the opportunity to affirm its sympathies for the more militant nationalism of Young Ireland by demanding the release of William Smith O'Brien, the best-known hero of the 1848 uprising.[52] The association further advanced Irish nationalism by promoting Irish sports and the use of the Irish language, another indication of Young Ireland's influence in Toronto Irish-Catholic circles.[53] Despite these promising beginnings, the YMSPA foundered on the rocks of partisanship in 1858, soon after Catholic Reformers took over the association and transformed it into a political club.[54]

The emergent nationalist consciousness embodied by the YMSPA culminated in the establishment of the Hibernian Benevolent Society by Michael Murphy at his Esplanade Street tavern in 1858. At first, the Hibernian Benevolent Society's primary aims were to patrol the streets in predominantly Catholic neighbourhoods and to keep watch over Catholics schools and churches, especially during the Orange festivals of 5 November and 12 July.[55] These patrols were, like other pastimes that involved camaraderie, a form of self-expression as well as an adaptation of traditional collective behaviour to new ends.[56]

Traditionally, collective action among Irish Catholics was typically directed as a protest against concrete grievances, an enforcement of communal mores, an expression of regional antipathy, or a demonstration of territorial control. Such collective action was primarily defensive in nature, and it frequently resulted in outbreaks of violence.[57] In Toronto, by contrast, only one Hibernian patrol resulted in violence between 1858 and 1868, suggesting not only restraint and discipline but also that the patrols were not specifically aimed at concrete challenges to the Irish-Catholic community. Indeed, the purpose of the Hibernians' patrols was essentially symbolic. By policing the city's streets with restraint and propriety, the Hibernians demonstrated that they, like all Irish Catholics, were worthy citizens of Toronto and hence entitled to equal protection under the law. These claims were not addressed primarily at Protestants, who for the most part were unaware of the Hibernians' existence until the early 1860s, but rather to the Hibernians' fellow Catholics. Hibernians' patrols were both an expression and affirmation of group pride. By taking to the streets of Toronto to uphold the rights of Catholics, the Hibernians made their claim to leadership in the Irish-Catholic community.

The very existence of the Hibernian Benevolent Society was an example of lay activism and initiative independent of the formal structures of the church. Yet the Hibernian Benevolent Society was a self-consciously Catholic organization and, as the Hibernians well recognized, the society's identification with the Catholic Church was essential if it was to gain a popular following. The official recognition of the church sought by the Hibernian Benevolent Society was thus yet another element of the society's strategy to secure its leadership among Irish Catholics. The Catholic Church was the dominant social and cultural institution in the Irish-Catholic community. While the clergy's failure to provide national leadership opened the way for the assertion of lay autonomy, the Hibernian leaders recognized that the most effective way to gain widespread influence and thereby consolidate their leadership in the community was to reach an accommodation with the Roman Catholic Church. Once recognized as patriotic and loyal sons of the church, the Hibernians could then make good their claim to represent the national aspirations of Toronto's Irish Catholics.

Bishop Charbonnel recognized the need for Irish Catholics to organize an association that would defend them against "un ennemi dévastateur que notre gouvernment, nos juges et partout nos juries protègent et encouragent." After meeting with representatives of the Hibernian Benevolent Society in December 1858, Charbonnel decided to consult with Bishop Ignace Bourget of Montreal before making a decision on the society's status. Bourget's advice convinced Charbonnel that the Hibernians' oath of secrecy was contrary to canon law. Such an oath, Charbonnel believed, would not allow the members of the Hibernian Benevolent Society to make a full and honest confession, and he ordered the Hibernians either to suspend their oath or to withdraw from the society.[58] No written response to Charbonnel's directive is to be found among the bishop's papers, but it would appear that the Hibernian Benevolent Society complied with the bishop's ruling and repealed its oath of secrecy. By the following November, the Hibernians were providing music for the annual charity sermons in the parish churches.[59] Although Bishop Charbonnel never made any official pronouncement, the laity could reasonably conclude that not only was the Hibernian Benevolent Society free from the church's ban on secret societies but that it now enjoyed the approbation of the clergy.

The Hibernians' new oath, though vague as to the exact purposes of their society, affirmed the members' loyalty to the Catholic

Church, "the faith of Saint Patrick patron Apostle of Ireland."[60] This affirmation persuaded Charbonnel's successor, Bishop Lynch, to support the society, while at the same time the Hibernians maintained their independence and freedom from clerical supervision.[61] Although Lynch left no record of his decision to approve the Hibernian Benevolent Society, it is possible to reconstruct his motives. Lynch's nationalism, the *Canadian Freeman* observed, bordered on enthusiasm. Like the Hibernians, Lynch believed that self-rule was the only solution for Ireland's grievances. In his view there could be no separation between Irish patriotism and the Roman Catholic faith, and on this score the Hibernians told Lynch exactly what he wanted to hear.[62]

The close association between religion and nationalism in Bishop Lynch's mind suggests that there was another, far more defensive, aspect to his decision. In his eyes, the existence of a nationalist society that was independent of the church was a challenge to the unrivalled leadership that the church had enjoyed in the Irish-Catholic community, particularly since the very existence of the Hibernian Benevolent Society made it that much more difficult for the church to exercise national leadership. While Lynch was far from pleased that an autonomous lay society existed in his diocese, he was convinced that any attempt to invoke sanctions against the Hibernians would simply alienate a large number of laymen and strip the church of its nationalist credentials.[63] Such considerations explain why the bishop apparently imposed no conditions, such as a measure of clerical supervision, in exchange for his support of the society.

After Lynch sanctioned the Hibernian Benevolent Society, the parish clergy forged closer ties with the organization. They now frequently accompanied the society's excursions, and the society regularly aided the clergy in organizing parish picnics, thereby winning the accolades of the clergy for its efforts to provide "healthful recreation."[64] The Catholic image of the Hibernian Benevolent Society was also reinforced by the presence of society members on the Toronto Separate School Board: of the eighteen lay members of the board in 1861, six were members of the Hibernian Benevolent Society.[65] However, it was the Saint Patrick's Day parade of 1862, the first since the attack on the National Hotel in 1859, that revealed the full extent of the Hibernians' success in securing the support of the clergy and in gaining public acceptance.

Ignoring protests led by Thomas D'Arcy McGee of Montreal and his Toronto ally, John O'Donohoe, Bishop Lynch lent his approval to the Hibernian Benevolent Society's plan to revive the annual Saint Patrick's Day parade and for the first time allowed its members to attend the now traditional Saint Patrick's Day High Mass as a group with their flags and regalia.[66] The opponents of the parade, declared James Moylan of the *Canadian Freeman*, were doing the work of the "mischievous and anti-Irish" Orange Order. Moylan's support for the Saint Patrick's Day procession reflected the popular appeal of the Hibernians' fusion of nationalism with Catholicism among Toronto's Irish Catholics. Because of this consensus, opposition to the Hibernian Benevolent Society could easily be branded as anti-Irish and, even more important, as anti-Catholic. By appropriating a religious festival the Hibernians simultaneously affirmed their close association with the church and advanced their claims to leadership in the Irish-Catholic community.

On Saint Patrick's Day the Hibernians stressed their allegiance to the Roman Catholic Church, offering their salutations to the parish clergy and praising Saint Paul's church as "the cradle of Catholicism in Toronto." The Hibernians existed, Michael Murphy explained, "to watch and take care of" those who insulted the Catholic clergy while they peaceably went about their ministry. Through its alliance with the Catholic Church, the Hibernian Benevolent Society could portray itself as the chief defender of Catholic rights. As a result of this stand, Irish Catholics soon saw the Hibernians as the natural embodiment of Irish nationalism in Toronto.[67]

The Hibernians clearly wished to demonstrate that there were no soberer, "nobler and honester," men than themselves, and in this they succeeded. "Our Irish population never before made a more creditable demonstration" commented James Beaty of the *Leader*, a statement that was high praise indeed since it was coming from a supporter of the Loyal Orange Order.[68] The Saint Patrick's Day parade with its twelve hundred to fifteen hundred marchers was an unmistakable expression of Irish-Catholic support for the Hibernian Benevolent Society. A mediocre verse published by the *Canadian Freeman* caught the prevailing Irish-Catholic sentiment:

Hibernians! March forth with banners of green –
Let no coward, no shame, in ranks be seen;

...

For your souls are pure and your hearts are true,
And you've arms strong to dare and do;
Who would oppose your strength must rue
The hour he insulted brave men like you.

...

Hibernians! Your spirit ne'er stoops to offend,
But you've altars and homes and you've got creed to defend;
To your friends be delight, to your foes be dismay,
When you're marching on Saint Patrick's Day!

...

Of your brothers, triumphant on many a field,
Where legions in armor before them oft reeled –
Of your martyrs, your chieftains, the storied array
Should swell up your pride on St. Patrick's Day!

...

Then, Hibernians! march on 'neath your banners of green,
And no varlet will dare insult you, I ween;
Let all cowards and slaves keep at home, far away
From your ranks, while you're feasting St. Patrick's Day![69]

The Hibernians were not only the embodiment of Irish manhood, but they also represented the hope of Ireland – what Irishmen could become in the new world. The Hibernian Benevolent Society thus represented the emergence of ethnic awareness. In its assertion of Irish-Catholic rights, the society instilled the conviction that Irish Catholics were a community apart, entitled to public recognition and equal status.

As an organization that affirmed Irish-Catholic respectability both as individuals and as a group, the Hibernian Benevolent Society was well placed to gain popular support. Its excursions now attracted some five hundred people, and prominent Irish-Catholic merchants willingly sold tickets to the events sponsored by the society.[70] The supporters and sympathizers of the Hibernian Benevolent Society represented a cross-section of the Irish-Catholic community. In addition, the founding of the society as an organization independent of the Roman Catholic Church was an open assertion of lay initiative and leadership by Irish-Catholic men, but an assertion nevertheless within the church's moral framework. The Hibernians' fusion of religion, patriotism, and lay autonomy was essential to their exercising ethnic leadership. With the launching of the Hibernians' weekly, the *Irish Canadian* on 7 January 1863, Irish nationalism assumed an ideological expression that was to strengthen further the Hibernian Benevolent Society's position in Toronto's Irish-Catholic community and establish it as a leading force among the Irish Catholics of Canada West.

Such unanimity was not to last, however. The Hibernian Benevolent Society had by this time developed clandestine ties with the Fenian Brotherhood, an American-based organization dedicated to insurrectionary nationalism. When this connection became common knowledge, it was to divide the Irish-Catholic community and jeopardize the Hibernians' relationship with their church.

8 "Loyal Hibernians?": Fenianism and the Hibernian Benevolent Society

During the late 1860s, "there were no more loyal citizens of the various colonies of British America than the Irish Catholics," W.L. Morton has observed.[1] Canadian historians have generally agreed that Irish-Catholic loyalism precluded widespread sympathy for Fenianism among the Irish Catholics of Canada.[2] Canadian Irish Catholics, Hereward Senior declared in an article written in 1967, "were, for the most part, indifferent to Fenianism," an impression that his more recent *The Fenians and Canada* has done little to change.[3] In his sweeping survey of Irish nationalism in Victorian Canada, Peter M. Toner questions whether these long-held generalizations faithfully reflect the diverse response of Irish Catholics in Canada to radical nationalism. Toner contends that in addition to Irish-Catholic loyalism, which found its most able exponent in the prominent Montreal politician Thomas D'Arcy McGee, revolutionary nationalism also gained a significant popular following in Canada. Anglophobia, an intense hostility to British institutions in Canada, and Fenianism, Toner suggests, enjoyed widespread Irish-Catholic support.[4] This observation is endorsed by George Sheppard's recent study of Irish Fenianism in Canada West.[5] Yet neither of these interpretations captures the complexity of the response among Toronto's Irish Catholics to Fenianism. In fact, that response was both more cautious and more enthusiastic than previously supposed. The following examination of the ambivalent Irish-Catholic attitude towards Fenianism throws further light on the nature and the well-springs of Irish nationalism in Toronto.

Irish Catholics in Toronto, many of whom had family and friends living in the United States, were in regular contact with their compatriots living south of the border. Not surprisingly, then, the lay nationalist leadership of the city came under the influence of the American revolutionary nationalist organization, the Fenian Brotherhood, soon after its founding in 1858. After its first convention in November 1863, the Fenian Brotherhood expanded quickly and began to drill its members in preparation for a general insurrection in Ireland. The Fenian Brotherhood thus became committed to a dual *modus operandi*: publicly it generated popular support for revolutionary nationalism and secretly it conspired to overthrow British rule in Ireland.[6] When the Fenian brotherhood was introduced to Canada, its insurrectionary program dictated a different line of action than that in the United States. Because it was a revolutionary organization plotting the overthrow of the British Crown in Ireland, the Fenian Brotherhood was of necessity an underground conspiracy in Canada. In these circumstances, the Hibernian Benevolent Society provided the brotherhood both with the necessary cover for secret operations and with much needed access to potential recruits. In 1859, a Fenian agent recruited the Hibernians' president, Michael Murphy, and the next year he began enlisting fellow Irishmen into the brotherhood.

The Canadian government was convinced that the Hibernian Benevolent Society was a Fenian organization. Despite a number of failures to infiltrate the society, it did succeed in hiring one informer, Patrick Nolan, whose brother was an Hibernian.[7] Nolan was certainly well placed to spy upon the society, but how reliable were his reports? Because he was a paid informer, he likely provided the government with unsubstantiated allegations and rumours in order to pander to his employer's suspicions, as did some of the other informers hired by the government.[8] Nevertheless, while much of Nolan's information was based on hearsay, his reports linking the Hibernians to the Fenian Brotherhood were borne out by the documents seized after the arrest in April 1866 of the Hibernians' president, Michael Murphy, when he attempted to join the brotherhood's attack on Campobello, New Brunswick. These documents, together with a few others that were intercepted by government agents, indicate that Nolan's reports over the years were accurate.[9]

A Toronto Fenian circle was established in 1860, two years after the founding of the Hibernian Benevolent Society, with Michael Murphy as Canadian centre.[10] Patrick Nolan claimed that there were two oaths, one for the Hibernian Benevolent Society, the other for the Fenian Brotherhood. Half of the 1300 members of the

Hibernian Benevolent Society, he added, "will not take the second oath."[11] It seems highly unlikely, however, that there were some 650 Fenians in Toronto. Had there been so many members, the government should have had little difficulty in discovering evidence that would have held up in a court of law, as it attempted to do from time to time.[12] A more realistic estimate would suggest that there were probably no more than one hundred Fenians in Toronto, a sufficient number to dominate the Hibernian Benevolent Society but not large enough to be easily infiltrated.[13] By 1862 or 1863, according to John Mulvey, Michael Murphy's brother-in-law, the Fenians had taken over the key executive positions and were in control of the society.[14] Viewed from this perspective, the Fenians were an inner, secret cabal within the Hibernian Benevolent Society. In short, the Hibernians, wittingly or not, were a front for the Fenian Brotherhood.

The organizational structure of the Hibernian Benevolent Society, which paralleled that of the Fenian Brotherhood, seems to support this conclusion. Like the circle of the Fenian Brotherhood, the Hibernian Benevolent Society was a secret organization divided into nine lodges or companies headed by captains. Each company was to be armed and well drilled, a standard that the Hibernians evidently met.[15] In theory, then, the Fenian sub-centers or captains were implanted within each of the Hibernian lodges; in practice, the relationship between the Hibernian Benevolent Society and the Fenian Brotherhood was closer and far more ambivalent than this description would suggest.

While the Hibernian Benevolent Society disavowed any connection with the Fenian Brotherhood, it did set out to generate public, if guarded, support for the organization. Fenian bonds were sold at the society's meetings, and during a three-month period in late 1865 the Hibernian lodges voted to send at least five hundred dollars to the Fenian Brotherhood headquarters in response to the final call for funds in aid of the planned uprising in Ireland.[16] Moreover, it was widely known that Michael Murphy, the Hibernians' president, attended the Fenian convention held in Chicago in 1863.[17] On Saint Patrick's Day, 1863, the Hibernian Benevolent Society for the first time publicly declared its support for the use of physical force in Ireland. Immediately after Bishop Lynch had blessed the society's members, Michael Murphy proclaimed that "Ireland's liberty must be obtained only by blood," and he was certain that 20,000 Irish Canadians "would not hesitate to sacrifice their lives" to gain Ireland's freedom.[18] The following year, in 1864, Murphy supported the Fenian Brotherhood by name in his Saint Patrick's Day oration. After the miserable failure of constitutional agitation, Murphy insisted that only the Fenians could now gain the redemption of Ireland.[19]

Murphy's declarations, though greeted with enthusiasm, were to involve the Hibernians in a long-drawn-out charade in which they denied any formal connection with the Fenian Brotherhood. In contrast to the situation in the United States, revolutionary republicanism in the Canadas was antagonistic to the imperial tie and members of the brotherhood risked entanglement in a treasonable conspiracy against British authority in Ireland. Subsequent events would show that few Irish-Catholic men wished to join a revolutionary conspiracy, but at the same time Irishmen in Canada had more scope than those in Ireland to express radical nationalist sentiments without incurring the charge of sedition. As long as the Hibernian Benevolent Society maintained the illusion that it had no formal connection with the Fenian Brotherhood, radical nationalism was free to cultivate Irish-Catholic support. How Toronto's radical nationalists responded to and coped with the contradictions inherent to their nationalist program and the ambivalence it engendered was probably best revealed in the nationalist newspaper, the *Irish Canadian*.

With the appearance in January 1863 of the *Irish Canadian*, which enjoyed the financial backing of the Hibernian Benevolent Society, the Hibernians finally gained a public platform for radical nationalism in Toronto. Published weekly by Patrick Boyle and his brother-in-law Edward Hynes, the paper apparently enjoyed a wide readership. Precise circulation figures are hard to come by, but by the mid-1870s Boyle claimed a circulation of 7,000, a figure that was to double by the time the paper folded in 1892.[20] Although one cannot be sure how large a circulation the *Irish Canadian* enjoyed in the mid-1860s, the paper most certainly did a brisk business, and some issues were sold out within hours of coming off the press.[21] Patrick Boyle was the Hibernian Benevolent Society's most prominent advocate and his persona captured the public's imagination.[22] A man unrestrained in his enthusiasms, who always wore his heart on his sleeve and whose graphic language was sentimental when it was not rambunctious or laced with vitriol, Boyle appeared to his readers as larger than life: the dedicated printer who worked late into the night, composing stick in hand, fighting on behalf of his compatriots. Because the *Irish Canadian* articulated the often contradictory hopes and aspirations of Irish nationalists in Canada, Patrick Boyle, who was to dominate the Irish nationalist movement in Toronto until the 1890s, quickly became the most influential English-speaking Roman Catholic editor in the United Canadas.

172 Piety and Nationalism

In the fall of 1863 Patrick Boyle openly declared in the pages of
the *Irish Canadian* his support for a rebellion in Ireland. "Moral suasion is nearly exhausted," Boyle insisted, "the only alternative that
remains ... is an appeal to the sword."[23] Ireland, Boyle promised,
will soon strike a blow for freedom and, he added, echoing Michael
Murphy's prophecy, thousands of Irish-Catholic men in Canada and
the United States would come to Ireland's aid.[24] Boyle's nationalist
vision was plainly derivative and, like much else of the Hibernians'
nationalist platform, owed much to the Fenian Brotherhood, which
at the time had just begun riding a wave of popularity among Irish
Americans. Following the familiar litany of the brotherhood, Boyle
claimed that Irish Catholics could redeem themselves and secure the
regeneration of their nationality only if they joined in the noble
struggle to liberate Ireland.[25]

Boyle attempted to deflect the subversive significance of these
statements by denying that there were fundamental differences in
either the aims or the methods of Fenianism and constitutional nationalism, a task made easier by the fluid lines between the Fenians
and what can be characterized as the left wing of the constitutionalist
movement in Ireland.[26] Boyle, in short, sought to create the impression of a united opposition to the legislative union of Ireland and
Britain, with the Fenians as merely one part of a broad Irish nationalist movement. To this end, he supported the constitutional agitation led by John Martin, who courted the advanced nationalist vote,
and Daniel O'Donoghue (popularly known as The O'Donoghue),
Daniel O'Connell's nephew.[27] At the same time, Boyle minimized
the differences that separated Martin and O'Donoghue from the advanced wing of the nationalist movement in terms both of their objectives and of the means they advocated to achieve those objectives.
Like the constitutional nationalists, Boyle misleadingly claimed, the
Fenians sought merely the repeal of the union and the restoration of
the Irish parliament, a claim made believable only because repeal
signified a rather vague goal.[28] Nor were such aspirations extreme,
Boyle assured his readers. "It is precisely the privilege that we enjoy
here – self-government," Boyle explained, "that we wish to see
extended to Ireland."[29]

Boyle further sought to bridge the breach between constitutional
and advanced nationalists over the question of means, the issue
of physical force. The Fenians, Boyle claimed, were only using
the threat of violence to wring concessions from Britain. Just as
O'Connell had frequently invoked the threat of violence during the
emancipation and repeal campaigns, a threat made all the more
credible by the agrarian disturbances that accompanied his agita-

tion, so too were the Fenians attempting to wrest concessions from the British.[30] By emphasizing the threat of violence and confusing the difference between that threat and actual violence – the act of rebellion – Boyle sought to place Fenianism in the constitutional tradition of Daniel O'Connell.

Yet even these explanations, as Boyle well knew, would not soothe Irish-Catholic uneasiness, and it became necessary to disassociate the Hibernian Benevolent Society from the Fenian Brotherhood. The brotherhood, Boyle disingenuously maintained, was strictly an American organization with which the Hibernian Benevolent Society had absolutely no connection. Furthermore, as an American association whose goals were limited to Ireland, Boyle contended, Fenianism had no bearing on the position of Irish Catholics in Canada. By so placing the scene of violence at a safe distance and securely in the future, Boyle deftly played upon the ambiguity that many Irish Catholics felt towards the prospect of insurrection.[31] This distinction between sympathy for armed revolution in Ireland and active involvement in the Fenian Brotherhood lay at the heart of Boyle's defence of the Hibernian Benevolent Society.[32]

Boyle's attempts to distance the Hibernians from the Fenian Brotherhood were patently transparent. Given the Hibernian Benevolent Society's public support of the Fenian Brotherhood, how was it possible for Boyle to skirt around the rather obvious implication of Michael Murphy's well-publicized attendance at the 1863 Fenian convention? And how could Boyle's apologetics gain credibility among the Irish Catholics of Toronto? The answer to these questions lies in Boyle's use of the past and how that past was constructed.

The *Irish Canadian* portrayed Ireland's past, prior to the Act of Union with Britain, as a golden one. In that time, Ireland had been the "great and inexhaustible source" of piety and learning.[33] Ireland's industrious people, her geographical position, climate, and soil were without match and well fitted her to "become the emporium of Europe." Yet, despite her impressive resources, Ireland was now a nation reduced to starvation. The *Irish Canadian* did not feel it had to look far for the cause of Ireland's decline. "Pitchfork bribery and corruption" robbed Ireland of independence and reduced "this fruitful island ... to beggary."[34] "What does England do," asked the *Irish Canadian*, "whilst the whole Irish people are sinking beneath the pangs of hunger?"[35] "The voracious Saxon" cut off all help from a starving people, and this "when men staggered and fell down in the midst of plenty from want of sustenance, when infants hung on dead mother's breasts and sought in vain the nourishment which starvation had drained away with life, when people fed like beasts on seaweed and the very wild herbs of the field, and when the dead lay unburied and noisome, because the living could not perform the last sad offices."[36] "The voracious Anglo-Saxon, untrue to most of the sentiments that dignify humanity," had driven a starving people into exile.[37] For the *Irish Canadian*, the Great Famine was not a past event but an ever-present reality and symbol of Ireland's degradation. In its pages, the famine assumed the status of a foundational myth.

The famine was indeed an horrific event, and for a good number of Irish Catholics in Toronto the trauma was such that their experiences must have been seared into their memories. But the significance of the famine for Irish nationalists lay in its power as a cultural symbol. According to Kerby Miller, the language of exile that grew out of the famine was an example of the estrangement that results when a people from a traditional culture attempt to cope with the mores and expectations of the modern world. Miller's emphasis is on cultural continuity. New cultural forms may emerge, such as nationalism, but the traditional world-view endures and so determines the shape that these newer cultural forms will assume. The idea of emigration as exile, Miller argues, was one such element of the traditional world-view of the Irish-Catholic emigrant, and it provided the leitmotif for their cultural self-definition.[38]

The image of the Irish Catholics abroad as the exiles driven from Erin was undoubtedly an important motif for Toronto's Irish nationalists. Yet the motif of exile did not come into common use in the city's Irish-Catholic press until the late 1850s, over ten years after the Great Famine, and it became a staple theme in nationalist speeches only in the early 1860s. The motif of exile and its associated picture of the famine were not original to the Irish Catholics of Toronto, who drew heavily on on the imagery formulated by the romantic leaders of Young Ireland and then later disseminated by the Fenian Brotherhood.[39] This development suggests that the image of exile was less the result of the persistence of an archaic world view than an appropriation of modern Irish nationalism by Toronto's Irish Catholics.

The image of enforced exile had a compelling appeal for so many Irish-Catholic immigrants and their children largely because it was integral to the nationalist framework to which it gave moral meaning. In brief, the elevation of the famine into the realm of mythology made it generic and prescriptive, and it is these characteristics that gave the mythology its moral force. This mythology offered Irish Catholics a ready explanation for their expatriation, as Miller suggests, but more important, it enabled them to define their social identity as a people and to do so in terms of ethnic separatism, another example of which was the radical nationalist's use of race.

The *Irish Canadian*'s attempt to portray the history of Ireland as the oppression of one racial group, the Celts, by another, the Saxons, had two consequences for the development of militant nationalism in Toronto. First, Irish-Catholic ethnicity was recast in racial terms. Race and religion in this view of Irish ethnicity were inextricably connected. To renounce one's religion was seen as a betrayal of one's race, a form of miscegenation.[40] Secondly, the *Irish Canadian*'s use of the language of purity and defilement also served to portray national independence as a symbol of racial pride. "The Saxon," asserted the *Irish Canadian*, "holds our heritage in his clutch" and as a result "we are unnoticed exiles in the far distant lands."[41] "Why are we," the *Irish Canadian* asked, "who are entitled to the fullest sisterhood, to be treated as the hand-maiden of England?"[42] A worse fate than starvation and oppression may befall us, warned the *Irish Canadian*, "if we still live on as a nation, without name or fame, honour or nationality."[43] "True men," the *Irish Canadian* maintained, "gained freedom because they have fought for it."[44] Because "the destiny of Ireland is ... in the hands of her children on this continent," let them like Wolfe Tone and Robert Emmet in "a noble emulation of the self-denial and fortitude of the patriot dead" make a sacrifice for their country.[45]

Radical nationalism was above all an ideology of hope. Fenianism, the *Irish Canadian* revealingly declared, "is the germ, the hope, the means of a *future* harvest, that shall give us life, strength, and health."[46] The prize that Fenianism promised was not simply the independence of Ireland. Rather, Irish national independence would result in the regeneration of the Irish people the world over. By creating a social myth, a complex of interrelated symbols, Fenianism gave the Hibernians the sense that they were actively and intimately involved in the affairs of Ireland and thereby shaping their own destiny as a people.[47] "It is time," the *Irish Canadian* concluded, for Ireland "to cast off the habiliments of wretchedness and come forth clothed in the manly garb of equality."[48] Because they were without a nation, Irish Catholics had been unjustly denied the status as a charter group in Canadian society that their longstanding settlement and loyalty had entitled them to.[49] Irish-Catholic industriousness and civic responsibility would reap its own reward, the *Irish Canadian* predicted, "for we Irish will yet stand erect in Canada."[50] And when they did, those who now insulted the sensibilities of Irish Catholics would pay the price. Irish nationalism, as the nationalists made plain, was to be directed to Canadian ends.

Irish radical nationalism influenced the way many Irish-Catholic men thought of their relationship to their newly adopted home. Canada, the *Globe* maintained, was a British colony, and the French Canadians and the Irish had no choice but to "become Britons in fact as well as in name."[51] By contrast, Irish nationalists advanced an alternative vision of Canada, one that opposed the prevailing consensus among the province's Protestant population. Canada, with its three races – the Saxons, the Gauls, and the Celts – was "neither fish, flesh, nor fowl."[52] "The identity of Canada ... is yet in a very shadowy condition," and the *Irish Canadian* intimated that it was very likely to remain so for quite some time.[53] Canada's diverse population and its lack of any one dominant national group led radical nationalists to draw a direct parallel between Britain's domination of Ireland and the British character of the United Canadas. Acceptance of Ireland's constitutional claims, it was believed, would result in public recognition of Canada's national diversity and the charter status of Irish Catholics as members of Canadian society. In this view, Canada was a community of communities, indeed it was a nation of cultural minorities, and thus Irish Catholics were entitled to public recognition as a distinct community with its own institutions and culture.[54]

Irish nationalism served to crystalize the ambivalent response of Irish Catholics to their situation in Canada. Most first-generation immigrants experience conflict between old ties and newly adopted loyalties, but what made the conflict particularly poignant for Irish Catholics was the comparison they could draw between their position in Ireland and that in Canada. Precisely because Irish Catholics appreciated the formal and constitutional liberties they enjoyed in Canada, they resented the Protestant image of Canada as a miniature Britain in which Irish Catholics were expected to forfeit their former allegiances and become assimilated.[55] While Irish Catholics were grateful that Canada offered them an opportunity to advance themselves economically, they were outraged that their accomplishments, which they felt should have earned them a standing in society as a separate community, were ignored by the Protestant majority.[56]

The moderate form of nationalism promoted by the clergy illustrates the consensus embodied in the nationalist program of the Hibernian Benevolent Society. Initially, the clergy had interpreted the history of Ireland's struggles solely in religious terms. After 1863, in response to the Hibernians' growing popularity, the priests of Toronto publicly called for the legislative independence of Ireland. Rather than ignoring Ireland's political struggles as they had done previously, the clergy now endeavoured to ally Catholicism with Ireland's national aspirations.[57] To do so, the clergy drew on many of the same motifs as the lay nationalists, and no motif was more central than that of enforced exile. The war of extermination waged by the British government drove the poverty-stricken Irish to foreign shores where they were "exposed to all the degradations which poverty and misery entail." Like the leaders of the Hibernian Benevolent Society, Bishop Lynch believed that Ireland's grievances – her starving people and ravaged economy – were the direct result of English rule.[58] As a result of this oppression, he warned that "a fearful retribution was in store for England."[59] Not surprisingly, Lynch agreed with the Hibernians that the only remedy for Ireland's ills lay in Irish self-government. Just as British rule was responsible for the degradation of the Irish people both at home and abroad, so too would self-government serve to advance them materially as well as in the estimation of others.[60]

By the early 1860s, therefore, a broad nationalist consensus had emerged among Toronto's Irish-Catholics. In this consensus, nationalism was now identified with the preservation of Irish-Catholic particularity and resistance to assimilation into the British mainstream of Toronto society. That the Hibernians forged this consensus in such a brief time was a considerable accomplishment. Almost every Irish county was represented among the city's Irish-Catholic population, and, for many immigrants, local allegiances and regional rivalries were of greater consequence than a putative nationality.[61] Besides being divided by traditional regional rivalries, Irish Catholics were dispersed in the countryside and various towns of Canada West. In these circumstances, nationalism, by invoking a shared past and a common destiny as a people, offered Irish Catholics a common heritage as well as a lens through which they could understand their relationship to the rest of Canadian society.

In declaring their sympathy for the Fenian cause, the Hibernian leaders located their ethnic identity outside the social and cultural framework of the city's Protestant majority. Yet, though the Hibernians frequently adopted an aggressive posture in advancing the claims of their nation and their religion that was quite in keeping with the manly independence favoured by revolutionary nationalists, their attitude to Canada was in fact riddled with ambivalence. In their rendition of the Irish past, the nationalists exhibited a kind of inferiority complex by pairing such opposing sentiments as pride and shame, accomplishment and dispossession, destiny and defeat, victory and victimization. Nationalism not only fostered these emotions, it gave them coherence and meaning by relating them to a sense of peoplehood and national destiny distinct from that of Britain. For those living in a British colony, nationalism would have pulled the emotional strings of ambivalence even tighter, especially since Irish-Catholic resentment at the lack of collective status in Canadian society was never far from the surface. The Hiberians' appeal to Irish-Catholic self-respect – and, its seeming corollary, defiance of Britain (frequently expressed in terms of hatred of all things British) – created a ground swell of sympathy for Fenianism. But at the same time, Irish Catholics desperately wanted to be reassured that this indirect support would not endanger their position in Canada. Boyle's apologetics – his attempts to narrow the differences between constitutional and revolutionary nationalism, his dissociation of the Hibernians from the Fenian Brotherhood, his portrayal of the Hibernians as a Catholic-defence society – were singularly transparent, but he told Irish Catholics just what they wanted to hear: that there was no fundamental conflict between Fenianism and constitutional nationalism. And for the moment, that reassurance was sufficient.

Weaving together various fragments of Irish-Catholic culture – the mores of the tavern, working-class aspirations to respectability, the romantic nationalism of Young Ireland – the Hibernian Benevolent Society attempted to recreate the communal bonds of the Irish village which were so important to the first-generation Irishmen. In mid-nineteenth century Ireland, the social identity of most Irish Catholics was defined by regional loyalties. Emigration shattered this allegiance to community and locality, and within a few years radical nationalist ideology had transcended Irish localism and provided in its place a national identity.[62] Communities, of course, are not built on ideology alone; they also emerge from a shared social life. Many Irishmen not only wished to socialize with other Irish Catholics; they also had the money as well as the time to engage in pastimes with their compatriots. This impulse from the grass roots found expression in the Hibernian Benevolent Society and its organization of recreation along national lines.[63]

The Hibernian Benevolent Society undertook to offer its members a way of life, a life apart. The regular meetings were held once a month, but special weekly meetings were often called, especially when the society was making preparations for its annual ball or the Saint Patrick's Day celebrations.[64] The society's meetings, however, were not limited to talk and endless planning. During the summer, the Hibernian companies frequently met after dark for drill practice.[65] If the society was to live up to its claim as the Irish-Catholic protective association, its men had both to display precision in their maneuvers, itself an example of the Hibernians' defiant demand for recognition, and to exemplify the new Irishman's manliness through athletics. The Hibernian Benevolent Society promoted its own rowing, football, and hurling teams, and these teams were determined to win.[66] The Hibernian football team, the *Globe* noted with disapproval, practised for days, while other teams, particularly the English one, hardly at all.[67] "If an Irishman fights, or dances, or works," the *Irish Canadian* proudly observed, "he does it with all his heart," and no doubt this was especially true when the Saint George Society was the challenger.[68] The advancement of team sports under the auspices of the Hibernian Benevolent Society was intended not only to exhibit athletic prowess and manliness but also to develop respectability. The sponsorship of the Hibernians guaranteed the respectability of the team's management, and so the society's athletic clubs were to be "conducted upon the strictest principles of morality and decorum."[69]

In its quest for respectability the Hibernian Benevolent Society soon ceased to hold its official meetings in Murphy's Esplanade Street tavern. After 1862 members met in the society's own meeting-hall at the Saint Lawrence Market or in the separate schools.[70] At its meetings the society promoted literary reunions, lectures, and other self-improving pursuits. The Hibernian Benevolent Society, explained Patrick Boyle, was a school where Irishmen could acquire and cultivate those social virtues, especially those of self-improvement, sobriety, and perseverance, that "are the means requisite to success."[71] The Hibernian Benevolent Society offered weekly dancing classes, annual balls, and annual excursions to promote "sober and regular habits."[72] It also provided music at the House of Providence for fund-raising events, parish charity sermons and picnics, and games and races at church-sponsored activities.[73] The respectability promoted by the radical nationalists certainly was similar to that sponsored by the Catholic Church, but it was an ethic which had its roots in male working-class culture.

The annual excursion, probably the only opportunity most of the society's members had to escape the city's summer heat, was a solid working-class form of recreation.[74] The average working-class family would have to exercise thrift, foresight, and discipline in order to afford the excursion boat's two-dollar per couple fare as well as the cost of the sit-down luncheon, treats, carriage ride, and drinks. Occasionally, as the *Globe* reprovingly pointed out, some indulged too freely in strong drink, but at least they did so in their Sunday best.[75] Toronto's Irish nationalists did not, of course, always live up to their professions of self-improvement and respectability. However, Irish nationalists probably did not view respectability in static and rigid terms but rather in a more limited and contextual manner that overlooked the occasional aberration.[76]

For the Hibernians, fighting hard and "healthful recreation" went hand in hand, and both were in their own way expressions of individual respectability, assertions of ethnic solidarity, and demands for collective recognition. Defiant Michael Murphy, always ready to stand up for his countrymen and to deliver a blow if need be, became the model of the "honest, industrious and independent citizen of Toronto."[77] Excursions, Irish national games, and military drilling were demonstrations of Irish manliness and working-class dignity. Similarly, during the week the Hibernians could meet with their friends at the taverns owned by the society's leading members, such as Charles Burns, Owen Cosgrove, and Michael Murphy.[78] With their nationalist toasts and the usual pub games, these taverns offered the Hibernians a convivial meeting-place where recreation, neighbourhood ties, and nationalism were combined.

The Hibernian Benevolent Society's emphasis on male camaraderie, which lay at the heart of the Hibernians' sociability, underscored the sexual segregation of leisure that existed in the Irish-Catholic community. Women cheered their men on at athletic competitions and thronged the sidewalks on Saint Patrick's Day, but only at specifically designated events open to the general public – such as the annual ball or summer excursion – could they participate in the Hibernians' social activities, and even then only as men's guests. That many women put on the green on Saint Patrick's Day – the *Globe* reported that among the spectators women outnumbered men – indicates that Irish nationalism enjoyed considerable popularity among Irish-Catholic women. Nevertheless, the social world of Irish nationalism, like popular pastimes in general, was sexually specific. The Hibernians had little desire to recruit Irish-Catholic women, which would have meant sacrificing their fraternal sociability, and the conventional sexual differentiation of leisure resulted in Irish nationalism remaining a movement dominated by men.[79] Women were involved in the nationalist movement: they participated in nationalist celebrations and helped organize such festivities. Such was their subordinate and ancillary role in the nationalist movement, however, that they were denied recognition as activists in their own right.

Although the Hibernians excluded women from their social world, their emphasis on male sociability made it possible for the society's pastimes to become a natural vehicle for the expression of ethnic pride and unity. The Hibernian Benevolent Society's pastimes,

Table 14
Members of the Hibernian Benevolent Association,
1862–66

Category	Number	Percentage
Unskilled	18	18.6
Semi-skilled	20	20.6
Skilled	19	19.6
Clerical	4	4.1
Business	36	37.1

Source: *Irish Canadian* and city directories.

which were rooted in the male sociability of street and tavern, affirmed its members' manliness and self-esteem while also expressing their aspirations for recognition. Recreation became the means for instilling nationalist pride and sentiment, as the popular image of Michael Murphy well illustrates. Murphy, who rose from a cooper to a proprietor of an inn and tavern, represented what Irishmen could become and what they ought to be – recognized and respected, through defiance if necessary. Murphy, then, embodied the independence and self-assertiveness that Irish-Catholic men sought in the fraternal life of the Hibernian Benevolent Society.

Still, with a fifty-cent initiation fee and membership dues of $1.20 per annum, the social world of the Hibernian Benevolent Society was not within reach of all Irish-Catholic men.[80] Although no Hibernian membership rolls have survived, contemporary newspaper accounts and detective reports frequently mention the activists in the society: members of the executive, parade marshals, picnic organizers, the annual ball committees, ticket sellers for one or another society function, and the like. The occupational profile of these activists, as summarized in table 14, reveals that the Hibernian Benevolent Society – unlike parochial societies such as the Saint Vincent de Paul Society or the FMTS – was predominantly a working-class organization. The majority of the working-class members of the society were either semi-skilled or skilled, and a large proportion had regular employment and were comfortably off compared to many other Irish-Catholic immigrants; many of the unskilled Hibernians had steady employment working in the Toronto Rolling Mills and other factories.[81] Joining the Hibernian Benevolent Society required discretionary income, and it is therefore not surprising that many of the society's members, unskilled workers included, were householders. Far from being marginalized immigrants, the radical nationalists had struck deep roots in Toronto and had achieved working-class success – a steady job and a house they could call their own.

Although primarily a working-class association, businessmen were the largest single occupational group among the Hibernians. This category, however, incorporates a very diverse range of wealth and status. Of all the businessmen, only one, Charles Burns, who owned a number of buildings in addition to his tavern, was wealthy.[82] None of these individuals was among the leading businessmen of the Irish-Catholic community, and a breakdown of the types of businesses operated by the Hibernians explains why. Tavern keeping was the most popular business among Toronto's Irish nationalists. Fourteen Hibernians, almost two-fifths of the total business membership, owned taverns. Eight, comprising a little less than a quarter of the Hibernian Benevolent Society's businessmen, were grocers. Among the business members there were also four shoe-store owners, two peddlers, a cab owner, a contractor, and a newspaper owner, the remainder being small shopkeepers.

That almost 40 per cent of the businessmen were tavern keepers underscores the Hibernian Benevolent Society's connection with working-class culture, and it is likely that tavern keepers were the most successful recruiters the society had. Tavern keeping was also a convenient and accessible form of upward mobility. Licensing requirements did not restrict the growth of taverns until the mid-1870s, when the police began to enforce liquor regulations consistently. Needing only a good-sized room, some furniture, and an ample stock of whisky and beer, the prospective tavern keeper required relatively little capital. By catering to his fellow countrymen, the tavern keeper was assured of a loyal clientele and, perhaps, modest prosperity for himself and his family. The large number of tavern keepers in the society reflected both the importance of the tavern in the lives of Irish-Catholic men and the Hibernian Benevolent Society's popular base in the Irish-Catholic community.

The central role of the tavern in the Hibernians' leisure also illustrates how radical nationalist ideology and recreation reinforced and gave meaning to one another.[83] For many of the members, middle-class notions of domesticity were neither attainable nor desirable. The club and the tavern, better still a club that held its unofficial gatherings in a tavern, were the preferred forms of recreation. At the same time, the Hibernian Benevolent Society articulated a form of self-help and respectability that suited its working-class membership. The members of the Hibernian Benevolent Society, with their skills and steady employment, were financially well off by working-class standards and had aspirations to respectability. This quest for respectability was both individual and collective: Irish-Catholic men insisted on their right to a position in the Canadian social order commensurate with their achievements as honest and industrious citizens.[84] Rather than celebrating the individual achievement of the self-made man, radical nationalism advocated a form of ethnic separatism in which individual recognition and collective rights were of a piece. The Hibernian Benevolent Society not only expressed the desire of many Irish-Catholic men for social autonomy from the dominant Protestant culture, but through its social life and its nationalist ideology it also fulfilled this desire.

The self-assertiveness of the Hibernians also led them to insist on their autonomy from their social superiors and the clergy in the conduct of their social life. Radical nationalists upheld popular sovereignty, insisting that communal leadership was to flow from "the bottom up."[85] As men of the people, the Hibernians believed that they well positioned to represent the grass roots and express the community's will. And many Irishmen agreed. Nationalist societies across the province, in places such as Hamilton, Guelph, and St Catharines, developed ties with the Hibernian Benevolent Society and looked to it for their lead.[86] Many more Irish Catholics in the countryside declared their support for the Hibernians by subscribing to its flagship, the *Irish Canadian*. Within a few years, the Hibernians had moved from being a tiny tavern society to an organization whose influence reached well beyond the municipal limits of Toronto.

Radical nationalists defined an area for lay leadership and initiative in which the clergy were to play a supportive but ancilliary role. Not only did the Hibernians claim effective control over their associational life, but they also claimed the right to exercise leadership and initiative independently of the church. This claim undoubtedly disturbed the clergy, even though the Hibernian leaders affirmed the centrality of Catholicism to the life of their community. Ultimately, the emergence of a broadly based lay leadership was to make possible the development of a consensus that was embraced by laymen and clergy alike. In the short term, however, the mixture of lay initiative and Fenian-inspired nationalism was a highly volatile one, and with Michael Murphy's penchant for incendiary speeches it was to be highly explosive indeed.

The rationalizations offered by the leaders of the Hibernian Benevolent Society to make radical nationalism acceptable to Irish Catho-

lics in Toronto were precarious jerry-building. Once the Hibernians'
flimsy attempts to distance themselves from the Fenian Brotherhood
were questioned by other Catholics, the apologetics for the society
would lose their plausibility, and clerical support could no longer be
taken for granted. Catholic unity was critical to the Hibernians' popularity. Once Thomas D'Arcy McGee, now the minister of agriculture, entered the lists in early April 1864, that unity was put into
question. Assailing the Hibernian Benevolent Society and the *Irish
Canadian* as Fenian organs, McGee called on Irish Catholics to root
out the traitors in their midst. If Irish Catholics did not place themselves squarely within the pale of the constitution, McGee warned,
no public office, "no private employment ... no professional patronage, no social recognition, no office of trust, no magisterial duty,
could be or would be entrusted" to them.[87] For the first time the
presence of Fenianism in Toronto had become a contentious issue
among Irish Catholics, and McGee's declaration marked the beginning of a newspaper war between the *Canadian Freeman* and the *Irish
Canadian* that was to last until the following September.

In a clear statement of support for Irish responsible government
and constitutional agitation, James Moylan denounced Fenianism as
a secret society condemned by the church. Laying before its readers
the condemnation of the Brotherhood of Saint Patrick by Archbishop Paul Cullen of Dublin and denunciations of Fenianism by
some members of the American hierarchy – all of which, Moylan neglected to point out, had force only in those ordinaries' dioceses – the
Freeman advised that "no Catholic Irishman worthy of the name, will
disregard or condemn the fatherly counsels of the Irish hierarchy."[88] Fenianism was also incompatible with the civic duty of Irish
Catholics in a British colony. Having settled in Canada, Catholics
were bound to be loyal and true to their adopted home. If the responsible government and full liberty of Canada were not to their
liking, they could leave; the trip to the United States was, after all, a
quick and easy one. But abuse of this liberty and conspiracy against
the British government could not be condoned by Irish Catholics.
Otherwise Irish Catholics would be unable to shake the stigma of
disloyalty. "Who would find fault with the Protestant community,"
Moylan asked, if they adopted "no Catholic need apply" as their
motto?[89]

By appealing to the insecurity of Irish Catholics and their longing
to put down roots in Canada, D'Arcy McGee and his Toronto ally,
James Moylan, had attacked the Hibernian Benevolent Society's
most vulnerable flank. Against such an attack Patrick Boyle's *Irish*

Canadian was forced to take the low road of character assassination to undermine McGee's and Moylan's credibility. McGee, Boyle charged, was an informer, no better than "Goula" Sullivan who had allegedly betrayed the Phoenix Society of Cork in 1858. This political adventurer and prostitute – to mention only two of the epithets Boyle slung at McGee – was not one to lecture others about loyalty. Having so dispatched McGee, Boyle then accused Moylan of being in the pocket of the Orange Order.[90] Such attacks hardly addressed the substance of McGee's and Moylan's accusations of disloyalty, but Boyle's counter-accusations probably succeeded in casting doubts on their motives.

As the chief apologist of the Hibernian Benevolent Society, the *Irish Canadian* was especially concerned with Moylan's accusation of infidelity. Fenianism had already been condemned by the bishops of Chicago, Philadelphia, and Buffalo, and in Montreal Bishop Ignace Bourget had declared the Fenians to be a secret society under the ban of the church.[91] In June 1864, Bishop Lynch once more publicly denounced the Fenians, but the impact of his censure was muted by his statement that the Fenian Brotherhood was an American organization.[92] Divisions within the Roman Catholic hierarchy both in Ireland and in North America over how best to respond to Fenianism delayed Rome's proscription of the Fenians by name until 1870.[93] The *Irish Canadian* exploited this situation to defend the Fenian Brotherhood as a thoroughly Catholic organization.[94]

It is difficult to measure the results of Boyle's polemics. They probably convinced the converted, and many Irish Catholics who disagreed with the Hibernians may well have preferred that McGee and Moylan had not made a public show of the community's dirty linen.[95] In any event, the Hibernians' credibility had suffered. Help came to them from the least likely source. Two months after the *Freeman*'s opening salvo, a Protestant attempt to disrupt the Corpus Christi procession unwittingly rescued the society from its predicament. By revealing the intensity of Protestant suspicion and antagonism towards Irish Catholics, the Corpus Christi riot gave the Hibernian Benevolent Society a new lease on life.

The *Canadian Freeman* announced on Thursday, 26 May 1864, that a Corpus Christi procession would be held the following Sunday in the garden adjoining the Episcopal Palace and Saint Michael's Cathedral. The Orange Order assumed that the procession of the host would take place on the city streets, and the next day it issued a protest denouncing this "insult to the Protestant community."[96] Bishop Lynch quickly made it known that the procession was to be confined to the garden of the cathedral. "We desire," the bishop declared, "to live in good and kindly feeling with our fellow-citizens, and we expect reciprocity."[97] In this Lynch was to be disappointed.

The Corpus Christi celebration on Sunday drew a large crowd which filled both the cathedral and the garden of the Episcopal Palace and overflowed onto the street. At first it seemed that the celebration would pass without incident. Although greeted by catcalls, the procession of the school children and sodalities as well as the celebration of the Mass at an outdoor altar proceeded without interruption.[98] When the monstrance emerged from the cathedral, a group of young men immediately attempted to force their way into the garden to break up the procession. In the mêlée that followed, the gate-crashers drew revolvers.[99] The school children, terror-stricken, broke ranks; the garden quickly emptied; some spectators sought safety in the cathedral vaults or the street; and in the crush a fence was pushed down. The ringing of a fire bell added to the confusion as the rumour went about that the cathedral was on fire.[100] The prompt intervention of the clergy prevented the panic from becoming anything worse, and the procession was resumed. Though the city police were present, they did not intervene to restore order.[101]

Catholic indignation was immediate. "Who gave the Orangemen of this city the power to dictate the course Catholics should pursue" by taking the law into their own hands, thundered the *Irish Canadian*. Boyle then rehearsed the litany of Orange outrages against Toronto's Irish-Catholic community – the murder of Matthew Sheedy and the attack on the National Hotel – to remind Irish Catholics that the Hibernians were essential to their self-defence.[102] Bishop Lynch agreed with the *Irish Canadian* that, if the government was not prepared to uphold their rights, Catholics would take matters into their own hands.[103] Lynch's determination to repeat the procession the following Sunday not only demonstrated how intent he was on asserting Catholic rights but also revealed that the Hibernian Benevolent Society could still count on Irish-Catholic suppport.[104] However much the *Canadian Freeman* feared and denounced the Fenian inclinations of the Hibernian Benevolent Society, that organization was now recognized as the only one capable of standing up for the Irish-Catholic community.

The Corpus Christi riot was a small affray compared to the Saint Patrick's Day riots of 1858, but an attack on Saint Michael's Cathedral, the seat of Catholicism of Toronto, and the disruption of a procession carrying the Sacred Host were sure to arouse Irish-Catholic indignation. That women and children were endangered in the attack only aggravated the already frayed emotions of Irish Catholics. The complacency of the civic authorities and the conspicuous indifference of the daily press led Irish Catholics to believe that Protestants at the very least condoned the actions of the mob. The attack on the Corpus Christi procession struck at the heart of Irish-Catholic attitudes towards British Canada. If they could not practice their religion on the grounds of their cathedral, Irish Catholics wondered, how could Irish Catholics hope to secure recognition as a distinct community? The social climate created by Irish nationalism and ultramontane Catholicism encouraged Irish Catholics to advance militantly the claims of their religion and nationality. Both taught Irish Catholics that consideration could be gained only if they had self-respect. As a consequence of this belief, Irish Catholics were convinced that they were never as virtuous as when they were nobly resisting the attacks of the world. How far Catholics were prepared to support the Hibernian Benevolent Society in this endeavour was to be tested by the Hibernians' midnight march on the night of 5 November.

Rumours quickly spread through the Catholic community that the Orange Order intended to burn effigies of Guy Fawkes, Pius IX, and Daniel O'Connell during its Guy Fawkes celebrations on Saturday, 5 November 1864.[105] When the Hibernian Benevolent Society made it known that Irish Catholics would not tolerate such an insult, the leaders of the Orange Order decided, in the interest of public peace, to forgo the annual burning of a Guy Fawkes effigy and to hold its festivities indoors. Although members of the Hibernian Benevolent Society were posted at the parish churches and watched over the homes of the society's leaders as a precautionary measure, the anniversary of the Gunpowder Plot had, it seemed, passed without a disturbance. Such hopes, however, were quickly shattered.

Around midnight, the Hibernians made their way to Queen's Park in groups of one or two dozen each. When about four hundred men, armed with shotguns, rifles, and revolvers arrived, they divided their forces, keeping a reserve at the park, while two companies marched off "four deep like a company of soldiers" along the principal streets to the east and west ends of the city. At about two o'clock, when a few shots were fired in the west end, the east-end Hibernians returned the signal and the marchers dispersed. In seizing control of the city streets, the Hibernian Benevolent Society was claiming that the city belonged as much to the Irish Catholics as to the Orange Order and that Catholic sensibilities had a legitimate claim to public respect. Nothing could have better rallied the support of the Irish-Catholic community.

The Hibernians' escapade, however, raised among Protestant Torontonians a Fenian scare which was to grip the city periodically until the Fenian raids of 1866. When Torontonians awoke the next morning, Sunday, 6 November 1864, to discover that during the night the Hibernian Benevolent Society had taken control of the city streets, the news, commented the *Leader*, "fell like a thunderclap." "The sensation was complete," the *Leader* continued, at the discovery that the citizens of Toronto "were in the hands of irresponsible and blood-thirsty bigots." The precision marching of the "Fenians" had yet another message for the *Leader*. Although the Fenian Brotherhood had still to plan its raid upon Canada, the *Leader* indirectly raised, for the first time, the spectre of an American invasion. Do they drill, asked the *Leader*, "for the defence of their country. Not a bit of it. Let the 'Grand Centre' of the organization in New York answer. Let the speeches of Mr. Murphy be produced as testimony. The whole conduct of these people rises up in judgement against them."[106] The reaction of the *Globe* was no less anxious. The demonstration, the *Globe* believed, proved the existence in Toronto of a Fenian circle, "an armed, secret organization, existing in defiance of the law" that held the city "completely at their mercy." Since Irish Catholics experienced neither civil nor religious disabilities, such an armed demonstration was an unwarranted attack on the public order.[107]

With public clamour at an unprecedented pitch, the municipal authorities were nonplussed. Not only had the marchers eluded the police, but the one case brought against a member of the Hibernian Benevolent Society quickly collapsed in court. In response, Toronto's mayor, F.H. Medcalf, attempted to turn attention away from the lamentable performance of his police force by fueling popular suspicions of Irish Catholics. Rumours and wild accusations increasingly gained credence; everything Catholic became suspect. Catholic churches (which some suspected had arms buried in their vaults), the Hibernian Benevolent Society, and the various Irish nationalist societies in the countryside around Toronto were all suspected of planning a Catholic uprising, which one correspondent to the *Globe* predicted would be like a second St Bartholomew's Day Massacre.[108]

In this atmosphere of public suspicion and hysteria the Catholic press immediately rallied to the defence of the Hibernian Benevolent Society. Law and order quickly became the focus of the Catholic apologetic. After the Orange-inspired Corpus Christi riot, the Catholics of Toronto, the *Irish Canadian* declared with not a little exaggeration, were not "such craven idiots as to trust their lives and their property to the care and protection of an Orange Mayor, when a howling mob of Orange fanatics threaten their destruction." If the civic authorities could not be relied on to uphold the law, the Catholics of Toronto, the *Irish Canadian* asserted, are "determined to protect it for ourselves."[109] Only the Hibernians, it seemed, would stand up for Irish Catholics. Nor did the *Canadian Freeman* disagree with the *Irish Canadian*'s assessment: both the civic authorities and public opinion had colluded with the Orange Order in its attack on the rights of Irish Catholics.[110] "Men will not stand being constantly insulted," the *Freeman* affirmed, and in its defence of Catholic rights, the Hibernian Benevolent Society had redeemed the pride and honour of Irish Catholics. The *Freeman* promptly repudiated its earlier accusations that the Hibernians harboured Fenians and accepted the society's explanation that it was simply a Catholic-defence organization.[111]

Bishop Lynch's response to the Hibernians' escapade was far more ambiguous than that of the *Canadian Freeman*. The Hibernians' march was both foolish and unwarranted, Lynch affirmed, but it would not have occurred had the Orange Order not been "a constant menace against the rights of Catholics." While he regretted the existence of organizations devoted to Catholic self-defence, such organizations were a natural response to the climate that the Orange Order had done so much to promote.[112] What the bishop had taken with one hand, he gave back with the other. The Hibernians had escaped with a light tap on the knuckles, while the Orange Order faced the bishop's full fury.

In light of the clear and unequivocal support of the *Canadian Freeman*, no friend of Patrick Boyle and the Hibernian Benevolent Society, and of Bishop Lynch's mild rebuke, the Hibernian Benevolent Society could well claim to have secured the confidence of Irish Catholics. Fortunately for the Hibernian Benevolent Society, the attack on the Corpus Christi procession was still fresh in the minds of Irish Catholics. Without the provocation of the Corpus Christi riot, it is doubtful that the society would have been recognized as the champion of Irish and Catholic rights. By making a show of defending the Catholic churches on the night of 5 November, the Hibernian Benevolent Society maintained the connection between nationalism and religion and transformed an armed midnight tramp through the city into a demonstration of Catholic rights. Boyle, the accomplished chameleon, who shifted his views and tactics as the situation demanded, had demonstrated himself to be an equally accomplished alchemist. By appealing to fears of the Orange Order, which embodied the forces that Catholics believed threatened their community, the *Irish Canadian* restored the Hibernian

Benevolent Society's standing in the Irish-Catholic community and made good its claim to be the guardian of that community's honour and integrity. In the process, however, the Hibernians had further alienated Protestant opinion. By the end of November, the debate in the daily press had begun to subside, but if Catholics expected the furore to settle down, they were to be sadly mistaken.

At the beginning of December, rumours circulated with increasing regularity that the American Fenians were conspiring with the Hibernians to annihilate Protestants in the countryside of southern Canada West.[113] Adjala and Tecumseh townships and the towns of Newmarket and Barrie were gripped by Fenian panics. In Toronto rumours of the Hibernians drilling on Bloor Street led to public protests. So seriously were the reports of a Fenian uprising taken that nine volunteer companies came forward to offer their services.[114] With the Fenian scare reaching a crescendo, the Toronto daily papers wisely ceased to publish rumours and the panic had largely abated by the end of the month.

With calm once more restored, the Hibernian Benevolent Society became even bolder in its flirtation with Fenianism. In 1865, the Hibernian Benevolent Society signalled its sympathy for Fenianism by inviting "Red Jim" McDermott, a well-known organizer for the Fenian Brotherhood and, as it turned out, a British informer, to give a Saint Patrick's Day speech.[115] The loud cheering that greeted his call for a free and independent republic erected on the ruins of the old kingdom led an emboldened McDermott to declare "that there are Fenians in Canada, too."[116] Despite the enthusiastic response that greeted McDermott's speech – the issue of the *Irish Canadian* containing his address soon sold out – Patrick Boyle continued to maintain that Fenianism was strictly an American movement.[117] As "we are not professed Fenians," Boyle declared, almost giving his game away, members of the Hibernian Benevolent Society derived all their knowledge of the Fenian Brotherhood from the newspapers.[118] Yet, their protestations of loyalty notwithstanding, Toronto's Hibernians could not disguise either their support for the Fenian Brotherhood or their hopes for a broad-based republican movement in Canada.[119]

Despite the Hibernians' boldness, they still enjoyed the support of the clergy and the vast majority of Irish Catholics. But they could not maintain this advantage for long. Michael Murphy, as always impetuous but usually astute, now blundered badly, leaving Bishop Lynch no choice but to condemn the Hibernian Benevolent Society.

The critical incident occurred in the summer of 1865. In May 1864, Bishop John Farrell of Hamilton had denounced the Hibernian Benevolent Society, declaring it to a subversive organization that fell under the church's ban on secret societies.[120] The following year, after the Hibernian Benevolent Society had announced its annual excursion in mid-July, Bishop Farrell repeated his condemnation of the society and urged the Catholics of Hamilton not to participate in the Hibernians' outing.[121]

On their way to Niagara Falls, the Toronto Hibernians stopped in Hamilton to pick up their Hamilton members. As there was a delay in boarding the train, Michael Murphy took the opportunity to address the crowd. Bishop Farrell's threats on a purely temporal question, Murphy declared, had no authority, be they "uttered by a Catholic bishop or a renegade or traitor."[122] Bishop Farrell immediately excommunicated the Hamilton members of the Hibernian Benevolent Society. The Fenians or Hibernians of Canada, he asserted, were led by irreligious men who opposed "the inalienable rights of the Roman Pontiff and of the whole Church."[123]

In responding to these developments, Bishop Lynch declared that the Hibernian Benevolent Society had fallen away from Catholic principles, and so it was the sacred duty of all good Catholics to quit the organization. "A Bishop has the undoubted right, and is the judge to decide what religious society or benevolent association may be established amongst his people," Bishop Lynch maintained. In defying Bishop Farrell's authority, Michael Murphy had rendered an unforgivable and highly offensive insult.[124] Given Murphy's provocation, Bishop Lynch was certainly justified in denouncing the Hibernians. The reason he had not done so sooner lies in the his ambivalent response to Fenianism.

Bishop Lynch first denounced the Fenian Brotherhood in June 1864.[125] Two years later, on 19 March 1866, Lynch repeated his denunciation of Fenianism, warning that the brotherhood was led by "misguided men who pretend to remedy the evils of Ireland by anarchy and bloodshed."[126] At no time, however, did the bishop believe that the Hibernian Benevolent Society was connected with the Fenian Brotherhood. Lynch maintained in private and in public that there was "no Fenian organization ... in Canada though there may be some sympathizers."[127] Even when Lynch condemned the Hibernian Benevolent Society, he insisted that the society was not a Fenian association.[128] Furthermore, it was only after many transgressions and many warnings that he finally called upon Catholics to quit the society.[129] In his mind, this denunciation of the Hibernian Benevolent Society had little to do with Fenianism. Rather, it was solely a response to the society's defiance of a member of the hierarchy. Lynch, the *Globe* wryly commented, "could endure Murphy's disloyalty with comparative equanimity, but when he went the length of attacking a right reverend father in God, episcopal patience gave way."[130] What the *Globe* failed to notice was that the bishop had not invoked a formal ban against the Hibernians, though he had claimed his right to do so. He simply asked Irish Catholics to demonstrate their fidelity to the church by leaving the society. Considering Murphy's challenge to episcopal authority, Lynch's response was temperate in the extreme.

The Hibernians had given Bishop Lynch ample grounds in the past for him to denounce their society. The society, as Lynch admitted, had proven intractable in its dealings with him over the years, which alone would have been sufficient for the bishop to withdraw his sanction of the organization. Moreover, bishops in Ireland, the United States, and Canada had proscribed organizations on the suspicion that they were affiliated with the Fenian Brotherhood. With the daily press hurling accusations of disloyalty at the Hibernian Benevolent Society, Lynch had good reason to distance himself from the Hibernians.

But several questions still remain. Why did Bishop Lynch accept the Hibernian Benevolent Society's patently transparent denials of affiliation with the Fenian Brotherhood? Why did he ignore the evidence provided by his own clergy linking the Hibernians to the Fenian Brotherhood?[131] Why did he go so far as to give his active support to the Hibernians by gracing their Saint Patrick's Day with his presence and allowing the Hibernian Benevolent Society to meet in Roman Catholic school rooms? Why, when the authority of a brother bishop was flouted, did he not impose ecclesiastical sanctions upon the society? In part, Bishop Lynch's acquiescence in the Hibernian Benevolent Society's presence in his diocese stemmed from his nationalist convictions and his implacable opposition to British rule in Ireland. "If by Fenians were meant those who objected to the oppression of Ireland and hated England," Lynch revealingly declared when he condemned the Hibernians, "those Fenians [were] everywhere."[132] The distinction between Fenianism and militant nationalism was a critical one for Lynch, as it was for many Irish Catholics. So, too, was the distinction between an active Fenian and a sympathizer of Fenianism. Much as he reprobated the means adopted by the Fenians, he could readily identify with the abiding hatred towards Britain that they expressed. To this extent, at least, Fenianism was "the suppuration of a deep chronic wound inflicted on Ireland" by Britain. While there may have been Fenian sympathizers in

Toronto, Bishop Lynch was certain that the Hibernians had not violated the church's ban on revolutionary organizations. The Hibernians may have been intemperate in their denunciations of Britain, but they were not disloyal subjects.[133]

These considerations reinforced Lynch's pastoral concerns, the grounds on which he had originally lent his support to the Hibernian Benevolent Society. As he admitted to a group of laymen in 1862, to oppose the Hibernians would have risked alienating them from the church and so dividing the Irish-Catholic community.[134] Independent lay associations made the bishop uneasy, but he feared even more the consequences of allowing a Catholic lay organization to operate outside the moral framework of the church. As long as the Hibernians professed to be loyal sons of the church, coexistence was possible. But when Murphy and the Hibernians explicitly denied the clergy's authority, Bishop Lynch had to exercise his prerogatives or risk losing them altogether. In his petulant diatribe against Bishop Farrell, Murphy had carelessly forfeited Lynch's confidence. In response to Lynch's open letter, the Hibernians rallied to the defence of their leader, claiming that Murphy had the right to act without the fetters of clerical control. As the society was organized for "protective and *quasi* political reasons," the Hibernians asserted, their "liberty of action and rights as citizens should not be deemed as within the influence of church authority."[135] Despite such provocation, and the undoubted challenge it posed to his leadership both in the church and in the community, Lynch was still ambivalent toward the Hibernians. As he confided only a few months later to Bishop Joseph-Eugène-Bruno Guiges of Ottawa, he could neither encourage nor condemn the Hibernian Benevolent Society.[136]

Lynch's action, guarded though it was, placed the Hibernian Benevolent Society in a difficult position, for it could defend its leader and justify its continued existence only by defying the authority of the church. The society's policy of maintaining its autonomy from clerical leadership while at the same time proclaiming its loyalty to the church had collapsed. The *Canadian Freeman* immediately denounced the Hibernians for placing themelves outside the Catholic fold.[137] A rift in the Irish-Catholic community appeared to be inevitable. Fortunately for Toronto's Catholics, events once more intervened, and the issue was again avoided.

Ironically, unity among Toronto's Irish Catholics was brought about largely by the dissensions within the Fenian ranks in the United States. The overthrow on 2 December 1865 of the head centre, John O'Mahony, by a wing of the movement led by William Roberts divided the Fenian Brotherhood into two rival factions. The

Roberts faction justified the coup on the grounds of O'Mahony's mishandling of an issue of Fenian bonds, but in fact this was only a convenient pretext. Disillusioned by O'Mahony's indecisiveness and his lack-lustre preparations for an uprising in Ireland, these men of action favoured an immediate attack on the British territory close to hand, Canada.[138]

The split in the brotherhood took the Hibernians by surprise, and at first, not realizing the profound differences between the two factions, they believed that the dispute could be amicably settled.[139] When it became apparent that the Roberts wing was set upon a Canadian invasion, the inner circle of the Toronto Fenians freely gave their support to the O'Mahony wing of the brotherhood, whose military objectives were limited to Ireland. The Canadian Fenians denounced "as the worst enemies of our motherland" the men who raised "the cry of 'to Canada,' instead of the cry 'to Ireland.'" To attack a friendly and self-governing people, such as Canada, was both "treacherous and fatal to Ireland, for to her delay is death."[140] As Patrick Boyle had long insisted, the object of Fenianism was not Canada, but the liberation of Ireland.[141]

The preparations of the Roberts faction to invade Canada unleashed yet another Fenian scare in Canada West. President Roberts and his secretary of war, Thomas Sweeny, on their tour in late January 1866 through Newark, Buffalo, and Cleveland, made it plain that they would soon launch an attack on Canada.[142] Sarnia was so gripped by reports of an imminent Fenian attack from Port Huron that the volunteers slept in their uniforms.[143] A rumour that Sweeny and Roberts were passing through Hamilton and London further fed the Fenian panic, and to the east, Cornwall was also obsessed by rumours of Fenian plans for a raid.[144] The *Canadian Freeman* promptly attempted to deflate the Fenian excitement. Roberts's and Sweeny's speeches, it insisted, were but empty gas. Fenianism, the *Freeman* observed, is dying a natural death and "will not venture to trouble us."[145] The Hibernian Benevolent Society, too, did not put much stock in the brotherhood's threat to invade Canada. "From the beginning we looked upon this project (if such was ever really intended)," Patrick Boyle declared, "as visionary and unproductive."[146] With Protestant hysteria in full flight, Irish Catholics closed ranks and sought to deflect the threat Fenianism posed to Canadian peace and security.

Although the Fenian scare was only gradually diminishing, the Hibernian Benevolent Society announced at the end of February 1866 that it would resume its custom of celebrating Saint Patrick's

Day with a parade.[147] The society's announcement could not have been more badly timed. Only a few days before the parade was to be held, the *Globe* revealed that a Fenian invasion was to coincide with the Saint Patrick's Day celebrations in Toronto.[148] By Saint Patrick's Day the Fenian panic had eased owing to the intervention of the authorities, who fortunately had access to more reliable information than the *Globe*,[149] and on 17 March about six hundred Hibernians marched on the city streets without incident.[150] Addressing the marchers, Murphy repeated his assurances that the Hibernians had no quarrel with Canada. "We have," he declared, "no sympathy with those who would bring war and attended horrors amongst peaceable and inoffensive people with whom our lot is cast." Yet Murphy could not resist asserting yet again that forty thousand Irish Catholics in Canada "were prepared to shed their blood for the redemption of Ireland."[151]

The *Irish Canadian* could proudly boast that by joining the procession at the risk of losing their jobs the Hibernians had sustained their honour. After Bishop Lynch's denunciation and the divisions that wracked the Fenian Brotherhood, Murphy badly needed a show of strength to boost the sagging morale of the Hibernian Benevolent Society. In his speech he offered the assurance that his followers sought: that radical nationalism, far from being inimical to the position of Irish Catholics in Canada, was the only sure way to gain respect in Canadian society. Under the protection of the Hibernian Benevolent Society, Murphy declared, Irish Catholics would no longer be shot down like dogs. His contention that radical nationalism was essential to maintaining the integrity and identity of Irish Catholics in Canada gained even more credibility when the schoolgirls of Saint Paul's separate school serenaded the Hibernians from the steps of Saint Paul's church.[152] Murphy had successfully minimized Bishop Lynch's half-hearted opposition to the Hibernian Benevolent Society and, by mustering six hundred Hibernians, had accomplished an impressive coup. It was, however, to be his last.

The Canadian government had been unable to uncover any evidence that would convict Michael Murphy or any of his colleagues.[153] But John O'Mahony's decision on 17 March 1866 to attack Campobello, New Brunswick, in order to steal the lead from the Roberts faction almost gave the Canadian authorities the conclusive proof they were looking for.[154] On 21 March, an operator for the Montreal Telegraph Company intercepted an easily decoded cipher to Philip Cullen, a clerk in the Toronto Savings Bank and a member of the Hibernian Benevolent Society: "Get twenty single men ready

196 Piety and Nationalism

for orders by tuesday chose drilled and temperance men if you can
pack equipment and ammunition ready for expressing where directed men to follow."[155]

Two weeks later, on 9 April, Michael Murphy and six other Hibernians set out for Portland, Maine, presumably to join O'Mahony's
expedition to Campobello, which was already under way. Although
Prime Minister John A. Macdonald gave express orders that Murphy and his associates were only to be tailed by "a confidential man,"
George-Étienne Cartier, attorney-general for Canada East, and Alexander Galt, the minister of finance, took it upon themselves to
order the arrest of Murphy and his companions when the train arrived at Cornwall.[156] Murphy and his fellow Hibernians, though
armed with revolvers, offered no resistance. The next day, a seventh
Hibernian who had eluded detection was also arrested.[157]

Cartier's and Galt's presumptuous action put Macdonald in an
awkward position. While he now had no choice but to prosecute the
prisoners, he also knew that the government had a poor case.[158]
Besides a cipher code, Cullen's telegram, and some hand guns, the
crown had no evidence of a treasonable conspiracy. The arrest of
Thomas Sheedy, the secretary of the Hibernian Benevolent Society,
brought the prosecution no closer to building a case, as Sheedy had
already destroyed whatever sensitive documents he had in his possession.[159] Despite the arrest of James Welsh, a treasurer of one of
the society's branches, and John Mulvey, Murphy's brother-in-law
and a former member of the society, the crown was unable to uncover any material evidence that would gain a conviction.[160]

The *Irish Canadian* immediately protested the arrest of Murphy
and his companions. In openly purchasing a ticket to Portland, the
Irish Canadian pointed out, Murphy had broken no law.[161] The arrest of Murphy on the flimsiest of pretenses only showed, the *Irish
Canadian* concluded, "that the boasted liberty of British subjects is a
sham."[162] The *Irish Canadian*'s suspicions were not allayed when the
crown attorney requested remand after remand. Finally, on 2 May,
upon hearing evidence *in camera*, the panel of local magistrates committed Murphy and his colleagues for trial at the fall assizes on the
charges of levying war against the Queen and conspiring with for-
eigners to invade Canada.[163]

O'Mahony's expedition to Campobello, New Brunswick, was a
fiasco. Although he had a force of over fifteen hundred under arms,
only a few parties managed to land near Campobello before stealing
back to the American side. A few burnt-out custom sheds and a sto-
len British flag were all the Fenians could show after weeks of frantic
military activity. Following the attack on Campobello, Canadians

looked on Fenianism as a spent force.[164] Both Protestants and Catholics were taken by surprise when Colonel John O'Neil of the Roberts wing of the brotherhood led a force of one thousand men across the Niagara River in an attack upon Fort Erie, Canada West, in the early morning hours of 1 June 1866. The Fenian invasion lasted little more than forty-eight hours, but in that time seven Canadians, including three college students, were killed in action.[165]

The radical nationalists of Toronto were shocked by O'Neill's raid on Canada.[166] "The possession of Canada by the Fenian followers of General Sweeney and President Roberts," Patrick Boyle complained, "could not advance an iota the cause of Ireland's freedom from misrule." The raid, Boyle repentantly declared, has caused Irish Catholics "a good deal of trouble ... and has helped to widen the breach between the inhabitants of the Upper Province already too much embittered with each other." With time, Boyle hoped, "we will again have peace."[167] The funeral for the five Toronto volunteers killed at Ridgeway, however, became a public demonstration of the Protestant and British character of English Canada.[168] Throughout the summer, despite John A. Macdonald's instructions, Irish Catholics were arrested for alleged membership in the Fenian Brotherhood and suspected Fenians were dismissed from their jobs.[169] Much to the relief of the Canadian government, during the night of 2 September, Michael Murphy and four other Hibernians escaped from the Cornwall jail and slipped across the border.[170] The three remaining prisoners were finally admitted to bail and were, for a lack of evidence, never brought to trial.[171] Though arrests of suspected Fenians continued throughout the fall, by December the Fenian fever had once again subsided.[172]

The Fenian invasion did not, as John A. Macdonald had hoped, break up the Hibernian Benevolent Society, even though the invasion had given credence to the *Freeman*'s attack on the Fenian Brotherhood as a threat to the security and prosperity of the Irish Catholics of Canada. Moreover, Bishop Lynch continued in his refusal to sanction the society.[173] Yet, while many had become disillusioned with the Fenian leadership, less than two years after the invasion the Hibernians could still muster four hundred members to celebrate Saint Patrick's Day.[174]

The assassination of Thomas D'Arcy McGee, the leading Irish-Catholic politician in Canada in the early morning hours of 7 April by James Whalen, in what the government alleged was a Fenian conspiracy, seriously compromised the Hibernian Benevolent Society's ability to maintain Irish-Catholic support. Though no convincing evidence of a Fenian conspiracy was to be forthcoming from the authorities, McGee's staunch opposition to the Fenians made them the objects of public suspicion.[175] With the arrest a month later of Patrick Boyle, now president of the Hibernian Benevolent Society, and John Nolan, the society's treasurer, in the government's desperate dragnet to uncover the Fenian connection with McGee's assassination, the Hibernians appeared to have received a fatal blow.[176] Nevertheless, the irrepressible Patrick Boyle was soon to demonstrate that under his leadership radical nationalism in Toronto could regain its popular following and become reconciled once again with the Roman Catholic Church.

9 "The Sacred Cause and the National Faith": The Resurrection of Irish Nationalism

Following Bishop Lynch's denunciation of the Hibernian Benevolent Society in 1865, the Fenian raids of 1866, and the assassination of Thomas D'Arcy McGee in 1868, radical nationalism lost much of its former influence among Irish Catholics in Toronto. Yet within three years the Hibernians had achieved a reconciliation with the Roman Catholic Church and had regained public support in the Irish-Catholic community. This turnaround in the fortunes of radical nationalism was the result of four profound changes in the character and organization of Irish nationalism in Toronto. First, radical nationalists moderated their stance significantly. Second, this shift in emphasis enabled the radicals to form an alliance with more moderate nationalists. Third, not only did Irish nationalism become more diverse ideologically, but it also became more institutionally varied as Irish-Catholic men established new nationalist societies. Fourth, these nationalist societies forged much closer ties with the Roman Catholic Church than the Hibernians had done in their heyday.

By advancing on these four fronts, the Hibernians and their radical allies in other nationalist societies consolidated their leadership of the nationalist movement in Toronto. Nationalism retained its populist ethos, and thus the issue of which spheres of leadership and initiative in the Irish-Catholic community properly belonged to laity and which to the clergy continued to be an object of negotiation – and, on occasion, of contention – between the radical nationalists and the clergy.

The assassination of Thomas D'Arcy McGee produced a wave of revulsion not only among Protestant Canadians but among many Irish
Catholics as well. Few could doubt the existence of a Fenian conspiracy to seek revenge on McGee; even fewer could countenance such
senseless violence. Whatever his faults, McGee was an Irishman, and
in death he was to become celebrated as a paragon of Canadian
patriotism.[1] Still, the Hibernians' earlier vitriolic denunciations of
McGee seemed to contradict their prompt condemnation and their
professed revulsion over McGee's tragic assassination. Though
genuinely shocked at the atrocity of McGee's murder, Patrick Boyle,
now the president of the Hibernian Benevolent Society, could not
shake the suspicion that fell upon radical nationalism. After the
arrest of Boyle and other members of the Hibernian inner circle,
that suspicion became even harder to dislodge.[2]

Both the Fenian invasions of 1866 and McGee's assassination had
undermined the credibility of the Hibernian Benevolent Society.
The Hibernians' procession on Saint Patrick's Day in 1869, the *Canadian Freeman* noted, was reduced to a remnant of its former
strength.[3] The following year, Patrick Boyle lamented that
"Cawtholics," those who trimmed their ideals to safeguard their
status, no longer attended Hibernian events. No doubt, Boyle observed with more than a touch of sarcasm, they would show up when
Irish nationalism was fashionable once more.[4] Faced with a rapidly
declining membership, deprived of its leaders (the result of Michael
Murphy's wild Campobello escapade), and cut off from the Catholic
Church, the outcome of yet another of Murphy's impetuous acts, the
very survival of the Hibernian Benevolent Society was at stake.[5] The
Hibernians could regain their former influence with the Irish-
Catholic community only if they repaired their alliance with the
church. That the breach could be healed was soon demonstrated
when James Moylan, Lynch's confidant, interceded with the authorities to secure Patrick Boyle's release from jail.[6]

But the renewal of good relations between the radical nationalists
and the Catholic Church was not to be accomplished overnight.
Bishop Lynch profoundly distrusted independent lay leadership. In
early July 1867, for example, Lynch strongly condemned a group of
Toronto Catholic Liberals for calling on their own authority a public
meeting for the Catholic electors of Ontario. "I have learned with
surprise that a certain number of gentlemen ... have taken upon
themselves the ecclesiastical office of issuing circulars to the *Catholics*
of the Province of Ontario," the bishop declared, "ignoring that
there are bishops and priests belonging also to the Catholic body
who are considered their leaders, and who consequently have a right

to speak to them as Catholics."[7] The Hibernian Benevolent Society most certainly had given the bishop good cause to be especially wary of Toronto's Irish nationalists. Still, he was eventually to effect a rapprochement with the society.

As the trial of James Whalen in the fall of 1868 approached, the anti-Fenian hysteria that had intermittently gripped southwestern Ontario abated.[8] As an example of this more relaxed attitude, both the *Leader*, an independent Conservative daily, and the *Globe*, a Reform organ, sought to take partisan credit for Patrick Boyle's release.[9] Confident that the Fenian Brotherhood was now a spent force, most Canadians quickly became preoccupied with other issues.[10] With calm restored, a more benign perception of the Hibernian Benevolent Society gained ground among Protestants and Catholics.

As usual, Bishop Lynch did not give his reasons for revoking his censure of the Hibernian Benevolent Society. Perhaps he believed that Fenianism was no longer a menace to Canadian security. One indication that Lynch believed Fenianism had run its course was his behind-the-scenes appeals to release some of the American prisioners captured in the Fenian raid on Canada West.[11] Lynch could also interpret developments in the Hibernian Benevolent Society as a portent of a more harmonious relationship between clergy and laity. Michael Murphy's disastrous foray to join the Fenians' Campobello expedition in April 1866 allowed the Hibernian Benevolent Society to replace its militant executive with more conciliatory members. At Lynch's request, the Hibernians marked the Saint Patrick's Day festivities of 1867 and 1868 in a far more muted manner than they had done when Mike Murphy headed the platform. Such conciliatory action probably convinced the bishop that the society would prove amenable in the future.[12] When, in February 1869, some sixty-five prominent Catholics petitioned the bishop to call off the Hibernian Benevolent Society's proposed Saint Patrick's Day march in order to prevent the "evil results that have, in years past, followed the annual procession of the 17th of March," Lynch not only refused their request but with the clergy stood in the portico of the episcopal palace to receive the cheers of the Hibernians for the first time since 1865.[13]

The Saint Patrick's Day celebrations in 1869 marked the rehabilitation of the Hibernian Benevolent Society not just within the Catholic community but also in the eyes of many Protestants. The Hibernians, commented the *Leader*, long a bitter foe of the society, "presented a very respectable and creditable appearance."[14] The fears of some Toronto Catholics that the Hibernians' procession would arouse antagonism and bring Catholics into disrepute proved to be without foundation. "The clans gathered in force," the *Irish Canadian* triumphantly proclaimed after the Hibernians' successful procession in 1869, and the day passed in "unity and harmony" between people and clergy as they celebrated their nation and their faith.[15] Indeed, the Hibernian Benevolent Society had so managed to regain the goodwill, not to mention the indulgence, of the clergy that the following year Bishop Lynch could dismiss the Hibernians' confrontation with the church in 1864 as "a little error of judgement and not of the heart." Michael Murphy's reckless actions had now become no more than "little imprudences."[16] Once the Hibernians had demonstrated themselves to be loyal sons of the church, Lynch was quite prepared to accept their patriotism as sincere.

Events in Ireland, which the Hibernians deftly exploited to their advantage, also contributed to the Hibernian Benevolent Society's rehabilitation. What the Irish Revolutionary Brotherhood's organizing drive in Ireland had failed to do in generating nationalist enthusiasm was accomplished by successive state trials in Ireland following its insurrection of 1867. By 1869 the unprecedented popular sympathy produced by the heavy sentences given to the Fenian prisoners was mobilized behind a broadly based nationalist movement under the leadership of Isaac Butt. Though Butt was an uncompromising supporter of agitation through constitutional means, his demand of amnesty for the Fenian prisoners quickly earned him the respect and support of many physical-force nationalists.[17] When he launched the Home Rule League in November 1873, Butt could count on Fenian support to transform the mounting amnesty agitation into a nationalist campaign for Home Rule on a federated basis with Britain. Such was Butt's stature and influence that the Irish Revolutionary Brotherhood, in the first of three departures from Fenian orthodoxy, endorsed the constitutional Home Rule movement. This departure was to give the Hibernians and other radical nationalists in Toronto a freer hand to regain their standing in the Irish-Catholic community.[18]

The Fenian raid in late May 1870 near Saint Albans, Vermont, convinced the inner circle of Hibernians to sever their ties with the Fenian Brotherhood.[19] The demise of the Hibernians' revolutionary cell set the stage for a significant change in the ideology of the radical nationalist movement. In the summer of 1870, Boyle's *Irish Canadian* shifted its support to the newly formed insurrectionary organization, the United Brotherhood or Clan na Gael. After this one declaration of support for the United Brotherhood, however, the *Irish Canadian* never explicitly endorsed either the United Brotherhood or the Fenian Brotherhood.[20] The Hibernians were now poised to capture the middle ground by identifying themselves with Isaac Butt.

By 1871 Toronto's radical nationalists had cautiously shifted their support to Isaac Butt's constitutional agitation for Home Rule.[21] Well aware that the revitalization of revolutionary nationalism would take a long time, these nationalists sought to take advantage of the patriotism stirred by the Home Rule movement in Toronto and to shape it to their own ends.[22] Irish Catholics had a sacred duty, Patrick Boyle declared, to support the Toronto Home Rule League, knowing full well that such support would redound to the radical nationalists benefit.[23] Butt's extraordinary eloquence, tact, and reasonableness, as well as his obvious reverence for parliamentary forms, gave Irish nationalism the legitimacy that Toronto's radical nationalists had long sought. Butt provided the radical nationalists, who were still under suspicion, with an excellent cover. "The lawful and legitimate attempt being made to benefit the people of Ireland," the *Irish Canadian* observed, "is well understood and duly appreciated ... in the Dominion of Canada."[24]

True to his revolutionary sympathies, Boyle nevertheless predicted that Butt's Home Rule campaign was doomed to failure. Justice could never be expected from England, he insisted, and when the impotence of constitutional agitation is finally exposed, "the Fenian doctrine ... will undoubtedly be regarded as the only true way." Meanwhile, the Hibernians' task was to nurse the grievances of the Irish people abroad and to bide their time.[25] With "*all* the 'big guns' of the Irish body" avoiding the Home Rule League's meetings, the Hibernians would show that somebody loved Ireland, "even though that love springs from the poor and humble of heart."[26] Though others may desert the cause, the Hibernians would keep the patriotic fires burning till the dawn of a new day.

Yet the radicals' declarations of sympathy for revolutionary nationalism became increasingly sporadic as the decade wore on. And the character of the radicals' sympathy for such nationalism changed as well. In the past such declarations had served to inspire hope for an imminent insurrection in Ireland; now they were occasions to honour patriots famous for the privations they had endured for the nationalist cause. When revolutionary nationalism was put in such terms, even moderate nationalists could lend their support: much as they disagreed with the methods of revolutionaries, their suffering was a standing testament to British misrule and enjoined the empathy of all patriotic Irishmen. By so capturing the middle ground, the radical nationalists ensured that they would continue to receive Archbishop Lynch's support.[27] In 1871 Lynch had unequivocally declared his support for Butt's Home Rule Movement,[28] and when a Toronto branch of the Home Rule League was founded in November 1873, the archbishop fully endorsed the move. The Irish, he insisted, have a right to Home Rule. When his country had need of his support, no Irishman should "forget the land of his birth, or that of his ancestors."[29]

By the time the radical nationalists launched the Home Rule League in 1873, there was a ready-made constituency for that movement. Although the Hibernians were slow to recover from the shock of D'Arcy McGee's assassination, two new nationalist societies, the Sons of Saint Patrick and the Young Irishmen's Catholic Benevolent Association, were founded in 1869.[30] Within one year, the Sons of Saint Patrick had organized three branches, but it was two years before the Young Irishmen launched a second society.[31] By 1876 the Young Irishmen's Catholic Benevolent Association had three city branches.[32] The Hibernians also benefited from this nationalist resurgence and by 1874 had formed two divisions.[33]

In this period Toronto's nationalist societies also forged a province-wide network. In 1873, the Toronto branches of the Young Irishmen initiated the creation of a Grand Council for the province of Ontario, which the Hibernian Benevolent Society eventually joined in 1876. As the Grand Council's responsibilities were limited to coordinating the various branches, the day-to-day business of the association was left to the local societies. When the Grand Council of the Young Irishmen's Benevolent Association voted to become affiliated with the Irish Catholic Benevolent Union of the United States (ICBU) in 1875, the Ontario Grand Council remained autonomous from the American organization, and control still resided with the individual societies. Nevertheless, the founding of the Grand Council was a telling indication of Toronto's metropolitan influence in the hinterland. Not only did Toronto's nationalists play an instrumental role in establishing the Grand Council, but their leadership helped to nurture among the members of nationalist societies in various towns across Ontario, such as those in St Thomas, Barrie, and Guelph, a shared sense of community.[34]

In 1874, a fourth nationalist society, the Emerald Benevolent Association, an American organization which had founded its first Canadian branch in Hamilton in 1872, was established in Toronto.[35] Before the end of the decade, the association had three branches in the city.[36] The various Canadian branches of the association withdrew from the American Grand Branch in 1876 to form a national federation that recognized local autonomy.[37] As in the ICBU, individual Emerald societies remained autonomous organizations responsible to their local memberships. Although Toronto's Emerald societies did not play as formative a role at the provincial level as did their counterparts in the ICBU, like the ICBU's Grand Council the Grand Branch of the Emeralds imparted to its members a communal identity that transcended geographical boundaries.

The proliferation of nationalist organizations in Toronto and the development of provincial organizational structures were accompanied by a broadening in the nationalist spectrum. Moderate nationalists, those who subscribed to the O'Connellite nationalist tradition, came to the fore, especially in the Emerald Benevolent Association. In the Young Irishmen, moderates as well as radicals held positions on the executive of the society's various branches. The emergence of moderate nationalism in Toronto's nationalist associations, together with the tempering of radical nationalism, led the nationalist societies to develop closer ties with the Catholic Church.

The new nationalist societies in Toronto were formally independent of the church, but they were also self-consciously Catholic. Only practising Catholics, those who attended Sunday Mass and performed their Easter duties, could join either the ICBU or the Emerald Benevolent Association, and the societies eagerly sought clerical approval.[38] The Young Irishmen, declared its president Bernard McMahon, sought to unite "the scattered Sons of Erin in a common brotherhood," bound by "the indissoluble tie of Faith." It was the society's truly Catholic spirit, McMahon maintained, that made it possible for Irishmen to "feel that we are indeed Brothers."[39] Similarly, the Emerald Benevolent Association, its promoters affirmed, was an "eminently practical Catholic association" devoted to "the sacred cause of Catholic unity." Membership in the association, they promised, would arouse Irishmen in the performance of their duties as members of the church.[40] To be patriotic was to be a devout Catholic.[41] Ireland's independence was "the sacred cause," but Catholicism was Ireland's "national faith": the two went together.[42]

The broad consensus forged by the nationalist fraternal organizations made it possible for Irish nationalists of all stripes to come together in the formation of the Home Rule League. Radical nationalist leaders from the Young Irishmen and the Hibernian Benevolent Society, such as Jeremiah Murphy, C.J. Murphy, and Patrick Boyle, shared the platform with moderate nationalists from the Young

Irishmen's Benevolent Association, such as William Mitchell, John Davey, and J.L. Troy, the editor of the semi-official diocesan weekly, the *Ontario Tribune*.

The forging of a nationalist consensus and the proliferation of nationalist societies resulted in a recovery of nationalist fortunes from the low point reached in the days after McGee's assassination, even though the nationalists were not to repeat the Hibernians' earlier successes at recruitment. In 1871, the combined enrolment of these nationalist societies reached 750 members, less than one-half of the Hibernian Benevolent Society's peak membership during the mid-1860s.[43] The dissolution of the Sons of Saint Patrick in 1874, however, resulted in a significant decline in the total nationalist society membership. In 1875 the Young Irishmen and Hibernians together had almost 350 members.[44] On the assumption that the Emerald Benevolent Association was equally successful in recruiting adherents, the total membership in the nationalist societies would have been 500 Irishmen, at most. Yet by 1877 the number had risen to perhaps 650.[45] During the 1870s, then, the membership of the nationalist societies reached a peak of over one-fifth of all Irish-Catholic men in 1871, although by 1877 it had declined to about one-sixth of Catholic adult males in the city.[46] Nevertheless, the segment of the male Irish-Catholic population the nationalist societies attracted was substantial, and it was among the Irish-Catholic working class that nationalists received the strongest support.

The overwhelming majority, nearly four-fifths of the officers and committeemen of the Hibernians and Young Irishmen, was from the working class. Workers in the trades comprised almost one-half of the executive members (table 15). Among those in semi-skilled occupations, almost half came from the building and printing trades, while shoemakers dominated the skilled category. The middle-class membership, a fifth of the societies' officers, was in fact somewhat less numerous than it would first appear. Three of the five clerical members were bartenders and the two professionals were students-at-law who did not retain their affiliation with the nationalist movement after entering into legal practice. The majority of the businessmen of the executive were small shopkeepers, mostly grocers, with tavern owners a distant second at three members. The almost complete absence of professionals and clerks in the Young Irishmen and the Hibernian associations, together with the low numbers of Irish-Catholic businessmen, meant that the nationalist

Table 15
Executive Members of the Hibernian Benevolent
Society and the Irish Catholic Benevolent Union,
1869–79

Category	Number	Percentage
Unskilled	32	32
Semi-skilled	30	30
Skilled	17	17
Clerical	5	5
Business	14	14
Professional	2	2

Source: Irish Canadian and city directories.

societies were led by Irish-Catholic workers for Irish-Catholic
workers.

Like the parish associations, nationalist societies forged a particular way of life, but unlike church groups they offered lay autonomy and working-class independence from the clergy as well as from the middle class. As part of their effort to create an inclusive way of life independent of the clergy, the nationalist societies began to offer a much wider range of wholesome and uplifting recreation than the Hibernian Benevolent Society had in the 1860s. In order to create a full associational life, individual branches of the nationalist societies collaborated in establishing permanent meeting-halls. In these halls, members could visit reading-rooms stocked with nationalist newspapers and Toronto dailies or participate in the weekly meetings of the dramatic groups, literary and debating clubs, and marching bands as well as the inevitable quadrille class.[47] In addition to the formal activities sponsored by the nationalist societies, these meeting-halls enabled Irish-Catholic men to socialize with one another informally, and it was not unusual for members to fraternize three, perhaps four, times a week.[48]

Besides offering conviviality and a rich social life independent of the church, nationalist societies provided attractive tangible benefits for working men. In the Young Irishmen, sick members received three dollars a week and in the case of death fifty dollars was paid to the family – twenty-five dollars for the funeral and twenty-five dollars towards the support of dependants – all for a two-dollar initiation fee and ten cents in dues a week.[49] Joining a nationalist society was a pragmatic decision, but it was much more than that. By providing these benefits a society helped a working man fulfil his role as provider and thereby increased his self-respect. Furthermore, a proper funeral, as much a social event as it was a religious rite, was an affirmation of social status.[50] A decent funeral demonstrated to all that a man had left his family well enough provided for that they could afford to perform the last rites properly. Thus the benefits of the nationalist societies were an assertion of respectability, independence, and moral worth. The last was an important issue in the nationalist societies. As the members of the Emerald Benevolent Association declared, the nationalist societies were devoted to the principles of "charity and brotherly love."[51] By charity they understood the help of peers rather than handouts from outsiders. Nationalist society members could avoid being dependent on charity of the latter kind. The benefits they received from their organizations were a form of working-class mutuality, an expression of ethnic solidarity, and an assertion of independence from those who would claim to be their social superiors.

Irish nationalists also continued to demand recognition for the Irish Catholics of Toronto, and one way that they did so was to take over the city's streets for parades and processions. With a renewed confidence and a rediscovered aggressiveness, the Irish nationalist societies, the Young Irishmen in particular, took to the streets to challenge the British and Protestant nature of Toronto's social order. This departure from the Hibernians' custom of parading only on Saint Patrick's Day was a challenge that met with a predictable response. Between 1870 and 1879, the Green and their Orange antagonists, the Young Britons, participated in some eighteen major street fights and riots.[52] Over two-thirds of the incidents between the Orange and the Green were prompted by parades, especially those held on Saint Patrick's Day or the Orange celebration of the Twelfth of July.

Marches were not simply recreational outings, though they were that too, but also demonstrations of territorial control. In Toronto this rarely took the form of a challenge to a neighbourhood.[53] Irish-Catholic parades were held on the major streets of the city. By marching in the business and commercial area, Irish Catholics were laying claim to the city, asserting that the city belonged as much to them as to anyone else. The unfurling of the green flag by the nationalist societies was a ritualized demand for recognition and an affirmation of ethnic solidarity in a predominantly Protestant city.

The role of Irish-Catholic demonstrations in sparking violence on Toronto's streets was especially apparent in the case of the city's two largest riots in the nineteenth century, the Jubilee riots of 1875 and the attack on Saint Patrick's Hall in March 1878 when O'Donovan Rossa came to Toronto.[54]

Pilgrimages to local churches in Toronto were held over the summer of 1875 to mark the jubilee proclaimed by Pope Pius IX. When unusually hot weather settled over the city, further pilgrimages were postponed until the fall. By then, however, the political and religious climate had heated up considerably. The burial of one Joseph Guibord, a *Rouge* excommunicated by Bishop Ignace Bourget, in early September had resulted in a riot at Montreal's Côte-des-Neiges cemetery when a crowd barred the cemetery gates. The sight of a large and unruly crowd of Catholics blocking a burial ordered by the courts of the land and upheld by the Privy Council produced intense indignation among many of Toronto's Protestants. Accusations of rule by Rome filled the air. Was the Catholic church, many wondered, to reign supreme over the state and render its writ null?[55]

The announcement that the opening of the first provincial council of bishops on the last Sunday of September was to be celebrated by an ecclesiastical procession was greeted by a storm of protest. The presence of "Bishops," "Priests," "Copes," "Dalmatics," "Full Pontificals," "Thurifers," the petitioners claimed, was "likely to lead to serious breaches of the public peace."[56] Archbishop Lynch refused the mayor's request that he cancel the procession opening the provincial council, which in any event passed off without incident. That afternoon over a thousand pilgrims, many of them women, resumed Jubilee pilgrimages that had been suspended over the summer, accompanied by an unusually large crowd of unfriendly spectators who regaled the pilgrims with shouts of "to h-ll with the Pope." When the pilgrims attempted to return to the cathedral a few hours later, the crowd, by then ready for trouble, placed the procession under constant siege, and a few shots were fired, fortunately without injury.[57]

The second Jubilee riot on the following Sunday, 3 October, was to be a much more violent affair. That day, a procession of over 1,500 men, accompanied by women and children on the sidewalks, made its way under police protection. As the procession left Saint Michael's Cathedral, it was briefly pelted with stones, but it was only when the pilgrims reached Queen Street that a riot finally broke out. The procession was greeted by a hail of stones, and when the attackers fired their guns into the procession, a few pilgrims fired back at the hostile crowd. Once the procession reached Adelaide Street and headed west towards Saint Mary's church, it came under almost constant attack, and gun-fire broke out on at least four occasions. At

Saint Mary's, the police managed to separate the pilgrims from their opponents, and the procession made its escape back to Saint Paul's church. The protestors, thinking that the pilgrimage was to proceed to Saint Patrick's church, rushed north, only to discover that their quarry had slipped away. The crowd then turned upon Owen Cosgrove's tavern, the Orangemen's favorite target. It was well after dark when the crowd finally tired of pelting Cosgrove's establishment and the mob dispersed.[58] The second Jubilee riot was the worst riot in the history of the city. More than eight thousand people participated in the affray, and the fighting took over whole neighbourhoods of the city for several hours. Though a few were seriously injured, there were, surprisingly, no deaths.

The second most violent riot of the decade erupted when the head centre of the Fenian Brotherhood, Jeremiah O'Donovan Rossa, visited Toronto at the invitation of the ICBU in 1878. Rossa's reputation as a cold-blooded terrorist who advocated dynamiting British targets preceded him. For many Torontonians, Rossa's presence in the city was itself a blatant attack on the cherished institutions of Canadian society. "It is not fair that Canada should be made the stamping ground on which these men may boast of their dastardly designs," declared the *Telegram*, referring to Rossa's Skirmishing Fund.[59] "Canada is as loyal as any country in the British Empire and Toronto as any city in the Dominion," wrote one correspondent to the *Mail*, "yet Fenians like Luby and Rossa are allowed to come here and deliver treasonable lectures with scarcely a protest." "How long," he asked, are we going "to allow this sort of thing?"[60] Saint Patrick's Day parades were one thing, O'Donovan Rossa advocating his plans for a no-holds-barred wave of terrorism against the British empire quite another. A loyalist crowd attempted to prevent Rossa's addressing the ICBU. When they failed in this, the crowd stoned the windows of Saint Patrick's Hall and then rushed up Jarvis Street to Queen Street, firing shots and smashing store windows as they went. Finally, the protestors visited Cosgrove's – no riot would be complete with recognizing this Irish establishment – and stoned the tavern.[61]

Knowing that violence was imminent, why did Irish Catholics march in the Young Irishmen's parades, participate in the Jubilee pilgrimages, and invite O'Donovan Rossa to Toronto? The letters Archbishop Lynch received after the Jubilee provide an invaluable glimpse into Irish-Catholic attitudes. T.P. French, a post office inspector, praised "the brave & noble stand" taken by Irish Catholics against "Toronto ruffianism." Irish Catholics, he affirmed, would neither be "cajoled or bullied into the surrender of one tittle of our rights as Citizens or as Catholics."[62] For many Irish Catholics, to stand up for their religion and nationality was a matter of pride. As one F.H. Hyland, whose jaw had been broken by a brick during the Jubilee riots, defiantly declared, "I have had the honor to be wounded severely."[63] The Jubilee riots and the riots involving the Young Irishmen and the Young Britons illustrate that Irish Catholics were determined to assert their ethnicity on the streets of Toronto. Their public demonstrations, as in the Jubilee processions or in the Young Irishmen parades, were deliberately provocative – a challenge to Toronto's Protestant majority to recognize Irish Catholics as a charter group of Canadian society whose nationality and religion had a purchase upon the public space of the city. But why Irish Catholics, moderate and radical nationalists alike, would court Protestant condemnation by inviting the likes of Rossa to Toronto can be understood only when the twin streams of moderate and radical nationalism are examined in greater depth.

The most visible division among Irish-Catholic nationalists in Toronto was that between those who sympathized with the use of physical force to obtain Irish independence and those who supported constitutional means exclusively. This distinction, however, concealed a far more fundamental division between radical and moderate nationalists. At the heart of each form of nationalism was a discrete interpretation of Irish-Catholic ethnicity. In both cases, religion and nationality were fundamental to Irish-Catholic ethnicity, but the emphasis of each was different. Radical nationalists emphasized ethnicity organized along national lines. By contrast, moderate nationalists saw nationalism as a means of instilling loyalty to the Catholic Church and emphasized ethnicity organized along religious lines. The two major expressions of Irish nationalism offered very different conceptions of Irish-Catholic ethnicity. In turn, the ways in which radical and moderate nationalists envisioned ethnicity was to shape their understanding of the place and scope of lay initiative in the Irish-Catholic community.

After the demise of the *Canadian Freeman* in 1873, the promotion of moderate nationalism was taken up by the *Ontario Tribune*, which after 1875 was edited by J.L. Troy, a leading member of the Young Irishmen and grand president of the ICBU in 1877.[64] As editor of the *Tribune*, the semi-official weekly of the Roman Catholic Archdiocese of Toronto, and as a long-time activist in the nationalist movement, Troy was one of the most influential lay advocates of moderate nationalism. Troy viewed nationalism primarily in religious terms. Only a devout Catholic could be truly Irish. Far from advocating national assimilation, Troy, like other moderates, viewed Irish nationalism as a means of preserving Catholic particularism. Nationalism was a bulwark of the faith: by strengthening Irish-Catholic solidarity and instilling a religious identity it would inhibit national assimilation and, in its train, apostasy.[65] Like the radical nationalists, Troy advocated a form of ethnicity in which Irish-Catholic social life was to be distinct and separate from that of the Protestant majority. But, while both moderate and radical nationalists sought to create an enclosed subculture, they differed as to what would form the best bulwark for the preservation of their community.

The religious cast of Troy's nationalism shaped not only his understanding of Irish-Catholic ethnicity but also his vision of Canadian society. The nationality of Canada ought not to be British, but rather a new nationality that recognized the diversity of Canada's communal groups and protected the religious integrity of each group. Troy supported Home Rule for Ireland because it would legitimatize Catholic claims for publicly funded communal institutions. Just as the Irish in Ireland were entitled to their own national institutions, so too were the Irish in Canada entitled to their own social institutions, such as separate schools and the like. Moderate nationalism, like its radical counterpart, advocated the collective rights of Irish Catholics. Yet the difference between the two forms of nationalism was nevertheless a critical one. Moderate nationalists hoped to secure those collective rights that pertained to the Irish as Catholics, and to this end they sought public funding for Catholic institutions.[66] They advocated a form of ethnic separatism that was primarily based on religion.

The moderate nationalists' conception of ethnicity had direct implications for the scope of clerical leadership and the place of lay initiative in the Irish-Catholic community. In this vision of Irish-Catholic ethnicity, the clergy were by virtue of their sacerdotal office the natural guardians of Catholic particularism. They and they alone could determine what was authentically Catholic, and hence they were the spiritual as well as the social leaders of the Irish-Catholic community. Lay initiative had its place, the moderate nationalists insisted, as did associations that were formally independent of the church and under the direction of the laity. Such organizations were necessary to strengthen lay commitment to the church and to sustain ethnic identity. Whether under the official structures of the church or not, however, the purpose of lay initiative was to assist the clergy and was therefore subject to their veto.[67]

The radical nationalists, on the other hand, emphasized national particularism. Not only did radical nationalists promote national particularism, but they also denounced moderate nationalism as an attempt to stamp out the Irish nationality, to rob the Irish people of their collective soul.[68] In their view, moderation in defence of one's nationality was no virtue, and only those who lacked self-respect could believe that it was. As Jeremiah Murphy declared in his characteristic manner, true Irish Catholics were "a people who cannot be shoved back."[69] For the radicals, religion was an important, perhaps even a necessary, element of their national particularism, but it could not furnish a sufficient basis for Irish-Catholic ethnicity.

The radical nationalists' conception of ethnicity also had implications for their vision of Canada. The Protestants of Canada, these nationalists argued, had sought to impose a quasi nationality on Canada. Because Britain had refused to recognize Ireland as a separate nation, Patrick Flanagan of the ICBU asserted, the British connection now served to deny the Irish their legitimate place as a founding people in Canada.[70] According to the radical nationalists, a single, homogeneous Canadian nationality simply did not exist.[71] Ethnicity along national lines was the social reality of Canada. It was this social diversity, the radical nationalists argued, that was denied by Protestant Canada's fetish for things British. Recognition for Irish-Catholics was therefore not to be gained by insisting on Catholic rights but rather by affirming Irish exclusivism.

The conflict between those in the ICBU who defined ethnicity primarily on religious grounds, the moderates, and those who defined it primarily on national grounds, the radicals, came to a head in fall of 1877. At the ICBU annual convention that year moderate nationalists defeated Patrick Boyle's ally Patrick Flanagan in his bid to remain grand president of the union, and they also captured key positions on the national executive. Encouraged by this electoral sweep, the new grand president, J.L. Troy, set out to change the purpose of the ICBU. Troy's plan was both simple and effective. The affiliation of the Young Irishmen with the ICBU of the United States had resulted in the appointment of a committee, dominated by Troy and his supporters, to revise the association's constitution. Hoping to circumvent the annual convention, Troy directed the committee to rewrite the sections of the ICBU's charter relating to Irish nationalism so that the organization would become a lay Catholic fraternal society, although it still would retain its independence from the church.

With Boyle's collaboration, Flanagan and the radical nationalists counter-attacked in a well-orchestrated and vigorous protest in Boyle's *Irish Canadian*. After suffering much personal abuse, Troy and his supporters were forced to back down. Troy realized that any further attempt to modify the ICBU's charter was futile. Most of the membership, even among the moderate nationalists, were not prepared to abandon their commitment to Ireland's national cause. At the annual convention in August 1878, Troy conceded defeat and declined the nomination for a second term as grand president.[72]

Troy's defeat in the ICBU helps to explain why radical nationalists invited well-known Irish revolutionaries to Toronto and why Irish Catholics did not oppose these invitations openly. As the Home Rule movement languished under Butt's indecisive leadership, many nationalists feared that nationalism might become irrelevant to the Irish Catholics of Toronto. At the same time, many Irish Catholics, moderate nationalists included, were ambivalent about Confederation and the new Canadian nationality. For many, the rise of the new Canadian nationality posed an assimilationist threat to Irish Catholics.[73] The presence of Irish revolutionaries such as Thomas F. Bourke (a leader in the 1867 uprising in Ireland), Thomas Clarke Luby (a veteran of the 1849 uprising and a well-known Fenian organizer), and Jeremiah O'Donovan Rossa assured Irish Catholics that the national struggle was indeed alive and gave them the vicarious experience of participating in Ireland's national destiny. In the struggle for the hearts and souls of Irish Catholics, the presence of well-known Irish firebrands was an affirmation that "we *are* yet Irish."[74] After Troy's debacle in the ICBU, moderate nationalists could scarcely dissent publicly from such sentiments. In fact, the moderates were all the more anxious to prove that they were far from lukewarm in their patriotism: when Rossa delivered his blistering harangue, Troy shared the podium with Patrick Boyle and his radical allies.[75]

A nationalist consensus did exist among moderate and radical nationalists, even though they disagreed as to the relative importance of nationalism and Catholicism. This consensus was possible because both moderate and radical nationalists advocated a form of ethnic separatism that was based on the fusion of nationalism and religion. Yet, if moderate and radical nationalists could agree on the necessity of ethnic separatism, they still disagreed fundamentally on the question of ethnic leadership: who could speak for the Irish-Catholic community, the clergy or the laity, and on what issues?

In their fight for Home Rule, radical nationalists in Toronto continually stressed the right of national self-rule and the sovereignty of the people. In this form of ethnicity, leadership and authority was democratic, populist, and lay. While the clergy were accepted as spiritual guides, the laity could still claim that nationalism was a lay responsibility.[76] Because ethnicity was defined largely on the basis of national particularity, radical nationalists contended that the laity had a prescriptive right to represent "the public interests of the Irish race in Canada." Authority flowed from the bottom up, that is, from the lay grass roots, rather than from the top down. If the clergy were to impose their views and to act without the consent of the laity in matters other than faith and morals, Patrick Boyle declared in his usual blunt manner, it would be a "presumptuous tampering with their personal rights, their individual independence, their political conscience."[77]

The radical nationalists' appeal to popular sovereignty and their ability to generate support from the grass roots enabled them to rival the clergy as leaders in the Irish-Catholic community. In making their bid for lay leadership, radical nationalists could usually rely on their more moderate confrères for support. The partnership between the radicals and moderates was an unequal one. The invitations to well-known Irish revolutionary nationalists, the preponderance of local radical nationalists on the platform at nationalist events, and the radicals' ability to control the direction of the ICBU on a fundamental matter of policy, all testified to the radicals' domination of the nationalist movement in Toronto. Unity in nationalist circles on issues that were potentially divisive lent credence to the radical nationalists' claim to represent the people and to express their communal aspirations and values.

The radical nationalists' populism together with their push for lay leadership that was independent of the clergy alarmed Archbishop Lynch. "We cannot conceive of a body of Irish Catholics," Archbishop Lynch declared, "to be anything else than men influenced by Irish & Catholic principles, the first of which is to be closely united and amenable to the authority of the Catholic church." In Lynch's view authority was hierarchical in nature, and leadership flowed from the clergy, by virtue of their sacerdotal rank and status, down to the laity. On both nationalist and religious grounds, Lynch insisted, Irish nationalist societies "must recognize it [the church] as their mother and Mistress" and so accept the direction of the parochial clergy in their internal affairs.

Lynch professed to be pleased that the Hibernians and the Young Irishmen had submitted their by-laws for ecclesiastical approval and had agreed to have chaplains appointed, but he saw clearly that these societies could not be controlled by the clergy.[78] Lynch was especially disturbed by the presence of radical nationalism in Toronto. He castigated its leading proponent, Patrick Boyle, for "causing dissentions [sic] and distrust amongst the Catholics of this Province by stirring up national prejudices."[79] The criticism of lay autonomy and national particularism as related threats to the church, which may seem odd coming from such a well-known and ardent nationalist as Archbishop Lynch, rested on the fact that the nationalist organizations were autonomous lay societies. If on occasion their leaders acceded to Lynch's wishes, they usually acted independently of the church. Although all the nationalist societies had chaplains appointed by the archbishop by 1873, there is no indication that these chaplains attended the societies' monthly meetings or, with the exception of the odd excursion, participated in other society activities. The chaplains' supervision of the nationalist societies was more formal than real, and the societies conducted themselves much as they had done previously. These societies, then, were associations run by the laity for the laity.

In secular and national questions the nationalist leaders expected the clergy to support automatically the decisions independently arrived at by the lay societies. This lay autonomy was also reflected in the commemoration of national festivals. The O'Connell centenary celebration in 1875, for example, was organized by the nationalist societies, and Archbishop Lynch was present as a guest only.[80] After 1877, rather than attending a church-sponsored charity concert on Saint Patrick's Day, the nationalists began holding their own lectures and concerts.[81] In 1878, the annual Saint Patrick's Day parade and salute to the clergy was discontinued.[82] The nationalist societies still attended the special Saint Patrick's Day Mass as a group, but these developments were unmistakable assertions of lay autonomy.

As Lynch's comments on the nationalist societies illustrated, lay independence was often confused with infidelity. That nothing could have been farther from the intentions of the radical nationalists was demonstrated by the close association of the nationalist societies with their church and their requirement that all members be practising Catholics. Yet so great was the clergy's zeal to establish their authority over the laity and to direct lay social life that they failed to understand that lay nationalists shared many of the same fundamental ideals as their priests. Temperance societies represented the clergy's most notable effort to incorporate male social life into the parish. With its emphasis on sobriety, patriotism, and piety, temperance was a natural way for the clergy to place lay social life under the auspices and supervision of the church. Nevertheless, even at its peak the temperance crusade scarcely put a damper on the nationalist societies' influence, and in any event the crusade proved to be a short-lived one.[83]

The founding of the Catholic Young Men's Association (CYMA) in November 1875 by Archbishop Lynch was yet another attempt by the clergy to create an associational life for men under the auspices of the church. Like the nationalist societies, this association promoted "mental and moral improvement," but unlike the nationalist organizations the CYMA was led by the clergy in their capacity as chaplains and officers of the association. The CYMA never fulfilled the hopes of the clergy, however, and it remained a predominantly middle-class organization with limited influence in the Irish-Catholic community.[84]

Although the clergy were unable to forge an associational life for men that offered a viable alternative to the nationalist societies, they still had the power of the pulpit. One of the clergy's most notable efforts to bolster their own leadership was their annual Saint Patrick's Day sermons, and here their vision of the religious destiny of the Irish people reached messianic proportions. In these sermons, the clergy explained how the Irish were a missionary people, a new children of Israel.[85] The conquest of Ireland, so the reasoning went, was providential. Because the Irish had been forced to learn English, they were now prepared "to convert their English masters, to spread the Faith in English colonies, and to gain the new world of America to the true faith." In promoting this religious form of Irish nationalism, the clergy were claiming that nationalism, far from being a purely lay affair, was above all a vital religious issue that came under the church's authority. Religion and nationalism went together, and the nature and extent of lay leadership in these, as in all other questions, were for the clergy to determine.

The clergy's fears of lay independence were most certainly exaggerated, and their efforts to reduce lay influence were largely ineffective. Radical nationalists were able to appropriate the clergy's nationalist vision, and to do so on their own terms. Perhaps the most notable lay proponent of Catholic messianism was Jeremiah Murphy, a radical nationalist perennial who, like Patrick Boyle, was a member of the Father Mathew Temperance Association. He, too, saw Irish Catholics as a missionary people of God destined to convert North America, but this belief in no way lessened his commitment to advanced nationalism or to the autonomy of lay leadership in nationalist matters.[86] For him, and for many other radical nationalists, militant nationalism and Catholicism were of a piece. While the nationalist societies fostered an identity that was self-consciously Catholic, they did so under lay auspices. By establishing a network of fraternal organizations, the nationalist societies established a social and cultural life that was largely outside the institutional framework of the church and its lines of authority. This selective appropriation of Catholicism enabled Irish-Catholic laymen to advance a form of

ethnicity that placed a premium on lay leadership and relegated the
clergy to a subordinate and essentially supportive role. Like two
ends of see-saw, the radical nationalists and the clergy were rarely in
equilibrium, and each hoped to gain the advantage.

As both church and nation could claim laymen's allegiances and
loyalty, under normal circumstances neither the clergy nor the radical nationalists could unilaterally impose their viewpoint on each
other or the Irish-Catholic community as a whole. Both the clergy
and the radical nationalists were therefore free to stake out their
claims and exercise leadership. While both the radical nationalists
and the clergy aspired to hegemony in the Irish-Catholic community, in practice both sought the support of the other in order to establish their respective religious and nationalist credentials. Such an
entente with the nationalist organizations was essential if the Roman
Catholic Church was to turn Irish-Catholic men into church-goers
and eventually become an inclusive institution in the Irish-Catholic
community that transcended both class and gender.[87] The drive by
the church and the radical nationalists to mobilize popular support
in Toronto led to the development of a form of ethnicity that was
based on a broad-based consensus among clergy and laity in which
nationalism and religion were integral to Irish-Catholic particularity. Whatever official reservations the clergy may have had, they
nonetheless entered into an alliance with the nationalist leadership
and so legitimized these men's claim that lay initiative had a proper
place in the public life of the Irish-Catholic community. This process
of negotiation and accommodation between the clergy and the nationalist leaders meant that the boundaries for independent lay initiative remained in flux, but one conflict – that between the clergy
and some of lay representatives on the Separate School Board – did
reveal the limits to lay initiative in terms both of its scope and of its
ability to garner popular support.

The conflict between some of the lay trustees and the clergy on the
Toronto Separate School Board in the late 1870s, it has been suggested, was a struggle between anti-clericals and the clergy.[88] The
clergy had little doubt that such was the case, but then the clergy frequently distrusted any form of lay initiative that did not in their view
adequately recognize their prerogatives. Once the issue of lay control of the school board was raised it was certain to be a contentious
one, for the school board occupied an important if ambiguous position in the Irish-Catholic community.

Like the public school system as a whole, the development of a separate schools system in which free schools were supported exclusively through public revenues resulted in the rise of central bureaucratic control and direction at the expense of local authorities and trustees.[89] While for public schools the educational bureaucracy was synonymous with the department of education, in the case of the separate schools much of this role was usually assumed by the ecclesiatical authorities, who in true ultramontane fashion insisted on the church's superiority over the state in educational matters. The Separate School Board was a public institution in which the laity had a role on the local level as parents, taxpayers, and school trustees, and at the same time a religious institution that was tied to the Catholic Church's structures of authority.

In early December 1877, six dissident trustees led by Remigius Elmsley, the son of John Elmsley, the church's greatest benefactor until his death in 1863, demanded that the property on Richmond Street, held in trust by the Roman Catholic Episcopal Corporation for the education of Catholic children, be turned over to the Toronto Separate School Board.[90] At the next meeting of the board, the dissidents made other demands. In addition to calling for a full account of the board's finances for the past decade, they insisted that the religious teachers should prove their competence to teach by obtaining provincial certificates.[91] Without teaching certificates, asked trustee J.E. Robertson, "what guarantees had they that their teachers were qualified?" George Evans immediately pressed the point home by reminding the board that, when the separate schools were inspected in 1876, it was revealed that some teachers were unable to spell even the name "Henry" correctly. Evans's comments drew such acrimonious denials from the parish clergy on the board that the meeting ended in chaos.[92]

The rancour generated by Elmsley's and Robertson's demands marred the Separate School Board election held in January 1878. The elections that year were so divisive that in five wards two sets of trustees were returned as each side in the controversy organized a separate poll. In response, Archbishop Lynch, as local superintendent, voided the polls organized by the dissident trustees.[93] The five remaining dissident trustees on the board quickly retaliated and moved that the archbishop be replaced as local superintendent. George Evans proclaimed that the issue was one of lay rights: "When the clergy placed themselves in the way of the educational progress of the children," he declared, the laity had "a right to protest against it."[94]

The conflict between the clergy and the opposition trustees was to become even more heated. In late March 1878, four trustees submitted their resignations in protest against Archbishop's Lynch's refusal to hand over the title of the Richmond Street property to the board.[95] When the by-election was finally called in May, the intervention of Patrick Boyle's *Irish Canadian* ensured that the central issue of the campaign was one of lay rights. While yielding "to no man in reverence for the Hierarchy and Priesthood of his church," Patrick Boyle insisted that the clergy were neither more nor less than citizens when they sat on the Separate School Board. "Is it to be said," he asked, "that we, another citizen, shall therefore have no voice in ... the expenditure of, and accounting for, money paid out of our pocket under the law of the land?" The election issue was obvious to Boyle: it was a question of the laity's rights as ratepayers, as parents, and as independent citizens.[96]

The clergy could not ignore such a challenge, and they set to work busily canvassing the Separate School Board electors.[97] The tone of the clergy's campaign, which unfortunately was not reported in the daily press, is perhaps best demonstrated by a letter to Patrick Boyle from Father J.J. McCann, Archbishop Lynch's secretary. The distinction between the clergy's sacerdotal office and their duties as trustees was dismissed by McCann as a wilful attack on clerical authority. "I am instructed to say," McCann informed Boyle, "that His Grace who is a competent Judge in this matter does not wish to accept the statement that you are at least at present an obedient son of the church."[98] In Lynch's juridical notion of the church, the education of Catholic children was to be directed by the clergy, whose counsels in such matters the laity were obliged to obey. It was on this basis that the clergy conducted their vigorous campaign against the dissident trustees. At the public poll performed in the presence of the parish priests, as was the custom in Separate School Board elections, only two of the four dissident trustees were returned by the electors.[99]

The three remaining opposition trustees on the board, though hopelessly outnumbered, still managed to keep the clergy and their lay supporters on the defensive. Besides demanding a detailed report of the board's accounts, they also insisted that separate schoolteachers improve their qualifications.[100] In response, Lynch denounced the dissidents as "Judases" seeking to betray the church.[101] Rather than excommunicating the dissidents, as he threatened to do, Lynch eventually adopted a more conciliatory approach. In early August 1878, the archbishop called a public meeting to explain the Roman Catholic Episcopal Corporation's financial contribution to the Toronto Separate School Board. To the satisfaction of all but two of the Catholics attending the meeting, Lynch explained that the board owed the corporation over three thousand dollars.[102] When the special committee to investigate the boards's accounts tabled its report in the middle of October, the archbishop's claim was vindicated. The board, the committee discovered, owed Archbishop Lynch almost twenty-eight hundred dollars, a finding that was accepted without demur by the trustees.[103]

But the resolution of the board's financial dealings with the Episcopal Corporation did not mark the end of the controversy. The annual school board election in January 1879 followed the same pattern set in 1878. Again, both camps held their own separate polls; and again, Lynch voided the dissidents' polls. Yet this time Lynch dealt the opposition trustees a resounding defeat by insisting that they not appeal his verdict through the civil courts, a decision that the archbishop reinforced with the threat of excommunication.[104] After crushing the dissidents, Lynch felt that he could concede on the original issue that had sparked the conflict without strengthening the dissidents' hand. In June 1879 he finally acceded to the board's request that the Richmond Street property be devoted solely to primary education and made subject to the board's control.[105] With the opposition trustees eliminated and the Richmond Street property transferred to the board, peace was restored.

The question of the Richmond Street property was a controversial one because it came to symbolize control over the separate schools in Toronto. The clergy and their supporters believed that education was a religious affair. The dissident trustees, Archbishop Lynch observed, seemed to think that they could do as they please without regard for the clergy's authority. "They forgot," the archbishop maintained, "that their duty was first to God and His Church." Catholic schools were part of the church's magisterium and therefore those "who attacked the schools also assaulted the church."[106] In this interpretation, the board was simply an adjunct of the church. Lay trustees were on the board to assist the clergy and were therefore bound to obey and carry out the directives of the clergy. In affirming their right to direct the intellectual as well as religious development of Catholic children, the clergy were asserting that leadership in the Irish-Catholic community belonged to them alone.

At no time did the dissident trustees and their supporters question the clergy's responsibility for the religious formation of Catholic children. They did, however, question the clergy's view of the role of laity on the Separate School Board. In part, their demand for lay control was a result of Catholic exclusion from local politics.[107] The

Separate School Board was the only political institution open to Irish Catholics. Far more important, however, was the rising confidence of the laity, especially the middle class. All the dissident trustees save one were from the middle class. The Separate School Board conflict signalled a new militancy for lay rights among this class, a cause that until then had been associated with the largely working-class constituency of the Irish nationalist societies. Appealing to the idea of popular sovereignty, the dissident trustees viewed education as a public matter of concern to all Catholic ratepayers. In keeping with this ideal, they believed that the school board ought to be controlled by the laity rather than, as had previously been case, by the clergy. The dissident trustees called for the laicizing of Catholic education, not, as some have supposed, its secularization.

The dissident trustees' demands for lay control over the school board also had implications for the clergy's role as ethnic leaders. Like the clergy, the dissident trustees saw separate schools as a means of maintaining Irish Catholics as a distinct people.[108] That the clergy had a role as ethnic leaders, few would deny. What was at issue was the nature and extent of that role. With their egalitarian and democratic concept of representation, the dissident trustees insisted that the clergy ought not to claim that they alone had the authority to decide matters of community-wide significance. In such matters, the dissident trustees contended, the consent of the laity was necessary, and to ensure that this consent was free and unfettered the clergy ought to respect the independence and integrity of the laity's representatives.

Once the clergy turned the 1879 School Board Election into a test of loyalty to the church, the dissident trustees were doomed to defeat, despite strong support for lay control. These trustees recognized that Catholicism was integral to Irish-Catholic ethnicity, and, in the face of the clergy's successful campaign to transform the bid for lay control into a religious question, they chose to submit rather than risk an irreparable break with the Catholic Church. Unlike the controversy that was to overtake the board in the 1880s, the trustees did not rely on Irish nationalism to legitimize their position and so polarize the Irish-Catholic community. Yet their position was not permanently abandoned. In February of 1879, some 140 Catholic householders signed a petition for the introduction of the secret ballot. This petition represented the ultimate demand for lay autonomy and control, a demand that was to divide Irish Catholics in 1887.[109] The check delivered to the dissident trustees during the winter of 1879 was a temporary one, and, rather than marking the end of demands for lay control in the schools, it represented a new point of departure.

When the separate school controversy came to an end, the issue of lay control was still unresolved and it would preoccupy Irish Catholics throughout the 1880s as the clergy and the lay nationalists vied for influence and position. In that decade as well, two other issues challenged the lay nationalists. Irish nationalism had secured popular support among Irish-Catholic men, but it nevertheless remained a working-class movement. Middle-class Catholics, especially professionals and successful businessmen, for the most part still shunned nationalism. In addition, the nationalists had to confront the implications of national exclusivism for sustaining ethnicity among an Irish-Catholic population that was becoming increasingly acculturated to Canadian society. As the Canadian-born generation came of age and as Irish Catholics developed, through work and friendship, ties outside the Irish-Catholic community, such an exclusive national identity lost its appeal for many. Upon what basis could Irish nationalism make its appeal? Could Irish nationalists continue to remain aloof from the larger social movements around them? In response to these questions Irish nationalists were to arrive at a different understanding of Irish-Catholic ethnicity and its relationship to Canadian society. Their new vision was to appeal to the middle class, but it was also to have profound consequences both for Catholic voluntary associations that were independent of the church and for the lay initiative that these associations represented.

10 New Departures

During the 1880s and the 1890s Toronto's Irish-Catholic population underwent a significant generational change. From being primarily a first-generation, immigrant population, the Irish-Catholic community became one in which the Canadian-born predominated.[1] As one might expect, this demographic development was accompanied by a shift from a militant form of ethnicity to a more conciliatory version in which Catholicism eventually displaced nationalism as the badge of ethnic allegiance. That change in Irish-Catholic self-definition, in turn, went hand in hand with a dramatic reorganization of associational life that saw the independent nationalist societies being eclipsed by church-affiliated associations for men. Such an outcome could hardly have been foreseen by contemporaries. In the early 1880s Irish nationalism enjoyed a resurgence in Toronto, as it did the world over, under the leadership and inspiration of Charles Stewart Parnell. Moreover, given Parnell's early reputation for extremism, many would have been surprised that a spirit of accommodation would so soon come to the fore in Toronto's nationalist circles.

By the end of 1875, physical-force nationalists in both Ireland and Britain were becoming disillusioned with the conciliatory ways of Isaac Butt, the leader of the Irish parliamentary party. Butt's lackadaisical efforts to introduce Home Rule and Irish land legislation deeply disturbed the revolutionary nationalists.[2] Charles Stewart

Parnell, a Protestant landlord from County Wicklow who was first elected to the House of Commons in 1874, soon replaced Butt in the Fenians' estimation.[3] While essentially conservative in his demand for Irish Home Rule, Parnell managed when it suited his purposes to convey the illusion of dangerous and exciting extremism.[4] His carefully designed strategy set the stage for "new departures" from Fenian orthodoxy.[5]

In October 1879, John Devoy of the Clan na Gael committed American revolutionary nationalists to a policy of collaboration with Parnell.[6] This departure laid the foundations for another, which was the bringing together of revolutionary and constitutional nationalists in a mass movement that would establish Parnell as the uncontested leader of the Irish people.[7] In the spring of 1879, after two bad harvests and a continuing decline in grain prices (the result of American grain imports), the prospect of yet another miserable harvest led to an outbreak of agrarian protest against what were now certain to be ruinous rents.[8] The formation of the Irish National Land League in October 1879 marked the beginning of a period in which American and Irish Fenians supported unconditionally a popular agrarian movement under Parnell's direction.[9] The Land League gave Parnell a grass-roots organization which, by riding the wave of popular enthusiasm engendered by the land agitation, would enable him to capture the leadership of the Irish parliamentary party in May 1880, exactly one year after Butt's death.[10]

Unlike the American Clan na Gael, radical nationalists in Toronto were slow to welcome Parnell's ascendancy.[11] When Butt died in early May 1879, the *Irish Canadian* mourned the passing of the only man it believed who could legitimately claim to express the national will of Ireland.[12] What changed the *Irish Canadian*'s opinion of Parnell was his involvement during the summer of 1879 in the agrarian agitation in County Mayo. For years Toronto's Irish nationalists had seared the image of the Great Famine into popular consciousness. The Irish Catholics of Toronto could thus easily identify themselves with the struggle against "a vicious system of property right" that had turned the Irish "upon the world to starve."[13] Parnell's resistance to "tyrannical injustice," the *Irish Canadian* observed with new-found sympathy for the man it had once denounced as a malcontent, "has already done much to restore popular faith in Home Rule."[14]

The clergy, however, were not among those who had faith in Parnell or his Land League. Archbishop Lynch had privately attempted to dissuade Parnell from visiting Toronto during his North American tour to collect funds for the Land League in the spring of

1880.[15] When Parnell ignored the archbishop's protests and delivered a speech at the Royal Opera House, neither Lynch nor any of his clergy would appear with him on the platform.[16] Later, when a Toronto branch of the Land League was founded in February 1881, neither Lynch nor his clergy would attend its meetings.[17] As was his habit when dealing with national matters, Archbishop Lynch offered no explanation for his decision to withhold his support from Parnell and his movement. It is possible that he was concerned that support for Parnell might inflame the sensitivities of Toronto's Protestants. Lynch may also have distrusted a lay movement over which he would have no control. Whatever the explanation, Lynch's attempt to distance himself and the church from the Land League was to give the laity yet another opportunity to act independently of the clergy. Such was their confidence in exercising ethnic leadership and taking the initiative that they were prepared to set off on a new and as yet uncharted course that was to broaden the appeal of Irish nationalism both inside and outside the Irish-Catholic community.

With the establishment of the Toronto Land League in February 1881, middle-class Irish Catholics became involved in a nationalist organization for the first time since their participation in the Hibernian Benevolent Society in the early 1860s. Among the leading members of the league were Peter Ryan, a former alderman and a dry goods dealer; George Evans, also a former alderman and a hardware store owner; John O'Donohoe, a lawyer and perhaps the leading Irish-Catholic politician in Toronto; Nicholas Murphy, a prominent criminal lawyer; and W.H. Riddell, manager of the *Ontario Tribune*.[18] Although membership lists have not survived, it would appear that the Land League, unlike the ICBU, was able to attract Irish-Catholic professionals as well as prosperous shopkeepers. For middle-class Irish Catholics the land question in Ireland became a symbol of upward mobility into the middle class, as the president of the Toronto Land League, John O'Donohoe argued. Land reform in Ireland, O'Donohoe believed, would return the land to its original owners, the farmers. Irish farmers would then be able to cultivate their own land and so demonstrate to the world that Irish Catholics were a hard-working people to whom middle-class status came quite naturally.[19] The Land League, then, reflected the quest of middle-class Irish Catholics for respectability and social acceptance.[20] These Irish-Catholics were conscious that they remained outsiders in a largely Protestant society, but they also knew that they had what it took to climb the social ladder.

If the entry of middle-class Irish Catholics into the nationalist ranks was a notable departure from the past, so too was the support the league drew from major Protestant labour activists such as Alfred Jury, a member of the Toronto Trades Assembly and an organizer for the Knights of Labor; A.W. Wright, a leader of the Knights of Labor and a "Beaverback" candidate in a federal by-election in 1880; and Phillips Thompson, a journalist and labour intellectual.[21] Their involvement indicated that Irish nationalism was still largely a working-class movement, but perhaps more important, it reflected the ties between Irish nationalism and social reform. At least $100 of the $550 collected by the Toronto Land League from its inception in February until the middle of May 1881 was forwarded to the league in Ireland through the *Irish World* of New York, a paper well known for its radical social criticism.[22] The publication of serial articles on the relationship between labour and capital, along with the Land League's hosting of the socialist thinker Henry George, provided further indication that many Irish-Catholic nationalists supported the cause of labour.[23]

The Land League formed a bridge between Irish-Catholic workers and working-class radicalism.[24] Labour leaders eagerly took advantage of this situation to recruit Irish-Catholic workers, and no union more assiduously cultivated Irish-Catholic support than the Knights of Labor, which spearheaded the wave of working-class militancy that swept the city during the 1880s. Such appeals met with a ready response among Irish Catholics. Both the Emerald Benevolent Association and the Irish Catholic Benevolent Union, for example, participated in labour parades.[25] This behaviour by Irish-Catholic fraternal societies demonstrated a profound change in attitude to Canadian society. Unlike the ICBU in the 1870s, these societies no longer walked the streets to claim possession of the city in an affirmation of Irish-Catholic exclusivism. On the contrary, instead of fostering a separatist mentality, Irish-Catholic organizations now provided their members with a springboard to participate in the larger society, in this case by demonstrating solidarity with the labour movement. At the same time, many Irish nationalists wished to affirm Irish-Catholic particularism, and the language of labour radicalism gave that particularism a moral purchase among labour activists by identifying Ireland's cause with the struggle against capital, be it in the form of landlordism or industrial capitalism.[26]

The Land League was a broad-based movement with a diverse constituency. All the same, radical nationalists, it would seem, were well placed to mold the Land League in their own image. The president of the league, John O'Donohoe, though not a radical nationalist, had long skirted the fringes of militant nationalism, and at least four members of the radical wing of the Irish Catholic Benevolent

Union were active on the Toronto Land League's executive: Patrick
Boyle and John Mulvey were vice-presidents of the league, C.J.
Murphy was its secretary, and Henry McKittrick was on the committee of management.[27] In short, radical nationalists together with
labour radicals dominated the Land League's executive. The former
found in labour's social criticism a convenient stick – the baneful
effects of landlordism – to excoriate British rule and a vocabulary to
express the dignity of Irish-Catholic workers.[28]

Yet the Land League did not in fact offer radical nationalists an
opportunity to continue their dominance of the Irish nationalist
movement in Toronto. Indeed, rather than reinforcing the radical
wing of the nationalist movement, the Land League's appearance
on the scene saw the end of radical nationalism as it had existed
in Toronto for twenty years. The Land League's platform of
thorough-going constitutional reform was enthusiastically embraced
by the city's Irish Catholics. As a result, not only was sympathy for
physical-force nationalism no longer expressed, it was in fact openly
discouraged.[29] Both the Emerald Benevolent Association and the
Irish Catholic Benevolent Union passed resolutions that declared
exclusive support for the constitutional-nationalist movement and
the Land League of Ireland.[30] Despite this endorsement, however,
the Land League of Toronto quietly ceased to meet in the fall of
1881, about the time that its counterpart in Ireland was suppressed
and a year before the American Land League was dissolved.

The Toronto Land League's existence was short, but before the
league disbanded it provided Irish nationalism with another constituency.[31] For decades, many Protestant Canadians had opposed
Irish nationalism because they believed that Irish nationalists, no
matter how moderate, were irresponsibly demanding special consideration for Ireland. Such preferential treatment, they feared, would
undermine not only imperial unity but also the British identity of
Canada. In the 1880s, however, the Protestant-Canadian perception
of Irish nationalism began to change. The Land League's campaign,
with its regular exposés of the plight of Irish farmers in the daily
press, revealed to the world that Irish society was experiencing a
mammoth structural crisis that went right to the heart of its social
and economic system: those who farmed the land were not those
who owned the land. At first in hesitant and muted tones and then
with the confidence gained by force of conviction, many Protestant
Canadians concluded that Ireland's unique social problems required
made-in-Ireland solutions. Home Rule became respectable, and
when Parnell undertook to support Gladstone's Liberal Party in the

Kilmainham compact of May 1882, Parnell's stock together with that of the Irish nationalist cause rose considerably in public estimation.[32] By the end of 1882, Senator Frank Smith, a Conservative Irish Catholic, Edward Blake, the Anglican leader of the Liberal Party, and Prime Minister John A. Macdonald supported the resolutions passed by the Canadian parliament in sympathy for Irish Home Rule.[33]

The success of the Land League in generating support both inside and outside the Irish-Catholic community demonstrated that the older nationalist organizations no longer could embody Irish nationalism as they had done in years past. Instead of being on the cutting edge of the nationalist movement, they had meekly followed the path forged by the Land League. After the demise of the Toronto branch of the Land League, the reawakening of the now moribund nationalist movement in Toronto would wait upon events in Ireland rather than upon the city's older nationalist organizations.

The land agitation had transformed the Irish parliamentary party into the recognized champion of the Irish people, but if Parnell was to make that party an effective political force he needed first to subdue the energies unleashed by the Land League and then to divert them into the conventional channels of constitutional politics.[34] While Parnell was engaged in the necessary but not spectacular task of building a national political machine, Irish Catholics in Toronto had little impetus to establish yet another nationalist organization. When in August 1885 it became clear that Parnell was finally launching his electoral campaign for Home Rule, a group of Irish Catholics, including long-time radical nationalists such as Patrick Boyle and Charles Burns and former Land Leaguers such as Bryan Lynch, founded a branch of the Irish National League in September 1885.[35]

At the first meeting of the Irish National League, the clergy were conspicuously absent. One month later, in October 1885, Archbishop Lynch gave the league his support in a letter he released to the press which was addressed to Archbishop Croke of Cashel, the most outspoken nationalist among the Irish hierarchy. The reasons for Lynch's change of heart towards Toronto's Parnellite nationalists remain mysterious, but two considerations surely entered into his calculations. After Gladstone entered into negotiations with Parnell, Irish nationalism was no longer the *bête noire* of Protestant public opinion in Toronto. As the religious leader of the Irish Catholics of Toronto, Lynch could hardly appear less fervent in his espousal of Irish nationalism and in his support of Parnell than Protestant politicians such as Edward Blake or John A. Macdonald. More seriously, if Archbishop Lynch did not catch up with popular Irish-Catholic sentiment for Home Rule and endorse the one organization that could legitimately claim a direct connection with that agitation in Ireland, his ability to act as an ethnic leader would have been seriously compromised. Under these circumstances, the archbishop may have felt it necessary to support the Irish National League, knowing full well that the laity would dominate the nationalist leadership, and hope for the best.

After Lynch had praised Parnell's efforts to secure Home Rule "as acts of religion and inspired by a merciful God," the clergy of Toronto could consider their participation in the Irish National League not only as a national duty but also as a religious obligation.[36] Thereafter, the parish clergy frequently took the platform at the league's meetings and headed its subscription lists.[37] How involved the clergy were in the National League activities is illustrated by Father Peter Gavan, a curate at Saint Mary's, who took the lead in founding the west-end branch of the Irish National League.[38] Control of the Irish National League nevertheless remained in lay hands. While the activists in the league respected the clergy's authority in religious matters and recognized them as influential figures in the community, they insisted that in the nationalist movement the clergy ought to defer to the laity.

The Irish National League, like the Land League, had a large working-class following and, like its predecessor, attempted to broaden the appeal of Irish nationalism. Both Protestant and Catholic labour leaders continued their support for Home Rule. D.J. O'Donoghue, the leading Catholic in the Knights of Labor, Bryan Lynch, another Catholic also active in the Knights, Alfred Jury, A.W. Wright, and Phillips Thompson regularly attended Irish National League meetings.[39] Now that the clergy supported the Irish National League, it began to attract to its meetings prominent and wealthy Catholics such as Frank Smith; George W. Kiely, Smith's partner in the Toronto Street Railway; Patrick Hughes, owner of one of the city's largest dry goods establishments; Timothy W. Anglin, former speaker of the House of Commons; William Petley, co-owner of a well-known dry goods emporium; and John O'Connor, a former federal cabinet minister and at the time a judge on the Court of Queen's Bench.[40] The participation of these well-to-do Irish Catholics in the Irish National League was as much a product of the respectability conferred on the league by the clergy as it was a reflection of Parnell's new reputation as a moderate and therefore legitimate leader of the Irish people.[41]

Naturally, it was Parnell's rehabilitation as a moderate leader seeking a realistic solution to Ireland's grievances, a point of view espoused in the editorial columns of the *Globe*, that induced leading politicians, who no doubt also had an eye to the Irish-Catholic vote, and other well-known Protestants to attend Irish National League meetings. Premier Oliver Mowat, Edward Blake, leader of the federal Liberal Party, Principal William Caven of Knox College, and William McMaster, president of the Canadian Imperial Bank of Commerce, all accepted invitations to Irish National League meetings.[42] "We are all Home Rulers," Oliver Mowat triumphantly declared.[43] This was something of an exaggeration, as Home Rule still caused many Protestants to fear for the integrity of the empire.[44] Nonetheless, Mowat's declaration was an unmistakeable affirmation of Irish nationalism's newly found respectability, which in turn was an indication not only of Parnell's stature as a leader but also of the changing nature of Irish nationalism in Toronto.

During the 1880s Irish nationalists assumed a new attitude towards Canada. Irish Catholics were now far more at home in Canadian society, as the quest for middle-class status by some nationalists and the support for labour radicalism by other nationalists illustrated. The nationalism of the Land League and its successor the Irish National League represented a shift towards ethnic accommodation with the larger culture and the adoption of a conciliatory stance towards the Protestant majority. This change in attitude is most clearly seen in the way Irish nationalists now praised the constitutional links that bound both Ireland and Canada to Britain. The best way to strengthen the British empire, John O'Donohoe announced, was to do justice to Ireland.[45] "Home Rule," Nicholas Murphy agreed, "did not mean ... the disintegration of the British Empire." Home Rule was not only compatible with being a British subject, it also fulfilled a Canadian's duty to preserve the empire. It was in Canada with its example of responsible government, Murphy boasted when referring to the Home Rule resolutions in the Canadian parliament, "that the first voice was raised to tell England how Ireland should be governed."[46] Irish Catholics in Canada had a special mission to show that the Confederation of the Canadian provinces could provide a model for the United Kingdom, a mission that placed a premium on loyalty to Canada. Moderate nationalists had long insisted that Irish Catholics could best contribute to Ireland's welfare by being loyal subjects, but in the past few had advocated that Irish Catholics should become Canadian patriots as well. Canada, "to which our affections cling," Nicholas Murphy confessed, "is dear to our hearts."[47] As M.W. Casey put it, national pride in the old land would make Irish Catholics "better citizens for the New."[48] Irish nationalism and Canadian patriotism were not only compatible, they were also in harmony with one another.

Irish nationalism, which since its inception in the later 1850s had fostered Irish separatism, was now prompting Irish Catholics to reach an accommodation with Canadian society. This shift did not mean, of course, that nationalism was becoming less relevant to Irish Catholics; in fact, the major object of the Irish National League was to develop "closer bonds of racial pride and affection, and to keep alive the holy flame of nationality."[49] Yet the Irish Catholics' perception of their ethnic identity had markedly altered: they now saw nationalism as a discrete commitment, one that could be easily accommodated to other loyalties. Their new outlook was reflected in the operations of the National League. Unlike previous nationalist organizations, the National League did not attempt to provide its members with a comprehensive social life. While the older nationalist societies expected their members to help organize and participate in a wide variety of activities, the National League asked no more of its rank and file than to attend its meetings, listen to its leaders' speeches, and make the occasional financial donation to the cause. This was simply a recognition that Irish Catholics, many of whom had been born and raised in Canada, lived and worked in a larger society and had formed new commitments and social bonds.

In 1860, some four-fifths of the Catholic adults who presented themselves to be married in the cities' parishes were Irish-born; two decades later, in 1880, one half of Irish-Catholic adults were born in Canada, and by 1890 that proportion was approaching 60 per cent.[50] The Canadian-born generation of Irish Catholics had come to maturity. In response to this generational change, lay ethnic institutions increasingly assumed specific functions. Rather than promoting ethnic exclusivism, with its self-contained social and cultural life, nationalism had become a means of forging an accommodation with the larger culture. This accommodation posed an immediate threat to the older nationalist societies, for it was to undermine the capacity of their leaders to act independently of the clergy.

The success of the Land League and the Irish National League, which signalled the triumph of constitutional nationalism in the 1880s, resulted in a fundamental reorganization of Irish-Catholic associations for men.

The decline of the Irish Catholic Benevolent Union illustrated the fate experienced by the older nationalist societies. Since 1877, when it had four branches, the Irish Catholic Benevolent Union had declined to two branches by 1881, a slump from which it never recovered.[51] Among the casualties was the ICBU branch number sixteen, the former Hibernian Benevolent Society. Membership figures for the ICBU also reveal a sharp decline: membership fell from some 300 members in 1877 to 154 in 1883. During the next three years, enrolment increased to between 200 and 220 members, but by 1889 the union had only 120 members – a mere fraction of its former strength.[52] The ICBU had long described itself as the conscience of Irish nationalism in Toronto. That claim, however, now properly belonged to the Land League and its successor, the Irish National League. With their direct connection to the Parnellite movement in Ireland, the Land League and the Irish National League were the living embodiment of the nationalist struggle against British rule and as such the recognized expression of the nation's will in exile. Their links to the Parnellite agitation enabled them to dominate the nationalist movement in Toronto, which reduced the ICBU to playing little more than an auxiliary role. At the same time, because of its wholehearted conversion to constitutional agitation, the union was unable to draw on the romantic allure of nationalist extremism to attract members, as it had done in the past.

The nature of the Land League's and the Irish National League's appeal also explains the ICBU's decline. Irish Catholics increasingly saw nationalism in terms that ran against the union's objective to provide a wide-ranging associational life with a nationalist ethos. In response to this development, the ICBU demonstrated remarkably indecisive leadership. In 1889, for example, the grand executive discussed dropping the word "Irish" from the union's name, a move that would have signalled a reorientation of the union's purpose. In the end no decision was made, not because of opposition, for there was none, but because of indifference.[53] If the leaders of the ICBU were uncertain how to respond to the changing expectations of the laity in general, they were even less sure how to go about recruiting the Canadian-born for whom the struggles of Ireland were a generation removed.[54] With no clear vision of ethnicity, the ICBU had little to offer this younger generation. The union's increased emphasis on cultural endeavours, such as reading-rooms and lectures, and recreational activities, including marching bands and gymnasiums, could not halt the association's decline when it so obviously lacked direction. The ICBU survived into the next century, but it had long ceased to be relevant.[55]

One of the reasons why the ICBU had become irrelevant can been seen in the story of the Emerald Benevolent Association after it be-

came affiliated with the Catholic Church. Unlike the leadership of
the foundering ICBU, the leaders of the Emerald Benevolent took
decisive action in response to laymen's changing expectations of
their fraternal organizations. Only a few months after the founding
of the Toronto branch of the Land League in February 1881, the association dropped its nationalist orientation and readily identified itself with the Catholic Church. D.A. Carey, the grand president,
stressed that the Emerald Benevolent Association was not a national
organization but a society for practising Catholics. This avowed
purpose evidently did not preclude oblique resolutions of support
for the Land League or open declarations in favour of constitutional
nationalism, but the association's attempt to distance itself from the
nationalist movement was nonetheless unmistakable.[56] The association, its recruiters repeatedly emphasized, was open to all nationalities; however, the vast majority of Catholics in Toronto were of Irish
extraction, and with the exception of a tiny French-Canadian minority, whom the Emeralds never attempted to attract, there
were few other potential Catholic recruits for the organization.
The Emerald Benevolent Association's professed ideal of uniting
Catholics of all nationalities was simply a way of discounting Irish
nationalism.[57]

"The Emerald Association," Jeremiah Murphy, an old Hibernian
firebrand, declared with evident disgust, "contains few friends of
Ireland." "I should esteem it the greatest pleasure," he continued,
obviously relishing the sensation he was about to create, "to empty
my cartridge pouch into the ranks of such a body." If Murphy had
hoped to shame the association, he missed his mark; for Emerald
members, such remarks were not only disloyal but also irreligious.
They could comfortably congratulate themselves on having chosen
the path of toleration, piety, and respectability, thereby distancing
themselves from embarrassments such as Jeremiah Murphy.[58]
Because they wished to be accepted as Canadian Catholics, they favoured conciliation, not confrontation.[59] "Our society is an aid to
our country," boasted D.A. Carey, who then pointedly added, "not
as, unfortunately, many others are, a detriment and a menace."
"The better Emerald a man is," Carey concluded, "so is he a better
citizen."[60] The Emerald Association had become a school for Canadian citizenship, eschewing Irish nationalism and with it the divided
loyalties that had had a purchase on Irish Catholics since the inception of the Hibernian Benevolent Society in the late 1850s.

As the Emerald Benevolent Association disavowed Irish nationalism, it also developed closer ties with the Catholic Church. The association reorganized its branches on a parochial basis, and the clergy

obtained representation on its executive at both the local and provincial levels.[61] Its recognition of clerical authority was evidently welcomed by the clergy, for now the association would conform to the church's ideal that Catholic social life should come under the supervision of the clergy. The Emerald's alliance with the clergy resulted in the association becoming devoted to specifically religious purposes. One major object of the association was now to nurture the participation of its members in the sacramental life of the church.[62] For example, like many other parish societies, the Emerald members received communion as a group and then attended vespers and the benediction of the Blessed Sacrament at their quarterly general meetings.[63] The recreational life of the Emerald Benevolent Association was to encourage Irish-Catholic men to become further involved in the religious practices of the church.[64]

That the Emerald Association had become part of the church's mission of outreach to Catholic men was made abundantly clear when Father Francis Rooney of Saint Mary's parish, the grand chaplain of the association, congratulated the society on its "obedience and docility" in aiding the clergy in their pastoral work.[65] The leaders of the association did indeed cooperate with the clergy, but their respect for the clergy's office should not be mistaken for docility. By and large the clergy acted in an advisory capacity, and though they could have have insisted on their pastoral prerogatives and assumed direction of the organization, they did not do so. Instead, they advised and supported the Emerald Association in its efforts to establish a Catholic fraternal life in the city. The laity continued to be responsible for running parish branches, founding new branches, and in general setting policy at the provincial level. In effect, day-to-day control of the organization remained with the laity, and if major changes in the association's structure were not to be made without consulting the clergy, they were nonetheless instigated by the laity themselves.[66] In forming an alliance with the Catholic Church, the lay leaders of the Emerald Benevolent Association had surrendered their former autonomy, but in exchange they secured their organization's survival and established an arena for lay initiative in the parish.

The Emerald Association's alliance with the church certainly contributed to its expansion. In early 1880, the association had only three city branches; by 1884, it had founded three new branches.[67] At mid-decade, then, the Emerald Association was well established in all the major city parishes: Saint Michael's, Saint Paul's, Saint Patrick's, Saint Mary's, Saint Helen's in the Junction Triangle, and Saint Joseph's to the east in Leslieville. Unfortunately, membership statistics are rare, but one surviving survey reveals that by 1886 the association had grown to some 570 members from an estimated 200 in 1877.[68] For many Canadian-born laymen, who unlike their parents were brought up in the atmosphere of devotional Catholicism, the Emerald Benevolent Association offered a familiar and reassuring form of belonging. After being exposed to confraternities and altar societies in the separate schools during their youth, many of these young men were drawn to a society that combined recreation and self-improvement with Catholic piety. The realignment of the Emerald Benevolent Association with the Catholic Church represented the triumph of the ultramontane conception of church and community among Irish-Catholic men. These Irish Catholics wished to maintain their particularity, but for them this was best achieved in associations affiliated with the Catholic Church in which the clergy took an active role in positions of leadership.

The Emerald Benevolent Association's success in bringing male social life under the auspices of the church demonstrated to the clergy that parish societies for men were not only desirable, on which point the clergy did not need much convincing, but also feasible. During the 1880s the clergy established a large number of different types of parochial organizations that together incorporated the social life of Irish-Catholic men into the parish and brought it within the ambit of the clergy's authority. After 1886, three parishes founded literary societies for Irish-Catholic young men. In 1888 the Knights of Saint John, a religious and semi-military mutual benevolent association, was introduced. This organization, however, managed to establish "commanderies" in only two parishes, Saint Paul's and Saint Patrick's. Later, in 1893, a branch of the Catholic Order of Foresters was founded, but its membership was limited to the French-Canadian parish of the Sacred Heart and thus remained small.[69]

The most successful fraternal association established by the clergy was the Catholic Mutual Benevolent Association (CMBA) founded in Niagara Falls, New York, by Bishop John Timon in 1876. Established at the instance of the clergy and under the supervision of the parish priests, the CMBA sought to bring scattered Catholics, who the clergy feared were "almost absorbed" by the non-Catholic population, into one "brotherhood, imbued with fervent love for the Holy Church, aiding her teachings, and helping her work."[70] To this end, the CMBA set out to rescue Catholics from the supposed corruption and vice of the Protestant society around them by providing a distinctly Catholic form of organized recreation located in the parish. The insurance benefits of the association were intended to save

Catholics from the temptation of joining "other benefit societies of doubtful and questionable morality" – a category that seems to have included any organization outside of the Catholic Church. In joining the CMBA instead, Catholics would be exposed to the teachings and sacraments of the church.[71]

The Catholic foundations of the CMBA, the association's promoters contended, made truly moral and intellectual improvement possible. The nurturing of sacramental piety was a central object of the association, and the CMBA encouraged its members to receive the sacraments frequently. Only through the sacraments, the clergy maintained, could the members be closely bound to God and to each other in fraternal love. The death benefit of the association, a substantial sum of two thousand dollars, was therefore a concrete expression of the virtues of charity and thrift. To elevate the intellectual as well as the religious and moral character of its members, the association also promoted "good Catholic reading" through its reading-rooms. Mutual benefit, self-improvement, and Catholicism were all inextricably connected in the CMBA's attempt to provide Catholic men with an associational life under the auspices of the parish. As a result, the wholesome leisure, self-improvement, and mutual benefit promoted by the association served to bind men to the sacramental life of the church and to incorporate their social life into the framework of the parish.[72]

The CMBA languished for six years after the founding of the first branch in 1881 because it lacked energetic leadership and had yet to gain the confidence of the clergy in Toronto. After the parochial clergy embraced the CMBA in 1888, however, it grew dramatically. In 1888 three parish branches were established, yet another in 1889, and in 1890 two more parishes branches were founded. By 1890, the association was operating in seven of the nine city parishes; the exceptions were the two smaller parishes, Sacred Heart and Saint Joseph's.

As no membership figures have survived, it is possible only to suggest lower and upper limits for the CMBA's membership after 1890. If the membership of the parish branches was equal to the Ontario-wide average, there would have been at least 280 members.[73] On the other hand, if each branch recruited sixty members, the enrolment of the association's more successful parish branches, the maximum membership would have been about 420. Since few workers could afford the annual membership fee of about seventeen dollars[74] – which represented almost three weeks' wages for an unskilled labourer and a minimum of a week and a half's earnings for the semi-skilled – it is unlikely that the association's enrolment approached the upper limit of 420; the total probably fell somewhere between 300 and 350. Still, by 1890, the CMBA was represented in more city parishes than any other Catholic voluntary association for men except the Saint Vincent de Paul Society.

The CMBA represented an interesting mix of clerical leadership and lay initiative. Though founded by a member of the American hierarchy, the association was introduced to the city by laymen, and three of city branches owed their inception to just one lay activist.[75] A few of clergy did hold executive positions above and beyond their role as spiritual advisers, a role that gave them pride of place in the CMBA. The CMBA was, in words of L.V. Byrne of Saint Basil's parish, "an auxiliary to the church," and as such it recognized the privileges and prerogatives of the clergy.[76] Parish priests, the leadership of the CMBA insisted, ought to be actively involved in the CMBA, but at its Grand Council – the only meetings for which accounts survive – clerical delegates were few, and the association's affairs were largely in lay hands. By 1888 the CMBA had over eighty branches stretching from the province of Quebec to the province of Manitoba, and the association was well on its way to providing its executive on the Grand Council with a national stage for lay leadership that was closely allied to the clergy.[77]

The second major fraternal association introduced in Toronto in the 1880s was the Ancient Order of Hibernians, a lay-led organization. First established in 1889, it had four city branches by 1890, and a fifth was launched in 1894. From 350 members in 1890, the order had expanded by 1893 to 715 members, making it the largest independent Catholic society for men in Toronto.[78] The order's relationship with the Roman Catholic Church differed from that of the CMBA and the Emerald Benevolent Association. Like the Emerald Benevolent Association, the individual branches of the Ancient Order of Hibernians were organized along parochial lines. However, although the order sought the approbation of the clergy and its members regularly received the sacraments in a body, it was nevertheless, like the ICBU, managed by the laity without the direct involvement of the clergy. The Ancient Order of Hibernians represented a compromise that balanced lay claims for independent initiative with a recognition that the parish now formed the primary framework for Irish-Catholic social life.[79]

Unlike the CMBA and the Emerald Benevolent Association, the Ancient Order of Hibernians sought to preserve the Irish heritage of Toronto's Catholics in addition to promoting the Catholic principles of "Friendship, Unity, and Christian Charity." Yet the order's leaders understood, as those of the ICBU did not, that an independent lay voluntary association could no longer simply rely on Irish nationalism to recruit members, especially among the rising generation of the Canadian-born. While seeking to promote awareness of Irish history and culture among its members, the Ancient Order of Hibernians eschewed the national particularism and exclusivism of its predecessors. The order encouraged Irish Catholics to cultivate their ethnicity, but the form of ethnic nationalism it expressed, unlike that of its sister branches in the United States, was far from militant. In its work, the cultivation of national heritage resembled the pursuit of family genealogy, a hobby as opposed to a way of life.[80]

The very strength of the Land League and the Irish National League had brought about a fundamental realignment of lay associations for men. Such was their dominance of the nationalist movement that male fraternal organizations either allied themselves with the Catholic Church, as in the case of the Emerald Association and, to a lesser degree, the Ancient Order of Hibernians, or did nothing and languished, as in the case of the ICBU. Organizations affiliated with the church thrived at the same time that the Land League and Irish National League prospered, and they did so for largely the same reasons. As Irish Catholics, the Canadian-born in particular, assumed a variety of new social obligations, they no longer expected their nationalist organizations to create an all-encompassing social life. For many Irish-Catholic men that social life was now furnished by fraternal organizations associated with the Catholic Church.

Although the Irish National League still held the allegiance of Irish Catholics, the vibrant state of church-related fraternal organizations was a portent of things to come. One such development was the founding of the Men's League of the Apostleship of Prayer in 1892. By 1895, the Men's League had gained over 760 members, making it the largest Catholic organization for men in the city. Like the parish devotional organizations for women, the purpose of the Men's League was to introduce its members to the devotional repertoire of the church. Devotionalism was quickly becoming a central feature of Catholic men's organizations, as the success of the Holy Name Society in recruiting thousands of laymen after 1900 confirmed.[81] With the launching of the Men's League, devotional organizations were in the process of consolidating their hold among Catholic men just as they had done a generation before among Catholic women. By this time, the moderate nationalism represented by the Land League and the Irish National League had experienced a dramatic reversal in fortunes, a development that few would have predicted when the lay nationalists began their drive for the secret ballot in Separate School Board elections.

The push for lay control of the Separate School Board, though checked by Archbishop Lynch in 1879, had not been defeated, and demands for lay management of education still simmered. During the fall of 1881, the board's meetings were wracked by accusations of jobbery and profiteering.[82] The following spring, while members of the board traded insults, the *Irish Canadian* published a lively exchange of letters questioning the competence of the teachers supplied by the religious orders. In the meantime, Robert Bell, an Orangeman, introduced in the provincial legislature in March 1882 a resolution for the separate school ballot, which the *Irish Canadian* energetically supported.[83] Though the bill was roundly defeated, Bell reintroduced the resolution the following year, but he met with no more success this time round. Over the next five years there were sporadic criticisms of the quality of education offered by the separate schools, and the occasional call for the ballot in the election of separate school trustees, but there was no discernible movement for greater lay involvement in the operation of the schools.[84]

Meanwhile, events in Ireland were leading up to an incident that would eventually revive the movement for the secret ballot in Separate School Board elections. In the fall of 1886, two of Parnell's lieutenants, John Dillon and William O'Brien, launched the Plan of Campaign to aid Irish farmers suffering from poor harvests and declining agricultural prices.[85] Under the plan, if a landlord refused to lower his rent, the tenants on the estate would pay a "fair rent" to trustees elected by the farmers, who would then use the funds to aid all those evicted for the non-payment of rent. Such a challenge could not go unanswered by Lord Salisbury's Conservative government. Several major estates were chosen by Arthur Balfour, the Irish chief secretary, as the battleground to destroy the Plan of Campaign. One of them was that of Lord Lansdowne, the governor-general of Canada.[86] Although the Toronto National League had endorsed the Plan of Campaign, William O'Brien's announcement in April 1887 that he would visit Canada to press Lord Lansdowne to settle with his tenants immediately divided Irish Catholics.[87]

Archbishop Lynch promptly cabled O'Brien to dissuade him from visiting Canada and secured an interview with the *Globe* condemning O'Brien's projected tour.[88] Leaving nothing to chance, Lynch also asked Archbishop Thomas Croke of Cashel to put pressure on O'Brien to cancel his visit.[89] Lynch's reasons for opposing O'Brien's planned visit were entirely pragmatic, as he explained through his secretary, Father Joseph McBride. "We here in Canada have already suffered severely in times past from the indiscreet action of a part of the extreme section of Irish patriots here," McBride declared, and

"O'Brien's coming would result in something similar now."[90] Many Irish Catholics shared the archbishop's fears that O'Brien's visit would stir up a "terrible excitement" among the city's Protestant population.[91] "The Governor General," Frank Smith observed in his usual semiliterate style, "is not heere an Irish Land Lord he is heere representing the British nation and we should not allow any one to come heere to hound him down." "We should as Catholics and true subjects of Canada," Smith insisted, "endeveour to continue the good feeling that now exists be all clases of Canadians."[92]

O'Brien's tour placed many Irish Catholics in a quandary. Criticism in Canada of Lord Lansdowne, who after all was the Queen's representative, was tantamount to displaying disrespect towards the British monarchy. Yet, as an evicting landlord, Lord Lansdowne was the very symbol of oppressive British rule in Ireland. For those nationalists anxious to demonstrate their loyalty to Canada, O'Brien's intentions were especially troublesome and inopportune.[93] Irish Catholics wished to be "true subjects of Canada," as Frank Smith put it, but for many Irish Catholics of his generation Ireland was still "our country." O'Brien's visit shattered the National League's claim that the Canadian loyalism and Irish patriotism were not only compatible loyalties but were also mutually reinforcing ones.[94] The leaders of the league would have preferred to avoid the issue entirely, but once O'Brien's decision had been publicly announced, they had little choice but to welcome the representative of the evicted Irish. Caught between Canadian loyalism and Irish patriotism, pragmatism and idealism, the executive of the league agreed to sponsor O'Brien's visit.[95]

Two days later, in response to the National League's announcement, a protest rally met under the chairmanship of Mayor William Howland. O'Brien's visit, declared an outraged H.E. Clark, the Conservative MPP for Toronto West, "was an attack upon Protestantism and upon their Protestant Queen." In criticizing the Queen's representative, Irish nationalists had committed an unpardonable offence against Canada's fundamental institutions and so had demonstrated themselves to be disloyal subjects. "All citizens of Toronto," the Anglican bishop of Algoma, Edward Sullivan explained, would "reprobate any insult" to the governor-general, for "his honor was our honor." The bishop proclaimed that "the heart of Canada still beats true to the mother that bore her" and assured the public that the citizens of Toronto would not countenance treason.[96] While the Irish Catholics of Toronto were just as opposed to treason, they did not believe that Lansdowne's office exempted him from criticism. Furthermore, nothing was better calculated to galvanize Catholic

support for the nationalist cause than a storm of Protestant indignation. To break ranks now would to be to endure the humiliation of
succumbing to Protestant opinion. If Irish Catholics were to avoid
such humiliation they would have to give O'Brien the most rousing
reception possible, and nowhere could they make their stand more
conspicuously than in Queen's Park – the public symbol of Toronto
the Good's devotion to the monarchy.[97]

Some four thousand people attended O'Brien's meeting at Queen's
Park on the following Tuesday. Despite Archbishop Lynch's instructions to the contrary, several priests were on the platform and later
attended the banquet held in O'Brien's honour. Although nearly
constant heckling rendered O'Brien's speech almost inaudible, the
Queen's Park meeting was not disrupted by any serious incidents.[98]
The next day, however, when O'Brien was out for a walk near his
hotel, he was set upon by a vengeful gang who only hours before
had escorted the governor-general's carriage. O'Brien escaped his
pursuers by running through a bicycle store to a back lane and then
taking refuge in a tailor's shop nearby.[99]

The attack on William O'Brien, commented the *Catholic Weekly
Review*, won over "the sympathy and respect of all liberty-loving people" to Ireland's cause.[100] Archbishop Lynch revealed what he really
thought of Lord Lansdowne when he refused to attend a reception
for the governor-general. "My nature resists," Archbishop Lynch explained, "against shaking hands with the oppressor of the poor."[101]
Few Irish Catholics would disagree, and since Protestant Canadians
were united in opposition to O'Brien, it became a matter of pride as
well as filial duty for all children of Ireland to come to his support.[102] Nonetheless, many Irish Catholics were ambivalent about
O'Brien's visit, and only under the pressure of events would they
chose Irish nationalism over Canadian patriotism.

O'Brien's appearance in Toronto had provoked strife and incited
a general attack on Irish Catholics, just as Archbishop Lynch had
predicted. Lynch's objections to O'Brien's presence in the city was
essentially pragmatic but, significantly, he had acted without consulting the leaders of the National League, implying that he alone spoke
for the Irish Catholics of Toronto. Having been so flagrantly
slighted, the leaders of the National League were anxious to seize
the initiative from the archbishop, and when the opportunity to do
so arose, they quickly exploited it.

As the celebration on 1 July in honour of Queen Victoria's golden
jubilee approached, the *Irish Canadian* observed that the Irish people
"can never forget the Victorian era, with its famine, its pestilence
and death; its coffin ships, its ocean graves, and its cemeteries along

the St. Lawrence."[103] The Queen's jubilee celebration triggered images of defeat and humiliation that the nationalist movement had seared into the collective consciousness of Irish Catholics over the past thirty years. With their paeans to British progress and expansion, the festivities were also another public affirmation of Irish-Catholic exclusion from the Protestant majority's national vision. For these reasons, Archbishop Lynch shared with Boyle's *Irish Canadian* the same antipathy to the jubilee celebrations. "I cannot see what obligation of gratitude we can have towards a ruler," the archbishop confided to Bishop John Walsh of London, "who, in this jubilee year of her reign, is occupied with forging new fetters for our country and its people."[104] Only "the more English and Catholic *Cawtholics*," those who had sold out and renounced their nationality, the archbishop had earlier predicted, would participate in the jubilee.[105]

Archbishop Lynch did not publicly express his bitterness towards the jubilee celebrations, though his decision not to follow the example of other denominations in marking the event with a religious service suggested where his sentiments lay. The majority of the separate school trustees, both clerical and lay, were apparently unaware of the archbishop's position and voted that the trustees should join the public celebrations on 1 July. The central issue debated by the trustees was similar to the one that arose over William O'Brien's visit to Toronto: could Irish Catholics remain true to the Emerald Isle and at the same time be loyal Canadian subjects? The nationalists were a minority among the lay members of the board, and their response to this question, especially after the O'Brien affray, was as predictable as it was certain of Irish-Catholic sympathy. Archbishop Lynch's private comments to Bishop John Walsh indicated that the nationalists could easily rely on Irish-Catholic support in an attack on the separate schools trustees who joined the jubilee celebrations.

The nationalist trustees vehemently attacked any official recognition of Queen Victoria's jubilee by the Separate School Board. "I cannot be a hypocrite and rejoice when I ought to feel sorrow," protested J.A. Mulligan, the Irish National League's president and separate school trustee. "Can we rejoice," he asked, "when we know that a million and half of our suffering fellow countrymen have been starved to death in the past fifty years ... by the English government? When eight hundred thousand more ... have been drawn out of their homes, and left to die in the wayside or in the poor-house?" "We are in Canada," trustee John Herbert replied, unmoved by Mulligan's passionate appeal. Ireland's plight, Herbert declared without hesitation, was of little concern to Canadian citizens, even if they were Irish-born. To the Irish Catholics of Canada "she has been a good Queen to us," Herbert concluded to the approval of the majority of the trustees, "and we ought to do her honor."[106] Such Canadian patriotism reflected the sentiments and aspirations of many Irish Catholics; however, as the trustees were soon to discover, this brand of Canadian patriotism was not acceptable to Irish Catholics if it involved sacrificing their national particularity and with that their self-respect.

Reaction to the trustees' decision was immediate. Their decision showed, the *Irish Canadian* observed, "bad taste and worse patriotism." Daniel P. Cahill, secretary of the Irish National League, was even less kind in his denunciation of the board. "In Toronto alone," he declared, "men are to be found who, like Peter, are willing to deny their Lord and master." Public acceptance, he warned, could never be gained by such duplicity. The school trustees, as the only Roman Catholic contingent at the celebrations on 1 July, had placed themselves in an impossible position. When the Orange Order band struck up the "Boyne Water" (a tune celebrating the defeat of the Catholic forces under King James II in 1690) as it passed the separate school trustees, the nationalists' fears were fully realized.[107]

In the fall, the nationalists on the board, most of whom were active in the Irish National League, resumed their attack on those lay trustees who had participated in the jubilee celebrations, and in this venture they were joined by one priest, Father Michael O'Reilly of Leslieville.[108] O'Reilly's actions posed a threat to clerical unity and discipline, which the Irish National League's meeting in Queen's Park that summer had revealed to be tenuous. Lynch disciplined his errant priest and at the same time took the opportunity to denounce the nationalists for introducing extraneous issues to the board's deliberations.[109] His intervention failed to neutralize the dissident trustees, however, and in fact by acting in this manner Lynch had conceded to the nationalists the one issue that they could effectively use to bypass the clergy and appeal to the grass roots of the Irish-Catholic community.

In December, the nationalists made their gambit to secure control of the Separate School Board. Daniel Cahill, who had resigned as secretary of the Irish National League when he ran for the Separate School Board in order to dissociate the league from the jubilee controversy, carefully avoided tangling with the clergy and directed his campaign at the lay trustees, questioning their competence to provide a good education. Cahill's veiled reference to the attendance of the separate school trustees at the jubilee as the squandering of public taxes for "pleasure trips" in carriages was the only hint at the real campaign issue.[110] The self-contradictory denial by James J. Travers, the National League's new secretary, to the charge that the league sought the defeat of the jubilee trustees gave the game away. "Some of them boast they are the true representatives of the Irish Catholics of Toronto," Travers declared, "although they have never yet identified themselves with anything Irish." "Their boast," Travers ominously vowed, leaving no doubt as to the league's true purpose, "will be put to the test."[111] The jubilee was transformed into a nationalist question because it was a convenient – perhaps the only – issue on which the nationalists could assert the claims of lay leadership in the Irish-Catholic community and in the realm of education in particular.

The strong nationalist campaign compelled the archbishop to resort to extraordinary measures. Lynch persuaded retiring trustees he could rely upon, all members of the Saint Vincent de Paul Society, to stand for re-election against the nationalists. He pressed other candidates to dissociate themselves from the nationalist camp. Nonetheless, the nationalists won three of the five wards in which polls were held, for a total of six seats.[112] The election campaign, surprisingly, did not result in a rift between the clergy and the Irish National League, as the clergy and the archbishop continued to lend the league their support.[113] But this harmony was abruptly shattered in mid-January 1888, when trustee D. Kelly moved that the board petition the Ontario legislature to grant the secret ballot for Separate School Board elections, a motion that was promptly ruled out of order by the chairman, Father Francis Rooney, who was also Lynch's vicar-general.[114]

In early February, Archbishop Lynch sent a circular letter to the trustees, which Daniel Cahill released to the press, roundly condemning the secret ballot. "There are in the Catholic church some followers of Judas," he warned, who would not hesitate to use the ballot as a shield for their hypocrisy and deception. The clergy are "by divine appointment, the guardians of the Catholic education of youth," Lynch affirmed, reminding the trustees of their duty, and "when laymen are introduced it is that they may help the clergy. In the church of Christ the shepherd leads the sheep!"[115] The subordinate position of the laity could hardly be made clearer. The secret ballot, the archbishop feared, would rob the clergy of their legitimate influence. Over the next two and half months, Archbishop Lynch demonstrated that he would brook no intervention by the pro-ballot trustees, even though they were only a small minority on the board, and that by insisting on the prerogatives of the clergy he would leave nothing to chance. The rift between the National League and the archbishop was now complete.

At the next meeting of the board, chairman Rooney refused to recognize Kelly's new motion for the ballot, although proper notice had been given.[116] The archbishop then followed up his circular letter by issuing veiled threats of excommunication to the recalcitrant trustees. Unmoved, the ballot supporters insisted that, as the ballot entailed no disrespect to the clergy, the laity should be free to support it.[117] Dissatisfied with this response, Lynch issued a pastoral letter to appeal directly to the Catholic population for its support. "So called Catholics," Archbishop Lynch warned, "are openly in league with the worst enemies of our faith in order to eventually break up our Catholic schools."[118] Two weeks later, in yet another pastoral read from the pulpit, the archbishop repeated his condemnation of the pro-ballot trustees. "Catholic education is essentially a religious affair," he announced, "to be managed with judgement and economy by the clergy, assisted by good Catholics."[119] Once Archbishop Lynch had defined the issue in terms of Catholic orthodoxy, the question was now who would dare to oppose the church's magisterium. After this salvo from their archbishop, the pro-ballot trustees recognized that they had been effectively isolated and so conceded defeat.[120]

This truce, however, was not to endure for long. With the sudden death of trustee Harry Nolan one month later, in early April 1888, the nationalist trustees could not pass up the opportunity to take their case to the Catholic electors once more. Archbishop Lynch had first selected E.A. Cullerton to fill Nolan's place on the board, a nominee whom the ballot trustees were confident of defeating. The energetic campaign put up by Samuel Dunbar, secretary of the Toronto Plasterers' Union and a former aldermanic candidate, persuaded the archbishop instead to nominate a much stronger candidate, Timothy W. Anglin, former speaker of the House of Commons and an experienced politician from the Maritimes well known to Toronto Catholics.

Archbishop Lynch spared little to ensure victory for his man. "A trustee," declared the archbishop in referring to Dunbar, "must be a conscientious and practical Catholic. To vote for a man to be a trustee who is seldom seen at Mass and never at the Altar of the Holy Eucharist, is a crime before God."[121] Father Francis Rooney followed up Lynch's attack on Dunbar with an assiduous canvassing of the electors, with visible results. The women electors, the pro-ballot advocates bitterly noted, were unanimous in their opposition to

Dunbar. Dunbar was also unable to retain the support of the working class, among whom he had once been very popular. As one cab driver noted, "I vote in accord wid me conscience. Me conscience tells me to vote for the church." For many electors, once Archbishop Lynch had insisted that the central issue of the election was one of Catholic orthodoxy, the matter was settled. Dunbar, who insisted that the election was purely a civic issue, did not stand a chance, and when the poll was held under the clergy's supervision, he was defeated by Anglin, 170 to 95 votes.[122]

Dunbar's defeat was an indication of the deep roots struck by the Catholic Church and its parish organizations. The loyal members of the Saint Vincent de Paul Society on the Separate School Board worked with the clergy to create a polarized atmosphere in which it was possible to stave off the nationalist advance. Moreover, Catholic women, in a vivid display of their parish confraternities' influence, almost without exception voted for Anglin, thereby transforming what would have otherwise been simply a solid victory into an electoral landslide. It was to be Lynch's last victory, however. While on his annual confirmation tour the archbishop caught a severe cold. Characteristically heedless of his health, he pushed on, but by the time he returned to Toronto, pneumonia had set in. Early Saturday morning, 12 May 1888, Archbishop Lynch's heart gave way to the strain.[123]

After Lynch's death the pro-ballot supporters hoped to take advantage of the resulting lack of clerical leadership to gain a working majority on the Separate School Board. Significantly, however, they now dropped their emphasis on nationalism. The rift between the clergy and the Irish National League slowly healed, and by the fall of 1888 the clergy had returned to their usual places on the platform at the National League meetings.[124] When in the fall of 1889 the pro-ballot trustees again sought to introduce a motion to petition the Ontario legislature for the ballot, the opposition led by the clergy succeeded in blocking the motion by making full use of the chairman's discretionary power and, when that failed, by seeking a court injunction.[125] Such tactics enabled the board to run the clock till the end of the year, and when the Separate School Board elections were held in January 1890 the pro-ballot candidates, including Daniel Cahill, were all defeated. Disheartened, the remaining pro-ballot trustees abandoned the agitation.[126] The provincial government granted the secret ballot for Separate School Board elections in 1894, but it did so as a concession to Protestant opinion rather than as a response to lay Catholic demands. Open voting in Separate School Board elections had simply become politically indefensible

for any Ontario government. The Roman Catholic hierarchy realized that any further attempt on their part to oppose the introduction of the secret ballot could only endanger the separate schools by
antagonizing Protestant opinion.[127]

The battle for the secret ballot was essentially an expression of the
lay effort to gain at least partial leadership of the Irish-Catholic community. But in this framework of lay-clerical dynamics, nationalism
in the late 1880s appears to have been more a strategic issue than an
ideological one. Irish nationalism provided lay Irish Catholics with
the only effective basis for independent leadership within the Irish-
Catholic community. Yet, because both the nationalists and the
clergy identified nationalism with Catholicism, disputes inevitably
arose over the limits of lay initiative and clerical authority, as Lynch's
unilateral attempt to dissuade O'Brien from visiting Toronto
illustrated. The nationalist reaction to Archbishop Lynch's authoritarianism was entirely predictable. Of all religious institutions controlled by the clergy, only one, the Separate School Board, was, in
legal theory at least, open to independent lay initiative. The struggle
between the lay advocates of the ballot and the clergy was over the
issue of jurisdiction. While the nationalists insisted on the primacy of
lay initiative, they did not question the clergy's spiritual authority;
what was in question, however, were the proper limits to that
authority.

Archbishop Lynch's endorsement of the jubilee trustees gave the
dissident trustees an issue custom-made to mobilize public sentiment
in their bid to gain control over the board. The conflict over the ballot owed its bitterness to the fact that both the pro-ballot trustees and
the clergy shared the same beliefs: Irish nationalism was essential to
Catholicism, and moral questions and religious formation were the
responsibility of the clergy. Far from being a manifestation of secu-
larism, the conflict over the ballot was a dispute over the place and
role of lay initiative in the Catholic Church and in the Irish-Catholic
community as a whole.[128]

Although the ballot controversy revealed the strength of Irish nationalism, it also underscored the movement's weakness. In the
spring of 1888, when Archbishop Lynch made full use of his spiritual authority, the fate of the pro-ballot candidates was sealed.
Forced to choose between Irish nationalism or the Roman Catholic
Church, Irish Catholics had no doubt that their loyalties lay with the
church. The demand for lay control of the school board would have
been a difficult one to carry even during the heyday of nationalism;
in the more sober climate of the late 1880s, when piety mattered
more than nationalism, such a campaign was doomed to fail. Al-

though the nationalists on the Separate School Board adroitly exploited an issue emotionally compelling to Irish Catholics, they not only lost the battle for the ballot but they also found themselves isolated and outmaneuvered by the clergy and their lay supporters on the board. In the past, the nationalists had experienced serious setbacks, but never had they been so marginalized in their own community. The experience of the nationalist trustees was an indication that nationalism increasingly offered an inadequate basis for lay leadership independent of the clergy. An equally telling portent of the future was the fact that the older nationalist societies, especially those affiliated with the ICBU, were even more unable to compete with the church and its network of voluntary associations.

In one sense, Irish nationalism was a victim of its own success. By binding Toronto's Irish Catholics to the agitation in Ireland, the Land League and Irish National League effectively dominated the nationalist movement. The older nationalist societies, which abandoned their former militant nationalism, at one time played a valuable role in the formation of a nationalist consensus. Once this consensus was formed, however, the nationalist societies could not hold their own against the Land League or the National League. Unable to offer a viable alternative to Parnellite nationalism, which only the Land League or the Irish National League could legitimately claim to represent, these societies either languished, as in the case of the Irish Catholic Benevolent Union, or allied themselves with the church, as the Emerald Benevolent Association had done.

In less than a decade, the domination of the nationalist movement by the Land League and the National League had resulted in the complete reorganization in the associational life of Irish-Catholic men. Unlike earlier lay associations outside the church, in which social life and nationalism were inextricably linked, the new fraternal societies promoted a social life that emphasized religious uplift, with little overt concern for nationalism. By the mid-1890s, fraternal and mutual-benefit societies with close connections to the church, parish young men's societies, and devotional organizations were the leading voluntary associations for men in the Catholic community. Catholic associational life had become firmly entrenched in the parish, within the reserved arena of the church.

Irish nationalist ideology had also undergone a dramatic change, a reflection of the experiences and aspirations of second-generation Irish Catholics. J.J. Curran, a member of parliament for Montreal Centre, proclaimed at a Saint Patrick's Day concert in Toronto that Canada was composed of "various classes, but one nationality – the Canadian."[129] "Our first duty is to Canada, the land we live in,"

declared Francis A. Anglin, son of Timothy W. Anglin, and later
chief justice of Canada, in his Saint Patrick's Day address to the Irish
National League. "By faithfully discharging the duties that loyalty to
Canada requires of us," Anglin explained,

we can render to the motherland an invaluable service ... In a country
endowed with free institutions we enjoy all the blessings of self-government.
We are Home Rulers. It is the privilege and it is the duty of every citizen to
interest himself in the affairs of this country, to assist in their management,
thus participating in its government. It is our duty to raise up from amongst
us as many public men as possible to take a prominent part in the government of the nation.

"We cannot afford to rely too much in our present position,"
Anglin warned, "in which we enjoy equal rights with all other citizens and the fullest measure of civil and religious liberty." By taking
a prominent role in public affairs, Anglin promised, "not only will
we discharge our duty as Canadian citizens, but believe me, we will
thus prove to Englishmen how ill founded is the charge of Irish in-
competence for self government." By "demonstrating that her sons
can be – that they are – successful Home Rulers," Anglin concluded,
"we shall have faithfully discharged our duty as Irish Canadians."
Getting ahead in Canadian society was the highest form of patriotic
service. Political and economic participation in Canadian life, not the
vicarious experience of Irish events, was the natural theatre for nationalist achievement, and Home Rule for Ireland was an incidental
by-product of Irish-Catholic political success and social mobility. Although Irish nationalists such as Anglin urged Irish Catholics to
make their weight and influence felt, the logical conclusion of their
exhortations was to encourage accommodation to Canadian society,
not nationalist militancy.[130]
    The associational life of the Irish National League reflected this
impulse to accommodation. Membership in the National League did
not imply, as in former nationalist societies, a complete way of life.
The inability of Irish nationalism to overcome this compartmental-
ization in Irish-Catholic social life meant that nationalism could not
provide Irish Catholics with a communal identity – only the church
could now supply that. This weakness, however, did not become apparent until after Parnell's fall. The revelation in the divorce court
in November 1890 of Parnell's liaison with Mrs Katherine O'Shea
split the Irish parliamentary party in two: an anti-Parnell majority
led by Justin McCarthy, and a rump that continued with Parnell
and, after his death in October 1891, with John Redmond as leader.

In supporting Parnell, the Irish nationalists had opted for pragmatism and realism; with the fall of Parnell and with the Irish parliamentary party in a shambles, realism had failed them, and hope – the promise of radical nationalism – was denied them. The demise of Patrick Boyle's *Irish Canadian* in December 1892 confirmed that nationalism had lost much of its appeal. Although the Parnellite Irish National League in Toronto continued to meet until 1893, it had long since dwindled into insignificance.[131]

The affiliation of the older nationalist societies with the Catholic Church and the ideological transformation of Irish nationalism that had preceded Parnell's fall had set the stage for the eclipse of Irish nationalism as an independent force in the Irish-Catholic community. With the rapid decline of the Irish National League and the Home Rule movement, laymen were deprived of the last independent organizational base in their community from which they could exercise leadership free from the supervision of the clergy. Nor could they now draw on Irish nationalist ideology to legitimatize lay initiative. "We ask no favors as a class," asserted D.A. Carey, president of the Emerald Benevolent Association, "we are all Canadians and as Canadians, loving our country and honoring her laws, do we desire to be judged."[132] Patriotism was now a Canadian, not an Irish, virtue.

In the last two decades of the nineteenth century, then, Irish nationalism in Toronto lost its sense of close connection to Ireland. Ireland was no longer "home," and Irish usage, such as the meaning of "friend" for relatives, had to be explained to Catholic readers.[133] Although this development was a reflection of the fact that the Irish-Catholic community lost its cultural ties with Ireland as the Canadian-born overtook the immigrant generation, it also indicated that Irish Catholics, whether Irish- or Canadian-born, now saw themselves as more Canadian than Irish. Even the Irish-born and -educated editor of the *Catholic Register*, Father J.R. Teefy, could declare, "our heart is large enough to sympathize most earnestly with our people – for they are our people in kinship and affection – in their struggle for Home Rule."[134]

The fight for Home Rule was no longer the struggle of the descendants of Irish Catholics in Canada. The intimate connection with Ireland instilled by radical nationalism was dead. The cause of Irish independence was remote, belonging to a related but essentially different people. Irish nationalism had become little more than an exercise in nostalgia. In the past, Irish nationalism had depended on the Catholic Church for part of its self-definition; indeed, nationalism had played a critical part in making Catholicism central to

Irish-Catholic ethnicity. At the same time, nationalism had also given Irish-Catholic ethnicity another, though complementary, dimension, a specifically Irish identity. Rather than supplanting Catholicism as the fundamental ground for Irish-Catholic ethnic identity, nationalism provided a complementary focus, one that enabled Catholic laymen to exercise leadership independently of the church while at the same time upholding the centrality of Catholicism to Irish-Catholic ethnicity. Competition between the laity and the clergy did not entail the rejection of Catholicism by the lay nationalists, for both the lay nationalists and clergy subscribed to the same fundamental beliefs – the indissoluble alliance between Irish nationalism and Catholicism. The dynamic interplay between nationalism and Catholicism, between two institutional arenas for lay activism and initiative, had defined Irish-Catholic ethnicity and so in a very real way contributed to the creation of an Irish-Catholic community in Toronto.

Irish nationalism in Toronto was living on borrowed time. The incorporation of lay fraternal organizations into the official structures of the Catholic Church and the emergence of mass-based devotional organizations for men represented the culmination of the devotional revolution inaugurated by Bishop Armand Charbonnel. In a sense, the Irish nationalist associations had been all too successful in promoting allegiance to the Catholic Church for them to continue as independent organizations. As nationalism ceased to have an independent organizational base, Irish Catholics increasingly defined their ethnicity by language and religion. Rather than looking to the past and the proud traditions of Ireland, laymen now embraced the present and the future as Canadians.

While the Catholic Church remained central to Catholic self-definition, and so still distinguished Irish Catholics from the Protestant majority, Catholics of Irish descent increasingly emphasized the fact that they spoke the English language, something they shared with Canadian Protestants. At the same time that the Roman Catholic Church extended its womb-to-tomb culture to incorporate male associational life, many laymen were to compartmentalize their loyalties and to exercise their initiative and leadership on a larger stage. English-speaking Catholics such as J.J. Foy entered into the political mainstream, gaining support well beyond their circle of co-religionists.[135] Others joined mainstream voluntary organizations such as the militia, which combined Canadian patriotism and recreation in equal measure.[136] As religion and language became the symbols of their self-definition, English-speaking Catholics insisted that they were fully Canadian. The language dispute in the 1920s between anglophone and francophone Catholics revealed that, in their anxiety to prove that they were English-speaking Canadians, Catholics of Irish descent would not be able to avoid the dangers of xenophobia.[137]

Conclusion

The Roman Catholic community in 1895 was a very different community from the one that greeted its second bishop, Armand de Charbonnel, in 1850. The Irish-Catholic community of 1850, composed mainly of recently arrived immigrants, and its lay associations and social institutions were in a rudimentary state. Even the Roman Catholic Church's parochial organization was still anaemic. This organizational vacuum opened the way for the town's small Catholic élite, many of whom were not Irish, to exercise lay initiative in church and community life. These lay men and women took a leading part in the administration of the parish and in the provision of the few but nonetheless essential social services that existed in the community, such as the care of orphans and the like. The lack of voluntary associations and social institutions was especially critical to the pastoral mission of the Roman Catholic church. Without these institutional means for social and spiritual outreach, the church had limited contact with the laity, many of whom were not regular church-goers. Not only was the church failing to achieve its pastoral mission, but it was also incapable of furnishing an adequate institutional framework for the development of an ethnic community.

By contrast, the vast majority of Catholics living in Toronto in 1895 attended church and regularly performed their devotions. Moreover, these second- and third-generation descendants of Irish-Catholic immigrants enjoyed an extensive network of religious, social, and recreational voluntary associations that were affiliated with or under the direct auspices of the Catholic Church, now unquestionably the dominant social institution in their community. These organizations transformed the Catholic Church into a comprehensive social and religious institution which offered something for almost everybody. The alignment of Catholic voluntary associations with the church also had implications for the laity's social identity. Lay people now defined their social identity in a way quite different from that which had taken root after the Irish nationalist awakening of the late 1850s. Irish nationalism could still pull on the heartstrings of the Canadian-born, but it lived on as a vestigial force, one that would soon be overtaken by language.

The seeds of these developments had been sown when Bishop Charbonnel launched his crusade for religious renewal in the 1850s. In keeping with its ultramontane ideals and objectives, this movement for renewal sought to make the church an inclusive institution that attended to the laity's spiritual regeneration and social improvement. With a primitive parish organization, few clergy, and very little in the way of financial resources, the church of necessity turned to the laity for assistance, and their voluntary associations would prove to be central to the church's achievement of its religious and cultural goals.

Devotional organizations were the largest parish voluntary associations, and they spearheaded the campaign for religious renewal in the parish. Although devotional organizations were in theory open to all, their membership was in fact largely made up of women. In becoming active in a devotional organization they served and saved others, a nurturing role for which it was thought women were particularly well suited by virtue of their sex. By identifying religion with women's capacity for nurture, devotional Catholicism gave women new authority in their personal relations, but it also restricted their options in the public arena of parish. The clergy relegated women to a subordinate role in the parish on account of both their lay status and their sex, which in the view of the clergy uniquely fitted them for service to others. Women of necessity had to exercise their initiative indirectly, by acting through the clergy, much as they often did with male family members at home. Through such means, women were able to carve out a sphere for lay leadership and initiative in the parish, making it possible for them to establish organizations of their own over which they maintained control even while they acknowledged the clergy's right to supervision.

Leadership in the parish devotional and charitable organizations was based on the hierarchy of class, but though these organizations were far from egalitarian, they did enable rank-and-file activists to fashion an associational life suited to their own needs. The close association between religion and female social roles led women to collaborate with each other in the creation of their own social world that joined female sociability with Roman Catholic piety. So successful were confraternity leaders and activists in this endeavour that their organizations quickly gained popular support among women, who became the principal constituency for devotional Catholicism.

The middle-class men who founded the Saint Vincent de Paul Society had a much easier time in obtaining the clergy's support of their leadership and initiative in the parish than did the activists in devotional organizations. From the society's inception, the clergy expected the Saint Vincent de Paul Society visitors to play an important role in the church's apostolate to the poor. To be sure, the leaders of the society consulted with the clergy, especially before undertaking new ventures, but usually they were left to their own devices. Having received a mandate from the church to provide the poor with religious succour and material assistance, these leaders demonstrated due deference to clerical authority and at the same time retained effective control over the operation of their society and its programs. As a result, a critical part of the church's outreach – especially home visiting – was in lay hands. Leadership of the Saint Vincent de Paul was oligarchical in nature, but the field for initiative open to this closely knit circle was wide indeed.

Lay initiative was far from being inherently subversive, as the women's charitable organizations and the Saint Vincent de Paul Society demonstrated. But no matter how it was exercised or how varied its scope, lay initiative transformed the parish. Lay leaders helped to establish a network of voluntary associations that radiated out from the parish church into the larger community to popularize new forms of public and private piety, especially among those who previously had little contact with the church. In providing essential social services to the community that invariably wedded social assistance to devotional discipline, lay activists made it possible for the church to become a comprehensive social and cultural institution that served the laity in Toronto and the surrounding countryside from the cradle to the grave. Not only did these organizations provide essential services for the many, but they also bound their members into "communities of belief and action," to borrow Timothy L. Smith's phrase. In these associations, lay activists forged new social relationships and engendered new loyalties among the rank and file, and so they created a comprehensive social life separate from that of the Protestant majority. The associational network of the parish, which was sustained by the initiative and activism of the laity, made possible the formation of an Irish-Catholic ethnic culture inseparable from the Roman Catholic Church.

Yet for the parish to assume its role as the institutional linchpin in the development of an ethnic culture, it had to become an inclusive institution. By the mid-1860s, when the first phase of Toronto's devotional revolution was coming to a close, religious behaviour and associational membership were sharply differentiated by sex. While women joined devotional and other organizations attached to the parish, men joined associations independent of the church and devoted to the cause of Irish nationalism. Like the devotional organizations, nationalist organizations also contributed to the development of Irish-Catholic solidarity, but they appealed to a very different constituency. In the nationalist societies, laymen – most of whom were from the working class – built an autonomous associational life that advanced lay leadership in the Irish-Catholic community. The nationalists' appropriation of politicized traditions of national resistance and freedom made them a potent force for ethnic pride and solidarity that, with its vindication of popular sovereignty, appealed directly to the grass roots in Toronto and in towns across Ontario. Their populist bid for ethnic leadership was a major challenge to the clergy's standing in the community, one that certainly made the clergy uneasy, for now nationalism enabled laymen to take the initiative in matters that the clergy would have preferred to remain in their own hands. Nevertheless, such independent lay leadership was not the incubus the clergy thought it to be.

Both the clergy and the nationalists leaders sought to shore up and, if possible, extend their followings, but each in their own way appealed to Catholicism and nationalism to bolster their leadership in the Irish-Catholic community. Parish-based organizations and national associations, therefore, did not promote exclusive forms of ethnic affiliation. Rather, they fostered Irish-Catholic ethnic consciousness in complementary ways that reinforced the centrality of Catholicism as a mark of ethnic distinction. Even among those laymen whose faith was more honoured in the breach than in the observance, nationalist societies did much to make Catholicism the touchstone for their communal identity. Similarly, parish-based voluntary associations fostered nationalist sentiments among their members. Lay activists in the parish and in the nationalist societies thus contributed to the emergence of a broad-based consensus that Catholicism and nationalism were the twin pillars for Irish-Catholic ethnicity, and it was this common ground that made possible an accommodation between the church and the independent nationalist societies.

At the same time that the clergy worked toward an accommodation with the nationalist societies and the constituency that these societies represented, they also sought ways to reach Irish-Catholic men more directly. Temperance societies were the most notable success in this direction, but they also illustrated the difficulties church-based organizations had in responding to the moral economy of men's social life. At the root of these organizations' failure was the clergy's ambivalence to lay initiative, especially when it ran outside the rule and the orbit of religion. The clergy hoped that the secular pastimes offered by temperance societies would appeal to Irish-Catholic men's aspirations to manly independence, which was essential if voluntary associations for men were to have a significant presence in the parish. Yet the clergy nonetheless distrusted the egalitarian ethos of these pastimes and so sought to keep these organizations on as close a rein as possible. The result was that most parishes failed to develop a cadre of lay activists whose leadership was essential for these organizations to sustain their support at the grass roots and to survive the disruption that usually followed the transfer of the pastor to another parish.

Within a generation, however, Catholic voluntary associations for men had become a fixed feature of parish life. Given the strength of the nationalist societies and their ability to maintain their autonomy in their earlier years, contemporaries could hardly have foreseen this outcome. The Irish nationalist societies' success in reaching an accommodation with the church consolidated their support at the grass roots, but this accommodation was eventually to contribute to their undoing. At first glance, it would appear that the nationalists had the upper hand in their relations with the clergy. In many instances, as in the case of the Hibernians' promotion of radical nationalism during the 1860s or the radical wing's adoption of moderate nationalism in the Irish Catholic Benevolent Union during the 1870s, the clergy were hard pressed to keep up with the advanced nationalists and to maintain the church's identification with Ireland's cause. Yet the nationalists' successes masked the true nature of the situation. In reaching an accommodation with the Catholic Church, the nationalist societies contributed to the cultural hegemony of the church, which in time would erode the ability of these organizations to function independently of the church and to form an effective counterweight to clerical leadership.

The church's cultural hegemony was graphically exemplified in the outlook and sensibilities of those Catholic men who came to maturity during the 1880s. Born and raised in Toronto, these men lived in a community in which the parish and its religious world and associational life had been an established fixture for a generation. Most of these young men grew up in a religious family environment, having been raised by mothers who were members of a devotional organization, and most of them had themselves been members of a devotional organization when they attended separate schools in their childhood. During their formative years, the piety and institutions of the church had defined their social world and culture as distinct and separate from that of the Protestant majority. For these men, an associational life under the auspices of the Catholic Church came quite naturally. Such an associational life was a familiar part of their social world, and it reflected the exclusive identity that was integral to that world.

In the late 1880s the controversy over the secret ballot in Separate School Board elections revealed the relative strengths of the clergy and of those who championed lay control over the Irish-Catholic community's public institutions. When the clergy presented the laity with a stark choice between their national or religious allegiances, the dissident trustees lost the battle for public opinion. Their defeat was intertwined with the decline of the Irish National League and, more particularly, with the brand of nationalism that it represented. The National League had fostered a spirit of accommodation to Canadian society, but in so doing it could not offer its members a complete way of life, as the older nationalist societies had done in their heyday. The fall of Parnell left a completely demoralized Irish National League unable to offer a viable alternative to the parish's rich associational life for men. By 1895 parish devotional organizations, such as the Men's League of the Apostleship of Prayer, had finally gained a mass following among Catholic men. Bishop Charbonnel's vision of an inclusive community based upon devotional Catholicism had finally triumphed.

Catholic voluntary associations no longer sustained lay initiative independent of the formal structures of the church, but lay initiative did persist, and in some respects its scope even expanded. Fraternal organizations affiliated with the church, such as the Catholic Mutual Benefit Association, were under lay control, though the clergy's right to supervision and counsel was well recognized. At the same time, such associations began to offer an expanded stage for lay leadership and initiative under Catholic auspices. In earlier Catholic organizations, such as the Irish nationalist associations, lay initiative flourished at the local level and eventually, as nationalists forged regional federations, at the provincial level. In the CMBA, however, the laity secured a national platform, much as they were to do later in the Knights of Columbus. For the descendants of Irish-Catholic immigrants – many of whom, as prosperous members of the middle class, wished to take their places in the mainstream of Canadian life – the CMBA offered suitable scope for and recognition of their talents and accomplishments.

The restructuring of Catholic voluntary associations during the late 1880s and early 1890s provided the institutional matrix for a new form of group consciousness among Toronto's Catholics. During this time Irish Catholics began to understand their ethnic identity in a new and different way. They no longer expected voluntary associations independent of the church to offer an inclusive way of life or to contribute fundamentally to their group consciousness. These responsibilities had now devolved to parochial organizations. The social world of the new generation was increasingly bounded by the parish on the one hand and the wider English-speaking Canadian society on the other. For this reason, they understood their particularity mainly in terms of Catholicism, in which nationalism was to play an auxiliary and ever decreasing role. As Irish nationalism declined in importance, Toronto's Catholics began to stress what they shared with other English-speaking Canadians: the English language. Language and religion were to become the primary foundations for their identity. At the same time that the laity became more engaged in Canadian society, their collective social life, and hence the primary basis for Catholic particularism, retreated to the comparatively private world of the parish. Among English-speaking Catholics, cultural separatism co-existed in an uneasy tension with the desire to become a part of the English-speaking Canadian mainstream. If Catholics of Irish origin found no easy resolution to this dilemma, it was because through their voluntary associations they had succeeded in creating a subculture and in so doing had forged their own exclusive identity.

APPENDIX

Occupational Categories*

Unskilled occupations include: cab driver, caretaker, carter, dairyman, drover, express man, farmer, gardener, gatekeeper, housekeeper, huckster, labourer, lamp lighter, marine sailor, milkman, nursery and seedsman, packer, peddlar, porter, railroad employee, sawyer, seamstress, servant, stuffer, teamster, waiter, washerwoman, watchman, wharfinger, whitewasher.

Semi-skilled occupations include: apprentice, axemaker, baker, barber, basket maker, blacking maker, blacksmith, boiler maker, brick maker, broom maker, builder (if not self-employed), butcher (if not self-employed), cabman, carpenter, carriage maker, cooper, cook, cordwainer, dyer, fareman, filemaker, fireman, fisherman, hostler, joiner, mason, mechanic, milliner, motor man, painter, polisher, press man, presser, printer, rope maker, roofer, sawmaker, shipwright, signmaker, steam fitter, tallow chandler, tanner, trimmer, turner, upholsterer, waggon maker, wheelwright, wood worker.

Skilled occupations include: armorer, artist, bell hanger, boat builder, bootmaker, book binder, brewer, bricklayer, brass founders, brass finishers, cabinet maker, carver, chair maker, chandler, clock or watch maker, coppersmith, cutler, distiller, dressmaker, edge-tool maker, engine driver, engraver, finisher, founder, gas fitter, goldsmith, guilder, gunsmith, glass cutter, glass stainer, harness maker, land surveyor, locksmith, lithographer, machinist, marble cutter, miller, moulder, musician, organ builder, paper

---

* This classification was developed by Peter G. Goheen, *Victorian Toronto, 1850–1900: Pattern and Process of Growth*, University of Chicago, Department of Geography, research paper no. 127 (Chicago 1970), 229–30.

hanger, pattern maker, piano maker, plasterer, plumber, saddler, shoe-maker, silversmith, stone cutter, tailor, telegraph operator, tinsmith, watch-maker, weaver, yardmaster.

Clerical occupations include: accountant, assessor, bailiff, barkeeper, bartender, bookkeeper, cashier, clerk, collector, commissioner, constable, customs collector, forwarder, goaler, letter carrier, notary public, photogra-phist, policeman, proofreader, salesman, traveller, turnkey.

Business occupations include: agent-general and insurance, auctioneer, banker, boarding-house keeper, bookseller and stationer, broker, cab owner, cattle dealer, chemist or druggist, clothier, confectioner, contractor, fruit-erer, furrier, grocer, hatter, hotel keeper, jeweler, jobber, manufacturer, merchant, publisher, shopkeeper, wholesaler.

Professional occupations include: architect, attorney, barrister, civil and other engineers, clergy, dentist, editor, medical doctor, professor, solicitor, student, teacher.

Private means include the following persons: gentleman, pensioner, re-tired, unemployed, widow.

Notes

INTRODUCTION

1 Mason Wade, *The French Canadians 1760–1967*, rev. ed. in 2 vols. (Toronto: Macmillan of Canada 1968), 1:360.
2 This campaign has been best documented in the case of the United States. See Patrick Carey's stimulating study *People, Priests, and Prelates: Ecclesiastical Democracy and the Tensions of Trusteeism* (Notre Dame, Indiana: University of Notre Dame Press 1987). Carey points out

that, though lay democracy may have been defeated, lay initiative nonetheless persisted.

3 Timothy L. Smith, "Lay Initiative in the Religious Life of American
Immigrants, 1880–1950," in *Anonymous Americans: Explorations in*
Nineteenth-Century Social History, ed. Tamara K. Hareven (Englewood
Cliffs, New Jersey: Prentice-Hall 1971), 235–6.

4 Emmet Larkin, "Church, State, and Nation in Modern Ireland," *Amer-*
ican Historical Review, 80 (1975), 1252–61, and Jacques Monet,
"French-Canadian Nationalism and the Challenge of Ultramontanism,"
Canadian Historical Association, *Historical Papers*, 41 (1966), 45–55.

5 Emmet Larkin, "The Devotional Revolution in Ireland, 1850–75,"
American Historical Review, 77 (1972), 635–8; David W. Miller, "Irish
Catholicism and the Great Famine," *Journal of Social History*, 9 (1975),
83–7.

6 Jay Dolan, *The Immigrant Church: New York's Irish and German Catholics,*
1815–1865 (Baltimore: Johns Hopkins University Press 1975),
163–5, and *The American Catholic Experience: A History from Colonial Times*
to the Present (Garden City, New York: Doubleday 1985), 213–14;
Lynn Hollen Lees, *Exiles of Erin: Irish Migrants in Victorian London*
(Ithaca, New York: Cornell University Press 1979), 177–9, 191–4,
and 207–12.

7 Dolan, *Immigrant Church*, 92–3; Lees, *Exiles of Erin*, 223–35; Dennis
J. Clark, *The Irish in Philadelphia: Ten Generations of Urban Experience*
(Philadelphia: Temple University Press 1973), 110–14; Thomas
N. Brown, *Irish-American Nationalism, 1870–1890* (New York:
J.P. Lippincott 1966), 34–7; Lawrence J. McCaffrey, *The Irish Diaspora*
in America (Bloomington: University of Indiana Press 1976),
110–37; E.R. Norman, *The Catholic Church and Ireland in the Age of*
Rebellion, 1859–1873 (Ithaca, New York: Cornell University Press
1965), 3, 6–7, and 86–134. For an important dissent from this view,
see Larkin, "Church, State, and Nation," 1260–2.

8 Kerby A. Miller, *Emigrants and Exiles: Ireland and the Irish Exodus to North*
America (New York: Oxford University Press 1985), 7–8, 273–8,
319–25, 340–2, 556, and 567–8; Clark, *Irish in Philadelphia*, 124;
Michael F. Funchion, *Chicago's Irish Nationalists 1881–1890* (New
York: Arno Press 1976), 18–22.

9 This summary of the primordialist approach is taken from Harold
R. Issacs, *Idols of the Tribe: Group Identity and Political Change* (New
York: Harper and Row 1975), 2, 4–5, 14, 24, 26, 32, 35–6, 107, 147–9,
154, 166–7, and 180–2, but Clifford Geertz, *The Interpretation of*
Cultures (New York: Basic Books 1973), 126–30, 167–8, 258–61,
269–70, and 308–10 is probably the best-known exponent of this
school of interpretation. My analysis of the primordialist interpretation
of ethnicity has been informed by Philip Gleason's perceptive

article, "Identifying Identity: A Semantic History," *Journal of American History*, 69 (1983), 910–31, and Nathan Glazer and Daniel Moynihan's introduction to *Ethnicity: Theory and Experience*, eds. Nathan Glazer and Daniel P. Moynihan (Cambridge, Mass.: Harvard University Press 1975), 19–20.

10 Orlando Patterson, "Context and Choice in Ethnic Allegiance: A Theoretical Framework and Caribbean Case Study," in *Ethnicity: Theory and Experience*, 305–49; Victor Greene, *For God and Country: The Rise of Polish and Lithuanian Ethnic Consciousness in America* (Madison: The State Historical Society of Wisconsin 1975), 4–13; Timothy L. Smith, "Lay Initiative in the Religious Life of American Immigrants," 214–49, "Religious Denominations as Ethnic Communities: A Regional Case Study," *Church History*, 35 (1966), 207–26, and "Religion and Ethnicity in America," *American Historical Review*, 83 (1978), 1157–60, 1168–9, and 1185; Michael Bainton, "Social Alignment and Identity in a West African City," in *Urbanization and Migration in West Africa*, ed. Hilda Kuper (Berkeley, California: University of California Press 1965), 131–47; Abner Cohen, "The Lessons of Ethnicity," in *Urban Ethnicity*, ed. Abner Cohen (London: Tavistock 1974), ix–xxiv.

11 Brown, *Irish-American Nationalism*, 179–82.

12 See Smith, "Religion and Ethnicity," 1168n.38, which cites some representative studies.

13 Donald Harman Akenson, "Ontario: Whatever Happened to the Irish?" in *Canadian Papers in Rural History*, ed. Donald Harman Akenson (Gananoque: Langdale Press 1982), 231–4; Donald Harman Akenson, *The Irish in Ontario: A Study in Rural History* (Kingston and Montreal: McGill-Queen's University Press 1984), 26–7 and 34–41; Donald Harman Akenson, *Being Had: Historians, Evidence, and the Irish in North America* (Port Credit, Ontario: P.D. Meany 1985), 84 and 94–5; A. Gordon Darroch and Michael D. Ornstein, "Ethnicity and Occupational Structure in Canada in 1871: The Vertical Mosaic in Historical Perspective," *Canadian Historical Review*, 61 (1980), 314, 323, and 325–6; Cecil J. Houston and William J. Smyth, *Irish Emigration and Canadian Settlement: Patterns, Links, and Letters* (Toronto: University of Toronto Press 1990), 21–3, 27, 122, 128, 207–8, and 337–40.

14 George Sheppard, "'God Save the Green' Fenianism and Fellowship in Victorian Ontario," *Histoire sociale/Social History*, 20 (1987), 131–4; *Report of the Superior Council of Canada for the Year 1886* (Quebec 1889), 18–19; *Canadian Messenger of the Sacred Heart* (1895), 80–1, 119, 201, and 253.

15 Gregory S. Kealey, *Toronto Workers Respond to Industrial Capitalism, 1867–1892* (Toronto: University of Toronto Press 1980), 98; Houston and Smyth, *Irish Emigration and Canadian Settlement*, 183.

CHAPTER ONE

1 Donald Harman Akenson, *The Irish in Ontario: A Study in Rural History* (Kingston and Montreal: McGill-Queen's University Press 1984), 26–8, 34, 36–39, and 43; Cecil J. Houston and William J. Smyth, *Irish Emigration and Canadian Settlement: Patterns, Links, and Letters* (Toronto: University of Toronto Press 1990), 4, 6, 21–8, and 73.

2 Oscar Handlin, *Boston's Immigrants: A Study in Acculturation*, rev. ed. (New York: Atheneum 1968), 29 and 38–48; Helen I. Cowan, *British Emigration to British North America: The First Hundred Years*, rev. ed. (Toronto: University of Toronto Press 1961), 36–7 and 176–8; William Forbes Adams, *Ireland and Irish Emigration to the New World from 1815 to the Famine* (New Haven, Connecticut: Yale University Press 1932), 2, 39–40, 65, 108, 132–3, 140–2, 163, 165, 224–6, 238–9, and 391; Gearóid Ó Tuathaigh, *Ireland Before the Famine 1798–1848* (Dublin: Gill and Macmillan 1972), 130, 135, and 140.

3 S.H. Cousens, "The Regional Variation in Emigration from Ireland between 1821 and 1841," *Institute of British Geographers, Transactions and Papers*, no.37 (December 1965), 15–30, and "The Regional Pattern of Emigration During the Great Irish Famine, 1846–51," *Institute of British Geographers, Transactions and Papers*, no.28 (1960), 126–9 and 132–3.

4 Lynn Hollen Lees, *Exiles of Erin: Irish Migrants in Victorian London* (Ithaca, New York: Cornell University Press 1979), 23–4 and 31–2.

5 Houston and Smyth, *Irish Emigration and Canadian Settlement*, 57–9 and 73.

6 S.H. Cousens, "Emigration and Demographic Change in Ireland, 1851–1861," *Economic Historical Review*, 2nd ser., 14 (1961), 284–6, and "Emigration from Ireland between 1821 and 1841," 28; Joel Mokyr, *Why Ireland Starved: A Quantitative and Analytical History of the Irish Economy, 1800–1850* (London: George Allen and Unwin 1983), 176–8 and 191–4; Raymond D. Crotty, *Irish Agricultural Production: Its Volume and Structure* (Cork: Cork University Press 1966), 36–7 and 42–3; Adams, *Ireland and Irish Emigration*, 188, 190, 219, and 221–3; Michael R. Beames, "Cottiers and Conacre in Pre-Famine Ireland," *Journal of Peasant Studies*, 2 (1975), 352–4; James S. Donnelly, Jr, *The Land and the People of Cork: The Rural Economy and the Land Question* (London: Routledge and Kegan Paul 1975), 20–2, 53, 57, and 126–8; Kerby A. Miller, *Emigrants and Exiles: Ireland and the Irish Exodus to North America* (New York: Oxford University Press 1985), 200, 208, and 216–19; and Houston and Smyth, *Irish Emigration and Canadian Settlement*, 57–60.

7 A. Gordon Darroch and Michael D. Ornstein, "Ethnicity and Occupational Structure in Canada in 1871: The Vertical Mosaic in Historical Perspective," *Canadian Historical Review*, 61 (1980), 314, 323, and 325.

8 Houston and Smyth, *Irish Emigration and Canadian Settlement*, 128–9 and 244–5.

9 Akenson, *Irish in Ontario*, 246–63, and Glenn J. Lockwood, "Success and the Doubtful Image of Irish Immigrants in Upper Canada: The Case of Montague Township 1820–1900," in *The Untold Story: The Irish in Canada*, 2 vols., eds. Robert O'Driscoll and Lorna Reynolds (Toronto: Celtic Arts of Canada 1988), 1:329–32 and 339–40.

10 Darroch and Ornstein, "Ethnicity and Occupational Structure," 324–5.

11 *Journals of the Legislative Assembly of Canada*, 1842, appendix M.

12 Gregory S. Kealey, *Toronto Workers Respond to Industrial Capitalism 1867–1892* (Toronto: University of Toronto Press 1980), 4–6, 18–25.

13 *Census of Canada, 1851–52* (Quebec 1853), 1:30–1 and 66–7. To arrive at the number of Irish Catholics I have begun with the census figure for the number of Catholics in the city, and then from this figure deducted the total number of Canadians of French origin, 3 per cent of those who reported they were from Scotland, 2 per cent of those from England and Wales, and 2 per cent of those from the natives of Canada, not of French origin, category. For a general discussion on using published census returns to estimate the number of Catholics of Irish ancestry, see Akenson, *Irish in Ontario*, 24–6.

14 *Census of Canada* (Quebec 1863), 1:48–9 and 128–9.

15 *Census of Canada, 1870–71*, (Ottawa 1873), 1:114–15. The procedure used to estimate the ratio of Irish Catholics is similar to the one used for earlier census returns, but for this census and for that of 1881 I have used the census figures for ancestry rather than for birth as the basis for my calculations.

16 *Census of Canada 1880–81* (Ottawa 1882), 1:174 and 276–7.

17 *Census of Canada, 1851–52*, 1:30–1.

18 *Census of Canada, 1871–2*, 1:267.

19 Kealey, *Toronto Workers Respond to Industrial Capitalism*, 98; Houston and Smyth, *Irish Emigration and Canadian Settlement*, 183.

20 Barrie Dyster, "Toronto, 1840–1860: Making It in a British Protestant Town" (PhD diss., University of Toronto 1970), 215 and 232–4.

21 Gilbert Tucker, "The Famine Immigration to Canada, 1847," *American Historical Review*, 36 (1931), 540; Houston and Smyth, *Irish Emigration and Canadian Settlement*, 27.

22 G.J. Parr, "The Welcome and the Wake: Attitudes in Canada West Toward the Irish Famine Migration," *Ontario History*, 66 (1974), 106–9.

23 John Elmsley to Rev. John Carroll, 18 August 1849, Charbonnel Papers, ARCAT; *Report of the Trustees of the House of Industry* (Toronto, 1853–1856).

24 Dyster, "Toronto 1840–1860," 442–7.

25 Parr, "The Welcome and The Wake," 112–13.

26 Houston and Smyth, *Irish Emigration and Canadian Settlement*, 27 and 60–2; Cousens, "Emigration during the Great Famine," 128 and 130–33; Cousens, "Emigration and Demographic Change," 275; Oliver Macdonagh, "The Irish Famine Emigration to the United States," *Perspectives in American History*, 10 (1976), 397, 400–1, 409, and 414.

27 Lynn Lees and John Model, "Irish Countryman Urbanized: A Comparative Perspective on the Famine Migration," *Journal of Urban History*, 3 (1977), 395–400.

28 Miller, *Emigrants and Exiles*, 364; Houston and Smyth, *Irish Emigration and Canadian Settlement*, 245.

29 Jacob Spelt, *Urban Development in South Central Ontario* (Ansem, The Netherlands: Van Gorcum 1955), 71–2, 81–92, 100–8, 114–20, 131–2; H.C. Pentland, *Labour and Capital in Canada, 1650–1860* (Toronto: James Lorimer 1981), 145–8; Peter Goheen, *Victorian Toronto, 1850–1900: Pattern and Process of Growth*, University of Chicago, Department of Geography, research paper no.127 (Chicago 1970), 64–5; Kealey, *Toronto Workers Respond to Industrial Capitalism*, 2–3 and 18–34; D.C. Masters, *The Rise of Toronto 1850–1890* (Toronto: University of Toronto Press 1947), 13–14 and 16–17; J.M.S. Careless, *Toronto to 1910: An Illustrated History* (Toronto: James Lorimer 1984), 86–89 and 109–10.

30 Kealey, *Toronto Workers Respond to Industrial Capitalism*, 37–52 and 64–82.

31 Eric James Jarvis, "Mid-Victorian Toronto: Panic, Policy, and Public Response, 1857–1863" (PhD diss., University of Western Ontario 1979), 274; J.E. Middleton, *The Municipality of Toronto*, 3 vols. (Toronto: Dominion Publishing 1923) 1:264; Bettina Bradbury, "Family Economy and Work in an Industrializing City: Montreal in the 1870s," Canadian Historical Association, *Historical Papers*, 1979, 87–9; Kealey, *Toronto Workers Respond to Industrial Capitalism*, 28.

32 Rev. J. Jamot, "Census of City Wards," *circa* early 1860s, ARCAT. Like Cecil J. Houston and William J. Smyth in their "The Irish Abroad: Better Questions Through a Better Source, the Canadian Census," *Irish Geographer*, 13 (1980), 1–18, I have used the occupation classification developed by Peter Goheen, *Victorian Toronto*, 229–30. See appendix.

33 Bradbury, "Family Economy and Work," 87–9; Kealey, *Toronto Workers Respond to Industrial Capitalism*, 28; *Globe*, 13 March 1860, 16 May 1861, and 24 April 1876.
34 Claudette Lacelle, "Les domestiques dans les villes canadiennes au XIX siècle: effectifs et conditions de vie," *Histoire sociale/Social History*, 15 (1982), 186; *Globe*, 16 June 1857, 20 October 1868, and 1 April 1876.
35 As almost 30 per cent of the Irish-Catholic male household heads in nearby Hamilton held skilled or semi-skilled jobs in 1851, it is likely that the results derived from Father Jamot's census are an accurate indication of Toronto's Irish-Catholic participation in the trades. See Michael B. Katz, *The People of Hamilton, Canada West: Family and Class in a Mid-Nineteenth-Century City* (Cambridge, Massachusetts: Harvard University Press 1975), 67.
36 Kealey, *Toronto Workers Respond to Industrial Capitalism*, 28 and 37–52.
37 *Globe*, 9 April 1858, 19 September 1864, 27 November 1866, 22 July 1867, and 28 October 1873; *Leader*, 20 April 1860 and 7 July 1865.
38 Rev. J. Jamot, "Census of City Wards," *circa* early 1860s, ARCAT. See also Captain W.S. Prince to John A. Macdonald, 20 October 1865, Macdonald Papers, NAC.
39 *Irish Canadian*, 14 November 1864 and 24 May 1865; *Globe*, 23 May 1860 and 19 March 1873; *Leader*, 27 February 1869 and 4 September 1871.
40 Unfortunately, detailed reports on wage rates and the cost of living in Toronto daily newspapers date from the 1880s, when the press became interested in the "labour question." Wage rates and cost of living are based on reports in *Globe*, 2 April 1881, 30 April 1881, 9 December 1882, 3 February 1883, 27 August 1883, 22 September 1883, 27 October 1883, and 17 November 1883. During the 1880s unusually high rates of employment combined with declining prices resulted in many families experiencing an improvement in their standard of living. Figures from the 1880s can therefore provide a rough indication of the standards of living experienced by families in earlier decades. See David Gagan and Rosemary Gagan, "Working-Class Standards of Living in Late-Victorian Urban Ontario: A Review of the Miscellaneous Evidence on the Quality of Material Life," *Journal of the Canadian Historical Association*, new series, 1 (1990), 176 and 184–5.
41 Not a few labourers were employed by fellow Irish Catholics. See *Globe*, 19 June 1855 and 17 May 1856.
42 Judith Fingard, "The Winter's Tale: The Seasonal Contours of Pre-industrial Poverty in British North America, 1815–1860," Canadian Historical Association, *Historical Papers*, 1974, 65–94; Bettina

Bradbury, "The Fragmented Family: Family Strategies in the Face of Death, Illness, and Poverty, Montreal, 1868–1885," in *Childhood and Family in Canadian History*, ed. Joy Parr (Toronto: McClelland and Stewart 1982), 109–28; Ian Davey, "The Rhythm of Work and the Rhythm of School," in *Egerton Ryerson and His Times*, eds. Neil McDonald and Alf Chaiton (Toronto: Macmillan of Canada 1978), 237–8.

43 My calculations are based on the Rev. Jamot's "Census of City Wards,"ARCAT, and *Census of Canada, 1860–61* (Quebec 1863), 1:48–9 and 128–9. My assumption is that the distribution of Irish-Catholic household heads approximated that of the population as whole, which are the only figures reported in the census.

44 *Globe*, 10 February 1855, 16 July 1856, 12 August 1856, 13 March 1860, 31 July 1862, 16 November 1867, 14 April 1869, 26 July 1870, 3 June 1871, 2 December 1872, 6 December 1872, 27 November 1880, 2 April 1881, 3 February 1883, and 24 December 1883.

45 *Census of Canada, 1860–61*, 1:128–9.

46 Goheen, *Victorian Toronto*, 7–10, 84–5, and 126–7. See also Katz, *People of Hamilton*, 23, 332–4, and 337–41.

47 Rev. J. Jamot, "Census of City Wards," *circa* early 1860s, ARCAT; Goheen, *Victorian Toronto*, 143, 151, 153–5, 187–8, and 213–15; Gerald J. Stortz, "John Joseph Lynch, Archbishop of Toronto: A Bibliographical Study in Religious, Political and Social Commitment" (PhD diss., University of Guelph 1980), 77–8; Dyster, "Toronto, 1840–1860," 36–7 and 169; Murray W. Nicolson, "The Catholic Church and the Irish in Victorian Toronto" (PhD diss., University of Guelph 1980), 16–20.

48 See the protest of the "respectable" residents of Dummer Street against the "rowdies" and "low" Irish on their street in *Globe*, 2 May 1878.

49 Bishop Lynch to an unidentified correspondent, 2 August 1866, Lynch Papers, ARCAT.

50 *Globe*, 18 January 1860, 13 March 1860, 27 December 1861, 25 October 1864, 26 February 1873, 24 April 1876, and 17 November 1883; *Leader*, 31 October 1865 and 15 April 1869.

51 *Globe*, 15 October 1866; Stortz, "John Joseph Lynch," 77; G.P. de T. Glazebrook, *The Story of Toronto* (Toronto: University of Toronto Press 1971), 146; Michael Piva, *The Condition of the Working Class in Toronto, 1900–1921* (Ottawa: University of Ottawa Press 1979), 125–6.

52 Since the census provides no information on Irish-Catholic family and household size, I have used the following estimates. In computing family size I have used an estimate of 3.7, which was the average family size for Irish Catholics in London, England. See Lees, *Exiles of Erin*, 136–8. I have assumed that household size among Irish Catholics was

five members, which is a low estimate. On household size, see Peter Laslett and Richard Wall, *Household and Family in Past Time* (Cambridge: Cambridge University Press 1972), 214 and 233, and A. Gordon Darroch and Michael Ornstein, "Family and Household in Nineteenth-Century Canada: Regional Patterns and Regional Economies," *Journal of Family History*, 9 (1984), 158–77. My calculations are based on the Rev. Jamot's "Census of City Wards," ARCAT, and *Census of Canada, 1860–61*, 1:48–9 and 128–9.

53 *Irish Canadian*, 7 January 1863 and 24 May 1865; *Canadian Freeman*, 7 January 1859 and 3 January 1861.

54 Goheen, *Victorian Toronto*, 169; G.J. Timperlake, *Illustrated Toronto: Past and Present* (Toronto: Peter Gross 1877), 147–9.

55 *Globe*, 9 April 1861, 20 April 1861, 22 October 1864, 14 February 1867, and 24 March 1869; *Leader*, 13 November 1860.

56 Dyster, "Toronto, 1840–1860," 169; Goheen, *Victorian Toronto*, 84.

57 *Globe*, 14 February 1866.

58 *Globe*, 15 September 1864.

59 *Globe*, 25 October 1864.

60 In the late 1850s and early 1860s, the Irish-Catholic mortality rate fluctuated from between one and a fifth to one and a quarter of the norm. See *Globe*, 1 January 1858 and 14 January 1861.

61 *Globe*, 1 June 1859, 12 March 1860, 17 May 1868, 28 September 1868, 26 June 1869, 17 January 1870, 20 October 1872, 12 April 1873, 10 July 1875, 21 January 1880, and 16 September 1882; *Leader*, 7 November 1864, 14 June 1865, and 28 June 1873; C.S. Clark, *Of Toronto the Good: A Social Study* (Toronto: Toronto Publishing 1898), 96; Timperlake, *Illustrated Toronto*, 147–9.

62 *Leader*, 23 January 1866.

63 *Globe*, 27 January 1865, 4 July 1865, 28 December 1865, and 1 September 1879; *Leader*, 15 February 1859, 10 May 1865, and 10 August 1866.

64 *Globe*, 11 May 1854, 9 April 1858, 29 January 1859, 10 April 1865, 18 August 1873, and 7 April 1881; *Leader*, 23 November 1865, 15 January 1867, and 2 August 1869.

65 *Globe*, 16 August 1856, 21 November 1856, 25 November 1856, 26 May 1860, and 24 May 1864; *Leader*, 11 January 1859, 15 and 17 November 1859, 28 September 1861, 24 August 1864, 6 February 1865, and 5 August 1875.

66 *Globe*, 11 October 1854 and 2 August 1869.

67 *Canadian Freeman*, 6 April 1865.

68 Kenneth Duncan, "Irish Famine Immigration and the Social Structure of Canada West," in *Canada: A Sociological Profile*, ed. W.E. Mann (Toronto: Copp, Clark 1966), 14–16.

69 Murray W. Nicolson, "Peasants in an Urban Society: The Irish
Catholics in Victorian Toronto," in *Gathering Place: People and
Neighborhoods of Toronto, 1834–1945*, ed. Robert Harney (Toronto:
Multicultural Historical Society of Ontario 1985), 58, "Irish Tri-
dentine Catholicism in Victorian Toronto: Vessel for Ethno-religious
Persistence," Canadian Catholic Historical Association, *Study
Sessions*, 50 (1983), 423 and 425, and "Catholic Church and the
Irish," 7, 548, and 553.
70 Paul C. Appleton, "The Sunshine and the Shade: Labour Activism
in Central Canada" (MA thesis, University of Calgary 1974), 32,
44, 46, 48, 69, 119–20, and 123–4.
71 J.A. Murphy, "The Support of the Clergy in Ireland, 1750–1850,"
Historical Studies, 5 (1965), 104–14.

CHAPTER TWO

1 Nive Voisine. "Jubilés, missions paroissiales et prédication au
XIXe siècle," *Recherches sociographiques*, 23 (1982), 125–37, and
Louis Rousseau, "Les missions populaires de 1840–42: acteurs prin-
cipaux et conséquences," Société canadienne d'histoire de l'Église
catholique, *Sessions d'étude*, 53 (1986), 7–21.
2 Murray W. Nicolson, "Ecclesiastical Metropolitanism and the Evolution
of the Catholic Archdiocese of Toronto," *Histoire sociale/Social History*, 15 (1982), 132–33. For a detailed account of the influence of the
Family Compact in church affairs and the intricate ties through
intermarriage that bound the families of the Compact, consult
Nicolson, "The Catholic Church and the Irish in Victorian Toronto" (PhD diss., University of Guelph 1980), chapter two. For an
analysis of the political role of the Family Compact and the roots
of their ideology, see S.F. Wise, "Upper Canada and the Conservative
Tradition," in *Profiles of a Province: Studies in the History of Ontario*
(Toronto: Ontario Historical Society 1967), 20–3.
3 John Bossy, *The English Catholic Community, 1570–1850* (New York:
Oxford University Press 1976), 254–64, 328, and 335–55; J. Derek
Holmes, *More Roman than Rome: English Catholicism in the Nineteenth
Century* (London: Burns and Oates 1978), 23–4.
4 Bossy, *English Catholic Community*, 306–16; Sheridan Gilley, "The
Roman Catholic Mission to the Irish in London, 1840–1860,"
Recusant History, 10 (1969), 123–42.
5 Emmet Larkin, "The Devotional Revolution in Ireland, 1850–75,"
American Historical Review, 77 (1972), 625–52; David W. Miller,
"Irish Catholicism and the Great Famine," *Journal of Social History*,
9 (1975), 80–98.
6 On the ultramontane movement in French Canada and the Catholic

revival of the 1840s, see Jacques Monet, "French-Canadian Nationalism and the Challenge of Ultramontanism," Canadian Historical Association, *Historical Papers*, 1966, 41–55; Robert Choquette,
"L'Église d'Ottawa sous Mgr. Guiges, 1848–1874," Société d'Histoire
de l'Église Catholique, *Sessions d'étude*, 44 (1977), 57–62; and
Gaston Carrière, "L'Église canadienne vers 1841," *Revue de l'Université
d'Ottawa*, 24 (1954), 66–89.

7 Bishop Ignace Bourget to Bishop Rémi Gaulin, 13 April 1841, Bishop
Gaulin to Bishop Bourget, 20 April 1841, Bishop Bourget to
Mgr. Carboli, 27 July 1841, Testimonial Letter of the Bishops of
Quebec, 29 April 1841, Testimonial Letter of the Bishops of
Montreal and Kingston, n.d., Power Papers, ARCAT; Robert Choquette,
L'Église Catholique dans l'Ontario français du dix-neuvième siècle
(Ottawa: Éditions de l'Université d'Ottawa 1984), 95–7.

8 Bishop Rémi Gaulin to Bishop Ignace Bourget, 25 April 1841, Bourget
Papers, ACAM.

9 Rev. J.J. Hay to Archbishop Joseph Signay, 3 October 1847,
Archbishop Signay to Bishop Bourget, 14 October 1847, Bishops of the
Province of Quebec to Pius IX, October 1849, Bourget Papers, ACAM.

10 Bishop Charbonnel to Bishop Bourget, 6 August 1855, Charbonnel
Papers, ARCAT; Choquette, *Église catholique*, 100–3; Murray
W. Nicolson and John S. Moir, "Armand-François-Marie de Charbon-
nel," *Dictionary of Canadian Biography* (Toronto: University of
Toronto Press 1990), 12:182–3.

11 J.R. Teefy, *Jubilee Volume: The Archdiocese of Toronto and Archbishop
Walsh* (Toronto: Geo. T. Dixon 1892), 179.

12 Bishop Lynch to Cardinal Alessandro Barnabo, 10 June 1868, Lynch
Papers, ARCAT. This letter clearly indicates that it was Toronto's
rise as the commercial, industrial, and governmental capital of Ontario
that dictated the choice of locating the archiepiscopal see in Toronto. The account in Edward McKeown, *The Life and Labors of Archbishop Lynch* (Toronto 1887), 263–4, which contends that Bishop
Lynch was made an archbishop in appreciation for his intervention
at the Vatican Council, must be rejected as spurious. That Lynch
did not deny the story reveals a curious flaw in character. For other
evidence of Archbishop Lynch's vanity, see Gerald J. Stortz, "John
Joseph Lynch, Archbishop of Toronto: A Biographical Study in Religious, Political and Social Commitment" (PhD diss., University
of Guelph 1980), 128–57.

13 Bishop Power to Rev. M.R. Mills, October 1843, Power Papers, ARCAT.
See also John Coglan to Bishop Charbonnel, 1 April 1854,
Charbonnel Papers, ARCAT.

14 Bishop Charbonnel to Cardinal Giacomo Filippo Fransoni, 26 May
1851, Charbonnel Papers, ARCAT.

15 John Elmsley and S.G. Lynn to Bishop Charbonnel, 18 October 1850, Charbonnel Papers, ARCAT.

16 Bishop Charbonnel to Cardinal Giacomo Filippo Fransoni, 26 May 1851, Charbonnel Papers, ARCAT.

17 Circular, 1850, Circular, 28 December 1852, Circular, 9 July 1853, Bishop Charbonnel to Rev. J. Walsh, 1 December 1854, Rev. M. O'Shea to Bishop Charbonnel, 5 January 1858, and Bishop Charbonnel to Rev. F. Rooney, 25 July 1858, Charbonnel Papers, ARCAT.

18 Bishop Charbonnel to Bishop Bourget, 6 August 1855, Bishop Charbonnel to an unidentified correspondent, 5 June 1852, Untitled Notes, 1855, Rev. M. O'Shea to Bishop Charbonnel, 14 March 1859, Charbonnel Papers, ARCAT; Bishop Charbonnel to Bishop Joseph-Eugène-Bruno Guiges, 31 July 1855, Guiges Papers, AAO; Bishop Power to Rev. W.P. McDonough, 22 February 1844, Bishop Power to Rev. W.P. McDonough, 29 April 1844, Power Papers, ARCAT; Canadian Freeman, 2 January 1862.

19 Bishop Charbonnel to Bishop Bourget, 30 October 1854, Charbonnel Papers, ARCAT; Bishop Power to J. Douglas Harrington, Power Papers, ARCAT; Dunigan's American Catholic Almanac (New York: Dunigan and Brother 1857); Sadlier Almanac & Credo (New York: Sadlier 1865); "Institutions," 1879, Lynch Papers, ARCAT.

20 Bishop Charbonnel to Bishop Bourget, 30 October 1854, and Bishop Charbonnel to Cardinal Giacomo Fransoni, 30 May 1853, Charbonnel Papers, ARCAT.

21 Bishop Power to Rev. S. Fergus, 9 May 1844, Bishop Power to Rev. M. McDonell, 28 May 1844, Rev. W.P. McDonough to Rev. J. Carroll, 19 July 1849, Power Papers, ARCAT; Archbishop Lynch to Bishop John Walsh, 9 September 1886, Lynch Papers, ARCAT.

22 Bishop Charbonnel to Cardinal Giacomo Fransoni, 30 May 1853, Charbonnel Papers, ARCAT.

23 Bishop Power to Rev. P. O'Dwyer, 30 September 1843, Power Papers, ARCAT; Circular, 28 December 1852, and Bishop Charbonnel to an unidentified correspondent, 5 June 1852, Charbonnel Papers, ARCAT.

24 Bishop Power to Rev. M.R. Mills, 9 November 1842, Bishop Power to Rev. P. O'Dwyer, 19 November 1842, Bishop Power to Rev. M. McDonnell, 14 December 1842, Rev. J. Carroll to an unidentified correspondent, 6 June 1849, Bishop Power to Rev. W.P. McDonough, 11 February 1843, Bishop Power to Rev. P. O'Dwyer, 23 March 1843, Bishop Power to Rev. P. O'Dwyer, 30 November 1843, Bishop Power to Rev. W.P. McDonough, 1 November 1844, Power Papers, ARCAT; Bartholomew Grattan to Bishop Charbonnel, 4 December 1854, Charbonnel Papers, ARCAT.

25 Bishop Power to Rev. M.R. Mills, 22 February 1846, Bishop
    Power to Rev. A. MacDonell, 22 November 1842, Rev. M.R. Mills
    to Bishop Power, 20 November 1846, Bishop Power to Rev.
    W.P. McDonough, 28 January 1843, Bishop Power to Rev.
    J. O'Flynn, 2 September 1842, Power Papers, ARCAT; and Rev.
    J.B. Proulx to Bishop Charbonnel, 1 February 1856, Charbonnel
    Papers, ARCAT.
26 Bishop Power to Rev. A MacDonell, 22 November 1842, Power Papers,
    ARCAT.
27 Bishop Charbonnel to Rev. C. Jubel, 27 June 1858, Charbonnel
    Papers, ARCAT; Rev. J.J. Hay to Samuel Brown, 12 June 1844,
    Bishop Power to Chas. Calquohn, 1 April 1843, Circular, 31 December
    1846, and Peter Mortagh to Rev. J.J. Hay, 3 February 1849, Power
    Papers, ARCAT.
28 Rev. R.A. O'Connor to Archbishop Lynch, 4 March 1862, Archbishop
    Lynch to Rev. J.J. McCann, 20 September 1876, Lynch Papers,
    ARCAT; Rev. M. O'Shea to Bishop Charbonnel, 20 December 1858,
    "Personal Effects of the Late, Reverend J. Synnot," 27 April 1857,
    Untitled Note, 1855 Charbonnel Papers, ARCAT; Bishop Power to Rev.
    J. O'Flynn, 13 February 1844, Rev. J. O'Flynn to Rev. J. Carroll,
    25 November 1849, Rev. J.J. Hay to Rev. P. O'Dwyer, 13 January 1849,
    Bishop Power to Rev. A. Vervais, 14 October 1843, Bishop Power
    to Rev. W.P. McDonough, 6 September 1842, and Bishop Power to
    Rev. J. O'Flynn, 1844, Power Papers, ARCAT; Gerald Stortz, "The
    Catholic Priest in Rural Ontario, 1850–1900," in *Religion and Rural
    Ontario's Past: Proceedings of the Fifth Annual Agricultural History of
    Ontario Seminar*, ed. Alan Brookes (Guelph: University School of Part-
    Time Studies and Continuing Education, University of Guelph
    1980), 36–7.
29 Archbishop Lynch to Rev. P. Keane, 20 January 1887, and Rev.
    P. Keane to Archbishop Lynch, 14 January 1887, Lynch Papers,
    ARCAT ; Rev. M. O'Shea to Bishop Charbonnel, 3 June 1859,
    Charbonnel Papers, ARCAT.
30 Bishop Power to Rev. M.R. Mills, 3 July 1845, Bishop Power to Rev.
    W.P. McDonough, 22 February 1844, Bishop Power to Rev.
    A. MacDonell, 22 November 1842, Circular, 8 May 1845, Power
    Papers, ARCAT; Circular, 1852, Charbonnel Papers, ARCAT.
31 Rev. J.J. Hay to Edward Smith, 9 August 1848, Bishop Power to Rev.
    M.R. Mills, 12 September 1842, Bishop Power to Rev. P. Connolly,
    25 October 1844, Rev. J. O'Flynn to Rev. J. Carroll, 1849, J.D. Bayes
    to Rev. J. Carroll, 31 December 1849, Bishop Power to Rev.
    W. Nightingale, 11 January 1847, Power Papers, ARCAT; Rev.
    M. O'Shea to Bishop Charbonnel, 3 July 1859, Bishop Charbonnel
    to Cardinal Giacomo Filippo Fransoni, 30 May 1853, Charbonnel

Papers, ARCAT; Archbishop Lynch to Rev. W. Harris, 30 December 1878, Archbishop Lynch to Rev. J. Bayle, 12 August 1864, Lynch Papers, ARCAT.

32 Rev. M. O'Shea to Bishop Charbonnel, 15 January 1858, Charbonnel Papers, ARCAT.

33 Rev. R.A. O'Connor to Archbishop Lynch, 27 August 1875, Lynch Papers, ARCAT; Stortz, "Catholic Priest," 35–6.

34 Archbishop Lynch to Rev. T. Morris, 1 September 1884, Archbishop Lynch to Rev. W. Bergin, 21 November 1887, Lynch Papers, ARCAT.

35 Rev. G. Northgraves to Messrs. Mallen and Fitzgerald, n.d., Rev. P. Keane to Archbishop Lynch, 14 January 1887, "Father Fell's Case," n.d., Rev. M. Fell to Archbishop Lynch, 24 October 1883, Lynch Papers, ARCAT.

36 Circular, 1842, Circular, 21 August 1845, Bishop Power to Rev. M.R. Mills, 8 August 1844, Bishop Power to Rev. W.P. McDonough, 29 April 1844, Bishop Power to Rev. W.P. McDonough, 22 February 1844, Bishop Power to Rev. P. O'Dwyer, 30 September 1843, Bishop Power to Rev. A. Vervais, 31 March 1843, Bishop Power to Rev. W.P. McDonough, 28 January 1843, Power Papers, ARCAT.

37 Bishop Power to Charles Baby, 22 August 1846, Circular, 19 September 1845, Power Papers, ARCAT. See also "An Act to Incorporate the Roman Catholic Bishops of Toronto and Kingston in Canada, in Each Diocese, LXXXII", 29 March 1845, Power Papers, ARCAT.

38 Circular, 31 December 1846, Power Papers, ARCAT.

39 Scope R. Birdsmore to Lt. Col. House, 27 January 1849, P. Phelan to Rev. J.J. Hay, 29 January 1849, Power Papers, ARCAT.

40 Circular, 28 December 1852, Bishop Charbonnel to Cardinal Giacomo Filippo Fransoni, 18 May 1852, Bishop Charbonnel to Cardinal Fransoni, 30 May 1853, Circular, 17 January 1855, Circular, 18 July 1853, Bishop Charbonnel to Cardinal Alessandro Barnabo, 26 May 1855, Charbonnel Papers, ARCAT.

41 Rev. R.A. O'Connor to Archbishop Lynch, 1 March 1862, Lynch Papers, ARCAT; Untitled note, 20 November 1859, Barth. Woodlock to Bishop Charbonnel, 15 December 1858, Rev. A. Montgolfier to Bishop Charbonnel, 20 December 1857, L.A. Barbarin to Rev. J.M. Soulerin, 29 August 1857, B.D. O'Brien to Bishop Charbonnel, 2 February 1857, Circular, 1852, Circular, 1 September 1856, Charbonnel Papers, ARCAT.

42 "Report of the Committee of Investigation on the Subject of the Salary to Rectors of Missions," 23 January 1883, Notes on the Provincial Council Decrees, 1875, Rev. R.A. O'Connor to Archbishop Lynch, 21 September 1887, "St. Michael's Association," 20 November

1861, "St. Michael's Association," 1863, Lynch Papers, ARCAT;
Nicolson, "Ecclesiastical Metropolitanism," 153.

43 Nicolson, "Catholic Church and the Irish," 60–89, gives a detailed
account of this conflict.

44 Barrie Dyster, "Toronto 1840–1860: Making It in a British Protestant
Town" (PhD diss., University of Toronto 1970), 203.

45 See the Catholic protest in *Globe*, 22 January 1853. See also *Globe*,
28 May 1855 and 25 September 1856.

46 See Stephen Speisman, "Munificent Parsons and Municipal Parsimony:
Voluntary vs. Public Poor Relief in Nineteenth Century Toronto,"
Ontario History, 65 (1973), 33–49.

47 Donald Harman Akenson, *Being Had: Historians, Evidence, and the Irish
in North America* (Port Credit, Ontario: P.D. Meany 1985), 160–2.

48 The most comprehensive account of the separate school controversy
is Franklin Walker's *Catholic Education and Politics in Upper Canada*
(Toronto: English Catholic Education Association of Ontario 1955).
For an important corrective to Walker's contention that the aims
of the Catholic bishops remained unchanged, see John S. Moir, *Church
and State in Canada West: Three Studies in the Relation of Denominationalism and Nationalism, 1841–1867* (Toronto: University of Toronto
Press 1959).

49 Akenson, *Being Had*, 174–5.

50 Akenson, *Being Had*, 177–80.

51 Circular, 9 July 1853, and Circular, 18 July 1853, Charbonnel Papers,
ARCAT; Walker, *Catholic Education in Upper Canada*, 104, 120,
124–5; Moir, *Church and State*, 150. Catholics had good reason to fear
the "common Christianity" taught in the schools with its Protestant,
particularly Methodist, bias. See Goldwin French, "Egerton Ryerson
and the Methodist Model for Upper Canada," and Albert S.
Fiorino, "The Moral Foundation of Egerton Ryerson's Ideas of
Education," in *Egerton Ryerson and His Times*, eds. Neil McDonald
and Alf Chaiton (Toronto: Macmillan of Canada 1978), 45–58 and
59–80.

52 Teefy, *Jubilee Volume*, 203–26.

53 Susan E. Houston, "Social Reform and Education: The Issue of
Compulsory Schooling, Toronto, 1851–1871," in *Egerton Ryerson
and His Times*, 261 and 263.

54 Susan E. Houston and Alison Prentice, *Schooling and Scholars in
Nineteenth-Century Ontario*, Ontario Historical Studies Series
(Toronto: University of Toronto Press 1988), 289 and 294.

55 *Canadian Freeman*, 17 January 1861.

56 John Elmsley to Rev. Hare, 27 October 1849, and Elmsley to Rev.
J. Carroll, 5 April 1850, John Elmsley Papers, ARCAT.

57 *Canadian Freeman*, 2 May 1861.

58 St Paul's Parish, Marriage Register, 1850–59; St Michael's Cathedral, Marriage Register, 1852–59; St Mary's Parish, Marriage Register, 1857–59, ARCAT. See also Terrence M. Punch, *Irish Halifax: The Immigrant Generation, 1815–1859* (Halifax: Ethnic Heritage Series 1981), 12–13.

59 Desmond Keenan, *The Catholic Church in Nineteenth-Century Ireland: A Sociological Study* (Dublin: Gill and Macmillan 1983), 125–8, and Kerby A. Miller "Emigrants and Exiles: Irish Cultures and Irish Emigration to North America, 1790–1922," *Irish Historical Studies*, 22 (1980), 108–10.

60 W.L. Morton, "Victorian Canada," in *The Shield of Achilles: Aspects of Canada in the Victorian Age*, ed. W.L. Morton (Toronto: McClelland and Stewart 1968), 316.

61 Monet, "French-Canadian Nationalism," 41–55.

62 Dyster, "Toronto 1840–1860," 364–5.

63 Dyster, "Toronto 1840–1860," 219–20, 233–4, 259, and 442–3, and Cecil J. Houston and William J. Smyth, *Irish Emigration and Canadian Settlement: Patterns, Links, and Letters* (Toronto: University of Toronto Press 1990), 185.

64 Houston and Prentice, *Schooling and Scholars*, 274–5.

65 *Globe*, 21 January 1851, 7 October 1851, and 18 December 1862; *Leader*, 14 August 1856.

66 *Canadian Freeman*, 5 January 1865; *Irish Canadian*, 9 March 1864 and 13 September 1869.

CHAPTER THREE

1 Emmet Larkin, "The Devotional Revolution in Ireland, 1850–75," *American Historical Review*, 77 (1972), 644–5. See also S.J. Connolly, *Priests and People in Pre-Famine Ireland, 1780–1845* (New York: St Martin's Press 1982), 98–9.

2 David W. Miller, "Irish Catholicism and the Great Famine," *Journal of Social History*, 9 (1975), 84–7, Larkin, "Devotional Revolution in Ireland," 628, 635, and 638.

3 Larkin, "Devotional Revolution in Ireland," 630; Connolly, *Priests and People*, 80–89 and 92–3; Desmond Keenan, *The Catholic Church in Ireland: A Sociological Study* (Dublin: Gill and Macmillan 1983), 148–52; K. Theodore Hoppen, *Elections, Politics, and Society in Ireland, 1832–1885* (Oxford: Oxford University Press, Clarendon Press 1984), 199–201; Miller, "Irish Catholicism and the Great Famine," 84–7. For an important rebuttal to Miller's estimates on church attendance, see Patrick J. Corish, *The Irish Experience: A Historical Survey* (Wilmington, Delaware: Michael Glazier 1985), 167.

4 Emmet Larkin, *The Historical Dimensions of Irish Catholicism* (1976; reprint ed., Washington, DC: Catholic University Press 1984), 5–9.

5 Miller, "Irish Catholicism and the Great Famine," 90–1; Connolly, *Priests and People*, 105–6; Seán Ó Súilleabháin, *Irish Folk Custom and Belief* (Cork: Mercier Press 1967), 67–8; Patrick Logan, *The Holy Wells of Ireland* (Gerrards Cross, U.K.: Colin Smythe 1980), 35–41; William Wilde, *Irish Popular Superstitions* (1852; reprint ed., Dublin: Irish Academic Press 1979), 54–7; E. Estyn Evans, *Irish Folk Ways* (London: Routledge and Kegan Paul 1957), 267–75.

6 Connolly, *Priests and People*, 148–59; Ó Súilleabháin, *Irish Folk Custom*, 51–8; Seán Ó Súilleabháin, *Irish Wake Amusements* (Dublin: Mercier Press 1967), 26–31, 85–6, 92, and 96–8.

7 Connolly, *Priests and People*, 101–4; Wilde, *Irish Popular Superstitions*, 121–5; Lady Gregory, *Visions and Beliefs in the West of Ireland* (1920; reprint ed., Gerrards Cross, Buckinghamshire: Colin Smythe 1970), 81, 84, 149–50, and 247–9.

8 Connolly, *Priests and People*, 109–10, 115, and 119–20; Miller, "Irish Catholicism and the Great Famine," 89–90. In making his case that a "general pattern of 'tridentine' religious observance" existed in pre-famine Ireland, P.J. Corish, *The Catholic Community in the Seventeenth and Eighteenth Centuries* (Dublin: Helicon 1981), 82–115, overlooks both the extent and significance of unofficial religious practices. Keenan, *Catholic Church in Ireland*, 19–24, curiously dismisses unofficial religious practices as "harmless," and by doing so he underestimates the dramatic change in the character of popular religion between 1830 and 1875.

9 Larkin, "Devotional Revolution in Ireland," 648–9, and "Church, State, and Nation in Modern Ireland," *American Historical Review*, 80 (1975), 1254; Connolly, *Priests and People*, 108 and 272–8; Miller, "Irish Catholicism and the Great Famine," 93; K. Theodore Hoppen, "National Politics and Local Realities in Mid-Nineteenth Century Ireland," in *Studies in Irish History Presented to R. Dudley Edwards*, eds. Art Cosgrove and Donal McCartney (Dublin: University College 1979), 225–7, and *Elections, Politics, and Society in Ireland*, 219–24; Kerby A. Miller, *Emigrants and Exiles: Ireland and the Irish Exodus to North America* (New York: Oxford University Press 1985), 67–79 and 121–7. For a reductionist explanation of the revolution in Irish popular religion, which stresses the importance of the stem family, see Eugene Hynes, "The Great Hunger and Irish Catholicism," *Societas*, 8 (1978), 137–56.

10 Cecil J. Houston and William J. Smyth, *Irish Emigration and Canadian Settlement: Patterns, Links, and Letters* (Toronto: University of Toronto Press 1990), 57–63; S.H. Cousens, "Emigration and

Demographic Change in Ireland, 1851–1861," *Economic History Review*, series 2, 14 (1961), 275–7.

11 Connolly, *Priests and People*, 277–8; "The Evils of Wholesale and Improvident Emigration from Ireland," 1864, Lynch Papers, ARCAT.

12 S.H. Cousens, "The Regional Pattern of Emigration during the Great Famine, 1846–51," Institute of British Geographers, *Transactions and Papers*, no.28 (1960), 128–33; J.M. Jamot, "Census of City Wards," *circa* early 1860s, ARCAT.

13 St Paul's Parish, Marriage Register, 1850–59; St Michael's Cathedral, Marriage Register, 1852–59; St Mary's Parish, Marriage Register, 1857–59, ARCAT.

14 Corish, *The Irish Experience*, 167, and Miller, "Irish Catholicism and the Great Famine," 87.

15 Corish, *The Irish Experience*, 174, 176, 181–2, 184, and 208–9; Miller, "Irish Catholicism and the Great Famine," 85–8; Connolly, *Priests and People*, 91–2.

16 James S. Donnelly, Jr, "Pastorini and Captain Rock," in *Irish Peasants: Violence and Political Unrest 1780–1914*, eds. Samuel Clark and James S. Donnelly, Jr (Madison, Wisconsin: University of Wisconsin Press 1983), 102–39.

17 Bishop Charbonnel to Cardinal Giacomo Filippo Fransoni, 30 May 1852, Charbonnel Papers, ARCAT.

18 Bishop Charbonnel to Monsignor Frédéric-François de Mérode, 12 July 1852, Charbonnel Papers, ARCAT.

19 Rev. M. O'Shea to Bishop Charbonnel, 13 April 1859, Charbonnel Papers, ARCAT.

20 Bishop Charbonnel to Cardinal Giacomo Filippo Fransoni, 26 May 1851, Circular, 28 December 1852, Bishop Charbonnel to Cardinal Fransoni, 30 May 1852, Bishop Charbonnel to John Wardy, 1 December 1854, and Bishop Charbonnel to Rev. F. Rooney, 25 July 1858, Charbonnel Papers, ARCAT.

21 Bishop Charbonnel to Cardinal Giacomo Filippo Fransoni, 18 May 1852, Charbonnel Papers, ARCAT.

22 Brian Harrison, "Religion and Recreation in Nineteenth-Century England," *Past and Present*, no.38 (December 1967), 98–125; Pastoral, 10 February 1859, Charbonnel Papers, ARCAT.

23 "Explication," October 1853, "Regulations for the Retreat preceding St. Patrick's Feast," 1859, Pastoral, 1858, and Circular, 15 August 1858, Charbonnel Papers, ARCAT.

24 Pastoral, 10 February 1859, and "Regulations for the Retreat preceding St. Patrick's Feast," 1859, Charbonnel Papers, ARCAT.

25 Bishop Charbonnel to Cardinal Giacomo Filippo Fransoni, 26 May 1851, Charbonnel Papers, ARCAT.

26 Bishop Charbonnel to city superintendent of common schools, 14 October 1850, Circular, 18 December 1852, Circular, 20 December 1852, Bishop Charbonnel to Cardinal Giacomo Filippo Fransoni, 30 May 1853, Bishop Charbonnel to Cardinal Alessandro Barnabo, 20 May 1854, Bishop Charbonnel to M. de Gessé, 30 September 1854, and Bishop Charbonnel to Cardinal Alessandro Barnabo, 26 May 1855, Charbonnel Papers, ARCAT.

27 Pastoral, 11 June 1853, and Bishop Charbonnel to Mayor George Allan, 2 March 1855, Charbonnel Papers, ARCAT; Connolly, *Priests and People*, 75–88 and 110–13.

28 Bishop Power to Rev. M.R. Mills, 9 November 1842, Bishop Power to Rev. P. O'Dwyer, 16 November 1842, and Bishop Power to Rev. A. McDonell, 14 December 1842, Power Papers, ARCAT; Circular, 20 December 1852, Circular, 28 December 1852, Rev. J.B. Proulx to Bishop Charbonnel, 9 June 1853, Rev. B. Grattan to Bishop Charbonnel, 14 January 1854, Rev. B. Grattan to Bishop Charbonnel, 21 December 1854, Rev. M. O'Shea to Bishop Charbonnel, 15 January 1858, Charbonnel Papers, ARCAT; Rev. J. Walsh to Archbishop Lynch, 5 April 1864, J. White to Archbishop Lynch, 23 January 1866, Rev. R.A. O'Connor to Archbishop Lynch, 25 January 1866, Rev. G. Northgraves to Archbishop Lynch, 27 May 1867, B. Cummings to Archbishop Lynch, 29 August 1867, Archbishop Lynch to Cardinal Giovanni Simeoni, n.d., and Bishop Timothy O'Mahony to Archbishop Lynch, n.d., Lynch Papers, ARCAT.

29 "Ordinations, Confirmations, Dispensations," Lynch Papers, ARCAT.

30 Bishop Power to Rev. A. McDonell, 14 December 1842, Power Papers, ARCAT; Circular, 26 December 1852, Charbonnel Papers, ARCAT; Rev. W.P. Harris to Archbishop Lynch, 5 February 1886, and Circular, 25 May 1887, Lynch Papers, ARCAT.

31 Saint Michael's Cathedral could hold at most 1,600 people; Saint Paul's had some 600 sittings. If it is assumed that two Masses were said at both churches on Sundays, the total capacity was 4,400.

32 Bishop Charbonnel to Cardinal Giocomo Filippo Fransoni, 26 May 1851, and List of Clergy, 1853, Charbonnel Papers, ARCAT; Miller, "Irish Catholicism and the Great Famine," 86–7.

33 Bishop Charbonnel to an unidentified correspondent, 25 July 1853, and Bishop Charbonnel to M. Gessé, 7 January 1854, Charbonnel Papers, ARCAT.

34 Rev. J. Jamot, "Census of City Wards," *circa* early 1860s, ARCAT; St Michael's Cathedral, Register of Pew Rents, 1867–1894, ARCAT; Peter G. Goheen, *Victorian Toronto, 1850–1900: Pattern and Process of Growth*, The University of Chicago, Department of Geography, research paper no.127 (Chicago 1970) 143, 151, 155, and 186–8.

35 Rev. J. Jamot, "Census of City Wards," *circa* early 1860s, ARCAT; Saint Vincent de Paul Society, "General Register," ARCAT; *Irish Canadian*, 15 December 1869; Goheen, *Victorian Toronto*, 213–15.

36 Unfortunately, complete financial accounts for this period are not available, but with the cathedral revenues running between £870 to £1,110 (or $3,480 to $4,440) a month, many Irish Catholics obviously contributed to the church at great personal sacrifice. See St Michael's Cathedral, Cash Book, 1855–59, and John Elmsley to Bishop Charbonnel, 1 January 1857, John Elmsley Papers, ARCAT.

37 *Irish Canadian*, 17 May 1876.

38 List of clergy, 1853, "clergy of the Diocese of Toronto," 1857, Charbonnel Papers, ARCAT; *The Metropolitan Catholic Almanac and Laity's Directory for the United States* (Baltimore: John Murphy 1860). In calculating these ratios I have assumed that two Basilians at Saint Michael's College were devoted to full-time parochial duties.

39 P.M. Larkin to an unidentified correspondent, 16 July 1849, Power Papers, ARCAT; Bishop Charbonnel to Rev. J. Walsh, 1 December 1854, Bishop Charbonnel to Rev. F. Rooney, 25 July 1858, Charbonnel Papers, ARCAT; and "Saint Paul's Parish, Toronto," 1876, Lynch Papers, ARCAT.

40 Rev. T.J. Morris to Archbishop Lynch, 14 February 1879, Archbishop Lynch to Rev. J. Shea, 9 September 1880, Rev. P.J. Harold to Archbishop Lynch, 7 August 1882, Archbishop Lynch to Rev. P. Conway, 5 August 1882, Archbishop Lynch to Rev. P. Conway, 15 August 1882, Lynch Papers, ARCAT.

41 *Irish Canadian*, 11 March 1886.

42 *Irish Canadian*, 13 May 1865, 29 July 1874, 10 March 1875, and 17 May 1876; *Canadian Freeman*, 12 August 1859.

43 Edward Kelly, *The Story of St. Paul's Parish, Toronto* (Toronto 1922), 44–6.

44 *Irish Canadian*, 10 December 1869.

45 Pastoral, 29 December 1847, Power Papers, ARCAT.

46 John Ross Robertson, *Landmarks of Toronto*, 6 vols. (Toronto: Toronto Telegram 1914), 4:310, 327, 332, 334, and 335; Mary Hoskin, *History of St. Basil's Parish, St. Joseph's Street* (Toronto: Catholic Register and Canadian Extension 1912), 56–7 and 82; Kelly, *St. Paul's Parish*, 140; Circular, n.d., Charbonnel Papers, ARCAT; *Canadian Freeman*, 28 January 1859; *Catholic Weekly Review*, 14 March 1891.

47 *Canadian Freeman*, 23 November 1871.

48 *Irish Canadian*, 1 March 1876.

49 John Elmsley to Bishop Charbonnel, 18 October 1850, John Elmsley Papers, ARCAT; *City of Toronto Directory for 1867–8* (Toronto 1867).

50 Robertson, *Landmarks of Toronto*, 4:307 and 324–5; *Globe*, 27 December

1869, 26 December 1879, and 16 April 1881; *Catholic Weekly Review*, 29 December 1888.

51 Robertson, *Landmarks of Toronto*, 4:307; *Globe*, 4 March 1867, 27 December 1869, 11 April 1879, 26 December 1879, 22 March 1880, 16 April 1881, and 25 December 1882; *Canadian Freeman*, 27 May 1859, 20 November 1862, 4 March 1867, and 6 October 1870; *Catholic Weekly Review*, 31 December 1887 and 29 December 1888.

52 *Irish Canadian*, 22 March 1870; Roger Aubert, *The Church in a Secularized Society*, vol. 5 of *The Christian Centuries* (New York: Paulist Press 1978), 222.

53 Robertson, *Landmarks of Toronto*, 4:325; *Canadian Freeman*, 11 May 1863.

54 *Canadian Freeman*, 23 May 1863 and 8 June 1871; *Globe*, 6 June 1861 and 29 June 1871.

55 For an excellent study of Catholic devotions, see Ann Taves, *The Household of Faith: Roman Catholic Devotions in Mid-Nineteenth Century America* (Notre Dame, Indiana: University of Notre Dame Press 1986); Jacques Gadille, "L'ultramontanisme français au XIXe siècle," in *Les ultramontains canadiens-français: Études d'histoire religieuse présentées en hommage au professeur Phillipe Sylvain*, eds. Nive Voisine and Jean Hamelin (Montreal: Boréal Express 1985), 41–4.

56 *Rules of the Society of St. Vincent of Paul* (Toronto 1861), 55–6 and 93; *Irish Canadian*, 17 January 1877.

57 Robertson, *Landmarks of Toronto*, 4:325; *Canadian Freeman*, 6 October 1870; *Globe*, 28 January 1880 and 1 October 1883.

58 *Canadian Freeman*, 2 May 1861, 2 January 1862, 13 March 1862, 20 March 1862, and 11 April 1867; *Irish Canadian*, 3 January 1872; *Catholic Weekly Review*, 12 March 1892.

59 Pastoral, 27 November 1847, Power Papers, ARCAT; Bishop Charbonnel to Cardinal Giacomo Filippo Fransoni, 27 September 1852, Charbonnel Papers, ARCAT; *Irish Canadian*, 7 May 1873; Circular, 18 February 1887, Lynch Papers, ARCAT.

60 *Exercise of the Via Crucis* (Rome: Propaganda Fide 1834), 6 and 22.

61 *Exercise of the Via Crucis*, 16.

62 *Exercise of the Via Crucis*, 11.

63 *Exercise of the Via Crucis*, 29.

64 *Catholic Weekly Review*, 12 May 1887.

65 See Jay P. Dolan, *Catholic Revivalism: The American Experience 1830–1900* (Notre Dame, Indiana: University of Notre Dame 1978), 12, 22, 31–2, and 74–5. For the role of parish missions in the ultramontane revival in Lower Canada, see Nive Voisine, "Jubilés, missions paroissiales et prédication au XIXe siècle," *Recherches*

sociographiques, 23 (1982), 125–37; *Irish Canadian*, 16 October 1869, 8 December 1870, 26 February 1873, 3 April 1878, 8 December 1880, and 10 November 1881; *Canadian Freeman*, 13 May 1859, 29 August 1861, 16 October 1862, and 20 November 1862; *Catholic Weekly Review*, 26 March 1892.

66 Dolan, *Catholic Revivalism*, 76.

67 *Canadian Freeman*, 25 May 1859 and 13 November 1862.

68 *Catholic Weekly Review*, 31 March 1888.

69 *Irish Canadian*, 10 February 1887.

70 *Canadian Freeman*, 9 April 1865, 7 December 1865, and 2 January 1868; *Irish Canadian*, 4 April 1877 and 4 September 1884; Circular, August 1869, and Circular, 28 August 1884, Lynch Papers, ARCAT.

71 *Globe*, 23 June 1882; *Irish Canadian*, 10 March 1875.

72 See the serial published in the *Irish Canadian* beginning on 3 January 1872.

73 Parish Reports, 1860–65, and "State of the Missions of the Diocese, 1865," Lynch Papers, ARCAT. My calculations are based on the assumption that the distribution of Irish Catholics by age was similar to that of the population as a whole. In the *Census of Canada, 1860–61* (Quebec 1863), 511–2, some 31 per cent of the total population are listed as under the age of twelve, the usual age among Catholics for confirmation and first communion. I have used this figure in estimating the number of Roman Catholics who were of age to fulfil their canonical duties.

74 Figures are calculated from *Census of Canada, 1880–81* (Ottawa 1882), 1:174–5 and 2:100–1. Almost 27 per cent of the city population was under age twelve. I have used this figure to calculate the rate of attendance from the results of the religious survey published in the *Globe*, 7 February 1882.

CHAPTER FOUR

1 For an overview of women's voluntary associations, see Alison Prentice, Paula Bourne, Gail Cuthbert Brandt, Beth Light, Wendy Mitchinson, and Naomi Black, *Canadian Women: A History* (Toronto: Harcourt Brace Jovanovich 1988), 170–4 and 176–9, and Christopher Headon, "Women and Organized Religion in Mid and Late Nineteenth Century Canada," *Journal of the Canadian Church Historical Society*, 20 (1976), 3–18.

2 Ruth Compton Brouwer, *New Women for God: Canadian Presbyterian Women and India Missions, 1876–1914* (Toronto: University of Toronto Press 1990), Rosemary R. Gagan, *A Sensitive Independence: Canadian Methodist Women Missionaries in Canada and the Orient, 1881–1925* (Montreal and Kingston: McGill-Queen's University Press

1992); Sharon Anne Cook, "'Continued and Persevering Combat':
The Ontario Woman's Christian Temperance Union, Evangelism, and
Social Reform, 1874–1916" (PhD diss., Carleton University 1990).
D.L. Pedersen's study, "The Young Women's Christian Association
in Canada, 1870–1920: A Movement to Meet Spiritual, Civic, and
National Need" (PhD diss., Carleton University 1988), was not available
to me as this book went to press. While there are relatively few
studies on religion and women in Canada, the field has flourished in
the United States since the publication of Barbara Welter's and
Ann Douglas's now classic studies. See Barbara Welter, "The Femi-
nization of American Religion: 1800–1860," in *Clio's Consciousness
Raised*, eds. Mary Hartman and Lois W. Banner (New York: Harper
and Row Publishers 1974), 137–57, and Ann Douglas, *The Femi-
nization of American Culture* (New York: Alfred A. Knopf 1977).

3 Jay Dolan, *The American Catholic Experience: A History from Colonial Times
to the Present* (Garden City, New York: Doubleday 1985), 213–14
and 232–4.

4 Confraternities are canonically erected devotional organizations.
Roman Catholic laity and clergy in the nineteenth century, as
today, rarely observed such formal distinctions in terminology.

5 For most of this period the only sources for the devotional organizations in the schools are the occasional items in the Catholic and
daily press reporting their participation in one or another religious
procession, most typically that of Corpus Christi. One later report
by a member of the Children of Mary in *Leaflets from Loretto* (April
1900), 62, reveals that the devotional activities of this sodality were
an integral part of the school's daily routine.

6 Bishop Charbonnel to Ignace Bourget, 10 October 1851, and
Charbonnel to Bourget, 5 November 1851, ACAM.

7 Bishop Charbonnel to Bishop Ignace Bourget, 10 October 1851,
ACAM; *Mirror*, 15 September 1854; St Paul's Parish Report, *circa*
1859, Charbonnel Papers, ARCAT; St Michael's Parish Report, *circa*
1861, and J.C. Puxel to Bishop Lynch, 23 November 1863, Lynch
Papers, ARCAT; *Canadian Freeman*, 1 June 1865; *Irish Canadian*, 31 May
1883.

8 Ann Taves, *The Household of Faith: Roman Catholic Devotions in Mid-
Nineteenth-Century America* (Notre Dame, Indiana: University of
Notre Dame Press 1986), 48–51, 81, and 83–8; Dolan, *American
Catholic Experience*, 208–11 and 219–20.

9 *Manual of the Archconfraternity of the Holy Family* (Bruges: Resclée,
de Brouwer 1884), 2.

10 Rev. M. O'Shea to Bishop Charbonnel, 15 January 1858, and Rev.
F. Rooney to Bishop Charbonnel, 1858, Charbonnel Papers,
ARCAT; E. Kelly, *St. Paul's Parish, Toronto* (Toronto 1922), 252.

11 See *Rules of the Society of St. Vincent of Paul* (Toronto 1861), 53–123.
12 Pastoral, 2 February 1855, Charbonnel Papers, ARCAT.
13 *Catholic Weekly Review*, 12 May 1887; *Exercise of the Via Crucis* (Rome: Propaganda Fide 1834), 30–1.
14 *Irish Canadian*, 1 March 1876; *Third Glorious Mystery, Fourth Glorious Mystery, Fifth Sorrowful Mystery*, and *Fifth Joyful Mystery* (Montreal: D. and J. Sadlier, n.d.)
15 *Apostleship of Prayer – Ticket of Admission* (n.p.).
16 *Apostleship of Prayer – Ticket of Admission; Archconfraternity of the Holy Family* (n.p.); St Michael's Cathedral, Book of Announcements, Third Sunday after Lent, 1882, and Second Sunday after Easter, 1884, ARCAT; Kelly, *St. Paul's Parish*, 262. In the 1860s, weekly communion was considered to be so exceptional as to be the mark of a saintly life. See the obituary of John Elmsley, thought by many to be a saint, in *Canadian Freeman*, 14 May 1863. In the 1860s, monthly reception of the sacraments was expected of confraternity members. Beginning in the 1880s, when the Apostleship of Prayer began the practice of receiving communion in a body on the first Friday of the month, the reception of the sacrament became more frequent still. By the late 1880s, weekly communion was common, though not as yet universal, among confraternity members.
17 H. Ramière, *The Apostleship of Prayer: Explanation and Practical Instruction* (Baltimore: John Murphy 1864), 6; *Bulletin of the Society of St. Vincent of Paul* (hereafter cited as *Bulletin*), September 1872, 218, and June 1879, 173.
18 Archbishop Lynch to Rev. T. Wardy, 9 December 1862, Pastoral, August 1869, and Rev. J.M. Jamot, "Confraternity of the Scapulary of Mt. Carmel," Lynch Papers, ARCAT; *Bulletin*, September 1872, 298; *Manual of the Archconfraternity of the Holy Family*, 106–12.
19 *Manual of the Archconfraternity of the Holy Family*, 9–10 and 127–9.
20 *Apostleship of Prayer – Ticket of Admission; Bulletin*, September 1872, 298; *Canadian Freeman*, 2 January 1862.
21 *Ticket of Admission to the Holy Tabernacle Association* (n.p.).
22 H. Ramière, *Apostleship of Prayer* (n.p.).
23 Ramière, *Apostleship of Prayer: Explanation*, 4–5.
24 *Manual of the Archconfraternity of the Holy Family*, 23.
25 Pastoral, 2 February 1843, and Pastoral, 2 February 1844, Power Papers, ARCAT; *Apostleship of Prayer – Ticket of Admission; Archconfraternity of the Holy Family*.
26 Taves, *Household of Faith*, 48–51, 62–3, and 83–6.
27 *Irish Canadian*, 20 March 1870.
28 *Canadian Freeman*, 30 January 1868; *Irish Canadian*, 4 October 1876 and 30 July 1879; *Canadian Messenger of the Sacred Heart*, August 1891, 264–5.

29 *Manual of the Archconfraternity of the Holy Family*, 63–4.

30 Louisa White to J.H. White, 20 April 1878, Lynch Papers, ARCAT.

31 *Manual of the Archconfraternity of the Holy Family*, 65 and 77–8; Taves, *Household of Faith*, 78–9, 81, and 104–5.

32 I am indebted to Peter G. Williams, *Popular Religion in America: Symbolic Change and the Modernization Process in Historical Perspective* (Englewood Cliffs, New Jersey: Prentice-Hall 1980), 73–4, for suggesting this line of interpretation.

33 Pastoral, 10 February 1859, Charbonnel Papers, ARCAT.

34 Roger Aubert, *Le Pontificat de Pie IX* (Paris: Bloud and Gay 1963), 465.

35 *Canadian Freeman*, 8 June 1871; *Irish Canadian*, 28 June 1871.

36 *Canadian Messenger of the Sacred Heart*, January 1894, 13.

37 See Jay P. Dolan, *Catholic Revivalism: The American Experience, 1830–1900* (Notre Dame, Indiana: University of Notre Dame Press 1978), 62 and 141.

38 St Paul's Parish, Book of Announcements, Second Sunday after Easter, 1871, ARCAT; Pastoral, August 1869, Lynch Papers, ARCAT.

39 *Apostleship of Prayer – Ticket of Admission*; Ramière, *Apostleship of Prayer: Explanation*, 6; *Bulletin*, April 1872, 126; *Work of the Holy Agony of Our Lord Jesus Christ* (n.p. 1863); Kelly, *St. Paul's Parish*, 254–63; Mary Hoskins, *History of St. Basil's Parish, St. Joseph Street* (Toronto: Catholic Register and Canadian Extension 1912), 63–6, 81–2, and 92.

40 *Apostleship of Prayer – Ticket of Admission*; Ramière, *Apostleship of Prayer: Explanation*, 6; *Bulletin*, April 1872, 126; *Work of the Holy Agony of Our Lord Jesus Christ* (n.p. 1863).

41 *Canadian Freeman*, 22 June 1865 and 22 June 1871; *Irish Canadian*, 21 September 1875; *Globe*, 7 February 1882.

42 *Globe*, 7 February 1882.

43 Aubert, *Le Pontificat de Pie IX*, 465.

44 I have borrowed the term from Dolan, *Catholic Revivalism*, 174.

45 St Mary's Parish Report, 15 August 1881, Lynch Papers, ARCAT.

46 "Register of the Saint Joseph's 'Bona Mors' Society," 1863–73, ARCAT.

47 These calculations are based on the sex ratio found in *Census of Canada, 1880–81* (Ottawa 1884), 1:73.

48 "Register of the Saint Joseph's 'Bona Mors' Society," 1863–73, ARCAT.

49 *Canadian Messenger of the Sacred Heart*, December 1896, 520–1. The total membership in the parish branches according to the *Messenger* was 5,740 but as three parishes with active branches – Saint Michael's, Saint Basil's, and Saint Peter's – did not send in returns, I have added 530 to the total, a conservative estimate given the size of these parishes. In order to estimate how many Catholic women were eligible for membership in the Apostleship of Prayer, I have relied on the sex and age distributions found in the general population, *Census of Canada, 1890–91* (Ottawa 1893), 1:74 and 2:11.

50 Peter Knights, *The Plain People of Boston, 1830–1860: A Study in City Growth* (New York: Oxford University Press 1971), 131.
51 St Michael's Cathedral, "Journal," 3 February 1867, and "Day Book," 5 October 1879, ARCAT. The parish clergy frequently gave out emergency relief. In 1878, the priests of Saint Michael's parish spent over $200 to provide such relief. St Michael's Cathedral Accounts, January 1879, ARCAT.
52 Joan W. Scott's "Gender: A Useful Category of Historical Analysis," in *Gender and the Politics of History* (New York: Columbia University Press 1988), 28–50, offers an incisive commentary on the question of gender and opens up new avenues for exploration.
53 Hasia R. Diner, *Erin's Daughters in America* (Baltimore: Johns Hopkins University Press 1983), 13, 16–17, 19–20, and 25; Conrad Arensberg, *The Irish Countryman* (1937; reprint ed., Garden City, New York: Natural History Press 1968), 56–7; Robert E. Kennedy, Jr, *The Irish: Emigration, Marriage, and Fertility* (Berkeley, California: University of California Press 1973), 53–4 and 65; J.J. Lee. "Women and the Church since the Famine," in *Women in Irish Society: The Historical Dimension*, eds. Margaret MacCurtain and Donncha Ó Corráin (Westport, Connecticut: Greenwood Press 1979), 37–9; Lynn Hollen Lees, *Exiles of Erin: Irish Migrants in Victorian London* (Ithaca, New York: Cornell University Press 1979), 34.
54 Prentice *et al.*, *Canadian Women*, 121–7; Joan W. Scott and Louise Tilly, "Women's Work and Family in Nineteenth-Century Europe," *Comparative Studies in Society and History*, 17 (1975), 43; Diner, *Erin's Daughters*, 13–14 and 19–20; Marjorie Griffin Cohen, *Women's Work, Markets, and Economic Development in Nineteenth-Century Ontario* (Toronto: University of Toronto Press 1988), 129–32.
55 Nancy F. Cott, *The Bonds of Womanhood: "Woman's Sphere" in New England, 1780–1835* (New Haven, Connecticut: Yale University Press 1977), 61–2 and 69; Barbara Welter, "The Cult of True Womanhood: 1820–1860," *American Quarterly*, 18 (1966), 152–3, 162–5, 170–2.
56 Brigitte Caulier, "Les confréries de dévotion et l'éducation de la foi," Société canadienne d'histoire de l'Église catholique, *Sessions d'étude*, 56 (1989), 108–11; Timothy J. Meagher, "Sweet Good Mothers and Young Women Out in the World: The Roles of Irish Women in Late Nineteenth and Early Twentieth Century Worcester, Massachusetts," *U.S. Catholic Historian*, 5 (1986), 328–30, Joseph G. Mannard, "Maternity ... of the Spirit: Nuns and Domesticity in Antebellum America," *U.S. Catholic Historian*, 5 (1986), 305–24; and Colleen McDannell, "Catholic Domesticity, 1860–1960," in *American Catholic Women: A Historical Exploration* ed. Karen Kennelly, CSJ (New York: Macmillan Publishing Company 1989), 48–65.

57 Christine Stansell, *City of Women: Sex and Class in New York, 1789–1860* (Urbana and Chicago: University of Illinois Press 1987), 42–3, 52, 56, and 81.

58 Scott, *Gender and the Politics of History*, 20–1 and 25–6, and Judith Newton, "*Family Fortunes*: 'New History' and 'New Historicism,'" *Radical History Review*, no.43 (1989), 11–12.

59 *Canadian Freeman*, 23 March 1871; *Irish Canadian*, 22 January 1879; "Register of the Saint Joseph's 'Bona Mors' Society," 1863–73, and Jamot, "Census of City Wards," *circa* early 1860s, ARCAT; Diner, *Erin's Daughters*, 51–2.

60 Cohen, *Women's Work*, 129–30.

61 Saint Vincent de Paul Society, Minutes of Our Lady Conference, 27 April 1856 and 30 January 1876, ARCAT; Saint Vincent de Paul Society, Minutes of St Patrick's Conference, 31 January 1874 and 1 December 1889, ARCAT.

62 *Globe*, 20 June 1860 and 26 July 1864.

63 John Francis Maguire, *The Irish in America* (London: Longmans, Green 1868), 123.

64 See Micheline Dumont-Johnson, "Les communautés religieuses et la condition féminine," *Recherches sociographiques*, 19 (1978), 79–102; Marta Danylewycz, "Changing Relationships: Nuns and Feminists in Montreal, 1890–1925," *Histoire sociale/Social History*, 15 (1981), 413–34.

65 *Irish Canadian*, 31 October 1877 and 22 January 1879.

66 *Irish Canadian*, 9 June 1879 and 24 May 1883.

67 *Manual of the Archconfraternity of the Holy Family*, 6, 7, and 127–8; Colleen McDannell, *The Christian Home in Victorian America, 1840–1900* (Bloomington, Indiana: Indiana University Press 1986), 64–6 and 75. In the early 1890s, one devotional organization, the Apostleship of Prayer, began to encourage family prayers. Such prayers, the promoters of the Apostleship of Prayer insisted, should be led by the wife since she was properly the "priestess" to her family. See *Canadian Messenger of the Sacred Heart*, March 1892, 81.

68 *Fifth Glorious Mystery* (Montreal: D. and J. Sadlier n.d.).

69 Pastoral, 1854, Charbonnel Papers, ARCAT.

70 Ramière, *Apostleship of Prayer: Explanation*, 5.

71 *Bulletin*, June 1879, 181.

72 Pastoral, 2 February 1855, Charbonnel Papers, ARCAT.

73 *Fourth Glorious Mystery* (Montreal: D. and J. Sadlier n.d.).

74 *Fourth Glorious Mystery*; Pastoral, 2 February 1855, Charbonnel Papers, ARCAT.

75 *Irish Canadian*, 29 April 1874, 27 October 1875, and 9 September 1875.

76 *Archconfraternity of the Holy Family*.

77 *Archconfraternity of the Holy Family*; *Prayer of the Holy Family* (n.p.).
78 "The Family," n.d., and Pastoral, 2 February 1846, Power Papers,
   ARCAT; Pastoral 2 February 1855, Charbonnel Papers, ARCAT;
   Irish Canadian, 22 March 1870; *Canadian Freeman*, 19 December 1872;
   Catholic Weekly Review, 17 March 1887.
79 Bishop Charbonnel to Lynch, 23 February 1863, Lynch Papers,
   ARCAT.
80 *Bulletin*, February 1890, 38.
81 Nancy F. Cott, "On Men's History and Women's History," in *Meanings
   For Manhood: Constructions of Masculinity in Victorian America*, eds.
   Mark C. Carnes and Clyde Griffen (Chicago: University of Chicago
   Press 1990), 206–7.
82 Joy Parr, "Nature and Hierarchy: Reflections on Writing the History
   of Women and Children," *Atlantis*, 11 (1985), 40–1.
83 Dolan, *American Catholic Experience*, 190.
84 Jay P. Dolan, *The Immigrant Church: New York's Irish and German
   Catholics, 1815–1865* (Baltimore: Johns Hopkins University Press
   1975), 165.
85 *Canadian Freeman*, 1 June 1865; *Catholic Weekly Review*, 28 November
   1891.
86 *Irish Canadian*, 11 March 1886.
87 *Archconfraternity of the Holy Family*; *Bulletin*, April 1872, 125; and
   June 1879, 173.
88 *Archconfraternity of the Holy Family*; *Canadian Freeman*, 28 November
   1861, 23 January 1862, 1 January 1863, and 1 June 1865; *Irish
   Canadian*, 16 June 1869, 16 February 1870, 19 July 1871, 4 February
   1874, 20 November 1878, 4 October 1883, 29 July 1886, and
   6 September 1888; *Globe*, 8 October 1874, 28 October 1880, and
   18 November 1884; *Catholic Weekly Review*, 19 November 1887,
   1 February 1890, and 18 April 1891; Hoskins, *St. Basil's Parish*, 96–8;
   Archbishop Lynch to Miss Banks and the Children of Mary, n.d.,
   and Helen Crawford *et al.* to Archbishop Lynch, 8 December 1874,
   Lynch Papers, ARCAT.
89 *Archconfraternity of the Holy Family*; *Apostleship of Prayer – Ticket of
   Admission*; Kelly, *St. Paul's Parish*, 263.
90 Kelly, *St. Paul's Parish*, 263.
91 St Paul's Parish, Book of Announcements, Second Sunday after Easter,
   1871, and Second Sunday after Advent, 1875, ARCAT.
92 St Paul's Parish, Book of Announcements, First Sunday in September,
   1872, Sixteenth Sunday after Pentecost, 1875, Second Sunday
   after Advent, 1875, and Fourth Sunday after Easter, 1876, ARCAT;
   St Michael's Cathedral, Book of Announcements, Twelfth Sunday
   after Pentecost, 1881, Third Sunday after Easter, 1882, and Fifth
   Sunday after Easter, 1882, ARCAT; *Globe*, 28 October 1880.

93 *Irish Canadian*, 7 July 1869, 13 December 1870, 10 September 1873, and 18 November 1886; *Canadian Freeman*, 29 December 1864, 6 June 1867, 4 June 1868, and 17 February 1870.

94 *Globe*, 16 May 1872.

95 *Irish Canadian*, 7 November 1877, 20 November 1878, and 19 November 1879; *Catholic Weekly Review*, 19 November 1887, 21 April 1888, 28 March 1891, 4 April 1891, and 25 April 1891; Helen Crawford *et al.* to Archbishop Lynch, 8 December 1874, Lynch Papers, ARCAT.

96 J.R. Teefy, *Jubilee Volume: The Archdiocese of Toronto and Archbishop Walsh* (Toronto: George T. Dixon 1892), 248; Saint Vincent de Paul Society, Hospital Board Minutes, April 1890, ARCAT.

97 Helen M. Crawford *et al.* to Archbishop Lynch, 8 December 1874, Lynch Papers, ARCAT; Hoskins, *St. Basil's Parish*, 63–4; "General Rules of the Sacred Heart and Our Lady of Perpetual Help," in *A Documentary Contribution to the History of The Saint Vincent de Paul Society, Toronto, 1850–1975*, ed. J.S. McGivern, SJ (Toronto 1975), 50–1.

98 Helen M. Crawford *et al.* to Archbishop Lynch, 8 December 1874, Lynch Papers, ARCAT.

99 "General Rules of the Sacred Heart and Our Lady of Perpetual Help," in *Documentary History*, 47–51.

100 Carroll Smith-Rosenberg, *Disorderly Conduct: Visions of Gender in Victorian America* (New York: Alfred A. Knopf 1985), 16.

101 *Globe*, 23 February 1882, 26 March 1883, and 21 April 1885.

102 *Irish Canadian*, 30 July 1879.

103 *Mirror*, 14 March 1851, 16 April 1852, and 14 November 1856.

104 *Canadian Freeman*, 3 and 10 April 1862; *Irish Canadian*, 4 September 1872, 2 November 1872, 16 November 1872, 5 March 1873, 2 April 1873, 9 April 1873, and 23 April 1873.

105 *Catholic Young Men's Association of Toronto: Constitution and By-Laws* (Toronto 1876), 2–3.

106 *Irish Canadian*, 2 February 1876, 24 November 1876, 25 January 1877, 7 November 1877, and 14 November 1877.

107 John O'Byrne to Rev. J. Carroll, 21 January 1850, Charbonnel Papers, ARCAT; Archbishop E.A. Taschereau to Archbishop Lynch, 12 May 1876, Circular, 20 January 1882, C.B. Doherty to Archbishop Lynch, 22 January 1884, Lynch Papers, ARCAT; *Globe*, 21 January 1884; and *Catholic Weekly Review*, 21 May 1892.

108 *Catholic Weekly Review*, 2 April 1892.

109 "List of Objections against having the girls of St. Bridget's School introduced in the new building destined for the Christian Brothers in Saint Catharines," 1 October 1887, Lynch Papers, ARCAT.

110 Archbishop Lynch to Rev. T. Wardy, 9 December 1862, Lynch Papers, ARCAT.

111 *Catholic Weekly Review*, 3 March 1887, 17 March 1887, and 6 October 1888.

112 *Catholic Weekly Review*, 6 October 1888.

113 *Catholic Weekly Review*, 17 March 1887, 10 January 1891, 7 November 1891, and 29 October 1892; *Irish Canadian*, 24 November 1892; *Catholic Young Men's Association of Toronto*, 4 and 9; *Catholic Register*, 16 November 1893.

114 *Catholic Weekly Review*, 17 March 1887.

115 *Catholic Weekly Review*, 30 January 1890, 6 February 1892, and 9 April 1892.

116 *Catholic Weekly Review*, 4 April and 31 October 1891.

117 *Catholic Weekly Review*, 7 February 1891 and 2 April 1892; *Irish Canadian*, 18 June 1879; *Catholic Register*, 8 February 1894.

118 *Catholic Weekly Review*, 1 February 1890 and 24 November 1892.

119 *Catholic Weekly Review*, 29 March 1890, 6 June 1890, 7 November 1890, 21 December 1890, and 31 October 1891.

120 *Canadian Freeman*, 26 May 1863; *Irish Canadian*, 31 May 1865, 5 June 1872, and 20 June 1877; *Catholic Weekly Review*, 27 July 1887 and 14 June 1890; and *Catholic Register*, 16 November 1893.

121 Marie Louise White to J.H. White, 3 February 1878, Lynch Papers, ARCAT.

122 *Catholic Weekly Review*, 31 January 1891 and 7 November 1891; *Irish Canadian*, 5 May 1892.

123 *Catholic Weekly Review*, 29 March 1890, 6 June 1891, 7 November 1891, 26 December 1891, 11 June 1892, and 25 June 1892.

124 *Catholic Weekly Review*, 2 April 1892.

125 *Catholic Weekly Review*, 3 March 1887, 27 July 1887, and 4 July 1891; Hoskins, *St. Basil's Parish*, 93–4.

126 *Catholic Weekly Review*, 6 October 1888, 31 October 1991, and 21 November 1991.

127 *Catholic Weekly Review*, 28 November 1891.

128 *Canadian Messenger of the Sacred Heart*, May 1892, 204–5; July 1892, 293; February 1893, 82–5; May 1894, 217–18; December 1895, 520.

129 Mark George McGowan, "'We Are All Canadians': A Social, Religious and Cultural Portrait of Toronto's English-Speaking Roman Catholics, 1890–1920" (PhD diss., University of Toronto 1988), 218–19.

CHAPTER FIVE

1 J.R. Teefy, *Jubilee Volume: The Archdiocese of Toronto and Archbishop Walsh* (Toronto: George T. Dixon 1892), 151–4.

2 Jean-Baptiste Duroselle, *Les Débuts du Catholicisme Social en France* (Paris: Presses universitaires de France 1951), 178.
3 *Manual of the Society of St. Vincent of Paul* (London 1867), 20, 30–3, and 112 (hereafter cited as *Manual*); John Elmsley and S.G. Lynn to Bishop Charbonnel, 18 October 1850, Charbonnel Papers, ARCAT.
4 *Irish Canadian*, 7 December 1872.
5 *Irish Canadian*, 1 November 1882.
6 *Canadian Freeman*, 22 December 1870.
7 *Manual*, 20; Saint Vincent de Paul Society, Minutes of Our Lady Conference, 18 June 1854, ARCAT (hereafter cited as OL).
8 *Manual*, 422.
9 *Manual*, 49–66.
10 OL, 8 February, 18 June, and 8 October 1854.
11 OL, 18 June 1854.
12 OL, 18 September 1853, 4 December 1853, and 16 November 1865.
13 OL, 8 February 1854, 18 June 1854, 8 October 1854, and 8 February 1857.
14 The members received a plenary indulgence, that is, the remission of the temporal penalty attached to a forgiven sin, on admission to the society. Once admitted, members were eligible for a plenary indulgence on three conditions. A plenary indulgence was awarded to members if they attended three-quarters of the meetings in a given month; a plenary indulgence was granted if members attended the general meeting, confessed, and received communion; and a plenary indulgence was also offered to members in the "hour of our death." An indulgence of seven years and seven quarantines (a quarantine was a period of forty days) was given if members attended a conference meeting, attended a funeral for a fellow member, or followed the hearse of a poor person.
15 *Globe*, 7 March 1860.
16 I have borrowed the term from Sheridan Gilley, "Heretic London, Holy Poverty, and the Irish Poor, 1830–1870," *Downside Review*, 89 (1971), 64–89. Gilley's brilliant exposition of the nature of Catholic charity in Victorian London is an essential contribution to the understanding of nineteenth-century Catholic social theory.
17 *Manual*, 225 and 234–5. The president of the Particular Council of Toronto, W.J. Macdonell, frequently emphasized this point when he addressed the membership. A representative report of one such speech appeared in the *Canadian Freeman*, 21 September 1871.
18 *Irish Canadian*, 5 February 1879.
19 *Bulletin of the Society of St. Vincent de Paul*, May 1877, 92 (hereafter cited as *Bulletin*).
20 *Bulletin*, June 1879, 173.

21 *Bulletin*, June 1887, 163.

22 "Twenty-Fifth General Meeting," 10 December 1865, in *A Documentary Contribution to the History of the St. Vincent de Paul Society in Toronto, 1850–1975*, ed. J.S. McGivern (Toronto 1975), 57.

23 *Canadian Freeman*, 26 January 1871.

24 *Manual*, 309–10.

25 *Bulletin*, September 1875, 260.

26 *Rules of the Society of St. Vincent de Paul* (Toronto 1861), 30 (hereafter cited as *Rules*); *Irish Canadian*, 15 December 1880.

27 "Twenty-Fifth General Meeting," in *Documentary History*, 57.

28 Gilley, "Heretic London," 66.

29 *Irish Canadian*, 5 February 1879.

30 *Irish Canadian*, 15 December 1880.

31 *Irish Canadian*, 21 November 1889.

32 *Irish Canadian*, 15 December 1880.

33 *Canadian Freeman*, 8 June 1871.

34 *Manual*, 30–1.

35 *Manual*, 24, 102, and 225.

36 "Twenty-Fifth General Meeting," in *Documentary History*, 57.

37 "Minutes of the First Meeting of the St. Vincent de Paul Society in Toronto," 10 November 1850, in *Documentary History*, 31.

38 "Summary Statement," 2 May 1851, in *Documentary History*, 35.

39 The occupational profile of the Saint Vincent de Paul Society has been compiled from the minute-books of the society. The members were then traced in the city directories using the occupation classification developed by Peter Goheen in his *Victorian Toronto: 1850–1900: Pattern and Process of Growth*, University of Chicago, Department of Geography, research paper no.127 (Chicago 1970) 229–30, and reproduced in the appendix. In reconstructing the occupational profile of the Saint Vincent de Paul Society's membership I have used the minute-books rather than the society's "General Register" of members, which is available at ARCAT. The "General Register" does not distinguish between those who joined the society and those who were nominated for membership but did not join the society. A comparison between the minute-books and the "General Register" reveals that many of those who were nominated but elected not to join the society were workers. As a consequence, the "General Register" inflates the working-class composition of the Saint Vincent de Paul Society.

40 Michael B. Katz, *The People of Hamilton: Family and Class in a Mid-Nineteenth-Century City* (Cambridge, Massachusetts: Harvard University Press 1975), 145–6; Clyde and Sally Griffen, *Natives and Newcomers: The Ordering of Opportunity in Mid-Nineteenth-Century*

Poughkeepsie (Cambridge, Massachusetts: Harvard University Press 1978), 133–4.

41 "Twenty-Fifth General Meeting," in *Documentary History*, 65.

42 *Société St. Vincent de Paul – Rapport du Conseil Supérieur de Québec pour l'année 1886* (Quebec 1887). In 1885 the society reported only 216 members. *Superior Council Report for the Year 1885* (Quebec 1886); *Report of the Superior Council of Quebec for the Year 1888* (Quebec 1889), 34.

43 *Superior Council of Canada – Report for the Year 1882* (Quebec 1883).

44 OL, 16 October 1853, 22 March 1867, 21 September 1874, 26 December 1880, and 20 January 1881; Minutes of the St Patrick's Conference, ARCAT (hereafter cited as StP), 31 December 1876, 31 March 1878, 5 January 1879, 4 October 1883, 4 May 1884, 12 April 1885, and 11 November 1888.

45 The "General Register" of the society reveals that clerks in particular were likely to be nominated by their employers.

46 OL, 19 October 1873; "Toronto Particular Council Report 1887–1888," *Bulletin*, October 1888, 344; "Suggestions on the use of Leaflet and Indulgence Card," Scrapbook, 3, J.J. Murphy Papers, SMC.

47 "Twenty-Fifth General Meeting," in *Documentary History*, 57; "Toronto Particular Council Report," *Bulletin*, March 1882, 91–2; "Toronto Particular Council Report," *Bulletin*, November 1890, 349.

48 *Manual*, 21, 66, 279, 310, and 370.

49 For an overview of middle-class perceptions of leisure during the mid-Victorian era, see Peter Bailey, *Leisure and Class in Victorian England: Rational Recreation and the Contest for Control, 1830–1885* (London: Routledge and Kegan Paul 1978), 56–72.

50 *Globe*, 19 June 1855, 17 May 1856, 26 July 1870, 12 October 1876, 2 April 1881, 30 April 1881, 3 February 1883, 22 September 1883, and 27 October 1883.

51 *Globe*, 9 December 1882; Bettina Bradbury, "Family Economy and Work in an Industrializing City: Montreal in the 1870s," Canadian Historical Association, *Historical Papers*, 1979, 78–82 and 86.

52 Gregory S. Kealey, *Toronto Workers Respond to Industrial Capitalism 1867–1892* (Toronto: University of Toronto Press 1980), 58; Bryan D. Palmer, *Working-Class Experience: The Rise and Reconstitution of Canadian Labour, 1800–1980* (Toronto: Butterworth 1983), 64–6; and Judith Fingard, "The Winter's Tale: The Seasonal Contours of Pre-Industrial Poverty in British North America, 1815–1860," Canadian Historical Association, *Historical Papers*, 1974, 66–72.

53 Ian Davey, "The Rhythm of Work and the Rhythm of School," in *Egerton Ryerson and His Times*, eds. Neil McDonald and Alf Chaiton (Toronto: Macmillan of Canada 1977), 237–8.

54 *Globe*, 3 February 1883.

55 OL, 27 April 1856, 26 January 1868, 30 January 1876, 10 December 1876, and 23 December 1877; stP, 31 January 1874, 28 February 1875, 3 January 1876, 2 March 1884, and 1 December 1889.

56 *Globe*, 8 December 1882.

57 *Globe*, 10 February 1855.

58 *Globe*, 11 February 1866.

59 *Globe*, 21 January 1880.

60 "Minutes of the First Meeting," in *Documentary History*, 32; OL, 11 December 1853, 14 January 1855, 21 January 1855, 1 February 1857, 9 February 1868, 4 January 1873, and 6 December 1874. There were four classes of relief: first class, twelve pounds of bread, two pounds of oatmeal or barley; second class, eight pounds of bread and two of grain; third class, six pounds of bread and one of grain; and fourth class, one pound of bread.

61 Saint Vincent de Paul Society, Families Relieved, 1850–1853, ARCAT; *Report Superior Council 1888*; *Globe*, 3 February and 27 October 1873. Average family size varied from 3.2 in 1850 to 3.8 for the years 1851 through to 1853 and the year 1888.

62 OL, 11 December 1853 and 2 December 1855; stP, 3 December 1877, 19 December 1878, and 9 February 1879; OL, 28 January 1854, 28 October 1866, 19 March 1871, 9 December 1872, and 3 October 1879; stP, 5 March 1876, 17 December 1876, 10 February 1878, and 21 January 1883.

63 "Minutes of the First Meeting," in *Documentary History*, 32.

64 OL, 26 March 1871 and 1 March 1876; stP, 25 September 1887.

65 *Irish Canadian*, 20 November 1878; OL, 30 January 1876; "Toronto Particular Council Report 1887–1888," *Bulletin*, October 1888, 345.

66 *Manual*, 45 and 485; OL, 24 December 1854, 25 February 1855, and 14 December 1879.

67 "St. Vincent de Paul Society, St. Mary's," n.d., Lynch Papers, ARCAT.

68 OL, 5 February 1854, 6 January 1856, 25 May 1856, 3 February 1868, and 24 December 1871; stP, 8 November 1874 and 8 March 1888. The rents paid by the society varied from $1.25 to $10. Moving expenses were also subsidized.

69 OL, 31 December 1854 and 5 January 1868; stP, 29 May 1887.

70 OL, 2 December 1877; stP, 13 December 1877.

71 "Summary Statement," 2 May 1851, in *Documentary History*, 36; OL, 7 November 1874 and 23 February 1879; stP, 18 May 1879, 2 April 1883, 11 January 1884, 13 November 1887, and 17 August 1890.

72 *Irish Canadian*, 11 May 1882.

73 OL, 10 December 1854, 10 February 1856, 15 December 1867, 12 June 1872, and 5 March 1876; STP, 4 May 1879. The society made arrangements with the railway companies to purchase tickets at half price. See *Canadian Freeman*, 27 September 1866.

74 The society paid for a nurse's attendance as well as for medicine. The society also had a doctor on retainer. OL, 12 March 1853, 24 March 1853, and 24 December 1871; STP, 8 November 1874 and 18 March 1888. On admittance to the General Hospital, see OL, 17 March 1872, 16 November 1873, and "Toronto – Hospital Committee – General Meeting July 21, 1889," *Bulletin*, March 1890, 75. For cab fares see OL, 30 March 1858.

75 OL, 4 May 1856 and 7 November 1880; STP, 13 July 1879, 2 March 1884, and 3 May 1885.

76 Saint Vincent de Paul Society, Hospital Board Minutes, 29 November 1885, 26 December 1886, and 30 November 1890, ARCAT (hereafter cited as HB); "Toronto Particular Council Report 1887–1888," *Bulletin*, October 1888, 349–51.

77 HB, 26 July 1885 and 24 February 1889.

78 OL, 30 October 1853, 30 April 1854, 31 December 1854, 2 September 1855, 22 March 1856, 4 May 1856, 13 July 1856, 22 September 1867, 15 December 1872, 16 February 1873, 24 December 1876, 14 January 1877, and 29 August 1880; STP, 14 February 1875 and 28 March 1886. The average cost of a pauper's funeral was five dollars but could go as high as ten dollars. See STP, 13 November 1887 and 29 January 1888.

79 *Manual*, 23.

80 *Manual*, 10–11; OL, 26 January 1868, 16 February 1868, 15 March 1868, 5 April 1868; STP, 24 January 1875, 2 January 1876, and 2 December 1883.

81 Figures cited in this paragraph and summarized in table 10 are taken from Saint Vincent de Paul Society, "Summary Statement," 2 May 1851, in *Documentary History*, 36; Families Relieved, 1850–53, ARCAT; "Minutes of the First General Meeting of the Saint Vincent de Paul Society in Toronto," July 1854, in *Documentary History*, 32; *Canadian Freeman*, 28 April 1864; "Twenty-Fifth General Meeting," in *Documentary History*, 60–1; *Superior Council Report 1882*; *Superior Council Report 1885*; *Rapport du Conseil Supérieur 1886*; *Report Superior Council 1888*.

82 A two-pound loaf of bread cost between seven and ten cents. OL, 2 December 1877; STP, 13 December 1877; "Summary Statement," 2 May 1851, in *Documentary History*, 36. In 1857 fuel accounted for half the society's expenditures ("Third General Meeting, Sunday, December 15th, 1857," in *Documentary History*, 54).

83 Clipping *circa* 1866, Scrapbook, 13, J.J. Murphy Papers, SMC; *Canadian Freeman*, 8 April 1861.

84 "Summary Statement," 2 May 1851, in *Documentary History*, 36; *Rapport du Conseil Supérieur 1886*; *Report Superior Council 1888*.

85 Untitled Report, *circa* Easter 1894, Scrapbook, 38–9, J.J. Murphy Papers, SMC; *Canadian Freeman*, 26 June 1862, 6 November 1862, 13 November 1862, 22 March 1871, and 28 March 1872; STP, 25 November 1877 and 10 March 1878.

86 *Canadian Freeman*, 10 June 1869.

87 J.M.S. Careless, "Mid-Victorian Liberalism in Central Canadian Newspapers," *Canadian Historical Review*, 31 (1950), 227–30.

88 *Globe*, 17 August 1870.

89 James Pitsula, "The Emergence of Social Work," *Journal of Canadian Studies*, 14 (1979), 36–8.

90 Pastoral, 1856, Charbonnel Papers, ARCAT.

91 "President's Address – St. Vincent de Paul Toronto – 8 December 1878," *Bulletin*, February 1879, 61.

92 On occasion, recommenders were appointed as visitors. OL, 26 January 1868 and 31 January 1869.

93 James Pitsula, "The Emergence of Social Work," 36. Still, if members were not discreet resentment could be quite bitter, an example of which was reported in STP, 27 January 1878, when the conference president cautioned members not to mention the names of informants.

94 "Twenty-Fifth General Meeting," in *Documentary History*, 59 and 63.

95 OL, 15 March 1868.

96 "Visitors' Report," Scrapbook, 4–5, J.J. Murphy Papers, SMC; OL, 31 March 1869, 30 November 1873, 1 April 1877; STP, 23 January 1873, 14 October 1883, 23 January 1887, and 30 September 1888.

97 The society did cooperate with the House of Industry in keeping a register of "doubtful cases."

98 OL, 4 June 1854, 17 December 1876, and 3 August 1879; STP, 31 January 1874 and 6 February 1876.

99 OL, 27 April 1856, 17 December 1871, 9 December 1877, 2 March 1879, and 25 April 1880; STP, 10 January 1875, 3 January 1876, 25 February 1878, 25 November 1883, and 22 June 1890.

100 *Canadian Freeman*, 21 December 1865.

101 *Canadian Freeman*, 5 January 1865.

102 OL, 22 June 1855, 23 February 1868, 10 March 1872, 1 April 1877, and 2 March 1879; STP, 24 January 1874, 31 January 1874, 9 September 1883, 27 January 1888, 6 January 1889, and 16 February 1890.

103 *Rules*, 29.

104 *Manual*, 9.

105 *Manual*, 225.
106 *Bulletin*, June 1887, 166.
107 *Manual*, 20–1.
108 *Manual*, 11.
109 *Manual*, 31.
110 *Manual*, 21, 273, and 413; *Bulletin*, August 1889, 228.
111 "Toronto Particular Council Report," *Bulletin*, March 1882, 92.
112 *Manual*, 57.
113 "Twenty-Fifth General Meeting," in *Documentary History*, 59 and 63.
114 "Visitors' Report," Scrapbook, 4–5, J.J. Murphy Papers, SMC.
115 *Irish Canadian*, 16 November 1870.
116 *Manual*, 477.
117 OL, 9 October 1853, 27 November 1853, 19 March 1854, 2 September
    1855, 27 January 1856, 13 April 1879, 27 April 1880; STP,
    23 December 1877, 28 October 1878, 2 March 1879, 28 January 1883,
    30 November 1884, 8 February 1885, and 9 November 1886;
    "President's Address – 8 December 1878," *Bulletin*, February 1879,
    61; "Toronto Particular Council Report 1887–1888," *Bulletin*,
    October 1888, 346; "Summary Statement," 2 May 1851, in *Documentary
    History*, 37; "Visitors' Report," Scrapbook, 4–5, J.J. Murphy Pa-
    pers, SMC.
118 OL, 3 September 1854, 10 December 1854, and 24 February 1874;
    STP, 10 February 1889; "Saint Vincent de Paul Society, Toronto,"
    Bulletin, November 1879, 301.
119 "Visitors' Report," Scrapbook, 4–5, J.J. Murphy Papers, SMC.
120 HB, 10 February 1884, 26 July 1885, 27 December 1885, and 29 May
    1887; *Bulletin*, March 1882, 93–4.
121 *Bulletin*, April 1871, 125–26, September 1872, 298–300; May 1873,
    152; June 1875, 161–3; June 1879, 172–81; April 1882, 100;
    and March 1888, 92. Also: *Superior Council Report 1882*, 20; STP,
    30 December 1883.
122 "Toronto Particular Council Report," *Bulletin*, March 1882, 92–3.
123 "Summary Statement," 2 May 1851, in *Documentary History*, 37; OL,
    30 October 1853, 4 May 1856, 22 September 1867, 15 December
    1872, 24 December 1876, 14 January 1877, and 29 August 1880; STP,
    14 February 1875 and 28 March 1886.
124 *Manual*, 225 and 234–5; *Bulletin*, May 1877, 165, and June 1879, 173;
    Canadian Freeman, 21 September 1871; *Irish Canadian*, 5 February
    1879.
125 Clipping, 22 December 1854, Scrapbook, 11, J.J. Murphy Papers, SMC.
126 STP, 25 February 1883 and 13 January 1884. By 1886 one other con-
    ference provided volunteers for teaching night schools. "Particular
    Council, Toronto," *Bulletin*, September 1886, 283.

127 "Particular Council Report 1887–1888," *Bulletin*, October 1888, 345–6.
128 *Manual*, 29.
129 "Saint Vincent de Paul Society, Toronto," *Bulletin*, November 1878, 345.
130 The definitive treatment of the Toronto Savings Bank is Gerald J. Stortz, "Archbishop Lynch and the Toronto Savings Bank," Canadian Catholic Historical Association, *Study Sessions*, 45 (1978), 5–19. See also J.E. Middleton, *The Municipality of Toronto: A History*, 3 vols. (Toronto: Dominion Publishing 1913), 1:489.
131 Saint Vincent de Paul Society, "General Register," ARCAT. Three of the five men attending the inaugural meeting were members of the Saint Vincent de Paul Society.
132 Memo, Toronto Savings Bank Meeting, 18 September, 1876, Lynch Papers, ARCAT. In 1859, for example, the bank gave $400 to Catholic charities. *Canadian Freeman*, 19 August 1859.
133 List of Toronto Savings Bank Directors, n.d., Lynch Papers, ARCAT.
134 Stortz, "Toronto Savings Bank," 10. See also *Canadian Freeman*, 5 September 1861.
135 "Memorandum of Losses Sustained and Doubtful and Unproductive Assets," 30 June 1872, Lynch Papers, ARCAT. For details on Archbishop Lynch's negotiations with the federal government see Stortz, "Toronto Savings Bank," 10–19.
136 *Globe*, 22 January 1853, 28 May 1855, and 25 September 1856; S.J. Connolly, *Priests and People in Pre-Famine Ireland, 1780–1845* (New York: St Martin's Press 1982), 75–6 and 109–10.
137 John Ross Robertson, *Landmarks of Toronto*, 6 vols. (Toronto: *Toronto Telegram* 1914), 4:307; *Globe*, 16 April 1881; *Irish Canadian*, 16 October 1869 and 14 March 1877.
138 "Toronto Particular Council Report," *Bulletin*, March 1882, 93.
139 *Bulletin*, January 1879, 179–80; "Particular Council Report," *Bulletin*, November 1888, 382–4; *Globe*, 23 February 1882, 26 March 1883, and 21 April 1885.
140 *Rules*, 10.
141 *Rules*, 26.
142 *Manual*, 233.
143 *Manual*, 6 and 26.
144 "An Act to Incorporate the Roman Catholic Bishops of Toronto and Kingston in Canada, LXXXII," 29 March 1845, Power Papers, ARCAT.
145 See for example St Michael's Parish, Report of the Committee on Ways and Means, 1876, Lynch Papers, ARCAT; Eugene O'Keefe to Archbishop John Walsh, 20 August 1890, Walsh Papers, ARCAT.

146 St Michael's Cathedral, Book of Announcements, 5 February 1882,
    21 August 1882, 9 August 1884, and passim, ARCAT; St Paul's
    Parish, Book of Announcements, 23 July 1871, Tenth Sunday after
    Pentecost, 1872, Fourth Sunday after Pentecost, 1874, ARCAT; OL,
    25 November 1855 and 13 April 1856; STP, 19 August 1877 and
    4 September 1887.
147 *Irish Canadian*, 29 April 1886.
148 OL, 19 September 1875, 10 June 1877, 24 June 1877, and 19 June
    1881; STP, 18 June 1875 and 17 June 1877; *Canadian Freeman*,
    22 June 1865 and 22 June 1871; *Irish Canadian*, 21 September 1875.
149 My account is based on the reports in the *Globe*, 5, 7, 8, and 10 January
    1881; "Our much Esteemed and Reverend Pastor," n.d. Lynch
    Papers, ARCAT.
150 G.M. Muir to M. Bilodeau, 16 November 1850, in *Documentary History*,
    30; "Minutes of the First Meeting of St. Vincent de Paul Society
    in Toronto," in *Documentary History*, 31 and 34; Teefy, *Jubilee Volume*,
    242–3.
151 OL, 9 October 1853, 21 October 1866, 23 December 1866, 10 October
    1869, 8 December 1872, 19 October 1873, and 22 November 1874.
152 "Presidential Address, Toronto Particular Council," *Bulletin*, February
    1879, 68.
153 *Manual*, 38–9.
154 "Twenty-Fifth General Meeting," in *Documentary History*, 56–65;
    "Toronto Particular Council Report 1887–1888," *Bulletin*,
    October 1888, 342–52; "Toronto Particular Council Report," *Bulletin*,
    November 1890, 348–9.
155 "Toronto Particular Council Report," *Bulletin*, January 1884, 20;
    "Toronto Particular Council Report," *Bulletin*, December 1886,
    365; "Toronto Particular Council Report 1887–1888," *Bulletin*,
    October 1888, 348.
156 "Toronto Particular Council Report 1887–1888," *Bulletin*, October
    1888, 349.

CHAPTER SIX

1 K.H. Connell, *Irish Peasant Society: Four Historical Essays* (London: Oxford University Press 1968), 12, 20, 26, and 49; James R. Barrett,
  "Why Paddy Drank: The Social Importance of Whiskey in Pre-Famine
  Ireland," *Journal of Popular Culture*, 12 (1977), 158–63.
2 T.P. O'Neil, "Rural Life," in *Social Life in Ireland, 1800–45*, ed. R.B.
  McDowell (Cork: Mercier Press 1957), 52.
3 *Globe*, 29 October 1874.

4 *Globe*, 15, 19, and 31 July 1865.

5 *Globe*, 20 January 1881.

6 *Globe*, 20 January 1881.

7 *Globe*, 28 February 1859, 14 November 1868, 18 November 1868, 17 March 1875, and 31 January 1881.

8 *Globe*, 10 July 1868.

9 *Globe*, 9 March 1859 and 31 January 1883.

10 *Globe*, 23 January 1859, 15 January 1869, and 12 February 1874; *Leader*, 14 March 1864.

11 *Globe*, 20 January 1857, 31 August, 19 November, 14 December 1868, and 10 May 1869.

12 *Globe*, 11 June 1864 and 31 January 1880.

13 *Globe*, 21 October 1868 and 21 January 1873; *Leader*, 6 January 1859 and 18 April 1864.

14 *Globe*, 8 and 9 March 1869. See also *Globe*, 23 May 1860 and 21 February 1876.

15 *Globe*, 29 July 1865, 15 April 1882, and 18 September 1882.

16 *Globe*, 24 April 1876, 25 June 1877, and 31 January 1880.

17 Elwood Jones and Douglas McCalla, "Toronto Waterworks, 1840–77: Continuity and Change in Nineteenth-Century Toronto Politics," *Canadian Historical Review*, 60 (1979), 300–23; J.G. Snell, "The Cost of Living in Canada in 1870," *Histoire sociale/Social History*, 12 (1979), 190; *Globe*, 8 February 1876 and 1 December 1881.

18 *Globe*, 27 October 1883.

19 *Globe*, 3 April 1869, 14 February 1873, and 24 April 1876; Christine Stansell, *City of Women: Sex and Class in New York, 1789–1869* (Chicago and Urbana: University of Illinois Press 1987), 57.

20 Gregory S. Kealey, *Toronto Workers Respond to Industrial Capitalism 1867–1892* (Toronto: University of Toronto Press 1980), 53–5, 75, and 350–1.

21 *Globe*, 1 January 1880.

22 Peter G. Goheen, *Victorian Toronto, 1850 to 1900: Pattern and Process of Growth*, University of Chicago, Department of Geography, research paper no.127 (Chicago 1970), 7–9 and 153.

23 *Globe*, 16 April 1857, 7 June 1859, and 21 October 1868; *Leader*, 13 November 1860 and 28 September 1864.

24 *Irish Canadian*, 1 October 1873.

25 *Globe*, 2 June 1860 and 29 June 1870; *Leader*, 29 April 1865.

26 *Globe*, 22 March 1855, 9 December 1856, 19 March 1858, 23 February 1860, 2 November 1863, 27 December 1868, and 29 December 1869.

27 *Leader*, 10 April 1864; *Globe*, 29 October 1867.

28 *Globe*, 20 June 1860, 26 July 1864, 14 April 1869, 12 February 1874, and 21 March 1885.

29 *Globe*, 20 June 1860 and 26 July 1864.

30 *Globe*, 24 April 1876 and 20 June 1882.

31 Temperance Pledge, 4 September 1876, and Temperance Pledge, 4 March 1882, Lynch Papers, ARCAT; *Globe*, 27 May 1882.

32 *Leader*, 24 August and 7 November 1864; *Globe*, 9 June 1862, 17 May 1865, 2 June 1865, 1 February 1868, 3 September 1868, 5 October 1868, 1 December 1868, 10 March 1869, 6 August 1870, and 17 June 1873.

33 *Irish Canadian*, 21 May 1873.

34 Joan Bland, *Hibernian Crusade: The Story of the Catholic Total Abstinence Union of America* (Washington, DC: Catholic University of America Press 1951), 22; A.E. Dingle and B.H. Harrison, "Cardinal Manning as Temperance Reformer," *Historical Journal*, 12 (1969), 489 and 496; and Jan Noel, "Dry Patriotism: The Chiniquy Crusade," *Canadian Historical Review*, 71 (1990), 191–4. In the nineteenth century, the terms temperance and total abstinence were used interchangeably. As all of the temperance societies in Toronto advocated total abstinence, I have followed this usage unless the distinction between temperance (moderation) and total abstinence is at issue.

35 Dingle and Harrison, "Cardinal Manning," 495.

36 Bland, *Hibernian Crusade*, 27–30 and 37; Elizabeth Malcolm, "The Catholic Church and the Irish Temperance Movement, 1838–1901," *Irish Historical Studies*, 23 (1982), 2.

37 Nive Voisine, "Mouvements de tempérance et religion populaire," in *Religion populaire, religion de clercs?*, eds. Benoit Lacroix and Jean Simard (Quebec: Institut québécois de recherche sur la culture 1984), 69 and 73–4.

38 Bland, *Hibernian Crusade*, 45–9; Dingle and Harrison, "Cardinal Manning," 495–6; Malcolm, "Irish Temperance," 11 and 13–15.

39 Bishop Charbonnel to Cardinal Giacomo Filippo Fransoni, 18 May 1852, Charbonnel Papers, ARCAT.

40 Pastoral, 10 February 1859, and "Regulations for the Retreat preceding St. Patrick's Feast," 1859, Charbonnel Papers, ARCAT.

41 *Mirror*, 20 February 1852, 5 November 1852, 13 May 1853, 30 December 1853, 17 March 1854, 12 May 1854, 9 March 1855, and 18 May 1855; Bishop Armand Charbonnel to Bishop Ignace Bourget, 10 October 1851, ACAM.

42 *Mirror*, 20 March 1857.

43 *Irish Canadian*, 13 January 1875.

44 *Irish Canadian*, 20 May 1874.

45 *Irish Canadian*, 20 November 1878.

46 *Irish Canadian*, 9 September 1874 and 18 December 1878.

47 *Canadian Freeman*, 23 March 1871.

48 *Irish Canadian*, 21 May 1873 and 27 October 1875.

49 *Irish Canadian*, 13 January 1875.

50 *Irish Canadian*, 27 October 1875.

51 *Irish Canadian*, 23 February 1876 and 19 July 1876.

52 *Irish Canadian*, 23 February 1876 and 19 July 1876.

53 *Irish Canadian*, 27 October 1875.

54 "St. John's Temperance Association of Toronto, C.W.," Lynch Papers, ARCAT; *Irish Canadian*, 1 April 1863 and 27 October 1875; *Canadian Freeman*, 4 April 1872.

55 *Irish Canadian*, 29 May 1872, 5 June 1872, 16 November 1872, and 5 October 1873; *Canadian Freeman*, 27 August 1863.

56 "St. John's Temperance Association of Toronto, C.W.," Lynch Papers, ARCAT. Only the regulations of the St John's Temperance Association of Saint Mary's parish have survived, but they could hardly have been unique.

57 *Catholic Weekly Review*, 21 April 1887.

58 *Irish Canadian*, 13 January 1875.

59 *Irish Canadian*, 13 January and 25 August 1875.

60 *Irish Canadian*, 28 February 1877.

61 *Irish Canadian*, 9 March 1864.

62 *Irish Canadian*, 17 February 1875.

63 *Irish Canadian*, 21 September 1872.

64 *Irish Canadian*, 15 May and 20 November 1878.

65 *Irish Canadian*, 21 May 1873.

66 *Irish Canadian*, 29 April 1874.

67 *Irish Canadian*, 27 October 1875 and 28 February 1878.

68 *Irish Canadian*, 29 April 1874 and 18 July 1877.

69 *Irish Canadian*, 28 February 1877.

70 My argument on this point is similar to that of Jay P. Dolan in his *Catholic Revivalism: The American Experience 1830–1900* (Notre Dame, Indiana: University of Notre Dame Press 1978), 162.

71 *Irish Canadian*, 20 December 1871, 10 January 1872, and 8 January 1873.

72 *Irish Canadian*, 20 December 1871 and 5 October 1872. Some of the temperance societies had juvenile branches for boys. Unfortunately, since the Irish-Catholic press ignored the junior temperance societies, almost nothing is known about them. For this reason, the figures cited here do not include the membership of the junior temperance branches.

73 *Irish Canadian*, 19 March and 20 August 1873.

74 *Globe*, 18 March 1875; *Irish Canadian*, 10 October 1877.

75 *Irish Canadian*, 16 and 30 March 1871; *Globe*, 7 January 1873.

76 *Globe*, 18 March 1875. No membership figures are available for the Saint Paul's Temperance Society. In estimating the total number of members city-wide I have assumed that the enrolment of the Saint Paul's Temperance Society was similar to that of the Saint Michael's Temperance Society and the Saint Mary's Temperance Society, both of which were smaller temperance societies.

77 Assuming the demographic profile of the Catholic population was similar to that of the city population as a whole, a little over half of the Catholic population was excluded from membership on the basis of sex, and some 45 per cent of all Catholics were too young to join. Thus, of the total Irish-Catholic population, only some 28 per cent were eligible for membership in the temperance societies. See *Census of Canada, 1870–71* (Ottawa 1873), 1:17, 114, and 2:30–3.

78 *Globe*, 8 February 1883.

79 See Dolan, *Catholic Revivalism*, 155.

80 *Irish Canadian*, 13 January 1875.

81 Patrick Boyle, editor and owner of the *Irish Canadian*, was certainly influential, but he was not among the élite of the Irish-Catholic community and perhaps he did not have any desire to be.

82 Dolan, *Catholic Revivalism*, 155; Bland, *Hibernian Crusade*, 267–8; and Kerby A. Miller, *Emigrants and Exiles: Ireland and the Irish Exodus to North America* (New York: Oxford University Press 1985), 535. For two important dissents from this view see Roy Rosenzweig, *Eight Hours for What We Will: Workers and Leisure in an Industrial City, 1870–1920* (Cambridge: Cambridge University Press 1983), 103–9, and Victor Anthony Walsh, "Across 'The Big Wather': Irish Community Life in Pittsburgh and Allegheny City, 1850–1885" (PhD diss., University of Pittsburgh 1983), 249–51, 253, and 257–9.

83 *Irish Canadian*, 19 July 1875, 27 October 1875, and 23 February 1876.

84 *Irish Canadian*, 27 October 1875 and 19 July 1876; *Canadian Freeman*, 24 September 1863.

85 *Canadian Freeman*, 5, 11, and 19 February 1863; *Irish Canadian*, 20 December 1871 and 7 February 1872.

86 *Canadian Freeman*, 5 March 1863, 4 February 1864, and 20 February 1872; *Irish Canadian*, 4 February 1863.

87 *Irish Canadian*, 9 December 1863 and 1 May 1872.

88 *Irish Canadian*, 31 January 1877.

89 *Irish Canadian*, 8 January 1873 and 23 January 1878.

90 *Irish Canadian*, 5 February 1879.

91 *Irish Canadian*, 5 October and 23 November 1872.

92 *Canadian Freeman*, 29 February 1872; *Irish Canadian*, 23 April 1873.

93 *Irish Canadian*, 15 July 1863, 17 July 1872, 20 August 1873, and
    25 August 1875; *Canadian Freeman*, 15 June 1871 and 5 June 1873.

94 *Irish Canadian*, 19 March 1873, 18 March 1874, and 17 March 1875.

95 *Irish Canadian*, 20 August 1873, 8 October 1873, 15 October 1873,
    15 July 1874, and 16 June 1875.

96 *Irish Canadian*, 25 August 1875.

97 *Irish Canadian*, 19 August 174.

98 *Irish Canadian*, 19 March 1873.

99 Geoffrey Crossick, "The Labour Aristocracy and Its Values: A Study
    of Mid-Victorian Kentish London," *Victorian Studies*, 19 (1976),
    301–28, and Peter Bailey, "'Will the Real Bill Banks Please Stand Up?'
    Towards a Role Analysis of Mid-Victorian Working-Class Respect-
    ability," *Journal of Social History*, 12 (1978), 336–53.

100 *Irish Canadian*, 5 November 1873, 23 January 1878, and 4 February
    1880. The FMTA began to offer illness and funeral benefits in 1874.
    The Saint Patrick's Temperance and Benevolent Society, as its name
    suggests, provided benefits since its inception in 1871. The initi-
    ation fee for the Saint Patrick's Temperance Society was twenty-five
    cents, for the FMTA a dollar.

101 *Irish Canadian*, 21 May 1879; "St. John's Temperance Association of
    Toronto, C.W.," Lynch Papers, ARCAT.

102 *Globe*, 9 December 1882.

103 *Irish Canadian*, 9 September 1874.

104 *Irish Canadian*, 17 February 1882.

105 *Irish Canadian*, 17 June 1863.

106 *Irish Canadian*, 27 September 1876 and 18 June 1879.

107 *Irish Canadian*, 18 October 1876.

108 *Irish Canadian*, 6 October 1887.

109 *Irish Canadian*, 27 October 1875.

110 *Irish Canadian*, 30 December 1874.

111 Ann Taves, *The Household of Faith: Roman Catholic Devotions in Mid-
    Nineteenth-Century America* (Notre Dame, Indiana: University of
    Notre Dame 1986), 86–7.

112 *Irish Canadian*, 9 September 1874.

113 *Irish Canadian*, 6 December 1888.

114 *Catholic Weekly Review*, 8 December 1888.

115 *Irish Canadian*, 20 November 1878.

116 *Canadian Freeman*, 24 September 1863.

CHAPTER SEVEN

1 Thomas N. Brown, *Irish-American Nationalism, 1870–1890* (Philadelphia: J.P. Lippincott 1966), 20–3, 30–1, 41, 46, 63, 134, 153–5,
   161, and 172–3.

2 Kerby A. Miller, *Emigrants and Exiles: Ireland and the Irish Exodus to North America* (New York: Oxford University Press 1985), 3, 7–8, 127–9, 340–2, 544–56, and 567–8.

3 Eric Foner, "Class, Ethnicity, & Radicalism in the Gilded Age: The Land League and Irish-America," *Marxist Perspectives*, 1 (1978), 6–55: Victor A. Walsh, "'A Fanatic Heart': The Cause of Irish-American Nationalism in Pittsburgh During the Gilded Age," *Journal of Social History*, 15 (1981), 187–204; Timothy J. Meagher "'Irish All the Time': Ethnic Consciousness Among the Irish in Worchester, Massachusetts, 1880–1905," *Journal of Social History*, 19 (1985), 273–303.

4 R.V. Comerford, "Patriotism as Pastime: The Appeal of Fenianism in the Mid-1860s," *Irish Historical Studies*, 22 (1981), 239–250, and *The Fenians in Context: Irish Politics and Society 1842–82* (Dublin: Wolfhound Press 1985), 65–6, 111–12, and 118–19.

5 Hereward Senior, *Orangeism in Ireland and Britain, 1795–1836* (London: Routledge and Kegan Paul 1966), 1–21, *Orangeism: The Canadian Phase* (Toronto: McGraw-Hill Ryerson 1972), 7–9 and 21, and "The Genesis of Canadian Orangeism," *Ontario History*, 60 (1968), 14–15; Marianne Elliott, *Partners in Revolution: The United Irishmen and France* (New Haven, Connecticut: Yale University Press 1982), 18–20; Peter Gibbon, "The Origins of the Orange Order and the United Irishmen: A Study in the Sociology of Revolution and Counter-Revolution," *Economy and Society*, 1 (1972), 155–8; David W. Miller, "The Armagh Troubles, 1784–95," in *Irish Peasants: Violence and Political Unrest 1780–1914*, eds. Samuel Clark and James S. Donnelly, Jr (Madison, Wisconsin: University of Wisconsin Press 1983), 179–81, 187, and 189.

6 Cecil J.Houston and William J. Smyth, *The Sash Canada Wore: A Historical Geography of the Orange Order in Canada* (Toronto: University of Toronto Press 1980), 3–5 and 12–13; Senior, *Orangeism: The Canadian Phase*, 45–7.

7 This estimate is based upon the 1871 census, the first to report on the cultural background of the Canadian population: *Census of Canada, 1870–71* (Ottawa 1873), 1:142–3 and 281. This estimate certainly underestimates the Irish Protestant population in the province during the 1850s, for by 1871 emigrants from England had overtaken those from Ireland. See Cecil J. Houston and William J. Smyth, *Irish Emigration and Canadian Settlement: Patterns, Links and Letters* (Toronto: University of Toronto Press 1990), 228–9, and Donald Harman Akenson, *Being Had: Historians, Evidence, and the Irish in North America* (Port Credit, Ontario: P.D. Meany 1985), 84–5 and 101–2.

8 Houston and Smyth, *Sash Canada Wore*, 18–19, 36–7, and 93–6.

9 Barrie Dyster, "Toronto 1840–1860: Making It in a British Protestant
   Town" (PhD diss., University of Toronto 1970), 404, 406–25, and
   432–42.
10 *Globe*, 6 September 1855.
11 *Globe*, 7 August 1857.
12 *Globe*, 13 February 1856.
13 *Globe*, 6 September 1853 and 25 May 1854.
14 Dyster, "Toronto 1840–1860," 83, 215, and 220.
15 Gregory S. Kealey, "Orangemen and the Corporation," in *Forging a
    Consensus: Historical Essays on Toronto*, ed. Victor L. Russell (To-
    ronto: University of Toronto Press 1984), 46–51 and 71–3; Nicholas
    Rogers, "Serving Toronto the Good," in *Forging a Consensus*,
    122–5; Eric Jarvis, "Mid-Victorian Toronto: Panic, Policy, and Public
    Response 1857–1863" (PhD diss., University of Western Ontario
    1979), 71–3. Even after the reform of 1858, about one third of the
    police force was enrolled in the Orange Order.
16 James S. Donnelly, Jr, "Pastorini and Captain Rock: Millenarianism
    and Sectarianism in the Rockite Movement of 1821–4," in *Irish
    Peasants: Violence and Political Unrest 1780–1914*, eds. Samuel Clark
    and James S. Donnelly, Jr (Madison, Wisconsin: University of
    Wisconsin Press 1983), 135–7; James A. Reynolds, *The Catholic Eman-
    cipation Crisis in Ireland, 1823–1829* (New Haven: Yale University
    Press 1954), 80–2, 133–5, and 141–4.
17 Desmond Bowen, *The Protestant Crusade in Ireland, 1800–70* (Kingston
    and Montreal: McGill-Queen's Press 1978), 135–7; Angus
    Macintyre, *The Liberator: Daniel O'Connell and the Irish Party, 1830–1847*
    (New York: Macmillan 1965), 111–17; Reynolds, *Catholic Eman-
    cipation*, 18–19, 46–7, 49, 51–4, 57, 60 and 97; Fergus O'Ferrall, *Cath-
    olic Emancipation: Daniel O'Connell and the Birth of Irish Democracy*
    (Dublin: Gill and Macmillan 1985), 74, 78, 106–7, 109, 141–2, 176–7,
    and 197–9.
18 Kevin B. Nowlan, *The Politics of Repeal: A Study in the Relations between
    Great Britain and Ireland, 1841–1850* (London: Routledge and
    Kegan Paul 1965), 6.
19 For a concise overview of one aspect of this festival, see Michael
    Cottrell, "St. Patrick's Day Parades in Nineteenth-Century To-
    ronto: A Study of Immigrant Adjustment and Elite Control," *Histoire
    sociale/Social History*, 49 (1992), 57–73.
20 *Mirror*, 25 March 1853, 24 March 1854, and 23 March 1855.
21 Pastoral, 1856, "Address of His Lordship to the Irish Catholics of
    Toronto," 1856, and Bishop Charbonnel to the President of the
    Montreal Saint Patrick's Association, 31 October 1854, Charbonnel
    Papers, ARCAT.
22 *Mirror*, 23 March 1855.

23 *Mirror*, 25 March 1853 and 23 March 1855.

24 R.F. Foster, *Modern Ireland 1600–1972* (New York and London: Penguin Books 1989), 316.

25 Elliott, *Partners in Revolution*, 366–7.

26 Mary Helen Thuente, "The Folklore of Irish Nationalism," in *Perspectives on Irish Nationalism*, eds. Thomas E. Hackey and Lawrence J. McCaffrey (Lexington: University Press of Kentucky 1989), 56–7, and Elliott, *Partners in Revolution*, 368–70.

27 J.H. Whyte, *The Independent Irish Party 1850–9* (London: Oxford University Press 1958), 111–16, 121, 136–7, 146–55, and 176–7; J.H. Whyte, "Fresh Light on Archbishop Cullen and the Tenant League," *Irish Ecclesiastical Record*, series 5, 99 (1963), 171–6; E.D. Steele, "Cardinal Cullen and Irish Nationality," *Irish Historical Studies*, 19 (1975), 248–52; J.H. Whyte, "The Influence of the Catholic Clergy on Elections in Nineteenth-Century Ireland," *English Historical Review*, 25 (1963), 249–52; Joseph Denieffe, *A Personal Narrative of the Irish Revolutionary Brotherhood* (1906; reprint ed., Shannon, Ireland: Irish University Press 1969), 2 and 25–6; John O'Leary, *Fenians and Fenianism*, 2 vols. (1896; reprint ed., Shannon, Ireland: Irish University Press 1969), 1:74 and 80–3.

28 J.M.S. Careless, *The Union of the Canadas: The Growth of Canadian Institutions, 1841–1857* (Toronto: McClelland and Stewart 1967), 198; John S. Moir, *Church and State in Canada West: Three Studies in the Relation of Denominationalism and Nationalism, 1841–1867* (Toronto: University of Toronto Press 1959), 18–19; Philippe Sylvain, "L'affaire Corrigan à Saint-Sylvestre," *Les cahiers des dix*, 42 (1979), 125–44.

29 *Globe*, 4 January 1856.

30 *Mirror*, 11 April 1856; *Irish Canadian*, 11 March 1863; "Orange Outrages," 1874, Lynch Papers, ARCAT.

31 *Globe*, 15, 16, 17, and 18 July 1857.

32 *Mirror*, 17 July 1857.

33 *Mirror*, 21 August 1857.

34 *Globe*, 18, 20, 23, 24, 28 March 1858, and 1 April 1858; *Leader*, 20 and 22 March 1858.

35 *Globe*, 18, 19, 22, 25, 27, 28 March 1858, 1, 2, 5, 6, 8, 12, and 14 April 1858; *Leader*, 18, 19, 20, 22, and 23 March 1858.

36 *Leader*, 11, 12, and 17 May 1858.

37 *Catholic Citizen*, 13 May 1858, as cited in Moir, *Church and State in Canada West*, 21, and *Mirror*, 30 April 1858.

38 *Globe*, 9 April 1858.

39 *Globe*, 22 April 1858.

40 James Moylan to Bishop Charbonnel, 12 February 1859, Charbonnel Papers, ARCAT; John A. Macdonald to Bishop Lynch, 7 July 1864, John A. Macdonald to Bishop Lynch, 30 September 1864, Untitled

Memo on the *Canadian Freeman* and *True Witness*, n.d., Lynch
Papers, ARCAT; *Canadian Freeman*, 5 and 19 August 1859.

41 *Canadian Freeman*, 13 May 1859. See also *Canadian Freeman*,
5 February, 22 and 29 April 1859.

42 *Canadian Freeman*, 22 April 1859.

43 *Canadian Freeman*, 13 and 20 May 1859.

44 *Canadian Freeman*, 26 March 1863.

45 *Canadian Freeman*, 18 November 1859.

46 *Canadian Freeman*, 9 December 1859.

47 *Canadian Freeman*, 6 May 1859.

48 *Canadian Freeman*, 18 November 1859 and 16 December 1859.

49 *Canadian Freeman*, 23 May 1861.

50 Barrie Dyster, "Toronto 1850–1860," 193–4: Murray W. Nicolson,
"The Catholic Church and the Irish in Victorian Toronto" (PhD
diss., University of Guelph 1980), 34–5.

51 *Mirror*, 16 November 1855, 30 November 1855, 21 December 1855,
21 March 1856, 14 November 1856, 20 February 1857, 20 March
1857, 9 October 1857, and 12 February 1858.

52 *Mirror*, 21 March 1856 and 20 March 1857.

53 Michael Cottrell, "Irish Catholic Political Leadership in Toronto,
1855–1862: A Study of Ethnic Politics" (PhD diss., University of
Saskatchewan 1988), 59.

54 *Mirror*, 11 June 1858, and 18 June 1858.

55 *Leader*, 16 and 17 July 1860; *Globe*, 16 July 1860 and 18 October 1860.

56 For another example of adaptation see Michael A. Gordon, "The
Labor Boycott in New York City, 1880–1886," *Labor History*, 16
(1975), 187–9 and 210–13.

57 David W. Miller, "The Armagh Troubles, 1784–87," in *Irish Peasants:
Violence and Political Unrest, 1780–1914*, eds. Samuel Clark and
James S. Donnelly, Jr (Madison: University of Wisconsin Press 1983),
175; Paul E.W. Roberts, "Caravats and Shanavests: Whiteboyism
and Faction Fighting in East Munster, 1802–11," in ibid, 64–101; Sybil
E. Baker, "Orange and Green in Belfast, 1832–1912," in *The Vic-
torian City: Images and Realities*, eds. H.J. Dyos and Michael Wolf, 2 vols.
(London: Routledge and Kegan Paul 1973), 2:790; Tom Garvin,
"Defenders, Ribbonmen and Others: Underground Political Networks
in Pre-Famine Ireland," *Past and Present*, no.96 (August 1982), 150.

58 Bishop Charbonnel to Bishop Ignace Bourget, 6 January 1859, and
Bishop Charbonnel to Bishop Bourget, 15 February 1859, ACAM.

59 *Canadian Freeman*, 18 November 1859.

60 "H.B.S. Oath," n.d., Lynch Papers, ARCAT.

61 Bishop Lynch to Bishop Joseph-Eugène-Bruno Guiges, 6 April 1866,
Lynch Papers, ARCAT.

62 *Canadian Freeman*, 23 October 1862 and 24 March 1864.

63 Lynch explained his reasons for allowing the Hibernian Benevolent Society to mark Saint Patrick's Day with a parade and a Mass in a meeting with a few prominent laymen held in February 1862. An account of this meeting is found in a letter by Rev. G.R. Northgraves to Bishop Lynch, 4 March 1865, Lynch Papers, ARCAT.

64 *Canadian Freeman*, 8 August and 19 September 1861.

65 *Canadian Freeman*, 17 January 1861.

66 *Canadian Freeman*, 20 February and 20 March 1862.

67 *Globe*, 18 March 1862; *Leader*, 18 March 1862; *Canadian Freeman*, 20 March 1862.

68 *Leader*, 18 March 1862.

69 *Canadian Freeman*, 13 March 1862.

70 *Leader*, 9 and 12 August 1862; *Canadian Freeman*, 24 and 30 July 1862.

CHAPTER EIGHT

1 W.L. Morton, *The Critical Years: The Union of British North America* (Toronto: McClelland and Stewart 1964), 183.

2 But see C.P. Stacey's pioneering study, "A Fenian Interlude: The Story of Michael Murphy," *Canadian Historical Review*, 5 (1934), 133–54.

3 Hereward Senior, "Quebec and the Fenians," *Canadian Historical Review*, 48 (1967), 28, and *The Fenians and Canada* (Toronto: Macmillan 1978), 56–7 and 143; Donald Harman Akenson, *The Irish of Ontario: A Study in Rural History* (Kingston and Montreal: McGill-Queen's Press 1984), 41–2.

4 Peter M. Toner, "The Rise of Irish Nationalism in Canada, 1858–1884" (PhD diss., National University of Ireland 1974), ii–iv, 73, 80, 85, 107–8, 121–2, 389–93, and 398–9. The most complete analysis of McGee's Canadian nationalism is found in Robin Burns, "D'Arcy McGee and the Economic Aspects of New Nationality," Canadian Historical Association, *Report*, 1967, 95–104. But see also Thomas N. Brown, "The Irish Layman," in *A History of Irish Catholicism*, ed. P.J. Corish, 6 vols. (Dublin: Gill and Macmillan 1970), 6, pt. 2:59–77, for a persuasive examination of the continuities that ran through McGee's seemingly diverse and disjointed career.

5 George Sheppard, "'God Save the Green' Fenianism and Fellowship in Victorian Ontario," *Histoire sociale/Social History*, 20 (1987), 129–44.

6 William D'Arcy, *The Fenian Movement in the United States: 1858–1886* (Washington, DC: Catholic University of America Press 1947), 33–4, 39–40, 43, and 45–6.

7 Captain W.S. Prince to Gilbert McMicken, 9 March 1866, Charles Clark to McMicken, 26 April 1866, Charles Clark to McMicken, 1864, Macdonald Papers, NAC. D'Arcy, *Fenian Movement*, 202. Gilbert McMicken was appointed stipendiary magistrate in December 1864 to establish a detective force to gather evidence against Union Army recruiters under the Foreign Enlistment Act. By early September 1865, McMicken had informers in Cincinnati and Chicago. Later in September, McMicken also placed detectives along the Canadian frontier. Patrick Nolan, who was McMicken's agent in Chicago, was ordered to Toronto, as was Charles Clark, who was later discovered by the Hibernian Benevolent Society. John McNab to Gilbert McMicken, 27 December 1864, "Special Order No. 1," Charles Clark to G. McMicken, 4 December 1865, and G. McMicken to John A. Macdonald, 27 December 1865, Macdonald Papers, NAC.

8 Charles Clark to Gilbert McMicken, n.d., 1864, G. McMicken to John A. Macdonald, 11 September 1865, and Charles Clark to G. McMicken, 4 December 1865, Macdonald Papers, NAC.

9 Gilbert McMicken to John A. Macdonald, 2 October 1865, Macdonald Papers, NAC.

10 The *Leader*, 30 April 1866, reprinted a Fenian Brotherhood membership card signed by Murphy. Fifty similar cards were intercepted by Canadian customs authorities in September 1863. Gilbert McMicken to John A. Macdonald, 18 April 1866, Macdonald Papers, NAC. In the Fenian Brotherhood, a "circle" was analogous to a regiment; the "centre" or A, equivalent to a colonel, chose nine B's, or captains, who chose nine C's, or sergeants, who chose nine D's, who constituted the rank and file. See John O'Leary, *Fenians and Fenianism*, 2 vols. (1896; reprint ed., Shannon, Ireland: Irish University Press 1969), 1:84.

11 P.C. Burton [Patrick Nolan] to Gilbert McMicken, 31 December 1865, Macdonald Papers, NAC.

12 John McNab to John A. Macdonald, 3 November 1865, John McNab to Gilbert McMicken, 2 January 1866, and Captain William S. Prince to Macdonald, 7 April 1866, Macdonald Papers, NAC.

13 D'Arcy, *Fenian Movement*, 202, and Senior, *Fenians and Canada*, 51, conclude that there were about sixty Fenians in Toronto. As the shipment of fifty membership cards in September 1863 was probably not the first and certainly not the last, D'Arcy's and Senior's estimates are probably somewhat low.

14 *Leader*, 19 April 1866.

15 P.C. Burton [Nolan] to Gilbert McMicken, 31 December 1866, Macdonald Papers, NAC; *Globe*, 19 December 1866; D'Arcy, *Fenian*

Movement, 55; *Leader*, 17 April 1866, reprinted excerpts from the "Constitution and By Laws [*sic*] of the Hibernian Benevolent Society," dated 1865. See also Erastus Burton [Nolan] to G. McMicken, 6 January 1866, Macdonald Papers, NAC, who reported that the Hibernian Benevolent Society had drilled frequently the previous summer.

16 Erastus Burton [Nolan] to Gilbert McMicken, 20 January and 8 March 1866, Macdonald Papers, NAC; E. Burton to G. McMicken, 27 March 1866, Macdonald Papers, NAC, lists the names of Fenian bond buyers, all of whom were members of the Hibernian Benevolent Society; *Leader*, 10 December 1865, citing a report in the *New York World*; *Globe*, 16 December 1865; D'Arcy, *Fenian Movement*, 70 and 72.

17 *Globe*, 12 December 1864.

18 *Irish Canadian*, 18 March 1863; *Leader*, 18 March 1863.

19 *Irish Canadian*, 23 March 1864.

20 *Irish Canadian*, 29 November 1876; *McKim's Directory of Canadian Publications* (Montreal: A. McKim 1892), 119.

21 John McNab to John A. Macdonald, 3 November 1865, NAC.

22 Charles Clarke to Gilbert McMicken, 10 May 1867, Macdonald Papers, NAC.

23 *Irish Canadian*, 18 November 1863.

24 *Irish Canadian*, 9 September 1863.

25 *Irish Canadian*, 2 September 1863.

26 R.V. Comerford, *Fenians in Context: Irish Politics and Society, 1842–82* (Dublin: Wolfhound Press 1985), 89–90.

27 *Irish Canadian*, 18 March, 22 March, 16 September, 18 November, and 4 December 1863.

28 *Irish Canadian*, 25 February 1863 and 27 April 1864.

29 *Irish Canadian*, 25 November 1863.

30 *Irish Canadian*, 25 March 1863, 10 February 1864, 18 May 1864, and 13 July 1864.

31 Mary Helen Thuente, "The Folklore of Irish Nationalism," in *Perspectives on Irish Nationalism*, eds. Thomas E. Hachey and Lawrence J. McCaffrey (Lexington: University Press of Kentucky 1989), 58.

32 *Irish Canadian*, 18 November 1866, 25 January 1865, 12 December 1865, and 20 December 1865.

33 *Irish Canadian*, 18 March 1863.

34 *Irish Canadian*, 18 and 25 March 1863.

35 *Irish Canadian*, 20 May 1863.

36 *Irish Canadian*, 10 May 1865.

37 *Irish Canadian*, 17 August 1864.

38 Kerby A. Miller, *Emigrants and Exiles: Ireland and the Irish Exodus to North America* (New York: Oxford University Press 1985), 103–7, 110–11, 114–30, 300–5, 315–24, 334–44, and 556–68. See also Oscar Handlin, *Boston's Immigrants: A Study in Acculturation*, rev. ed. New York: Atheneum 1968), 55, 125–6, and 188–9.

39 Kevin B. Nowlan, *The Politics of Repeal: A Study in the Relations between Great Britain and Ireland, 1841–1850* (London: Routledge and Kegan Paul 1965), 124, 148–54, 157–8, and 205–6. For a typical example of how Patrick Boyle drew on the imagery developed by Young Ireland and propagated by the Fenian Brotherhood, see *Irish Canadian*, 4 February 1863.

40 *Irish Canadian*, 11 March 1863, 1 April 1863, 22 April 1863, and 7 September 1864.

41 *Irish Canadian*, 28 December 1864.

42 *Irish Canadian*, 25 March 1863.

43 *Irish Canadian*, 26 July 1865.

44 *Irish Canadian*, 2 September 1863 and 10 May 1865.

45 *Irish Canadian*, 10 May, 27 September, and 6 December 1865.

46 *Irish Canadian*, 9 August 1865.

47 I have borrowed the term social myth from Georges Sorel, *Reflections on Violence*, trans T.E. Hulme and J. Roth (1950; reprint ed., New York: Collier Books 1961), 49–52.

48 *Irish Canadian*, 27 September 1865.

49 *Irish Canadian*, 18 March 1863, 17 February 1864, 23 March 1864, 6 April 1864, 18 May 1864, 23 May 1864, 16 November 1864, and 23 November 1864.

50 *Irish Canadian*, 4 February 1863.

51 *Globe*, 21 and 27 November 1861.

52 *Irish Canadian*, 17 February, 3 April, and 17 August 1864.

53 *Irish Canadian*, 3 April, 17 August, and 21 October 1864.

54 *Irish Canadian*, 25 March 1863; *Canadian Freeman*, 24 March 1864.

55 *Canadian Freeman*, 20 March 1862 and 30 October 1862.

56 *Irish Canadian*, 6 May 1863.

57 *Irish Canadian*, 18 March 1863 and 23 March 1864.

58 *Canadian Freeman*, 19 March 1863, 24 March 1864, and 11 April 1867.

59 *Canadian Freeman*, 23 October 1862; Bishop Lynch to O'Donohoe, 28 February 1866, Lynch Papers, ARCAT.

60 *Canadian Freeman*, 24 March 1864; "The Evils of Wholesale and Improvident Emigration from Ireland," 1864, ARCAT.

61 Miller, *Emigrants and Exiles*, 54–5 and 78; Theodore K. Hoppen, "Rural Politics and Local Realities in Mid-Nineteenth Century Ire-

land," in *Studies in Irish History Presented to R. Dudley Edwards*, eds. Art Cosgrove and Donal McCartney (Dublin: University College 1979), 211–13; Cecil J. Houston and William J. Smith, *Irish Emigration and Canadian Settlement: Patterns, Links, and Letters* (Toronto: University of Toronto Press 1990), 170–1.

62 David W. Miller, "Irish Catholicism and the Great Famine," *Journal of Social History*, 9 (1975), 93; K. Theodore Hoppen, "Rural Politics and Local Realities in Mid-Nineteenth Century Ireland," in *Studies in Irish History Presented to R. Dudley Edwards*, 217; Miller, *Emigrants and Exiles*, 54–60 and 115–16.

63 For a perceptive analysis of the relationship between nationalism and leisure in Ireland that offers interesting parallels to developments in Toronto, see R.V. Comerford, "Patriotism as Pastime: The Appeal of Fenianism in the Mid-1860s," *Irish Historical Studies*, 22 (1981), 247–9, and *Fenians in Context*, 111–13.

64 P.C. Burton [Nolan] to Gilbert McMicken, 31 December 1865, Macdonald Papers, NAC; *Irish Canadian*, 19 October, 26 October, 16 November, 7 December, and 28 December 1864, 11 January, 25 January, 8 February, 15 February, and 22 February 1865.

65 *Globe*, 19 December 1866.

66 How important that could be is illustrated by the *Irish Canadian*'s humorous comment that some Hibernians' "sweethearts would not see them home" after their dismal performance at a football game. See *Irish Canadian*, 27 May 1863. *Canadian Freeman*, 4 February 1859, 16 September 1859, 20 August 1862, 16 October 1862, and 30 October 1862; *Globe*, 27 August 1859, 9 September 1859, and 17 October 1863.

67 *Globe*, 9 September 1859.

68 *Irish Canadian*, 19 April 1865.

69 *Canadian Freeman*, 14 February 1859.

70 P.C. Burton [Nolan] to Gilbert McMicken, 31 December 1865, Macdonald Papers, NAC.

71 *Irish Canadian*, 18 November 1863 and 7 September 1862; *Canadian Freeman*, 14 March 1864.

72 *Irish Canadian*, 8 April 1863, 22 July 1863, 12 August 1863, 20 July 1864, 10 August 1864, 26 October 1864, 19 April 1865, and 15 November 1865; *Canadian Freeman*, 4 February 1859, 8 April 1859, 8 August 1861, 24 April 1862, 24 July 1862, 14 August 1862, and 12 August 1863. The press reported that between twelve hundred and fifteen hundred people went on the Hibernians' excursions, but a more realistic estimate would put the figure between six hundred and a thousand.

73 *Canadian Freeman*, 18 November 1859, 19 September 1861, 28 August 1862, 15 October 1863, and 18 August 1864.

74 Hugh McLeod, *Class and Religion in the Late Victorian City* (Hamden, Connecticut: Archon Books 1974), 159.

75 *Globe*, 12 September 1866.

76 Peter Bailey, "'Will the Real Bill Banks Please Stand Up?' Towards a Role Analysis of Mid-Victorian Working-Class Respectability," *Journal of Social History*, 12 (1978), 336–53.

77 *Irish Canadian*, 4 November 1863.

78 Captain W.S. Prince to John A. Macdonald, 7 April 1866, Macdonald Papers, NAC.

79 *Irish Canadian*, 8 April 1863, 27 May 1863, 12 August 1863, 23 March 1864, 10 August 1864, and 26 July 1865; *Globe*, 18 March 1864.

80 Erastus Burton [Nolan] to Gilbert McMicken, 20 January 1866, Macdonald Papers, NAC.

81 "List of names in the h.b.s.," and Captain W.S. Prince to John A. Macdonald, 20 October 1865, Macdonald Papers, NAC.

82 Some did become successful businessmen. For example, J.J. Landy was later a leading contractor and Patrick Boyle prospered with the growth of the *Irish Canadian*.

83 Compare this argument to that advanced in Comerford, *Fenians in Context*, 65–6, 69, 81, and 111–12.

84 *Irish Canadian*, 4 February 1863, 4 November 1863, and 18 November 1863.

85 Emmet Larkin, "The Irish Political Tradition," in *Perspectives on Irish Nationalism*, eds. Thomas E. Hackey and Lawrence J. McCaffrey (Lexington: University Press of Kentucky 1989), 101 and 111.

86 Sheppard, "'God Save the Green,'" 132–4.

87 *Canadian Freeman*, 31 March, 7 April, and 14 April 1864.

88 *Canadian Freeman*, 14 April 1864.

89 *Canadian Freeman*, 7 April 1864.

90 *Irish Canadian*, 30 March and 13 April 1864.

91 D'Arcy, *Fenian Movement*, 49; *Canadian Freeman*, 14 April 1864.

92 *Irish Canadian*, 8 June 1864.

93 P.J. Corish, "Political Problems, 1860–78," in *A History of Irish Catholicism*, ed. P.J. Corish, 6 vols. (Dublin: Gill and Son 1967), 5, pt. 3:8, 11, 12, and 17–22; Emmet Larkin, *The Consolidation of the Roman Catholic Church in Ireland, 1860–1870* (Chapel Hill: University of North Carolina Press 1987), 260–1, 399–400, and 655–63.

94 Donal McCartney, "The Church and the Fenians," in *Fenians and Fenianism*, ed. Maurice Harmon (Dublin: Specter Books 1968), 16; *Irish Canadian*, 17 August 1864.

95 For one such reaction to McGee's tactics in 1865, see William M. Baker, *Timothy Warren Anglin, 1822–96, Irish Catholic Canadian* (Toronto: University of Toronto Press 1977), 125–6.

96 *Canadian Freeman*, 26 May 1864; *Leader*, 30 May 1864.

97 *Globe*, 30 and 31 May 1864.

98 *Globe*, 30 May 1864.

99 *Leader*, 30 May 1864.

100 *Leader*, 30 May 1864; Bishop Lynch to E.P. Taché, 3 June 1864, Lynch Papers, ARCAT.

101 *Leader*, 30 May 1864.

102 *Irish Canadian*, 1 June 1864.

103 Bishop Lynch to E.P. Taché, 3 June 1864, and Bishop Lynch to Lord Monck, 8 June 1864, Lynch Papers, ARCAT; *Irish Canadian*, 8 June 1864.

104 *Canadian Freeman*, 2 and 9 June 1864.

105 My account is based on the reports in the *Leader*, 7 and 10 November 1864, *Globe*, 7 and 9 November 1864, and *Irish Canadian*, 9 November 1864.

106 *Leader*, 8 November 1864.

107 *Globe*, 8 November 1864.

108 *Globe*, 19, 23, and 26 November 1864.

109 *Irish Canadian*, 9 November 1864.

110 *Canadian Freeman*, 10 November 1864; *Globe*, 8 and 18 November 1864.

111 *Canadian Freeman*, 23 November 1864.

112 Bishop Lynch's letter was published in the *Globe*, 12 November 1864, *Leader*, 12 November 1864, *Canadian Freeman*, 17 November 1864, and *Irish Canadian*, 16 November 1864.

113 *Leader*, 2 December 1864.

114 *Leader*, 7, 16, and 19 December 1864; *Globe*, 17 and 19 December 1864.

115 *Irish Canadian*, 15 March 1865; D'Arcy, *Fenian Movement*, 41 and 96–7.

116 *Irish Canadian*, 22 March 1865.

117 *Irish Canadian*, 15 February, 22 March, 11 May, and 13 September 1865.

118 *Irish Canadian*, 25 January, 12 December, and 20 December 1865.

119 *Irish Canadian*, 4 and 11 January 1865.

120 *Irish Canadian*, 23 May 1864.

121 *Irish Canadian*, 12 July 1865; *Canadian Freeman*, 3 August 1865.

122 *Irish Canadian*, 26 July 1865.

123 "Pastoral Letter of His Lordship the Rt. Rev. John Farrell, Bishop of Hamilton," 6 August 1865, Lynch Papers, ARCAT.

124 *Canadian Freeman*, 17 August 1865; *Globe*, 14 and 17 August 1865.

125 *Irish Canadian*, 8 June 1864.

126 Circular, 9 March 1866, Lynch Papers, ARCAT.

127 Bishop Lynch to Archbishop Thomas Connolly, 1 February 1866, Lynch Papers, ARCAT.

128 *Leader*, 14 August 1865.

129 *Canadian Freeman*, 17 August 1865.

130 *Globe*, 17 August 1865.

131 Rev. George Northgraves to Bishop Lynch, 19 November 1863, Lynch Papers, ARCAT.

132 *Leader*, 14 August 1865.

133 Bishop Lynch to Archbishop T. Connolly, 1 February 1966, Lynch Papers, ARCAT; Bishop Lynch to Bishop Joseph-Eugène-Bruno Guigues, 7 April 1866, Guigues Papers, AAO.

134 An account of this meeting is given in the Rev. George Northgraves's letter to Bishop Lynch, 4 March 1865, Lynch Papers, ARCAT.

135 *Irish Canadian*, 23 August 1865.

136 Bishop Lynch to Bishop Joseph-Eugène-Bruno Guigues, 7 April 1866, Guigues Papers, AAO.

137 *Canadian Freeman*, 10 August, 17 August, and 24 August 1865.

138 D'Arcy, *Fenian Movement*, 103–7 and 113–17.

139 *Irish Canadian*, 3 and 17 June 1864.

140 *Irish Canadian*, 7 and 14 February 1866.

141 *Irish Canadian*, 1 November 1866.

142 *Leader*, 27, 29, and 31 January 1866; *Globe*, 27 and 29 January 1866.

143 James Allen and William Caldwell to Gilbert McMicken, 27 January 1866, James Allen and William Caldwell to G. McMicken, 30 January 1866, James Allen and William Caldwell to G. McMicken, 31 January 1866, Macdonald Papers, NAC.

144 *Leader*, 3 and 5 February 1866.

145 *Canadian Freeman*, 1 March 1866.

146 *Irish Canadian*, 7 February 1866.

147 *Irish Canadian*, 21 February 1866.

148 *Globe*, 9 March 1866. Captain William S. Prince of the Toronto police force warned the government that he believed "riot and bloodshed" would occur if the Hibernian Benevolent Society proceeded with their march. Captain W.S. Prince to John A. Macdonald, 8 March 1866, Macdonald Papers, NAC.

149 Gilbert McMicken to John A. Macdonald, 18 March 1866, Macdonald Papers, NAC; *Globe*, 19 March 1866.

150 The *Globe* reported 618 marchers, the *Leader* 680, McMicken "only 532," and Ogle Gowan 584. See *Globe*, 18 March 1866; *Leader*, 19 March 1866; Gilbert McMicken to John A. Macdonald, 18 March

1866, and Ogle Gowan to John A. Macdonald, 19 March 1866, Macdonald Papers, NAC.

151 *Irish Canadian*, 21 March 1866.

152 *Irish Canadian*, 21 March 1866.

153 John McNab to John A. Macdonald, 3 November 1865, Gilbert McMicken to John A. Macdonald, 27 December 1865, J. McNab to John A. Macdonald, 2 January 1866, G. McMicken to John A. Macdonald, 23 March 1866, and G. McMicken to John A. Macdonald, 28 March 1866, Macdonald Papers, NAC.

154 D'Arcy, *Fenian Movement*, 135.

155 H.P. Dwight to William McDougal, 12 April 1866, Macdonald Papers, NAC; *Globe*, 20 April 1866. The original is without punctuation and capitalization.

156 G.-É. Cartier to John A. Macdonald, 10 April 1866, A.J. Galt to John A. Macdonald, 10 April 1866, John A. Macdonald to Col. Edward Ermatinger, 9 April 1866, and Captain W.S. Prince to John A. Macdonald, 7 April 1866, Macdonald Papers, NAC.

157 *Globe*, 11 April 1866.

158 William Cox Allen to John A. Macdonald, 10 April 1866, and J.J. Pringle to John A. Macdonald, 20 April 1866, Macdonald Papers, NAC.

159 *Leader*, 11 April 1866.

160 Gilbert McMicken to John A. Macdonald, 17 April 1866, Macdonald Papers, NAC; *Leader*, 19 April 1866.

161 *Irish Canadian*, 18 April 1866.

162 *Irish Canadian*, 2 May 1866.

163 *Leader*, 3 May 1866.

164 *Globe*, 7 and 15 May 1866.

165 For the definitive account of the Battle of Ridgeway, see W.S. Neidhardt, *Fenianism in North America* (University Park, Pennsylvania: Pennsylvania University Press 1975), 59-75.

166 *Irish Canadian*, 6 June 1866.

167 *Irish Canadian*, 13 June 1866.

168 *Globe*, 6 June 1866; *Leader*, 6 June 1866.

169 *Globe*, 30 June 1866; *Leader*, 6, 8, 13, 14, and 29 June, 2, 10, and 12 July 1866.

170 Lord Monck to John A. Macdonald, 18 September 1866, Macdonald Papers, NAC; *Leader*, 3 and 7 September 1866; *Globe*, 3, 4, and 5 September 1866.

171 *Leader*, 30 October and 12 November 1866; *Globe*, 17 November 1866.

172 *Globe*, 14 September, 25 September, 5 October, 9 November, 6 December, and 15 December 1866; *Leader*, 9 November, 15 November, and 25 December 1866.

173 *Leader*, 29 June 1866; *Canadian Freeman*, 21 March 1867.

174 *Leader*, 18 March 1868.

175 *Leader*, 18 April and 27 April 1868; *Globe*, 18 April 1868. T.P. Slattery, in his *"They Got to Find Mee Guilty Yet"* (Toronto: Doubleday 1972), offers a probing investigation of Whalen's Fenian connections and his role in McGee's assassination. While the crown's case for a Fenian conspiracy is now open to serious doubt, Slattery has yet to convincingly establish convincingly Whalen's innocence.

176 *Globe*, 6 and 8 May 1868; Charles Follis to Gilbert McMicken, 20 May 1868, Macdonald Papers, NAC.

CHAPTER NINE

1 *Canadian Freeman*, 23 April 1868 and 18 February 1869.

2 *Irish Canadian*, 15 January 1868, 15 April 1868, 2 September 1868, 16 September 1868, 23 September 1868, and 13 January 1869.

3 *Canadian Freeman*, 25 March 1869.

4 *Irish Canadian*, 20 April 1870.

5 Unfortunately, it is impossible to determine precisely the decline in the Hibernian Benevolent Society's membership, but as some thirty members decamped to Philadelphia alone, the losses must have been considerable. See *Irish Canadian*, 29 April 1868.

6 *Canadian Freeman*, 23 July 1868; *Leader*, 21 July 1868 and 24 July 1868.

7 *Leader*, 10 July 1867.

8 See, for example, *Globe*, 28 October 1868.

9 *Globe*, 22 July 1868 and 6 August 1868; *Leader*, 2 July 1868 and 14 July 1868.

10 *Globe*, 8 June 1870.

11 John A. Macdonald to Bishop Lynch, 17 July 1869, Lynch Papers, ARCAT; Bishop Lynch to John A. Macdonald, 4 October 1869, Macdonald Papers, NAC; Bishop Lynch to Bishop Joseph-Eugène-Bruno Guigues, 27 July 1869, Guigues Papers, AAO.

12 *Canadian Freeman*, 21 March 1867; *Globe*, 18 March 1867; *Irish Canadian*, 18 March 1868.

13 Petition to Bishop Lynch, February 1868, Lynch Papers, ARCAT; *Irish Canadian*, 17 March 1869; *Canadian Freeman*, 23 March 1869.

14 *Leader*, 18 March 1869.

15 *Irish Canadian*, 17 March 1869.

16 *Irish Canadian*, 21 September 1870.

17 David Thornley, *Isaac Butt and Home Rule* (London: MacGibbon and Kee 1964), 53 and 83–9.

18 T.W. Moody, *Davitt and Irish Revolution, 1846–82* (Oxford: Oxford University Press, Clarendon Press 1981), 123.

19 Edward Thornton to Sir John Young, 25 April 1870, Macdonald Papers, NAC.

20 *Irish Canadian*, 31 August 1870.

21 *Irish Canadian*, 31 May 1871.

22 *Irish Canadian*, 21 July 1868, 13 October 1868, and 7 April 1870.

23 *Irish Canadian*, 14 January 1874.

24 *Irish Canadian*, 2 November 1873.

25 *Irish Canadian*, 29 April 1874.

26 *Irish Canadian*, 21 January 1874.

27 *Irish Canadian*, 15 April 1874.

28 *Canadian Freeman*, 23 March 1871 and 28 November 1872.

29 *Irish Canadian*, 15 April 1874

30 *Irish Canadian*, 24 February 1869 and 3 March 1869.

31 *Irish Canadian*, 19 May 1868, 2 March 1870, and 14 February 1872.

32 *Irish Canadian*, 19 January 1876.

33 *Irish Canadian*, 28 January 1874.

34 *Globe*, 5 December 1873; *Irish Canadian*, 22 September 1875, 12 September 1877, 28 November 1877, and 4 September 1878.

35 *Irish Canadian*, 29 April 1874.

36 *Irish Canadian*, 3 February 1876 and 29 January 1879.

37 *Irish Canadian*, 15 November 1876.

38 *Irish Canadian*, 9 September 1874 and 28 November 1877; Archbishop Lynch to Rev. Sir, 2 August 1873, Lynch Papers, ARCAT.

39 *Irish Canadian*, 4 February 1874.

40 *Irish Canadian*, 9 September 1874.

41 *Irish Canadian*, 15 February 1873, 19 September 1877, and 21 December 1879; *Tribune*, 4 November 1875.

42 *Irish Canadian*, 16 March 1870 and 11 February 1874.

43 *Leader*, 18 March 1871.

44 *Globe*, 18 March 1875.

45 *Irish Canadian*, 12 September 1877. The combined total for the Young Irishmen and the Hibernian Benevolent Society was 460. Figures for the Emeralds are not available. I have assumed that the association had some 200 members, certainly a conservative estimate.

46 If the demographic profile of the Irish-Catholic population resembled the city population as a whole, 45.5 per cent of the Irish were too young to join the nationalist societies and 50.9 per cent were excluded on the basis of sex. Only 27.7 per cent of the Irish-Catholic population was eligible for membership in the nationalist societies. See *Census of Canada, 1870–71* (Ottawa 1873), 1:17 and 2:30–3.

47 *Irish Canadian*, 2 November 1872, 24 November 1875, 19 January 1876, 3 October 1877, 30 January 1878, 13 February 1878, and 28 April 1880.

48 *Irish Canadian*, 8 May 1878.
49 *Irish Canadian*, 5 February 1873.
50 Pastoral, 2 April 1876, Lynch Papers, ARCAT.
51 *Irish Canadian*, 19 February 1873.
52 For a path-breaking analysis of the conflict between Orange and Green, see Gregory S. Kealey, *Toronto Workers Respond to Industrial Capitalism 1867–1892* (Toronto: University of Toronto Press 1980), 115–23. My count differs from that offered by Kealey because I have included only significant riots.
53 David W. Miller, "The Armagh Troubles, 1784–95," in *Irish Peasants: Violence and Political Unrest 1780–1914*, eds. Samuel Clark and James S. Donnelly, Jr (Madison, Wisconsin: University of Wisconsin Press 1983), 175; Sybil E. Baker, "Orange and Green: Belfast, 1832–1912," in *The Victorian City: Images and Realities*, eds. H.J. Dyos and Michael Wolf, 2 vols. (London: Routledge and Kegan Paul 1973), 2:790; *Globe*, 9 and 11 July 1870, 11 and 14 July 1876, 19 and 21 June 1877, 13 and 14 July 1877; *Leader*, 18 July 1877.
54 *Globe*, 18 March 1871, 21 March 1871, 19 March 1872, 28 July 1874, 27 September 1875, and 4 October 1875; *Leader*, 2 September 1870, 20 March 1871, and 30 July 1873; *Mail*, 19 March 1877.
55 See *Globe*, 4, 6, 8, 11, 14, 16, 21, 22, 23, and 25 September 1875.
56 *Mail*, 27 September 1875.
57 *Globe*, 27 September 1875; *Leader*, 27 September 1875; *Mail*, 27 September 1875; *Irish Canadian*, 29 September 1875. Martin Galvin's "The Jubilee Riots in Toronto, 1875," Canadian Catholic Historical Association, *Report*, 26 (1959), 93–107, is the definitive study of the Jubilee riots.
58 *Globe*, 4, 5, 9, and 13 October 1875, 14, 18, 19, 20, and 25 January 1876; *Leader*, 4 October 1875; *Mail*, 5 October 1875.
59 *Telegram*, 21 February 1878.
60 *Mail*, 23 February 1873.
61 *Globe*, 19 March 1878; *Mail*, 19 March 1878.
62 T.P. French to Archbishop Lynch, 7 October 1875, Lynch Papers, ARCAT.
63 F.A. Hyland to Archbishop Lynch, 16 October 1875, Lynch Papers, ARCAT.
64 For the background to the founding of the *Tribune* see Gerald J. Stortz, "The Irish Catholic Press in Toronto, 1874–1887," Canadian Catholic Historical Association, *Study Sessions*, 47 (1980), 43–4.
65 *Tribune*, 13 July 1876.
66 *Tribune*, 17 September 1874, 3 December 1874, 10 December 1874, 4 February 1875, 29 April 1875, 16 September 1875, 2 December

1875, 13 January 1876, 20 January 1876, 17 February 1876, 25 May 1876, 10 August 1876, and 9 October 1877.

67 *Tribune,* 17 September 1874, 1 December 1876, 19 January 1877, and 19 October 1877.

68 *Irish Canadian,* 9 February 1870.

69 *Irish Canadian,* 19 March 1873.

70 *Irish Canadian,* 10 November 1869, 7 January 1874, 4 February 1874, 28 October 1874, 8 December 1875, 22 December 1875, 3 January 1877, 4 July 1877, and 18 July 1877.

71 *Irish Canadian,* 28 May 1877.

72 *Irish Canadian,* 24 October 1877, 31 October 1877, 14 November 1877, 28 November 1877, 5 December 1877, 19 December 1877, 9 January 1878, and 6 February 1878.

73 *Irish Canadian,* 1 January 1873; *Tribune,* 10 December 1874 and 3 September 1876.

74 *Irish Canadian,* 19 February 1873.

75 *Irish Canadian,* 20 March 1878.

76 *Irish Canadian,* 16 June 1869, 10 August 1870, 17 January 1872, 19 February 1873, 19 March 1873, and 11 July 1877.

77 *Irish Canadian,* 26 June 1878.

78 Archbishop Lynch to Rev. Sir, 2 August 1873, and James Phalen to Archbishop Lynch, 22 October 1874, Lynch Papers, ARCAT.

79 "To whom it may concern," 6 December 1876, Lynch Papers, ARCAT.

80 *Irish Canadian,* 11 August 1875.

81 *Irish Canadian,* 21 March 1877.

82 *Globe,* 19 March 1878.

83 *Irish Canadian,* 19 March 1873, 27 September 1876, and 18 June 1879.

84 *Irish Canadian,* 24 November 1875, 2 February 1876, and 6 December 1876.

85 *Canadian Freeman,* 23 March 1871.

86 *Irish Canadian,* 19 March 1873.

87 Emmet Larkin, "Church, State and Nation in Modern Ireland," *American Historical Review,* 80 (1975), 1262.

88 See Franklin Walker, *Catholic Education and Politics in Ontario* (Toronto: English Catholic Education Association of Ontario 1964), 30–59, for a detailed account of the conflict.

89 Susan E. Houston and Alison Prentice, *Schooling and Scholars in Nineteenth-Century Ontario,* Ontario Historical Studies Series (Toronto: University of Toronto Press 1988), 118–21 and 154–5; Donald Harman Akenson, *Being Had: Historians, Evidence, and the Irish in North America* (Port Credit: P.D. Meany 1985), 163.

90 *Globe,* 5 December 1877.

324 Notes to pages 219–25

91 *Globe*, 19 December 1877. Under the Scott Act of 1863, teachers of religious orders who taught in the separate schools were exempted from the usual requirement that teachers in state-supported schools hold a provincial teaching certificate.

92 *Globe*, 23 December 1877.

93 *Irish Canadian*, 16 January 1878; *Globe*, 10 January 1878.

94 *Telegram*, 17 January 1878.

95 *Globe*, 23 March and 4 April 1878.

96 *Irish Canadian*, 15 May 1878.

97 *Irish Canadian*, 15 and 22 May 1878.

98 Rev. J.J. McCann to Patrick Boyle, 7 June 1878, Lynch Papers, ARCAT.

99 *Globe*, 17 May 1878.

100 *Globe*, 5 and 19 June 1878.

101 *Telegram*, 15 June 1878.

102 *Globe*, 8 August 1878.

103 *Globe*, 16 October 1878.

104 *Telegram*, 1 February 1879.

105 Walker, *Catholic Education in Ontario*, 57–8.

106 *Telegram*, 13 January 1879.

107 In 1877, for example, there were no Catholics on city council. The following year, in 1878, out of twenty-seven aldermen, only one was a Catholic.

108 *Irish Canadian*, 26 December 1877, 30 January 1878, 15 May 1878, 22 May 1878, and 26 June 1878.

109 "To the Legislative Assembly of Ontario," 1879, Lynch Papers, ARCAT; Walker, *Catholic Education in Ontario*, 61.

CHAPTER TEN

1 For an important analysis of the relationship between generational differences and ethnic identity, see Timothy J. Meagher, "'Irish All the Time:' Ethnic Consciousness Among the Irish in Worcester, Massachusetts, 1880–1905," *Journal of Social History*, 19 (1985), 273–303, and "Irish, American, Catholic: Irish-American Identity in Worcester, Massachusetts, 1880–1920," in *From Paddy to Studs: Irish-American Communities in the Turn of the Century Era, 1880 to 1930*, ed. Timothy J. Meagher (New York: Greenwood Press 1986), 75–92.

2 David Thornley, *Isaac Butt and Home Rule* (London: MacGibbon and Kee 1964), 236–7, 255–8, 269, 277, and 290–1.

3 F.S.L. Lyons, *Charles Stewart Parnell* (London: Collins 1977), 60–5 and 68; Thornley, *Isaac Butt*, 317–29.

4 T.W. Moody, *Davitt and Irish Revolution, 1846–82* (Oxford: Oxford University Press, Clarendon Press 1981), 130.

5 For this distinction I am indebted to Moody's magisterial biography of Davitt. The first "new departure" was the Irish Revolutionary Brotherhood's tacit support for Isaac Butt's parliamentary party between 1873 and 1877. See Moody, *Davitt*, xv, xvi, and 249–53.

6 Thomas N. Brown, *Irish-American Nationalism, 1870–1890* (New York: J.P. Lippincott 1966), 87 and 91; Lyons, *Parnell*, 80–2.

7 Moody, *Davitt*, 249–53 and 286–8.

8 Samuel Clark, *Social Origins of the Irish Land War* (Princeton, New Jersey: Princeton University Press 1979), 227–32, 236, and 246–9.

9 Moody, *Davitt*, 296–302 and 325–6; Lyons, *Parnell*, 84, 88–91, and 98.

10 T.W. Moody, "The New Departure in Irish Politics, 1878–9," in *Essays in British and Irish History in Honour of James Eadie Todd*, eds. Henry Cronne, T.W. Moody, and D.B. Quinn (London: Frederick Muller 1947), 322; Conor Cruise O'Brien, *Parnell and His Party 1880–90* (Oxford: Oxford University Press, Clarendon Press 1957), 38.

11 *Irish Canadian*, 2 August 1876, 9 September 1876, 13 September 1876, 4 October 1876, 29 August 1877, 26 September 1877, and 3 October 1877; Brown, *Irish-American Nationalism*, 81.

12 *Irish Canadian*, 7 May 1879 and 25 June 1879.

13 *Irish Canadian*, 2 and 10 July 1879; Moody, *Davitt*, 328–9.

14 *Irish Canadian*, 20 August 1879 and 21 January 1880.

15 C.S. Parnell to Archbishop Lynch, 1 March 1880, Lynch Papers, ARCAT.

16 *Irish Canadian*, 10 March 1880.

17 *Globe*, 20 and 23 May 1881.

18 *Irish Canadian*, 17 February 1881, 10 March 1881, and 12 May 1881.

19 *Irish Canadian*, 17 February, 10 March, and 24 March 1881.

20 Thomas N. Brown, *Irish-American Nationalism*, 154, 166, 168–9, and 172–3.

21 *Irish Canadian*, 17 February 1881, 17 March 1881, and 19 May 1881; *Globe*, 2 March 1881, 15 March 1881, and 9 May 1881; Gregory S. Kealey, *Toronto Workers Respond to Industrial Capitalism, 1876–1892* (Toronto: University of Toronto Press 1980), 179, 325, and 328–9.

22 *Irish Canadian*, 17 February 1881, 3 March 1881, and 12 May 1881; James Paul Rodechko, *Patrick Ford and His Search for America: A Case Study of Irish-American Journalism, 1870–1913* (New York: Arno Press 1976), 62–88; Brown, *Irish-American Nationalism*, 49–52.

23 *Irish Canadian*, 16 July 1879, 30 July 1879, 20 September 1879, and 23 June 1881.

24 Gregory S. Kealey and Bryan D. Palmer, *Dreaming of What Might Be: The Knights of Labor in Ontario, 1880–1900* (Cambridge: Cambridge University Press 1982), 313–16; Eric Foner, "Class, Ethnicity, and Radicalism in the Gilded Age: The Land League and Irish America," *Marxist Perspectives*, 1 (1978), 6–55.

25 *Globe*, 24 July 1882, 21 July 1884, 11 May 1886, and 2 October 1887; *Mail*, 13 September 1886.

26 *Irish Canadian*, 20 October 1880, 16 May 1881, 27 July 1882, 22 May 1884, 25 June 1885, 26 July 1886, 25 November 1886, and 20 July 1888.

27 *Irish Canadian*, 11 February 1881.

28 *Irish Canadian*, 12 November 1879, 17 December 1879, 21 April 1880, 12 January 1882, 25 June 1885, and 20 July 1888.

29 *Irish Canadian*, 24 March 1881, 25 August 1881, 5 January 1882, and 3 May 1883; *Globe*, 23 April 1881.

30 *Irish Canadian*, 28 April 1881 and 25 August 1881.

31 *Tribune*, 3 October 1880, 31 December 1880, and 24 June 1881.

32 This trajectory in Protestant English-Canadian opinion can be traced in the *Globe*, 3 August 1877, 13 October 1879, 17 December 1879, 19 December 1879, 8 March 1880, 22 June 1880, 31 March 1881, 11 November 1881, 22 April 1882, 4 May 1882, 15 May 1882, and 23 June 1882.

33 *Irish Canadian*, 13 April 1882; Stanley W. Horrall, "Canada and the Irish Question: A Study of the Canadian Response to Irish Home Rule, 1882–1893" (MA thesis, Carleton University 1966), 13–33, explores the partisan motives for the Home Rule resolutions and examines in detail the legislative debates on these resolutions.

34 R.F. Foster, *Modern Ireland 1660–1972* (New York and London: Penguin Books 1989), 415–17; O'Brien, *Parnell and His Party*, 77–9.

35 *Globe*, 29 September 1885.

36 *Irish Canadian*, 29 October 1885.

37 *Irish Canadian*, 12 November 1885, 19 November 1885, 18 March 1886, and 1 July 1886; *Globe*, 23 November 1886 and 17 March 1887.

38 *Irish Canadian*, 20 October 1887.

39 *Irish Canadian*, 1 October 1885, 25 November 1886, and 20 January 1887; Kealey, *Toronto Workers Respond*, 240.

40 *Irish Canadian*, 1 October 1885, 4 March 1886, 6 May 1886, 1 July 1886, and 15 July 1886.

41 *Globe*, 10 July 1883, 24 September 1883, 5 May 1884, 23 November 1885, and 2 December 1885.

42 *Irish Canadian*, 1 July 1886 and 23 November 1886.

43 *Globe*, 23 November 1886.

44 *Mail,* 9 March 1886, 10 March 1886, 5 May 1886, 4 October 1886, 9 November 1886, and 12 November 1886.

45 *Irish Canadian,* 24 March 1881.

46 *Globe,* 19 March 1883.

47 *Irish Canadian,* 22 March 1883.

48 *Catholic Weekly Review,* 10 December 1887.

49 *Irish Canadian,* 1 October 1885.

50 These figures have been derived from the marriage registers of Saint Paul's, Saint Michael's, Saint Mary's, and Saint Patrick's parishes.

51 *Irish Canadian,* 12 September 1877, 24 March 1881, 19 January 1882, and 8 January 1891; *Catholic Weekly Review,* 27 December 1894 and 23 May 1895.

52 *Irish Canadian,* 20 September 1883, 12 August 1886, and 12 September 1889; *Globe,* 5 July 1884.

53 *Irish Canadian,* 12 September 1889.

54 *Irish Canadian,* 23 March 1881.

55 *Irish Canadian,* 9 August 1883; *Globe,* 21 May 1884 and 16 July 1884.

56 *Irish Canadian,* 28 April 1881, 4 August 1881, and 23 July 1885.

57 *Irish Canadian,* 8 January 1885 and 13 June 1889.

58 *Irish Canadian,* 1 October 1885.

59 *Globe,* 23 October 1881; *Irish Canadian,* 27 April 1882.

60 *Catholic Register,* 18 May 1893.

61 *Irish Canadian,* 4 August 1880, 28 April 1881, 27 April 1882, 21 August 1884, and 14 May 1885; *Catholic Weekly Review,* 26 March 1892.

62 *Irish Canadian,* 27 April 1882.

63 *Irish Canadian,* 9 April 1885 and 3 September 1886.

64 *Irish Canadian,* 20 June 1889 and 12 September 1889; *Catholic Weekly Review,* 26 March 1892.

65 *Irish Canadian,* 12 September 1889.

66 *Globe,* 23 April 1884; *Irish Canadian,* 14 May 1885.

67 *Irish Canadian,* 4 August 1880, 1 October 1885, and 13 November 1890. A seventh branch was founded sometime during 1890.

68 *Irish Canadian,* 12 August 1886.

69 *Irish Canadian,* 5 April 1888, 17 March 1892, and 30 June 1892; *Catholic Weekly Review,* 2 March 1891; *Catholic Register,* 12 October 1893, 23 November 1893, 11 January 1894, 14 March 1895, and 8 May 1895.

70 *Catholic Weekly Review,* 13 September, 15 November, 22 November, and 13 December 1890; *Irish Canadian,* 26 December 1889; *Catholic Record,* 1 April 1881.

71 *Catholic Weekly Review,* 5 January 1890 and 22 November 1890.

72 *Irish Canadian,* 25 August 1888; *Catholic Weekly Review,* 13 September

1890, 6 December 1890, 21 February 1891, and 13 February 1892; *Catholic Record*, 1 April 1881 and 8 June 1883.

73 *Irish Canadian*, 25 August 1888.

74 *Catholic Record*, 14 October 1881, 8 June 1882, and 5 October 1882.

75 *Irish Canadian*, 25 August 1888.

76 *Catholic Weekly Review*, 13 February 1892.

77 *Catholic Record*, 8 August 1884; *Irish Canadian*, 25 August 1888.

78 *Irish Canadian*, 18 July 1889 and 23 October 1890; *Catholic Weekly Review*, 28 October 1890 and 23 March 1893; *Catholic Register*, 31 May 1894.

79 *Irish Canadian*, 23 April 1891 and 10 September 1891.

80 *Irish Canadian*, 20 August 1891; *Catholic Weekly Review*, 13 September 1890; John O'Dea, *History of the Ancient Order of Hibernians and Ladies' Auxiliary* (Philadelphia: National Board of the Ancient Order of Hibernians 1929), 2:1006, 1147–8, and 1156.

81 *Canadian Messenger of the Sacred Heart*, May 1892, 204–5, and December 1986, 520; Edward Kelly, *The Story of St. Paul's Parish, Toronto* (Toronto 1922), 266–76; Mark George McGowan, "'We are all Canadians': A Social, Religious and Cultural Portrait of Toronto's English-speaking Catholics, 1890–1920" (PhD diss., University of Toronto 1988), 218–20.

82 *Globe*, 12 October 1881, 7 December 1881, and 20 December 1881; *Irish Canadian*, 23 May 1882.

83 *Globe*, 8 February 1882 and 8 March 1882; *Irish Canadian*, 26 January, 2 March, 9 March, 16 March, 30 March, 6 April, 13 April, and 4 May 1882.

84 *Irish Canadian*, 9 March 1882; Franklin Walker, *Catholic Education and Politics in Ontario* (Toronto: English Catholic Education Association of Ontario 1964), 62–3.

85 Lyons, *Parnell*, 360–8.

86 William O'Brien, *Evening Memories* (Dublin: Maunsel 1920), 219–22.

87 *Irish Canadian*, 25 November 1886 and 21 April 1887; *Globe*, 21 April 1887. For an account of O'Brien's visit to Toronto, see Gerald J. Stortz, "An Irish Radical in a Tory Town: William O'Brien in Toronto," *Eire-Ireland*, 14 (1984), 35–58.

88 Frank Smith to Archbishop Lynch, 18 May 1887, Rev. Joseph McBride to Frank Smith, 21 April 1887, and H.M. Pardon to Rev. J. McBride, 4 May 1887, Lynch Papers, ARCAT; *Globe*, 22 April 1887.

89 Archbishop Lynch to Archbishop Thomas W. Croke, 20 April 1887, Lynch Papers, ARCAT.

90 Rev. Joseph McBride to Rev. Michael O'Reilly, 1887, Lynch Papers, ARCAT.

91 *Catholic Weekly Review*, 5 May 1887; Eugene O'Keefe to Archbishop Lynch, 4 May 1887, Lynch Papers, ARCAT.

92 Frank Smith to Archbishop Lynch, 9 May 1887, Lynch Papers, ARCAT.

93 *Catholic Weekly Review*, 5 May 1887.

94 *Catholic Weekly Review*, 12 and 19 May 1887.

95 *Irish Canadian*, 5 May 1887.

96 *Mail*, 16 May 1887.

97 *Globe*, 13 and 14 May 1887.

98 *Mail*, 18 May 1887; *Globe*, 18 May 1887: *Irish Canadian*, 19 May 1887; Rev. Joseph McBride to Rev. J.L. Hand, 16 May 1887, Lynch Papers, ARCAT.

99 *Globe*, 19, 20, and 21 May 1887; *Mail*, 19 May 1887.

100 *Catholic Weekly Review*, 19 May 1887.

101 *Catholic Weekly Review*, 19 May 1887.

102 *Catholic Weekly Review*, 26 May 1887; *Irish Canadian*, 19 and 26 May 1887.

103 *Irish Canadian*, 23 June 1887.

104 Archbishop Lynch to Bishop John Walsh, 18 June 1887, Lynch Papers, ARCAT.

105 Archbishop Lynch to Bishop John Walsh, 15 June 1887, Lynch Papers, ARCAT.

106 *Irish Canadian*, 30 June 1887.

107 *Irish Canadian*, 30 June 1887 and 7 July 1887: *Globe*, 2 July 1887.

108 *Irish Canadian*, 8 September 1887.

109 Archbishop Lynch to Rev. Michael O'Reilly, 19 September 1887, Lynch Papers, ARCAT, which was published in *Catholic Weekly Review*, 8 October 1887.

110 "To the Electors of the Separate Schools within St. George's Ward," Lynch Papers, ARCAT. The separate school board controversy has been extensively documented in Franklin Walker's pioneering study, *Catholic Education and Politics in Ontario*, 64–81. Walker, however, considers the lay nationalist demand for the ballot to be a manifestation of anti-clericalism. In fact, he has mistaken lay initiative for hostility towards the Catholic Church, just as Archbishop Lynch and his clergy had done.

111 *Irish Canadian*, 29 December 1887.

112 Archbishop Lynch to Patrick Curran, 27 December 1887, Archbishop Lynch to J.A. Mulligan, 27 December 1887, Archbishop Lynch to Charles Burns, 27 December 1887, Archbishop Lynch to Rev. M. O'Reilly, 27 December 1887, Lynch Papers, ARCAT; *Telegram*, 5 January 1888; *Irish Canadian*, 12 January 1888. Polls were held for only five of the twelve vacant seats; the trustees for the remaining

seven seats were elected by acclamation. Only one of the trustees elected by acclamation supported the secret ballot. Although there were twenty-four seats on the board, most trustees rarely attended board meetings. With only slightly more than half of the board usually present, the six pro-ballot trustees regularly posed a threat to the clergy's control of the board.

113 *Irish Canadian*, 5 January 1888.

114 *Irish Canadian*, 19 January 1888.

115 *Globe*, 6 February 1888; Circular, 3 February 1888, Lynch Papers, ARCAT.

116 *Mail*, 8 February 1888; *Irish Canadian*, 16 February 1888.

117 Archbishop Lynch to D. Kelly, 14 February 1888, Archbishop Lynch to P. Curran, 27 February 1888, and T.J. McMahon to Archbishop Lynch, 23 February 1888, Lynch Papers, ARCAT; *Globe*, 18 February 1888. Some of the trustees' replies to the archbishop have not survived. See Walker, *Catholic Education in Ontario*, 69.

118 "To the Catholic People of Toronto," 18 February 1888, Lynch Papers, ARCAT.

119 *Mail*, 5 March 1888.

120 J.A. Mulligan to Archbishop Lynch, 10 March 1888, Lynch Papers, ARCAT.

121 *Globe*, 26 October 1883, 1 January 1884, and 18 April 1888; "To the Honorable T.W. Anglin," 15 April 1888, Lynch Papers, ARCAT.

122 *Globe*, 18, 24, and 25 April 1888; *Mail*, 17 and 25 April 1888; *Telegram*, 24 April 1888.

123 *Mail*, 14 May 1888; *Globe*, 14 May 1888; J.R. Teefy, *Jubilee Volume: The Archdiocese of Toronto and Archbishop Walsh* (Toronto: George T. Dixon 1892), 194.

124 *Irish Canadian*, 27 September 1888, 4 October 1888, 18 October 1888, and 29 November 1888.

125 *Telegram*, 26 December 1888 and 2 January 1889.

126 *Telegram*, 2 October 1889; *Mail*, 25 September 1889 and 25 November 1889.

127 Walker, *Catholic Education in Ontario*, 171–3.

128 But see Gerald J. Stortz, "John Joseph Lynch, Archbishop of Toronto: A Biographical Study in Religious, Political and Social Commitment" (PhD diss., University of Guelph 1980), 28 and 264.

129 *Irish Canadian*, 22 March 1888.

130 *Irish Canadian*, 23 March 1890.

131 *Irish Canadian*, 15 October 1891; *Catholic Register*, 23 March 1893.

132 *Catholic Register*, 18 May 1893.

133 *Catholic Weekly Review*, 21 July 1888.

134 *Catholic Register*, 5 January 1893.

135 McGowan, "'We Are All Canadians,'" 321–2, and Charles
W. Humphries, *'Honest Enough to Be Bold': The Life and Times of Sir
James Whitney*, Ontario Historical Studies Series (Toronto: University
of Toronto Press 1985), 79 and 99.
136 McGowan, "'We Are All Canadians,'" 429.
137 Robert Choquette, *Language and Religion: A History of English-French
Conflict in Ontario* (Ottawa: University of Ottawa Press 1975),
161–95.

Index

Act of Union, 155, 173
Adjala Township, 190
Akenson, Donald H., 8
alcohol: availability of, 129; and social life, 130; and violence, 131–2
alcoholism, 36–7, 39, 50
Ancient Order of Hibernians, 238–9
Anglin, Francis A., 250
Anglin, Timothy W., 230, 246, 250
anglophobia, 168
anti-Catholicism, 32
Apostleship of Prayer, 63, 66, 71–2, 83–4, 95, 239, 259
Archconfraternity of the Holy Family, 63–4, 83
Arnold, Brother, 135, 138, 145
Association of the Childen of Mary, 63–4
Association of the Sacred Heart, 87–8
Aubert, Roger, 70

Balfour, Arthur, 240
Barrie, 190

Beaty, James, 165
Bell, Robert, 240
Benediction of the Blessed Sacrament, 45, 58, 61
Blake, Edward, 229–31
Board of Education, 40
Bourget, Ignace, 3, 33, 37, 132, 163, 185, 209
Bourke, Thomas F., 214
Boyle, Patrick, 146–7, 149, 171–4, 178, 184–5, 189–90, 197–8, 200, 203, 205, 213–15, 217, 220, 228–9
Britton, James, 81
Brotherhood of Saint Patrick, 184
Brown, George, 160
Brown, Thomas, 7, 152
Burns, Charles, 20, 180, 182, 229
Burns, Mrs Patrick, 82
Burns, William, 123
Butt, Isaac, 202–4, 214
Byrne, L.V., 238

Cahill, Daniel P., 92, 244–5, 247
Campobello (New Brunswick), 169, 195–6, 200

Canada: relationship of, to Ireland, 231–2, 251
Canadian Freeman, 58, 80, 99, 102, 114, 116, 160–1, 164–5, 184–6, 189, 193–4, 200, 211
Carey, D.A., 234, 251
Cartier, George-Étienne, 196
Casey, M.W., 231–2
Cathedraticum, 38
Catholic Church. *See* Roman Catholic Church
Catholic churches, 53–4, 55–6. *See also* names of individual churches
Catholic clergy. *See* clergy
Catholic emancipation, 155
Catholic Irish. *See* Irish Catholic
Catholic Literary Association (1847), 90, 155
Catholic Mutual Benevolent Association (CMBA), 236–8, 259–60
Catholic Order of Foresters, 236
Catholic priests. *See* clergy

Propaganda Fide, 49
Protestant nationalists, 32
Protestant population (Canada West), 42
Protestant teetotalers, 139
Provincial Council of Quebec (1868), 34
public school system, 40, 43

Quarant'Ore (Forty Hours), 45, 58–9. *See also* Forty Hours
Queen Victoria's Golden Jubilee, 242–4
Queen's Park, 242

radical nationalism, 175–6, 183–4, 199, 203–5, 211–15, 228, 258; and the clergy, 212–13; and Roman Catholic Church, 217–18. *See also* Irish nationalism; militant nationalism; moderate nationalism
recreational clubs and societies, 91–5
Redmond, John, 251
Reformers, 160
retreats, 37, 60, 63
Ribbon societies, 157
Riddell, W.H., 226
Ridgeway: battle of, 197
riots, 158–9, 185–7, 208–10.
Ritchey, John, 159
Roberts, William, 193–4, 197
Robertson, J.E., 219
Robertson, John Ross, 56, 58
Roman Catholic Church: and Irish nationalism, 155, 164; and radical nationalism, 217–18; reform of, chapter 2
Roman Catholic Episcopal Corporation, 219–20
Rooney, Francis, 55, 82, 116, 235, 246
rosary, 45, 60, 64–5
Rossa, Jeremiah O'Donovan, 209–10, 214
Royal Opera House, 226
rural deans, 38
Ryan, Peter, 220

sacraments: frequent reception of, 65
Sacred Heart Church (1886), 53
Sacred Heart of Jesus, 61, 66, 68
Saint Alphonsus Young Men's Literary Society (1888), 92
St Bartholomew's Day Massacre, 188
Saint Basil's Church (1855), 53, 82, 87, 92, 100
St Catharines, 144
Saint Cecilia's Church (1895), 53
Saint David's Ward, 23–4
Saint George Society, 179
Saint George's Ward, 23
Saint Helen's Church (1872), 53, 139, 235
Saint Helen's Conference (Saint Vincent de Paul Society), 106
Saint Joseph's Bona Mors Society, 71–4
Saint Joseph's Church (1878), 53, 235
Saint Joseph's Conference (Saint Vincent de Paul Society), 106
Saint Joseph's Society (1862), 90
Saint Lawrence Hall, 159
Saint Lawrence Market, 179
Saint Lawrence Ward, 20, 23–4
Saint Mary's Church, 53–5, 71, 82, 209–10, 230, 235
Saint Mary's Conference (Saint Vincent de Paul Society), 111
Saint Mary's Temperance Society, 140
Saint Michael's Cathedral (1848), 52–5, 82, 87, 104, 140, 209, 235
Saint Michael's College, 38, 53
Saint Nicholas Institute, 4, 120
Saint Patrick's Church (1858), 53–54, 92–3, 104, 210, 235–6
Saint Patrick's Conference (Saint Vincent de Paul Society), 104–6
Saint Patrick's Day, 144, 147, 155–6, 158, 161–2, 164–5, 170, 178, 190, 194–5, 197, 201, 208, 216–17, 249–50
Saint Patrick's Day riots (1858), 186–7
Saint Patrick's Hall, 209–10
Saint Patrick's school, 120
Saint Patrick's Society, 161
Saint Patrick's Temperance and Benevolent Society, 140–1, 146
Saint Paul's Church (1826), 39, 52, 55, 70, 92, 99, 140, 195, 210, 235–6
Saint Paul's Literary and Debating Society, 92
Saint Paul's separate school, 195
Saint Peter's Church (1872), 53, 139
Saint Peter's Conference (Saint Vincent de Paul Society), 106, 110
Saint Sylvestre's Church, 158
St Thomas, 104
Saint Vincent de Paul Society, chapter 5; 10, 84–6, 95–6, 181, 238, 245, 247, 256; authority in, 124–5; charitable